Canola oil = Rapeseed
Cilantro = coriander

Quinoa 333

Enjoy 333 Days with Amazing Quinoa Recipes in Your Own Quinoa Cookbook

(Quinoa- Volume 1)

Lily Li

Copyright: Published in the United States by Lily Li/ © LILY LI

Published on November 6, 2018

All rights reserved. No part of this publication may be reproduced, stored in retrieval system, copied in any form or by any means, electronic, mechanical, photocopying, recording or otherwise transmitted without written permission from the publisher. Please do not participate in or encourage piracy of this material in any way. You must not circulate this book in any format. LILY LI does not control or direct users' actions and is not responsible for the information or content shared, harm and/or actions of the book readers.

In accordance with the U.S. Copyright Act of 1976, the scanning, uploading and electronic sharing of any part of this book without the permission of the publisher constitute unlawful piracy and theft of the author's intellectual property. If you would like to use material from the book (other than just simply for reviewing the book), prior permission must be obtained by contacting the author at *cheflilyli@gmail.com*

Thank you for your support of the author's rights.

Contents

CONTENTS 3

INTRODUCTION 9

333 AMAZING AND HEALTHY QUINOA RECIPES 10

1. African Quinoa Soup 11
2. Amandas Quinoa Salad 11
3. Amazing Chocolate Quinoa Cake 12
4. Apple OatQuinoa Granola 12
5. Asian Breakfast StirFry 13
6. Asian Fusion Quinoa 13
7. Asian Quinoa Salad 14
8. BabyandMe Pilaf 15
9. Bacon Spinach Quinoa 15
10. Balsamic and Herb Quinoa Salad 16
11. Banana Quinoa Rice Pudding 16
12. Best Greek Quinoa Salad 17
13. Black Bean and Quinoa Enchilada Bake 17
14. Black Bean and Tomato Quinoa 18
15. Black Bean Corn and Quinoa Salad 19
16. Black Bean Quinoa Burgers 19
17. Black Bean Quinoa Veggie Burgers 20
18. Blackberry Pomegranate Quinoa Parfait 20
19. Blackened Chicken with Avocado Cream Sauce 21
20. Blueberry Lemon Breakfast Quinoa 22
21. Blueberry Lemon Sprouted Rice and Quinoa Cereal 22
22. Blueberry Quinoa with Lemon Glaze .. 23
23. BroccoliQuinoa Casserole 23
24. Brown Rice and Quinoa Sushi Rolls 24
25. Buddha Bowl 25
26. Buffalo Chicken Quinoa Bites 25
27. Buffalo Veggie Quinoa Meatloaf 26
28. Butternut Squash Chicken and Quinoa Soup 27
29. Butternut Squash Turnip and GreenBean Quinoa 27
30. Cabbage Rolls with Quinoa 28
31. Carons Kickin Quinoa Salad 29
32. Carrot Cake Quinoa 29
33. Carrot Tomato and Spinach Quinoa Pilaf 30
34. Carrot Tomato and Spinach Quinoa Pilaf with Ground Turkey 30
35. Cauliflower With Quinoa Prunes and Peanuts 31
36. Cheesy Broccoli Quinoa 32
37. Cheesy Quinoa Patties with Kale and Spinach 32
38. Cheesy Quinoa Pilaf with Spinach 33
39. Cheesy Stuffed Peppers 34
40. Cheesy VeggieQuinoa Bites 34
41. Chicken Quinoa Stuffed Peppers 35
42. Chicken and Quinoa Paella 35
43. Chicken Chorizo on Quinoa with Peppers 36
44. Chicken Quinoa 37
45. Chicken Quinoa Casserole 38
46. Chicken Quinoa Salad 38
47. Chicken Quinoa Salad with Apples and Mozzarella 39
48. Chicken Quinoa Soup 39
49. Chicken with Peas Quinoa 40
50. Chicken with Quinoa and Veggies 41
51. Chickpea and Quinoa Salad with Lemon and Tahini 41
52. Chili with Quinoa 42
53. CiderGlazed Carrot and Quinoa Salad . 42
54. Cilantro Lime Quinoa 43
55. CinnaCoco Quinoa Bites 44
56. Coconut Quinoa 44
57. Coconut Quinoa with HarissaRoasted Sweet Potatoes 45
58. CoconutCurry Lentil Stew Served over Quinoa 45
59. Cold Chicken Quinoa Avocado Salad .. 46
60. Copycat First Watch Quinoa Power Bowl 47

61. Cranberry and Cilantro Quinoa Salad .. 47
62. Cranberry Apple Pecan Quinoa Salad .. 48
63. Cranberry Lentil and Quinoa Salad 48
64. Cranberry Quinoa Salad with Broccoli. 49
65. Cream of Broccoli Soup with Quinoa .. 50
66. Creamy Quinoa Risotto 50
67. Crunchy Lemon Quinoa and Asparagus Bowl 51
68. CrunchySweet Quinoa Couscous with Fresh Herbs 51
69. Curried Quinoa 52
70. Curried Quinoa Salad with Mango 53
71. Curried Quinoa with Red Lentils and Kale 53
72. Curry Couscous and Quinoa Pilaf Vegetarian 54
73. Curry Quinoa and Couscous Salad 55
74. Delicata Delish 55
75. Diannes LemonFeta Quinoa Salad 56
76. Easy Broccoli Quinoa Soup 56
77. Easy Quinoa Tabbouleh 57
78. Fall Salad with Quinoa Brussels Sprouts and Pomegranate 58
79. Fresh Taco Salad withCreamy AvocadoLime Dressing 58
80. Fruity Curried Lentil Salad 60
81. Garbanzo Bean and Quinoa Salad 60
82. Garlic Cheese Quinoa 61
83. Garlic Kale Quinoa 61
84. Garlic Quinoa 62
85. Gingery QuinoaStuffed Acorn Squash . 62
86. GlutenFree Apple Crisp 63
87. GlutenFree Moist Chocolate Cake 64
88. GlutenFree Multigrain Bread 64
89. Grain Bowl Soup 65
90. Grain Bowl With Spiced Squash Mushrooms and Curried Yogurt 66
91. Grape Lime and Quinoa Salad Surprise 66
92. Green Quinoa Tabbouleh 67
93. Grilled Steak Vegetable and Quinoa Salad with YogurtTahini Dressing 68
94. GuacamoleStyle Quinoa 69
95. Healthy AfterSchool Granola Bars 69
96. Healthy Quinoa Salad 70
97. Hearty Multigrain Bread 70
98. HighProtein Quinoa Breakfast Bowl 71
99. HighProtein Vegan StirFry 71
100. Instant Pot Chicken Quinoa Tortilla Soup 72
101. Instant Pot Mexican Quinoa 73
102. Instant Pot Vegan Quinoa and Kale Minestrone Soup 73
103. Italian Quinoa Salad 74
104. ItalianStyle QuinoaStuffed Sole 74
105. Jans Brown Rice and Quinoa Cheesy Rice Balls 75
106. JicamaLime Salad 76
107. Kale and Quinoa Patties with Herb Dipping Sauce 76
108. Kale and Quinoa Salad 77
109. Kale Carrot and Sunflower Seed Salad . 77
110. Kale Quinoa and Avocado Salad with Lemon Dijon Vinaigrette 78
111. Kale Quinoa Salad 78
112. Kale Tabbouleh with Quinoa 79
113. LeekTomato Quinoa 80
114. Lemon Herb Quinoa 80
115. LemonBasil Quinoa Salad 81
116. LemonScented Quinoa 81
117. Lemony Quinoa 82
118. Lemony Quinoa with Chickpeas and Huckleberries 82
119. Little Quinoa Patties 83
120. LowCarb Turkey Quinoa Lasagna 84
121. LTF DTox Mediterranean Chicken Quinoa Salad 84
122. MakeAhead Spinach Salad in a Jar 85
123. Mango Quinoa Salad 85
124. Mediterranean Quinoa 86
125. Mediterranean Quinoa Salad 87
126. Mediterranean Quinoa Salad with Shrimp 87
127. Mexican Quinoa 88
128. Mexican Quinoa Salad 88
129. MexiQuinoa Chicken Casserole 89
130. Micheles Thai Chicken Soup 89
131. Mini Baked Quinoa Patties 90
132. Miso Stew 91
133. MolassesAlmond Quinoa Vegan Cookies 91
134. Moms Quinoa Burgers 92
135. Moroccan Quinoa Salad 93
136. Mushroom Meatballs 93

137. Mystic Mushroom and Quinoa Chowder 94
138. New Years Soup 95
139. NoBake Quinoa Bars 95
140. NoBake Quinoa Protein Bars 96
141. Nothing Id Rather Eat Quinoa Patties. 96
142. Oat and Quinoa Breakfast Cake 97
143. OMG Quinoa Patties 98
144. One Skillet Mexican Quinoa 98
145. OnePan Mexican Quinoa 99
146. OneSkillet Quinoa and Chicken Dinner 99
147. Pad Thai Quinoa Bowl 100
148. Pantry Curried Quinoa with Garbanzo Beans and Roasted Peppers 101
149. Parsley Walnut Pesto Quinoa Salad 101
150. Perfectly Crunchy Granola 102
151. Pesto Quinoa 102
152. Pineapple Fried Quinoa 103
153. Pomegranate Steak with Quinoa 103
154. Pork Fried Quinoa 104
155. Power Salad Bowl 105
156. ProteinPacked Spicy Vegan Quinoa with Edamame 105
157. Pumpkin Quinoa Muffins 106
158. Puree of Green Things Soup with Quinoa and Pepper Relish 107
159. Quick Coconut Curry Bowls 108
160. Quinoa Almond Pilaf 108
161. Quinoa and Black Bean Chili 109
162. Quinoa and Black Bean Chili from GOYA 110
163. Quinoa and Black Bean Salad 110
164. Quinoa and Black Beans 111
165. Quinoa and Broccoli Brunch Cups 111
166. Quinoa and Dill Flatbread 112
167. Quinoa and GrilledPepper Salad 112
168. Quinoa and Honey Mustard Chicken Slow Cooker Meal 113
169. Quinoa and Lentil Salad 113
170. Quinoa and Pepper Pilaf 114
171. Quinoa and Red Lentil Burgers 114
172. Quinoa and Spinach Pilaf 115
173. Quinoa and SteelCut Oats Crunchy Granola 116
174. Quinoa and Sweet Potato Bakes 116
175. Quinoa and Turkey Stuffed Tomatoes 117
176. Quinoa Asparagus and Feta Salad 118
177. Quinoa Bean and Ground Turkey Chili 118
178. Quinoa Beet and Arugula Salad 119
179. Quinoa Biryani 120
180. Quinoa Black Bean Burgers 120
181. Quinoa Black Bean Tacos Vegan 121
182. Quinoa Bowl 121
183. Quinoa Breakfast Cereal 122
184. Quinoa Broccoli Casserole 122
185. Quinoa Brown Rice Sushi 123
186. Quinoa Burgers 124
187. Quinoa Cakes with EggplantTomato Rag and Smoked Mozzarella 125
188. Quinoa Chard Pilaf 126
189. Quinoa Chicken 126
190. Quinoa Chicken Sausage and White Bean Stew 127
191. Quinoa Chili 127
192. Quinoa Chocolate Treats 128
193. Quinoa Chorizo 128
194. Quinoa Couscous and Farro Salad with Summer Vegetables 129
195. Quinoa Crab Salad 130
196. Quinoa Dijon and Swiss Burger 130
197. Quinoa Fried Rice 131
198. Quinoa Grape and Prune Salad 131
199. Quinoa GreekInspired Salad 132
200. Quinoa High Protein Muffins 132
201. Quinoa Jambalaya 133
202. Quinoa Lasagna 133
203. Quinoa Lime and ChiliCrumbed Snapper With Sweet Potato Wedges 134
204. Quinoa Milk 135
205. Quinoa Mushroom Risotto 135
206. Quinoa Peanut White Bean Soup 136
207. Quinoa Pilaf 136
208. Quinoa Pilaf With Mushrooms 137
209. Quinoa Pilaf with Shredded Chicken. 137
210. Quinoa Pilaf with Veggies and Chickpeas 138
211. Quinoa Pilau 138
212. Quinoa Pudding 139
213. Quinoa Raisin Breakfast Bites 139
214. Quinoa Risotto with Mushrooms and Thyme 140

215. Quinoa Salad 140
216. Quinoa Salad Vegan 141
217. Quinoa Salad with Beets Blue Cheese and Nutty Herb Vinaigrette 141
218. Quinoa Salad with Dried Fruit and Nuts 142
219. Quinoa Salad with Grapefruit Avocado and Arugula 142
220. Quinoa Salad with Mint Almonds and Cranberries 143
221. Quinoa Salad with Roasted Yams 143
222. Quinoa Salad with Winter Veggies and Buffalo Chicken Sausage 144
223. Quinoa Side Dish 145
224. Quinoa Squash Muffins 145
225. Quinoa Stuffed Peppers 146
226. Quinoa Stuffed Pork Tenderloin 147
227. Quinoa Stuffing 147
228. Quinoa Summer Salad 148
229. Quinoa Summer Salad with Feta 148
230. Quinoa Tabbouleh 149
231. Quinoa Tabbouleh Salad 149
232. Quinoa Tabbouleh Salad GlutenFree . 150
233. Quinoa Tuna Casserole 150
234. Quinoa Tuna Salad 151
235. Quinoa Turkey Stuffing 152
236. Quinoa Vegetable Medley 152
237. Quinoa Vegetable Salad 153
238. Quinoa Vegetable Soup 153
239. Quinoa Veggie Salad with Zesty Vinaigrette 154
240. Quinoa with Asian Flavors 154
241. Quinoa with Butternut Squash Chicken and Goat Cheese 155
242. Quinoa with Carrots and Raisins 156
243. Quinoa with Chicken Asparagus and Red Peppers 156
244. Quinoa with Chickpeas and Tomatoes 157
245. Quinoa with Feta Walnuts and Dried Cranberries 157
246. Quinoa with Ground Turkey 157
247. Quinoa with Mango and Curried Yogurt 158
248. Quinoa with Moroccan Winter Squash and Carrot Stew 159
249. Quinoa with Mushrooms 160
250. Quinoa with Peas 160
251. Quinoa with Salmon and Swiss Chard 161
252. Quinoa with Sweet Potato and Mushrooms 161
253. Quinoa with Sweet Potatoes and Broccoli 162
254. Quinoa with Veggies 163
255. Quinoa Zucchini Protein Muffins 163
256. QuinoaCranberry Salad with Pecans .. 164
257. QuinoaFennel Pilaf 164
258. QuinoaMushroom Frittata With Fresh Herbs 165
259. Red Quinoa and Avocado Salad 165
260. Red Quinoa and Tuscan Kale 166
261. Red Quinoa Pilaf with Caribbean Flavors 166
262. Rice and Quinoa Breakfast Pudding .. 167
263. Rice Cooker Chicken Quinoa with Sundried Tomatoes 168
264. Ricks Sauteed Salmon over Quinoa ... 168
265. Roasted Butternut Squash Quinoa with Pumpkin Seeds 169
266. Roasted Sweet Potato Quinoa Salad .. 169
267. Robins Quinoa with Mushrooms and Spinach 170
268. Saffron Quinoa with Dried Cherries and Almonds 171
269. Savory Rice and Quinoa Pilaf 171
270. Scots Thai Soup 172
271. Seeded Flatbread 173
272. Seedy CherryQuinoa Bars 173
273. Sesame Kale Glow Bowl 174
274. Shrimp and Quinoa 174
275. Shrimp Quinoa 175
276. Simple Mexican Quinoa 175
277. Simple Savory Quinoa 176
278. Skillet Chicken and Quinoa with Fresh Salsa 176
279. Slow Cooked Chicken Stew 177
280. Slow Cooker Chicken Curry with Quinoa 178
281. Slow Cooker Quinoa Sweet Potato Chicken 178
282. Soft Polenta with Spicy Tomato Sauce 179
283. Solterito De Quinua Quinoa Solterito 179
284. Southwestern Quinoa Salad 180

285. SpanishStyle Quinoa 181
286. Speedy Mexican Black Beans and Quinoa 181
287. Spiced Quinoa................................. 182
288. Spiced Quinoa Porridge 182
289. Spicy Chicken Quinoa 183
290. Spicy Quinoa and Spinach Pulao Pilaf 183
291. Spicy Quinoa Bean and Pepper Salad. 184
292. Spicy Vegan Lentil Quinoa Soup 184
293. Spinach Quinoa Burgers 185
294. Spinach Tomato and Feta Quinoa Salad 185
295. Sriracha Quinoa Burger Melt 186
296. SteelCut Oats and Quinoa Breakfast .. 187
297. Stovetop Butternut Squash and Chicken Stew with Quinoa 187
298. Stuffed Peppers with Quinoa 188
299. Stuffed Red Pepper with Quinoa and Chickpeas 189
300. Stuffed Red Peppers with Quinoa Mushrooms and Turkey 189
301. Summer Squash and Red Quinoa Salad with Walnuts 190
302. Super Breakfast Apple and Quinoa Oatmeal 191
303. Super Pasta e Ceci 191
304. Suzys Special Red Quinoa 192
305. Sweet Potato Quinoa Patties 192
306. Tabbouleh Salad with Quinoa and Shredded Carrots 193
307. TexMex Quinoa Salad 193
308. Toasted Quinoa Granola 194
309. Tomato and Spinach Quinoa Skillet ... 194
310. TomatoMint Quinoa Salad 195
311. Tropical Coconut Quinoa Pudding 195
312. Tropical Quinoa 196
313. Tropical Quinoa Salsa Salad 196
314. Turkey and Quinoa Meatballs.............. 197
315. Turkey and Quinoa Meatloaf 197
316. Turkey Quinoa and Zucchini Mini Meatloaves 198
317. Turkey Quinoa Baked Burgers 199
318. Uncle Bobs Soybean Bread 200
319. Vegan Curry Quinoa Salad 200
320. Vegan Mexican Quinoa Bowl with Green Chile Cilantro Sauce 201
321. Vegan Quinoa and Guac Bowl 201
322. Vegan Quinoa Chili 202
323. Vegan Quinoa Oatmeal 202
324. Vegan QuinoaStuffed Peppers 203
325. Vegetarian Quinoa Frittatas 203
326. Veggie Almond and Raisin Quinoa Salad 204
327. Veggie Quinoa.................................... 205
328. Veggie Quinoa Bake............................ 205
329. Veggie Quinoa Burgers....................... 206
330. Warm Cinnamon Raisin Quinoa 207
331. What I Did With Quinoa 207
332. Zesty Quinoa Salad 208
333. Zucchini Noodle and Cannellini Bean Quinoa Bowl... 209

INDEX 210
CONCLUSION 221
LILY LI 221

Introduction

***

With life being fast-paced nowadays, it's difficult to make time to cook meals from scratch. But it's essential enough for me to make it my priority. Cooking at home is good not only for my family but also for me. I make a lot of creative and business decisions at work that I couldn't shake those thoughts off my mind even when I'm home. So it's hard for me to be fully present because the things that happened during the day often cross my mind.

However...

When I busy myself in the kitchen (like peeling potatoes or mixing ingredients in a bowl for baking a pie crust), my thoughts suddenly begin to slow down. I start to become relaxed. I open the kitchen window, blast my favorite music, and listen to the background sound of children playing with Chip. They all ease my mind. These sounds make me feel that indeed, I am home.

Working in the kitchen is no different from working in the garden. You work with your hands and take care of whatever you're working on. When it's time to harvest, you get so much in return. Such is the reward coming from working with your hands regardless of where it is: it could be your home, garden, or kitchen. We can choose to see our daily routines as either gifts or chores. Just a tiny shift in perspective can turn a dreadful thing into something you're excited about. I look forward to home cooking the most. Nothing can replace my time in the kitchen.

Consider this book "Quinoa 333 Volume 1" a celebration of bringing people together through good food. Sharing here most of my personal favorites, as well as some recipes I got from my family and friends. In each recipe, preparation, cooking, serving and cooling times are included. They're estimates only, so no need to follow them to a T. Those time estimates just work for me when I cook for my family. A dish that takes me half an hour to make may take you just 15 minutes or an hour. Just as some ovens heat faster and some people slice ingredients more quickly than others. Don't be disheartened if it takes you longer to prepare a dish or the outcome doesn't look like the one in the photo. What matters more is owning and enjoying the cooking experience. Just like my design philosophy (which is making your space reflect your own personality), I want to inspire you to make these recipes uniquely yours and tweak them to suit your taste, as well as your family's. Is there an ingredient in the recipe that you dislike? Omit it! If there's something you really like, add more of it! Just because you found a recipe in the breakfast section doesn't mean it's meant only for breakfast. Actually, I urge you to change things up frequently. Don't take everything here as gospel truth. Far from being a professional chef, I'm just an on-the-go, working mom who's fond of cooking and sharing recipes.

Also, I'm not the type who seeks perfection in the kitchen. If I were, I'd be too tired and drained come meal time. That defeats the purpose of enjoying food with the family. So you'll see things here that probably seem inconsistent, but these really are the ways I cook dishes for my family. For instance, I grow many of the veggies I use for my recipes and use organic meat a lot. Yet at the same time, I'm happy to use store-bought boxed broth and refrigerated dough (They're so convenient!). On my free time, I like to create pie crust from scratch, but I usually stock up on store-bought crust for baking a quick quiche. I fill my pantry with all the ingredients for making pancakes from scratch, but more often than not (especially when I'm rushing in the morning), I reheat frozen waffles or use a pancake mix. When I'm too busy to make a fresh pie for dessert, I just purchase a pie at the store and prepare fresh whipped cream for the topping on my own.

More than the recipes and food photos in this book, I hope to inspire you to unlock ways to cook meals that are truly yours, whether you just want to experiment in the kitchen as a beginner or you're looking to learn new recipes to add to the selection of meals you've been serving for years. Regardless, just enjoy cooking. In case you mess up, you can always order pizza.

You also see more different types of ingredient recipes such as:
- Cooking with Sesame Oil
- Herbs & Spices
- Whole Grains
- Nuts & Seeds
- Mozzarella
- ...

Thank you for choosing "Quinoa 333 Volume 1". I really hope that each book in the series will be always your best friend in your little kitchen.

Let's live happily and cook yourself every day!

Enjoy the book,

333 Amazing and Healthy Quinoa Recipes

***

1. African Quinoa Soup

"Hearty vegetarian soup with unique flavor. Leave out the jalapeno pepper for a more kid-friendly version. Taste and adjust seasonings if necessary."

Serving: 6 | Prep: 15 m | Cook: 40 m | Ready in: 55 m

Ingredients

- 2 tablespoons butter
- 1 onion, chopped
- 1 sweet potato, chopped
- 1 red bell pepper, chopped
- 2 stalks celery, chopped
- 2 zucchini, chopped
- 1 jalapeno pepper, minced
- 2 cloves garlic, minced
- 6 cups vegetable stock
- 1/2 cup quinoa
- 1 teaspoon ground cumin
- 1 teaspoon ground oregano
- 1 teaspoon salt
- 1 pinch ground black pepper
- 1 pinch cayenne pepper
- 1/2 cup peanut butter

Direction

- Heat butter in pot over medium heat; cook and stir onion, sweet potato, red bell pepper, celery, zucchini, jalapeno pepper, and garlic in the melted butter until vegetables are softened, about 10 minutes.
- Stir vegetable stock, quinoa, cumin, oregano, salt, black pepper, and cayenne pepper into vegetable mixture; bring to a boil. Reduce heat, cover pot, and simmer soup until quinoa is tender, 10 to 15 minutes. Stir peanut butter into soup and simmer until flavors have blended, about 20 more minutes.

Nutrition Information

- Calories: 292 calories
- Total Fat: 16.4 g
- Cholesterol: 10 mg
- Sodium: 1006 mg
- Total Carbohydrate: 29.1 g
- Protein: 10.3 g

2. Amandas Quinoa Salad

"This is my stepdaughter Amanda's concoction, I had it once and was hooked! Keep it in the fridge all the time!"

Serving: 9 | Prep: 15 m | Cook: 15 m | Ready in: 4 h 30 m

Ingredients

- 2 cups water
- 1 cup quinoa
- 5 ounces mango salsa
- 1 bunch green onions, chopped (green parts only)
- 1/3 cup dried cranberries
- 1 1/2 ounces sunflower kernels
- 2 tablespoons champagne vinegar
- 1 tablespoon French vinaigrette (such as Briannas Home Style®)

Direction

- Bring water and quinoa to a boil in a saucepan. Reduce heat to medium-low, cover, and simmer until quinoa is tender and water has been absorbed, 15 to 20 minutes. Transfer quinoa to a bowl and fluff with a fork.
- Stir mango salsa, green onions, cranberries, sunflower kernels, champagne vinegar, and French vinaigrette into the quinoa. Cover bowl with plastic wrap.
- Refrigerate salad at least 4 hours before serving.

Nutrition Information

- Calories: 166 calories
- Total Fat: 5.3 g
- Cholesterol: 0 mg
- Sodium: 204 mg
- Total Carbohydrate: 27.4 g
- Protein: 4.2 g

- Sodium: 375 mg
- Total Carbohydrate: 37 g
- Protein: 5.8 g

3. Amazing Chocolate Quinoa Cake

"This delicious cake is made with quinoa and no flour! Enjoy!"

Serving: 12 | Prep: 15 m | Cook: 40 m | Ready in: 1 h 25 m

Ingredients

- 2 cups cold cooked quinoa
- 3/4 cup melted butter
- 4 eggs
- 1/3 cup milk
- 1 1/2 teaspoons vanilla extract
- 1 1/4 cups white sugar
- 1 cup cocoa powder
- 1 1/2 teaspoons baking powder
- 1 teaspoon baking soda
- 1/2 teaspoon salt
- 1/2 cup chocolate chips
- 1/2 cup chopped pecans (optional)

Direction

- Preheat oven to 350 degrees F (175 degrees C). Grease a rectangular cake pan.
- Blend quinoa, butter, eggs, milk, and vanilla extract together in a blender until smooth.
- Combine sugar, cocoa powder, baking powder, baking soda, and salt together in a large bowl. Stir quinoa mixture into sugar mixture until batter is well combined. Fold chocolate chips and pecans into batter; pour into the prepared pan.
- Bake in the preheated oven until a toothpick inserted in the center of the cake comes out clean, 40 to 45 minutes. Cool cake on a wire rack.

Nutrition Information

- Calories: 332 calories
- Total Fat: 20.5 g
- Cholesterol: 93 mg

4. Apple OatQuinoa Granola

"Delicious, low-fat, high-fiber, and super-easy to make."

Serving: 20 | Prep: 20 m | Cook: 1 h 20 m | Ready in: 2 h 15 m

Ingredients

- Apples:
- 3 apples, cored and diced
- 2 teaspoons ground cinnamon
- 1 teaspoon ground nutmeg
- Granola:
- 1/3 cup honey
- 1/4 cup applesauce
- 1/4 cup coconut oil
- 1 tablespoon ground cinnamon
- 1 teaspoon ground nutmeg
- 1 teaspoon ground ginger
- 1/2 teaspoon ground cloves
- 1 cup quinoa
- 2 cups rolled oats
- 1/2 cup coarsely ground almonds
- 1/2 cup flaked coconut

Direction

- Preheat oven to 300 degrees F (150 degrees C). Line a baking sheet with aluminum foil.
- Spread diced apples on baking sheet. Sprinkle 2 teaspoons cinnamon and 1 teaspoon nutmeg on top.
- Bake apples in the preheated oven, stirring at 10-minute intervals, until tender but not over-crisp, about 40 minutes total.
- Mix honey, applesauce, coconut oil, 1 tablespoon cinnamon, 1 teaspoon nutmeg, ginger, and cloves together in a large bowl. Stir in quinoa. Let sit, about 5 minutes.

- Stir oats, almond, and coconut into the honey mixture. Spread evenly over baked apple pieces.
- Bake in the preheated oven, stirring at 10-minute-intervals, until granola is golden brown and crispy, about 40 minutes. Cool completely before storing, 30 minutes to 1 hour.

Nutrition Information

- Calories: 147 calories
- Total Fat: 6.3 g
- Cholesterol: 0 mg
- Sodium: 7 mg
- Total Carbohydrate: 21.2 g
- Protein: 3.2 g

5. Asian Breakfast StirFry

"Here is an under-an-hour recipe for an Asian-inspired, veggie-rich, breakfast stir-fry that could also work as a main dish lunch or dinner for 1."

Serving: 1 | Prep: 20 m | Cook: 35 m | Ready in: 55 m

Ingredients

- 1 cup water
- 1/2 cup quinoa
- 1 large carrot, peeled and chopped
- 1/2 cup broccoli florets
- 1/4 cup chopped onion
- 1 (1 inch) piece ginger, peeled, or to taste
- 1 tablespoon sesame oil
- 1 tablespoon minced garlic
- 1 cup kale
- 1 tablespoon reduced-sodium soy sauce
- 1 tablespoon water
- 1/2 cup shredded boneless, skinless baked chicken breast
- 1 cooking spray (optional)
- 2 large eggs
- 1 teaspoon chile-garlic sauce (such as Sriracha®), or to taste (optional)
- 1 teaspoon fresh cilantro, or to taste (optional)
- 1 teaspoon sesame seeds, or to taste (optional)

Direction

- Bring water and quinoa to a boil in a saucepan. Reduce heat to medium-low, cover, and simmer until quinoa is tender, 15 to 20 minutes.
- Combine carrot, broccoli, and onion in the bowl of a food processor and chop.
- Heat sesame oil in a large skillet over medium heat and add garlic. Stir until fragrant, about 1 minute. Add chopped vegetable mixture from food processor. Cook and stir until onions are translucent, 3 to 5 minutes. Add kale; cook until wilted, about 1 minute. Add soy sauce and water; cook for 5 minutes more.
- Add chicken and 1/4 cup cooked quinoa to the skillet with the vegetable mixture. Cook and stir until heated through, 2 to 3 minutes. Transfer stir-fry to a plate.
- Spray the skillet with cooking spray and cook eggs to preference, 3 to 5 minutes. Place cooked eggs on top of stir-fry in the plate. Garnish with chile-garlic sauce, cilantro, and sesame seeds.

Nutrition Information

- Calories: 814 calories
- Total Fat: 36.1 g
- Cholesterol: 424 mg
- Sodium: 1015 mg
- Total Carbohydrate: 75.4 g
- Protein: 48.2 g

6. Asian Fusion Quinoa

"Quinoa mixed with Asian flavors of sweet and salty. Be careful not to burn the garlic! And feel free to add chopped peanuts as a garnish."

Serving: 2 | Prep: 10 m | Cook: 10 m | Ready in: 20 m

Ingredients

- 1 1/2 tablespoons coconut oil

- 1/2 onion, chopped
- 2 green onions, chopped
- 3 cloves garlic, chopped
- 1 cup cooked quinoa
- 2 tablespoons chopped fresh cilantro
- 2 tablespoons orange marmalade
- 1 tablespoon soy sauce, or to taste
- 1 pinch garlic salt
- 1 egg, beaten

Direction

- Melt coconut oil in a skillet over medium-high heat; add onion. Cook and stir until soft, about 3 minutes. Add green onions and garlic to skillet. Cook and stir until garlic is slightly crispy, about 2 minutes.
- Reduce heat to medium; add cooked quinoa, cilantro, marmalade, soy sauce, and garlic salt to the skillet. Cook and stir until heated through, about 2 minutes. Make a well in quinoa-veggie mixture; add egg and cook and stir until egg is firm, about 3 minutes. Stir cooked egg into quinoa-veggie mixture.

Nutrition Information

- Calories: 323 calories
- Total Fat: 14.6 g
- Cholesterol: 93 mg
- Sodium: 675 mg
- Total Carbohydrate: 41.5 g
- Protein: 9 g

7. Asian Quinoa Salad

"An Asian-inspired vegetarian salad made with quinoa, cabbage, edamame, and a spicy sweet dressing."

Serving: 4 | Prep: 15 m | Cook: 10 m | Ready in: 1 h 10 m

Ingredients

- 2 cups vegetable broth
- 1 cup quinoa
- 1 1/2 cups thinly sliced purple cabbage
- 1 cup chopped carrots
- 1 cup frozen shelled edamame (green soybeans)
- 4 green onions, thinly sliced
- Dressing:
- 1 1/2 tablespoons rice wine vinegar
- 1 tablespoon vegetable oil
- 2 teaspoons sriracha sauce
- 2 teaspoons soy sauce
- 1 teaspoon minced fresh ginger
- 1 1/2 teaspoons white sugar
- 1/2 teaspoon Asian-style mustard

Direction

- Bring vegetable broth to a boil in a saucepan. Add quinoa, reduce heat to medium, and simmer, stirring occasionally, until quinoa is tender and liquid is absorbed, 10 to 15 minutes. Remove saucepan from heat and cool.
- Mix cabbage, carrots, edamame, and green onions together in a large bowl.
- Whisk vinegar, oil, Sriracha sauce, soy sauce, ginger, sugar, and mustard together in a bowl until dressing is smooth; drizzle over cabbage mixture. Stir quinoa into salad and toss to coat. Refrigerate until chilled, at least 30 minutes.

Nutrition Information

- Calories: 335 calories
- Total Fat: 10.8 g
- Cholesterol: 0 mg
- Sodium: 594 mg
- Total Carbohydrate: 46.2 g
- Protein: 15.9 g

8. BabyandMe Pilaf

"Dairy- and gluten-free, complex in texture and flavor, this recipe is gentle on the digestive tract and can be enjoyed by all family members 7-months and up."

Serving: 4 | Prep: 10 m | Cook: 30 m | Ready in: 40 m

Ingredients

- 1/4 cup millet
- 1/4 cup amaranth
- 1/4 cup quinoa
- 1/4 cup brown rice
- 1 cup soy milk
- 3/4 cup water
- 1 tablespoon olive oil
- 1/2 teaspoon sea salt (optional)
- 1/4 teaspoon roasted garlic (optional)
- 1 pinch dill (optional)

Direction

- Preheat oven to 350 degrees F (175 degrees C).
- Combine millet, amaranth, quinoa, and brown rice in a bowl and rinse in warm water thoroughly, changing water 2 or 3 times.
- Stir soy milk, water, and oil together in a baking dish. Stir sea salt, roasted garlic, and dill into the soy milk mixture; add grains mixture and stir gently.
- Bake in preheated oven until most of the liquid is absorbed, 30 to 45 minutes.

Nutrition Information

- Calories: 238 calories
- Total Fat: 6.7 g
- Cholesterol: 0 mg
- Sodium: 257 mg
- Total Carbohydrate: 37 g
- Protein: 7.6 g

9. Bacon Spinach Quinoa

"This is a quick and easy meal!"

Serving: 6 | Prep: 10 m | Cook: 25 m | Ready in: 35 m

Ingredients

- 1 1/2 cups chicken broth
- 1 cup quinoa
- 1 pound bacon, cut into bite-sized pieces
- 1 onion, chopped
- 1 (10 ounce) package baby spinach
- 1 tablespoon chopped fresh cilantro

Direction

- Bring chicken broth and quinoa to a boil in a saucepan. Reduce heat to medium-low, cover, and simmer until the quinoa is tender and broth has been absorbed, about 15 minutes.
- Cook and stir bacon and onion in a skillet over medium heat until bacon is cooked and onion is softened, 5 to 10 minutes. Transfer and drain mixture on a paper towel-lined plate. Cook spinach in the remaining bacon drippings until wilted, 2 to 3 minutes. Stir quinoa, onion-bacon mixture, and cilantro into spinach until evenly blended.

Nutrition Information

- Calories: 261 calories
- Total Fat: 12.4 g
- Cholesterol: 29 mg
- Sodium: 853 mg
- Total Carbohydrate: 22.2 g
- Protein: 15 g

10. Balsamic and Herb Quinoa Salad

"Serve this cold salad as a delicious summer side to your favorite grilled meat or try it alone as a great light lunch. I have been experimenting a lot with quinoa recently, and this is by far my favorite recipe. It's such a nice, healthy alternative to pasta and rice!"

Serving: 4 | Prep: 15 m | Cook: 25 m | Ready in: 1 h 20 m

Ingredients

- Salad:
- 2 cups water
- 1 cup quinoa
- 1 teaspoon chicken bouillon granules
- 1/2 cup frozen baby lima beans
- water to cover
- salt and freshly ground black pepper to taste
- 1/3 cup slivered almonds
- 3 Campari tomatoes, diced
- 2 tablespoons thinly sliced scallions
- 2 ounces fresh mozzarella cheese, cut into small chunks
- Dressing:
- 3 tablespoons balsamic vinegar
- 3 tablespoons almond oil
- 2 tablespoons extra-virgin olive oil
- 2 teaspoons Italian seasoning
- 2 teaspoons dried basil
- 1 teaspoon minced garlic
- 1/4 teaspoon salt

Direction

- Bring 2 cups water, quinoa, and bouillon granules to a boil in a saucepan. Reduce heat to medium-low, cover, and simmer until quinoa is tender and water has been absorbed, 15 to 20 minutes. Spread quinoa onto a baking sheet and refrigerate until cooled, about 30 minutes. Rinse saucepan.
- Place lima beans into the saucepan and add enough water to cover beans by 1 inch; season with salt and pepper. Cover saucepan with a lid and bring water to a boil. Reduce heat to medium and simmer until beans are cooked through but still tender, 3 to 4 minutes. Drain water and rinse beans under cold water to stop the cooking process; refrigerate until cool, about 10 minutes.
- Cook and stir almonds in a skillet over medium heat until toasted, about 5 minutes. Remove skillet from heat and cool almonds to room temperature, about 5 minutes.
- Mix quinoa, lima beans, almonds, tomatoes, scallions, and mozzarella cheese together in a large bowl.
- Whisk vinegar, almond oil, olive oil, Italian seasoning, basil, garlic, and salt together in a bowl until smooth; pour over quinoa mixture and stir to coat.

Nutrition Information

- Calories: 453 calories
- Total Fat: 27.5 g
- Cholesterol: 11 mg
- Sodium: 308 mg
- Total Carbohydrate: 39.7 g
- Protein: 12.6 g

11. Banana Quinoa Rice Pudding

"Quinoa is a complete protein that's also high in fiber. Banana 'rice' pudding makes an excellent snack or meal for a toddler, and a delicious dessert for an adult."

Serving: 6 | Prep: 5 m | Cook: 25 m | Ready in: 1 h

Ingredients

- 3/4 cup quinoa
- 1 1/2 cups water
- 2 ripe bananas
- 1 cup whole milk
- 1 cup coconut milk
- 4 tablespoons honey, divided
- 1 tablespoon butter
- 1 teaspoon ground cinnamon, divided
- 1/4 teaspoon salt

Direction

- Rinse quinoa in a paper towel-lined colander until water is no longer milky. Transfer quinoa to a saucepan, add 1 1/2 cups water and soak for 30 minutes.
- Bring quinoa and water to a boil, reduce heat to low, cover, and simmer until water is absorbed, about 15 minutes.
- Blend bananas, whole milk, coconut milk, 3 tablespoons honey, butter, 1/2 teaspoon cinnamon, and salt together in a blender until smooth.
- Stir milk mixture into quinoa, raise heat to medium; cook and stir constantly until pudding becomes thick, about 10 minutes.
- Transfer pudding to serving dish and refrigerate until cold, about 1 hour. Drizzle 1 tablespoon honey over pudding; sprinkle with 1/2 teaspoon cinnamon.

Nutrition Information

- Calories: 278 calories
- Total Fat: 12.7 g
- Cholesterol: 9 mg
- Sodium: 136 mg
- Total Carbohydrate: 38.7 g
- Protein: 5.6 g

12. Best Greek Quinoa Salad

"This is my absolute favorite quinoa recipe! It's so flavorful and always a big hit with my family and friends. Trust me, you'll want to eat every single bite!"

Serving: 10 | Prep: 15 m | Cook: 15 m | Ready in: 1 h 40 m

Ingredients

- 3 1/2 cups chicken broth
- 2 cups quinoa
- 1 cup halved grape tomatoes
- 3/4 cup chopped fresh parsley
- 1/2 cup sliced pitted kalamata olives
- 1/2 cup minced red onion
- 4 ounces chopped feta cheese, or more to taste
- 3 tablespoons olive oil
- 3 tablespoons red wine vinegar
- 2 cloves garlic, minced
- 1 lemon, halved
- salt and ground black pepper to taste

Direction

- Bring broth and quinoa to a boil in a saucepan. Reduce heat to medium-low, cover, and simmer until quinoa is tender and water has been absorbed, 15 to 20 minutes. Transfer quinoa to a large bowl and set aside to cool, about 10 minutes.
- Mix tomatoes, parsley, kalamata olives, onion, feta cheese, olive oil, vinegar, and garlic into quinoa. Squeeze lemon juice over quinoa salad, season with salt and pepper, and toss to coat. Chill in refrigerator, 1 to 4 hours.

Nutrition Information

- Calories: 227 calories
- Total Fat: 10.6 g
- Cholesterol: 12 mg
- Sodium: 666 mg
- Total Carbohydrate: 25.8 g
- Protein: 7.4 g

13. Black Bean and Quinoa Enchilada Bake

"Great dish for Mexican night with lots of different possibilities. The best thing about this recipe is it can be served by itself for a main dish on Mexican night, or be eaten with tortilla chips as a dip or even rolled up in a tortilla as a taco, burrito, or enchilada. Garnish with green onions, avocado, tomatoes, or/and sour cream. Very versatile recipe. So enjoy and learn the many uses of oh so healthy quinoa."

Serving: 6 | Prep: 15 m   Cook: 1 h | Ready in: 1 h 15 m

Ingredients

- 2 cups water

- 1 cup quinoa
- 1 tablespoon olive oil
- 1 small onion, diced
- 1 yellow bell pepper, diced
- 1 orange bell pepper, diced
- 1 jalapeno pepper, minced
- 2 cloves garlic, minced
- 1 (15 ounce) can black beans, rinsed and drained
- 1/3 cup chopped fresh cilantro
- 1 tablespoon chili powder
- 1 teaspoon lime juice
- 1 teaspoon ground cumin
- salt and ground black pepper to taste
- 1 (10 ounce) can enchilada sauce
- 2 cups shredded Cheddar cheese

Direction

- Preheat oven to 350 degrees F (175 degrees C).
- Bring water and quinoa to a boil in a saucepan. Reduce heat to medium-low, cover, and simmer until quinoa is tender and water has been absorbed, 15 to 20 minutes.
- Heat olive oil in a skillet over medium heat; cook and stir onion, yellow bell pepper, orange bell pepper, jalapeno pepper, and garlic in the hot oil until softened, about 10 minutes.
- Mix black beans, pepper mixture, quinoa, cilantro, chili powder, lime juice, cumin, salt, and pepper together in a bowl; transfer to a casserole dish. Pour enchilada sauce over quinoa mixture, spreading sauce evenly over the top. Sprinkle Cheddar cheese over sauce. Cover dish with aluminum foil.
- Bake in the preheated oven for 20 minutes. Remove foil and continue baking until cheese is bubbling, 10 to 15 minutes.

Nutrition Information

- Calories: 388 calories
- Total Fat: 18 g
- Cholesterol: 40 mg
- Sodium: 673 mg
- Total Carbohydrate: 38.6 g
- Protein: 19.2 g

14. Black Bean and Tomato Quinoa

Quinoa is a fast-cooking, protein-packed whole grain. Steamed, it makes a perfect partner for lime-spiked black beans and fresh tomato.

Serving: Makes 4 (side dish) servings | Prep: 20 m | Cook: 45 m

Ingredients

- 2 teaspoons grated lime zest
- 2 tablespoons fresh lime juice
- 2 tablespoons unsalted butter, melted and cooled
- 1 tablespoon vegetable oil
- 1 teaspoon sugar
- 1 cup quinoa
- 1 (14- to 15-ounce) can black beans, rinsed and drained
- 2 medium tomatoes, diced
- 4 scallions, chopped
- 1/4 cup chopped fresh cilantro

Direction

- Whisk together lime zest and juice, butter, oil, sugar, 1/2 teaspoon salt, and 1/4 teaspoon pepper in a large bowl.
- Wash quinoa in 3 changes of cold water in a bowl, draining in a sieve each time.
- Cook quinoa in a medium pot of boiling salted water (1 tablespoon salt for 2 quarts water), uncovered, until almost tender, about 10 minutes. Drain in sieve, then set sieve in same pot with 1 inch of simmering water (water should not touch bottom of sieve). Cover quinoa with a folded kitchen towel, then cover sieve with a lid (don't worry if lid doesn't fit tightly) and steam over medium heat until tender, fluffy, and dry, about 10 minutes. Remove pot from heat and remove lid. Let stand, still covered with towel, 5 minutes.
- Add quinoa to dressing and toss until dressing is absorbed, then stir in remaining ingredients and salt and pepper to taste.

- Per serving: 382 calories, 12 g fat (4 g saturated), 15 mg cholesterol, 446 mg sodium, 55 g carbohydrate, 10 g fiber, 14 g protein
- Nutritional analysis provided by Nutrition Data
- See Nutrition Data's complete analysis of this recipe ›

Nutrition Information

- Calories: 250 calories
- Total Fat: 7.1 g
- Cholesterol: 2 mg
- Sodium: 622 mg
- Total Carbohydrate: 38.3 g
- Protein: 9.8 g

15. Black Bean Corn and Quinoa Salad

"This is a wonderful Southwestern style salad that is quick and easy to make."

Serving: 6 | Prep: 15 m | Cook: 20 m | Ready in: 40 m

Ingredients

- 2 cups chicken broth
- 1 cup uncooked quinoa
- 1 cup frozen corn
- 1 tablespoon lime juice
- 1 teaspoon red wine vinegar
- lime, zested
- 1/2 teaspoon ground cumin
- 2 tablespoons avocado oil
- 1 (15 ounce) can black beans, drained
- 1 small red bell pepper, seeded and chopped
- 1 small red onion, chopped
- 1/4 cup chopped fresh cilantro
- salt and ground black pepper to taste

Direction

- Bring chicken broth to a boil in a 2-quart saucepan. Stir in quinoa. Reduce heat to low; simmer, covered, until broth is absorbed, 15 to 20 minutes. Remove from heat; stir in corn. Cover and let stand until corn is warmed through, about 5 minutes.
- Whisk lime juice, red wine vinegar, lime zest, and cumin together in a large bowl. Whisk in avocado oil. Add black beans, red bell pepper, red onion, and cilantro. Season with salt and pepper. Stir in quinoa and corn.

16. Black Bean Quinoa Burgers

"These burgers make up a complete vegetarian protein, and are both delicious and low fat. Add all your burger fixings to your bun, serve, and enjoy."

Serving: 4 | Prep: 20 m | Cook: 33 m | Ready in: 53 m

Ingredients

- 1/2 cup uncooked quinoa
- 1 cup water
- 2 tablespoons vegetable oil, or as needed, divided
- 1 small red onion, chopped
- 1 clove garlic, minced
- 1 cup frozen corn
- 1/3 teaspoon chili powder
- 1/8 teaspoon ground cumin
- 1/8 teaspoon ground cayenne pepper, or to taste (optional)
- salt and ground black pepper to taste
- 1 (15 ounce) can black beans, rinsed and drained
- 2 eggs
- 1/3 cup dry bread crumbs

Direction

- Combine water and quinoa in a pot. Bring to a boil; simmer until water is absorbed, 10 to 15 minutes.
- Heat 1 tablespoon oil in a saucepan over medium heat. Add onion and garlic; cook and stir until onion is translucent and soft, about 5 minutes. Add corn, chili powder, cumin, cayenne pepper, salt, and black pepper. Cook

- and stir until corn is defrosted, about 5 minutes.
- Mash beans in a bowl using a fork. Add quinoa and corn mixture; mash until well combined. Add eggs; mix well. Stir in bread crumbs. Form mixture into 4 flat, round patties.
- Heat the remaining 1 tablespoon oil in a skillet; cook patties until golden brown, about 4 minutes per side.

Nutrition Information

- Calories: 352 calories
- Total Fat: 11.8 g
- Cholesterol: 93 mg
- Sodium: 555 mg
- Total Carbohydrate: 48.5 g
- Protein: 15.3 g

17. Black Bean Quinoa Veggie Burgers

"A hearty, protein-rich veggie burger that's really satisfying. The quinoa gives this burger a texture similar to ground beef. Serve just like your favorite burger."

Serving: 8 | Prep: 15 m | Cook: 26 m | Ready in: 41 m

Ingredients

- 2 cups vegetable broth
- 1 teaspoon hoisin sauce
- 1/2 teaspoon sesame oil
- 1 cup uncooked quinoa
- 1 cup canned black beans - drained, rinsed, and mashed
- 2 eggs
- 1 slice bread
- 2 tablespoons water
- 1 small clove garlic, minced
- 1/2 teaspoon salt
- 1/4 teaspoon ground black pepper
- 3 tablespoons canola oil, or as needed

Direction

- Bring vegetable broth, hoisin, and sesame oil to a boil in a saucepan; add quinoa. Reduce heat to low, cover, and cook until quinoa is tender, about 20 minutes. Remove from heat; cool slightly.
- Combine black beans, eggs, bread, water, garlic, salt, and pepper together in a bowl; mash thoroughly. Add 1 1/2 cup cooled quinoa and mix well.
- Heat canola oil in a large skillet over medium-high heat. Form each burger patty using about 1/2 cup of the burger mixture; transfer to the skillet. Cook until golden brown; about 3 minutes per side. Drain on paper towel-lined dish.

Nutrition Information

- Calories: 190 calories
- Total Fat: 8.4 g
- Cholesterol: 47 mg
- Sodium: 426 mg
- Total Carbohydrate: 22 g
- Protein: 6.9 g

18. Blackberry Pomegranate Quinoa Parfait

"Loaded with fresh fruit and fruit spread, these whole grain and chia seed parfaits with creamy Greek yogurt make delicious snacks or desserts."

Serving: 4 | Prep: 20 m | Ready in: 20 m

Ingredients

- 1/2 cup Santa Cruz Organic® Blackberry Pomegranate Fruit Spread
- 1 tablespoon truRoots® Organic Chia Seeds
- 1 (6 ounce) container fresh blackberries
- 1 (6 ounce) container fresh raspberries
- 1 cup cooked truRoots® Accents® Organic Sprouted Quinoa Trio
- 1 1/3 cups vanilla Greek yogurt

- 1/2 teaspoon grated fresh lemon peel
- 4 lemon slices, for garnish

Direction

- Combine fruit spread and chia seeds in medium bowl. Stir in berries and quinoa. Combine yogurt and lemon peel in small bowl.
- Divide half of quinoa mixture evenly into 4 parfait glasses. Reserve 2 tablespoons yogurt for garnish. Top quinoa mixture with 1/3 cup yogurt. Divide and spoon remaining quinoa mixture over yogurt. Top with dollop of yogurt and lemon slice. Chill.

Nutrition Information

- Calories: 342 calories
- Total Fat: 8 g
- Cholesterol: 6 mg
- Sodium: 38 mg
- Total Carbohydrate: 62.6 g
- Protein: 10.8 g

19. Blackened Chicken with Avocado Cream Sauce

"This recipe will kick your taste buds into high gear! The perfect blend of paprika, cumin, and cayenne pepper will have your mouth buzzing with flavor and heat, but don't worry, the addition of the avocado and Greek yogurt cream sauce acts as a cooling agent for all that fire! The quinoa adds a gentle basic flavor to this intense dish and contributes a satisfying amount of nutritious fiber and protein to keep you and your family full and happy!"

Serving: 4 | Prep: 10 m | Cook: 30 m | Ready in: 40 m

Ingredients

- Quinoa:
- 2 cups reduced-sodium chicken broth
- 1 cup quinoa
- 1/2 cup chopped scallions
- 1 1/2 teaspoons lemon juice
- Blackened Chicken:
- 1 teaspoon paprika
- 1 teaspoon ground cumin
- 1 teaspoon onion powder
- 1 teaspoon ground black pepper
- 1/2 teaspoon cayenne pepper
- 1/2 teaspoon sea salt
- 4 (4 ounce) skinless, boneless chicken breast halves
- non-stick cooking spray
- Avocado Cream Sauce:
- 1/2 avocado
- 1/4 cup plain non-fat Greek-style yogurt
- 1 1/2 teaspoons lemon juice
- 1/2 teaspoon garlic powder

Direction

- Bring chicken broth to a boil in a saucepan. Stir quinoa into the broth and bring again to a boil; reduce heat to medium-low, cover, and simmer until quinoa is tender and broth has been absorbed, 15 to 20 minutes.
- Stir scallions and 1 1/2 teaspoons lemon juice into the quinoa.
- Mix paprika, cumin, onion powder, black pepper, cayenne pepper, and sea salt together in a small bowl; rub onto chicken breasts to season completely.
- Prepare a large skillet with cooking spray and heat over medium-high heat.
- Lay chicken breasts into the hot skillet, cover skillet with a lid, and cook until chicken is no longer pink in the center and the juices run clear, about 7 minutes per side. An instant-read thermometer inserted into the center should read at least 165 degrees F (74 degrees C).
- Blend avocado, yogurt, 1 1/2 teaspoons lemon juice, and garlic powder in a food processor until smooth.
- Spread quinoa onto a serving platter. Arrange chicken breasts onto the platter. Drizzle avocado cream sauce over the chicken breasts.

Nutrition Information

- Calories: 367 calories
- Total Fat: 10.3 g

- Cholesterol: 71 mg
- Sodium: 356 mg
- Total Carbohydrate: 33.2 g
- Protein: 35 g

20. Blueberry Lemon Breakfast Quinoa

"Sweet blueberries and tart lemon pair well in this alternative to oatmeal. High in protein and fiber, quinoa is a great start to your day! I made this up one morning when I had a craving for quinoa and was looking for a change from the usual. Top with extra milk for a thinner consistency. Also good with a sprinkle of cinnamon or nutmeg."

Serving: 2 | Prep: 5 m | Cook: 25 m | Ready in: 30 m

Ingredients

- 1 cup quinoa
- 2 cups nonfat milk
- 1 pinch salt
- 3 tablespoons maple syrup
- 1/2 lemon, zested
- 1 cup blueberries
- 2 teaspoons flax seed

Direction

- Rinse quinoa in a fine strainer with cold water to remove bitterness until water runs clear and is no longer frothy.
- Heat milk in a saucepan over medium heat until warm, 2 to 3 minutes. Stir quinoa and salt into the milk; simmer over medium-low heat until much of the liquid has been absorbed, about 20 minutes. Remove saucepan from heat. Stir maple syrup and lemon zest into the quinoa mixture. Gently fold blueberries into the mixture.
- Divide quinoa mixture between 2 bowls; top each with 1 teaspoon flax seed to serve.

Nutrition Information

- Calories: 538 calories

- Total Fat: 7.3 g
- Cholesterol: 5 mg
- Sodium: 112 mg
- Total Carbohydrate: 98.7 g
- Protein: 21.5 g

21. Blueberry Lemon Sprouted Rice and Quinoa Cereal

"Breakfast hot cereal has never been this delicious--a rice and quinoa combo is cooked in almond milk and served with a lemony maple syrup and almond milk blend and fresh blueberries."

Serving: 4 | Prep: 10 m | Cook: 35 m | Ready in: 45 m

Ingredients

- 2 1/2 cups vanilla-flavored almond milk
- 1 cup truRoots® Sprouted Rice Quinoa Medley
- 1/8 teaspoon fine sea salt
- 3 tablespoons pure maple syrup
- 1/2 teaspoon finely grated lemon peel
- 1 cup blueberries

Direction

- Combine 2 cups milk, rice quinoa medley and salt in large saucepan. Bring to boil over medium-high heat. Reduce to simmer. Cover and cook about 32 minutes or until liquid is absorbed. Remove from heat. Let stand, 10 minutes. Fluff with fork.
- Heat remaining 1/2 cup milk. Blend milk, syrup and lemon peel into rice quinoa medley. Gently stir in blueberries.

Nutrition Information

- Calories: 256 calories
- Total Fat: 2.7 g
- Cholesterol: 0 mg
- Sodium: 150 mg
- Total Carbohydrate: 55.4 g
- Protein: 3.9 g

22. Blueberry Quinoa with Lemon Glaze

"Healthy alternative if you want some dessert. Good to make night before if using it as a dessert or breakfast item."

Serving: 12 | Prep: 10 m | Cook: 20 m | Ready in: 3 h

Ingredients

- Blueberry Quinoa:
- 6 cups apple juice
- 3 cups quinoa
- 1 tablespoon vanilla extract
- 1 pint blueberries
- Lemon Glaze:
- 1 cup almond milk
- 2 tablespoons water
- 1 tablespoon cornstarch
- 1 lemon, juiced
- 1 tablespoon maple syrup

Direction

- Combine apple juice, quinoa, and vanilla extract in a large pot; bring to a boil. Reduce heat to medium-low, cover, and simmer until quinoa is tender and liquid is absorbed, about 15 minutes.
- Gently fold blueberries into hot quinoa. Pour blueberry mixture into a 9x13-inch baking dish. Cool until quinoa is set.
- Whisk almond milk, water, and cornstarch together in a small saucepan over high heat. Add lemon juice and maple syrup; cook, stirring constantly, until glaze is thick, 2 to 3 minutes. Pour hot glaze over quinoa to cover it completely. Cool to room temperature. Cover baking dish with plastic wrap and refrigerate for at least 2 hours.

Nutrition Information

- Calories: 247 calories
- Total Fat: 3 g
- Cholesterol: 0 mg
- Sodium: 20 mg
- Total Carbohydrate: 48.6 g
- Protein: 6.4 g

23. Broccoli Quinoa Casserole

"A high-protein dish made with rotisserie chicken--and a great way to sneak some veggies in, too!"

Serving: 8 | Prep: 10 m | Cook: 58 m | Ready in: 1 h 8 m

Ingredients

- 1 1/2 cups water
- 3/4 cup quinoa
- 1/4 teaspoon salt
- 2 cups broccoli florets
- cooking spray
- 1 pound shredded rotisserie chicken
- 1 (10.75 ounce) can cream of broccoli soup
- 1 1/4 cups shredded reduced-fat Cheddar cheese
- 1/3 cup reduced-fat mayonnaise
- 2 tablespoons milk
- 1/2 teaspoon stevia powder
- 1/4 teaspoon black pepper
- 1 dash freshly grated nutmeg
- 3 tablespoons freshly grated Parmesan cheese, or to taste

Direction

- Rinse quinoa in a fine-mesh sieve until water runs clear. Combine 1 1/2 cups water, quinoa, and salt in a small saucepan. Bring to a boil. Reduce heat to low and cover. Cook until tender, 18 to 20 minutes. Fluff with a fork.
- Preheat oven to 350 degrees F (175 degrees C). Coat a shallow 8-inch baking dish with cooking spray.
- Place a steamer insert into a saucepan and fill with water to just below the bottom of the steamer. Bring water to a boil. Add broccoli, cover, and steam until tender, about 3 minutes. Drain.

- Combine chicken, cream of broccoli soup, Cheddar cheese, mayonnaise, milk, stevia powder, pepper, and nutmeg in a large bowl. Stir in quinoa and broccoli. Spoon mixture into the prepared baking dish. Sprinkle Parmesan cheese on top.
- Bake in the preheated oven until top is bubbly and edges are golden, 35 to 40 minutes.

Nutrition Information

- Calories: 282 calories
- Total Fat: 12.7 g
- Cholesterol: 52 mg
- Sodium: 385 mg
- Total Carbohydrate: 18 g
- Protein: 23.5 g

24. Brown Rice and Quinoa Sushi Rolls

"I have omitted white sugar and flour from my diet and wanted to come up with a new way to make sushi, since being half Japanese, I still wanted to be able to enjoy sushi but wanted an option. I love it! Adds that extra bit of protein to make this a well-rounded light meal or snack. I like organic sugar in this recipe."

Serving: 4 | Prep: 30 m | Cook: 45 m | Ready in: 1 h 25 m

Ingredients

- 2/3 cup short-grain brown rice
- 2 1/3 cups water
- 1 pinch sea salt
- 2 tablespoons rice vinegar
- 1 tablespoon cider vinegar
- 1 tablespoon mirin (Japanese sweet wine) (optional)
- 2 tablespoons turbinado sugar
- 1/2 teaspoon sea salt
- 1/2 cup quinoa
- 4 sheets nori (dry seaweed)
- 1/2 carrot, shredded
- 1/2 cucumber, cut into thin strips
- 1 avocado - peeled, pitted, and cut into thin strips

Direction

- Rinse and drain brown rice and bring to a boil in a saucepan with water and a pinch of sea salt. Reduce heat to low, cover pan, and simmer rice for 30 minutes. Rice will not be dry.
- Meanwhile, stir rice vinegar, cider vinegar, mirin, sugar, and 1/2 teaspoon sea salt in a bowl until sugar and salt have dissolved. Set the vinegar mixture aside.
- Stir quinoa into rice and cooking liquid, bring to a boil, and reduce heat to low again; simmer until rice and quinoa are both tender and liquid is absorbed, about 15 more minutes. Transfer rice and quinoa into a large bowl and gently mix the vinegar mixture into the rice, spreading the grains out a little as you mix to help dry and cool the rice and quinoa. Let rice mixture cool until warm, about 10 minutes of stirring and fanning.
- Place a nori sheet onto a sushi mat. With wet fingers, lightly press about 1/4 the rice mixture onto the nori sheet in an even layer, leaving about 1/2-inch uncovered at the top of the sheet. Place about 1/4 the shredded carrot, cucumber strips, and avocado slices in a line across the bottom of the rice.
- Pick up the edge of the bamboo rolling sheet, fold the bottom edge of the sheet up, enclosing the filling, and tightly roll the sushi into a thick cylinder. Once the sushi is rolled, wrap it in the mat and gently squeeze to compact it tightly. Unwrap the roll and cut into 6 pieces to serve; repeat with remaining ingredients to make 4 rolls.

Nutrition Information

- Calories: 315 calories
- Total Fat: 9.4 g
- Cholesterol: 0 mg
- Sodium: 320 mg
- Total Carbohydrate: 51.6 g
- Protein: 7 g

25. Buddha Bowl

"Tasty healthy meal in under 1 hour."

Serving: 4 | Prep: 10 m | Cook: 48 m | Ready in: 58 m

Ingredients

- 3 cups chicken broth
- 1 1/2 cups quinoa
- 1 large sweet potato, diced
- 1 large red onion, diced
- 1/4 cup olive oil, divided
- kosher salt to taste
- freshly ground black pepper to taste
- 3 cloves garlic, minced, divided
- 1 tablespoon minced fresh ginger root
- 1 pound skinless, boneless chicken breast halves
- 1/4 cup lime juice
- 2 tablespoons smooth peanut butter
- 1 tablespoon soy sauce
- 1 tablespoon honey
- 1 tablespoon sesame oil
- 2 cups baby spinach
- 1 avocado - peeled, pitted, and thinly sliced
- 1 tablespoon chopped fresh cilantro
- 1 teaspoon toasted sesame seeds

Direction

- Bring chicken broth and quinoa to a boil in a saucepan. Reduce heat to medium-low, cover, and simmer until quinoa is tender and broth is absorbed, 15 to 20 minutes.
- Preheat oven to 425 degrees F (220 degrees C).
- Spread sweet potato and red onion onto a baking sheet. Drizzle 1 tablespoon olive oil over mixture and season with salt and pepper; toss to coat.
- Bake in the preheated oven until sweet potatoes are tender, 20 to 25 minutes.
- Heat 1 tablespoon olive oil in a skillet over medium heat; cook and stir 2 cloves garlic and ginger until fragrant, about 1 minute. Add chicken and cook until no longer pink in the center and the juices run clear, about 6 minutes per side. An instant-read thermometer inserted into the center should read at least 165 degrees F (74 degrees C). Cut chicken into 1-inch pieces.
- Whisk 1 garlic clove, lime juice, peanut butter, soy sauce, and honey together in a bowl. Whisk 1 tablespoon olive oil and sesame oil into mixture until dressing is smooth.
- Divide quinoa among bowls; top with chicken, sweet potato mixture, spinach, and avocado. Sprinkle cilantro and sesame seeds over the top and drizzle dressing over each bowl.

Nutrition Information

- Calories: 796 calories
- Total Fat: 35.9 g
- Cholesterol: 68 mg
- Sodium: 1223 mg
- Total Carbohydrate: 81.7 g
- Protein: 39.7 g

26. Buffalo Chicken Quinoa Bites

"These little bites are a crowd-pleaser for social events, but we also like to make a big batch and freeze them to take to work during the week. They reheat in 20 to 40 seconds in the microwave. Very versatile!"

Serving: 6 | Prep: 15 m | Cook: 20 m | Ready in: 35 m

Ingredients

- 1 1/2 cups shredded cooked chicken
- 1/4 cup hot Buffalo wing sauce (such as Frank's® REDHOT Buffalo Wing Sauce), or to taste
- 2 ounces cream cheese, softened
- 1 egg, beaten
- 1 egg white
- 1 cup shredded Cheddar cheese
- 2 tablespoons sliced green onion
- 1 cup cooked quinoa

Direction

- Preheat oven to 350 degrees F (175 degrees C). Grease 24 mini-muffin cups.
- Stir chicken, Buffalo wing sauce, cream cheese, egg, and egg white together in a large bowl until well-mixed. Add Cheddar cheese and green onion; stir. Stir quinoa into chicken mixture. Spoon mixture into prepared mini-muffin cups.
- Bake in the preheated oven until browned around the edges, 18 to 22 minutes.

Nutrition Information

- Calories: 236 calories
- Total Fat: 13.9 g
- Cholesterol: 87 mg
- Sodium: 467 mg
- Total Carbohydrate: 8.9 g
- Protein: 18.4 g

27. Buffalo Veggie Quinoa Meatloaf

"Well it's hard to make a healthy meatloaf with 'traditional' ingredients. So this recipe is hearty, healthy, and guilt-free."

Serving: 4 | Prep: 15 m | Cook: 1 h 20 m | Ready in: 1 h 35 m

Ingredients

- 1/2 cup water
- 1/4 cup quinoa
- 1 tablespoon olive oil, or as needed
- 1 small sweet yellow onion, chopped
- 1 sweet potato, chopped
- 1 cup chopped kale, or more to taste
- 1/2 red bell pepper, chopped, or more to taste
- 1 pound ground buffalo meat
- 2 eggs
- 1 tablespoon Worcestershire sauce, or more to taste
- 1 tablespoon minced garlic, or more to taste
- 1 tablespoon ketchup, or more to taste
- 1 1/2 teaspoons salt
- 1 teaspoon ground black pepper
- 1 pinch dried oregano, or more to taste
- 1 pinch dried basil, or more to taste
- 1 pinch dried thyme, or more to taste
- 1 tablespoon barbeque sauce, or to taste

Direction

- Preheat oven to 375 degrees F (190 degrees C). Grease a 9x5-inch loaf pan.
- Bring water and quinoa to a boil in a saucepan. Reduce heat to medium-low, cover, and simmer until quinoa is tender and water has been absorbed, 10 to 15 minutes.
- Heat olive oil in a skillet over medium heat; cook and stir onion, sweet potato, kale, and red bell pepper until tender, 10 to 15 minutes.
- Combine buffalo meat, eggs, Worcestershire sauce, garlic, ketchup, salt, black pepper, oregano, basil, and thyme together in a bowl. Add vegetable mixture and quinoa to buffalo mixture and mix well. Transfer mixture to the prepared loaf pan; top with a thin layer of barbeque sauce.
- Bake in the preheated oven until no longer pink in the center, about 1 hour. An instant-read thermometer inserted into the center should read at least 160 degrees F (70 degrees C).

Nutrition Information

- Calories: 265 calories
- Total Fat: 8.1 g
- Cholesterol: 136 mg
- Sodium: 1103 mg
- Total Carbohydrate: 22.4 g
- Protein: 25.4 g

28. Butternut Squash Chicken and Quinoa Soup

"This tasty, healthy, and filling soup is the perfect comfort food. Serve with crusty rolls or bread."

Serving: 8 | Prep: 15 m | Cook: 1 h 35 m | Ready in: 2 h

Ingredients

- 1 1/2 pounds whole skinless, boneless chicken breasts
- salt and ground black pepper to taste
- 1 1/2 pounds butternut squash, quartered and seeded
- 2 teaspoons olive oil
- 1 onion, minced
- 4 cloves garlic, crushed
- 3 1/2 cups chicken broth
- 1 (14 ounce) can canned diced tomatoes
- 2/3 cup quinoa
- 1 1/2 teaspoons dried oregano
- 1/2 teaspoon salt

Direction

- Preheat oven to 400 degrees F (200 degrees C).
- Sprinkle chicken with salt and ground black pepper. Wrap in aluminum foil and place on a baking sheet.
- Place butternut squash pieces cut-side down in a 9x13-inch baking dish. Add about 1/2-inch water to the dish and cover with aluminum foil.
- Bake chicken and squash in the preheated oven until butternut squash is tender and chicken breasts are no longer pink in the center, about 30 minutes. An instant-read thermometer inserted into the center of the chicken should read at least 165 degrees F (74 degrees C).
- Heat oil in a skillet over medium heat. Add onion and garlic; cook and stir until softened, about 5 minutes.
- Scoop cooked squash flesh into a large pot. Pour in chicken broth and mash together until smooth using an immersion blender or potato masher.
- Cube cooked chicken and add to the pot. Stir in onion, garlic, canned tomatoes, quinoa, oregano, and 1/2 teaspoon salt. Bring soup to a gentle boil; reduce heat and simmer until quinoa is tender and flavors are well-blended, about 1 hour.

Nutrition Information

- Calories: 224 calories
- Total Fat: 4.5 g
- Cholesterol: 51 mg
- Sodium: 703 mg
- Total Carbohydrate: 24.8 g
- Protein: 21.8 g

29. Butternut Squash Turnip and GreenBean Quinoa

Can be prepared in 45 minutes or less.

Serving: Serves 4

Ingredients

- 2/3 cup quinoa
- 1 1/3 cups water
- 1/2 teaspoon salt
- 1 medium turnip
- 1 large garlic clove
- 4 scallions
- 2 ounces green beans
- 1 cup 1/3-inch cubes butternut squash

Direction

- In a sieve rinse quinoa under cold running water until water runs clear
- In a small saucepan bring water to a boil with quinoa and salt and simmer mixture, covered, over moderately low heat until just cooked through, 5 to 10 minutes. Drain quinoa in sieve (do not rinse) and spread out on a plate to cool.

- Peel turnip and cut into 1/3-inch cubes. Mince garlic. Slice scallions thin on the diagonal and cut beans into 1/3-inch pieces.
- In a steamer set over 1 inch boiling water combine squash, turnip, and garlic and steam vegetables, covered, 7 minutes, or until almost tender. Add beans, quinoa, and salt and pepper to taste and steam 3 minutes, or until beans are crisp-tender. Transfer mixture to a bowl and toss with scallions.

30. Cabbage Rolls with Quinoa

"Cabbage is nutritious, low in calories, and can be super filling! If you want to lose weight, cabbage should be on your menu! I recently bought the rainbow quinoa from Target® and decided this would be a perfect recipe to utilize this very popular superfood."

Serving: 8 | Prep: 15 m | Cook: 1 h 20 m | Ready in: 1 h 35 m

Ingredients

- 1 large head cabbage
- 2 cups water
- 1 cup quinoa
- 2 tablespoons olive oil, divided, or as needed
- 1 large onion, chopped
- 1 carrot, sliced
- 1/2 pound ground beef
- 1/2 pound ground pork
- 1 cup pasta sauce, divided
- 2 eggs
- 2 tablespoons finely chopped dill
- 1 tablespoon garlic powder
- 1 tablespoon onion powder
- 1 teaspoon paprika
- salt and ground black pepper to taste
- 1 cup low-sodium chicken broth
- 2 cloves garlic, minced
- 2 tablespoons sauerkraut, drained
- 2 tablespoons chopped fresh dill

Direction

- Bring a large pot of lightly salted water to a boil. Place cabbage on a flat work surface. Cut a circle around the stem and remove the core. Place cabbage in the boiling water. Cover and cook until tender, 8 to 10 minutes. Remove cabbage leaves with tongs as they cook; pat dry with paper towels.
- Bring water and quinoa to a boil in a saucepan. Reduce heat to medium-low, cover, and simmer until quinoa is tender, 15 to 20 minutes.
- Preheat the oven to 375 degrees F (190 degrees C).
- Heat 1 tablespoon olive oil in a skillet over medium-high heat. Add onion and carrot; sauté until softened, about 5 minutes. Let cool.
- Transfer most of the onion-carrot mixture to a bowl, reserving a small portion of the mixture for the sauce. Add the remaining olive oil, quinoa, beef, pork, 1 tablespoon pasta sauce, eggs, 2 tablespoons dill, garlic powder, onion powder, paprika, salt, and pepper. Mix until filling is well combined.
- Cut out the thick part of the rib from the bottom of each cooked leaf so it will be easier to roll. Spoon a portion of the filling onto a leaf. Fold the stem up over the filling and fold the sides toward the middle. Roll filling up the rest of the leaf. Repeat until the filling is used. Finely shred the remaining cabbage.
- Combine remaining pasta sauce with chicken broth, garlic, sauerkraut, and 2 tablespoons dill in a bowl. Spread a few tablespoons of the sauce over the bottom of a baking pan. Add the shredded cabbage. Place cabbage rolls seam-side down in a single layer on top. Pour remaining sauce over the rolls. Cover with aluminum foil.
- Bake in the preheated oven until cabbage rolls are tender, 60 to 90 minutes.

Nutrition Information

- Calories: 324 calories
- Total Fat: 14.5 g
- Cholesterol: 84 mg
- Sodium: 244 mg
- Total Carbohydrate: 31.7 g
- Protein: 18 g

31. Carons Kickin Quinoa Salad

"An easy way to use that tuna you have sitting around and that weird quinoa stuff you got at the health food store. This is great if you want a tuna salad sandwich but don't or can't have bread, or also if you like sushi because it has a nice wasabi kick and a texture reminiscent of sticky rice. And, it has a good crunch and flavor with chopped celery and onion. Quinoa (KEEN-wa) is a 'grain that's not really a grain' used by the ancient Incas. It is especially good for people with wheat or gluten allergies, and can be doctored up with anything for every meal of the day. Try serving on a salad or lettuce leaves for a complete meal and presentation."

Serving: 2 | Prep: 15 m | Cook: 10 m | Ready in: 1 h

Ingredients

- 1/2 cup uncooked quinoa
- 1 cup water
- 1/4 cup chopped celery
- 1/4 cup chopped onion
- 1/4 cup low fat mayonnaise (such as Hellman's® Light)
- 1 teaspoon wasabi powder
- 2 teaspoons lemon juice, or to taste
- salt and ground black pepper to taste
- 1 (5 ounce) can tuna, drained

Direction

- Stir the quinoa and water together in a microwave-safe bowl. Cover; cook in the microwave on High until the water has been absorbed and the quinoa is tender, about 9 minutes. Uncover and place into the refrigerator to cool.
- Place the celery, onion, and mayonnaise together in a bowl. Season with wasabi, lemon juice, salt, and pepper; stir to mix. Fold in the tuna and chilled quinoa until evenly blended.

Nutrition Information

- Calories: 293 calories
- Total Fat: 5.1 g

- Cholesterol: 19 mg
- Sodium: 410 mg
- Total Carbohydrate 38.6 g
- Protein: 22.5 g

32. Carrot Cake Quinoa

"Gluten-free and vegan! A great lunch for work. Healthy and delicious! Serve hot or cold."

Serving: 4 | Prep: 10 m | Cook: 20 m | Ready in: 35 m

Ingredients

- 4 cups water
- 1 cup quinoa
- 3/4 cup amaranth
- 1/4 cup wild rice
- 2 teaspoons ground cumin
- 1 teaspoon salt
- 2 stalks celery, diced
- 1 large carrot, grated
- 1/2 cup canned chickpeas (garbanzo beans) (optional)
- 1/2 cup raisins
- 1 tablespoon olive oil
- 1 clove garlic, minced
- salt and ground black pepper to taste

Direction

- Bring water, quinoa, amaranth, wild rice, cumin, and 1 teaspoon salt to a boil in a saucepan. Reduce heat to medium-low, cover, and simmer until grains are tender and water has been absorbed, 20 to 25 minutes. Let stand for 5 minutes.
- Mix celery, carrot, chickpeas, raisins, olive oil, garlic, salt, and pepper together in a bowl; add grain mixture and mix well.

Nutrition Information

- Calories: 472 calories
- Total Fat: 9.2 g
- Cholesterol: 0 mg

- Sodium: 721 mg
- Total Carbohydrate: 85.1 g
- Protein: 15.4 g

33. Carrot Tomato and Spinach Quinoa Pilaf

"I remember my aunt telling me about quinoa, saying it was such a wonderfully healthy food and what do you know? It's kosher for Passover! I decided to beef up my quinoa with some fresh vegetables, cooked until they are just tender without becoming mushy. As a side dish this serves 4-5, but I've been known to eat half of it as a meal on its own."

Serving: 5 | Prep: 10 m | Cook: 25 m | Ready in: 35 m

Ingredients

- 2 teaspoons olive oil
- 1/2 onion, chopped
- 1 cup quinoa
- 2 cups water
- 2 tablespoons vegetarian chicken-flavored bouillon granules
- 1 teaspoon ground black pepper
- 1 teaspoon thyme
- 1 carrot, chopped
- 1 tomato, chopped
- 1 cup baby spinach

Direction

- Heat the olive oil in a sauce pan over medium heat; cook and stir the onion in the hot oil until translucent, about 5 minutes. Lower the heat, stir in quinoa, and toast, stirring constantly, for 2 minutes. Stir in the water, bouillon granules, black pepper, and thyme; raise heat to high and bring to a boil. Cover, reduce heat to low, and simmer for 5 minutes.
- Stir in the carrots. Cover and simmer until all water is absorbed, about 10 more minutes. Turn off the heat, add the tomatoes and spinach, and stir until the spinach is wilted and the tomatoes have given off their moisture, about 2 minutes.

Nutrition Information

- Calories: 165 calories
- Total Fat: 4.1 g
- Cholesterol: 0 mg
- Sodium: 52 mg
- Total Carbohydrate: 27 g
- Protein: 5.7 g

34. Carrot Tomato and Spinach Quinoa Pilaf with Ground Turkey

"I took some leftover quinoa pilaf and added black beans and ground turkey. It made an excellent one-dish meal that hits the table in a hurry. I found it was a good way to use up the leftovers from another dinner. We have the pilaf as a side dish for the two of us, and it is always too much. Adding ground turkey and black beans makes another unique meal that is quick to prepare. Enjoy!"

Serving: 5 | Prep: 20 m | Cook: 40 m | Ready in: 1 h

Ingredients

- 2 teaspoons olive oil
- 1 cup quinoa
- 1/2 onion, chopped
- 2 cups water
- 2 tablespoons chicken-flavored vegetable bouillon
- 1 teaspoon ground black pepper
- 1 teaspoon ground thyme
- 1 carrot, chopped
- 1 tomato, chopped
- 1 cup baby spinach
- 2 tablespoons olive oil
- 1 pound ground turkey, or more to taste (optional)
- 1 (14.5 ounce) can black beans, rinsed and drained

Direction

- Heat 2 teaspoons olive oil in a saucepan over medium heat; cook and stir onion in hot oil until translucent, about 5 minutes. Reduce heat to medium-low, stir quinoa with the onion, and cook, stirring constantly, until the quinoa is lightly toasted, about 2 minutes.
- Pour water into the saucepan; add bouillon granules, black pepper, and thyme. Bring the liquid to a boil, place a cover on the saucepan, reduce heat to low, and cook at a simmer until the quinoa softens, about 5 minutes.
- Stir carrot into the quinoa mixture, replace cover, and continue to cook at a simmer until water is completely absorbed, about 10 minutes more.
- Remove saucepan from heat. Stir tomato and baby spinach into the quinoa mixture until the spinach wilts, about 2 minutes.
- Heat 2 tablespoons olive oil in large skillet over medium-high heat. Cook and stir turkey in the hot skillet until browned and crumbly, 5 to 7 minutes; drain and discard grease. Reduce heat to medium-low. Stir black beans with the turkey; cook and stir until the beans are hot, 2 to 3 minutes; add the quinoa mixture, stir, and cook until heated through, about 5 minutes more.

Nutrition Information

- Calories: 422 calories
- Total Fat: 16.6 g
- Cholesterol: 67 mg
- Sodium: 396 mg
- Total Carbohydrate: 40.8 g
- Protein: 28.6 g

35. Cauliflower With Quinoa Prunes and Peanuts

Serving: 4-6 servings

Ingredients

- 3 tablespoons olive oil
- 1/4 red onion, minced
- 1 shallot, minced
- 1 garlic clove, minced
- 1/2 cup quinoa
- 2 cups vegetable broth or water
- 1 sprig thyme
- Salt and pepper
- 1 head cauliflower
- 1/3 cup finely diced prunes
- 2 tablespoons chopped unsalted roasted peanuts, plus 1 tablespoon crushed nuts
- 1 tablespoon onion puree (2 tablespoons olive oil, 1 onion, very thinly sliced, 1 tablespoon sherry vinegar, Salt pepper)
- 1 tablespoon unsalted butter
- 2 tablespoons finely chopped cilantro, plus a handful of whole leaves
- 1 tablespoon finely chopped chives

Direction

- For the Onion Puree: In a medium saucepan, heat the oil over medium-low heat. Add the onions and cook, stirring often, until they are completely soft but have not taken on any color, 15 to 20 minutes. A bit of water helps here. Add the vinegar and cook for 5 more minutes. Season with salt and pepper. Transfer to a blender and process until satiny-smooth. The puree can be cooled, covered, and stored in the refrigerator for up to 2 days.
- For the Cauliflower with Quinoa, Prunes Peanuts: Preheat the oven to 400°F.
- In a small saucepan, heat 1 table-spoon of the oil over medium-low heat. Add the onion, shallot, and garlic and cook, stirring often, until the onion is softened, about 5 minutes. Add the quinoa and toast, stirring constantly, for about a minute.

- Increase the heat to high, add 1 cup of the broth and the thyme, season with salt and pepper, and bring to a simmer. Cook, covered, until almost all the liquid has been absorbed, about 15 minutes. Remove from the heat and let stand for 5 minutes. Discard the thyme sprig.
- Trim the stem of the cauliflower so that the head sits flat on a cutting board. Cut down through the center of the head, making 4 thick slices. Most of the slices will still have a bit of stem still attached and that's good.
- Heat 2 tablespoons of the olive oil over medium-high heat in the largest skillet you have. Working in batches, brown the cauliflower slices on both sides, about 3 minutes per side. Transfer to a baking pan.
- Season the cauliflower with salt and pepper, transfer to the oven, and roast until tender, about 15 minutes.
- Meanwhile, add the prunes, chopped peanuts, and onion puree to the quinoa and gently heat through, stirring. Add the remaining 1 cup broth to moisten the quinoa, then stir in the butter and chopped cilantro. Season with salt and pepper.
- Lay the cauliflower slices on plates and spoon the quinoa on top. Sprinkle with crushed peanuts, chives and cilantro leaves.

Nutrition Information

- Calories: 328
- Total Fat: 18 g (28%)
- Saturated Fat: 4 g (20%)
- Cholesterol: 8 mg (3%)
- Sodium: 772 mg (32%)
- Total Carbohydrate: 36 g (12%)
- Protein: 9 g (17%)
- Fiber: 6 g (23%)

36. Cheesy Broccoli Quinoa

"The classic Cheddar cheese and broccoli combo served in quinoa."

Serving: 4 | Prep: 5 m | Cook: 20 m | Ready in: 25 m

Ingredients

- 2 cups chopped broccoli
- 1 3/4 cups vegetable broth
- 1 cup quinoa
- 1 cup shredded Cheddar cheese
- salt and ground black pepper to taste

Direction

- Combine broccoli, broth, and quinoa in a saucepan; bring to a boil. Reduce heat to medium-low, place a cover on the saucepan, and cook at a simmer until the broth has been absorbed and the quinoa is tender, 15 to 20 minutes.
- Stir Cheddar cheese into the quinoa, replace the lid, and set aside until the cheese melts, 2 to 3 minutes; season with salt and pepper.

Nutrition Information

- Calories: 299 calories
- Total Fat: 12.3 g
- Cholesterol: 30 mg
- Sodium: 394 mg
- Total Carbohydrate: 32.9 g
- Protein: 14.8 g

37. Cheesy Quinoa Patties with Kale and Spinach

"Very healthy recipe with tons of superfoods."

Serving: 12 | Prep: 30 m | Cook: 54 m | Ready in: 1 h 24 m

Ingredients

- 1 cup uncooked quinoa
- 1 1/2 cups water

- 1 teaspoon salt
- 1 teaspoon ground black pepper
- 1 clove garlic
- 1 tablespoon vegetable oil
- 1/4 onion, chopped
- 3/4 cup finely chopped kale
- 3/4 cup finely chopped spinach
- 1 cup grated mozzarella cheese
- 1/2 cup bread crumbs
- 1 tablespoon flaxseed meal (optional)
- 1 egg, beaten
- 1/4 cup vegetable oil

Direction

- Bring water and quinoa to a boil in a saucepan. Add salt, black pepper, and garlic. Reduce heat to medium-low, cover, and simmer until quinoa is tender, 15 to 20 minutes.
- Heat 1 tablespoon oil in a skillet over medium heat; add onion. Cook and stir until translucent, about 2 minutes. Transfer to a bowl. Add kale and spinach to hot skillet; cook and stir until tender, 2 to 3 minutes.
- Combine cooked quinoa, onions, kale, spinach, mozzarella cheese, bread crumbs, and flaxseed meal in a bowl; stir to combine. Add beaten egg; mix well.
- Preheat oven to 350 degrees F (175 degrees C). Oil a baking sheet.
- Form golf-ball-size portions of the quinoa mixture into patties. Place on the prepared baking sheet.
- Bake in the preheated oven until golden brown and crusty, about 15 minutes per side.

Nutrition Information

- Calories: 156 calories
- Total Fat: 9 g
- Cholesterol: 22 mg
- Sodium: 294 mg
- Total Carbohydrate: 13.5 g
- Protein: 5.7 g

38. Cheesy Quinoa Pilaf with Spinach

"This creamy pilaf incorporates the fluffy, nutty-flavored grain, quinoa, with a decadent and delicious goat cheese gouda. This has an amazing flavor and texture. Try serving with steamed salmon. I think this would work well with pine nuts as well as a variety of other cheeses. Try regular goat, Parmesan, blue, etc."

Serving: 3 | Prep: 10 m | Cook: 30 m | Ready in: 40 m

Ingredients

- 1/4 cup quinoa
- 3 tablespoons olive oil
- 2 tablespoons raw sunflower seeds
- 2 cloves garlic, minced
- 1/2 cup fresh spinach leaves
- 2 teaspoons lemon juice
- 1/3 cup grated goat gouda cheese

Direction

- Bring a pot of lightly salted water to a boil over high heat. Add the quinoa, and cook until the quinoa is tender, 15 to 20 minutes. Drain in a mesh strainer, and rinse until cold; set aside.
- Heat the olive oil in a skillet over medium heat, stir in the sunflower seeds, and cook until lightly toasted, about 2 minutes. Stir in the garlic, and cook until the garlic softens and the aroma mellows, about 2 minutes. Stir in the cooled quinoa and spinach; cook and stir until the quinoa is hot, and the spinach has wilted. Stir in the lemon juice, and all but a pinch of the cheese. Stir until the cheese has melted. Serve sprinkled with the remaining cheese.

Nutrition Information

- Calories: 233 calories
- Total Fat: 18.9 g
- Cholesterol: 13 mg
- Sodium: 49 mg
- Total Carbohydrate: 10.5 g
- Protein: 6.1 g

39. Cheesy Stuffed Peppers

Serving: Makes 1 serving

Ingredients

- 1 large poblano pepper, seeded
- 2 teaspoons olive oil, divided
- 1/2 cup cooked quinoa
- 1/2 cup shredded reduced-fat Mexican-blend cheese
- 1/2 cup chopped onion
- 3 teaspoons chopped garlic, divided
- 1/2 teaspoon cinnamon
- 1/2 teaspoon ground cumin
- 1/2 cup low-sodium chicken broth
- 2 tablespoons marinara sauce
- 1/2 teaspoon chili powder
- 1/2 ounces chopped dark chocolate
- Vegetable oil cooking spray
- 2 cups baby spinach
- 3/4 cup sliced onion
- 1/2 cup sliced portobellos
- 1/2 cup black beans, rinsed and drained
- 4 ounces red wine

Direction

- Heat oven to 375°F. Brush poblano with 1 teaspoon oil. Mix quinoa with cheese; stuff inside poblano; cook in a baking dish 20 minutes. In a pan, sauté chopped onion, 2 teaspoons garlic, remaining 1 teaspoon oil, cinnamon and cumin over medium heat 5 minutes. Stir in broth, marinara and chili powder; bring to a boil; reduce heat and simmer 15 minutes. Add chocolate; stir until melted, 2 minutes. In a second pan coated with cooking spray, sauté spinach, sliced onion, portobellos, beans and remaining 1 teaspoon garlic. Pour sauce over poblano; serve with spinach and glass of wine.
- Per serving: 555 calories, 19 grams fat 6 grams saturated, 59 grams carbohydrates, 14 grams fiber, 23 grams protein

- Nutritional analysis provided by Self

40. Cheesy VeggieQuinoa Bites

"This is by far my favorite vegetarian quinoa recipe. My 2-year-old went crazy eating them. He couldn't even tell there were veggies in it! He asked for seconds... and thirds."

Serving: 32 | Prep: 10 m | Cook: 30 m | Ready in: 50 m

Ingredients

- 2 teaspoons vegetable oil, or as needed
- 1 1/3 cups water
- 2/3 cup quinoa
- 1/2 cup cauliflower florets, or more to taste
- 3 carrots, shredded
- 1 cup shredded Cheddar cheese, or more to taste
- 2 large eggs
- 1/4 cup chopped fresh kale
- 2 tablespoons all-purpose flour
- 1 tablespoon flax seeds (optional)
- 1 tablespoon chia seeds (optional)
- 2 teaspoons minced garlic
- 2 teaspoons onion powder
- salt and ground black pepper to taste

Direction

- Preheat the oven to 350 degrees F (175 degrees C). Grease a mini muffin tin with oil.
- Bring water and quinoa to a boil in a saucepan. Reduce heat to medium-low, cover, and simmer until quinoa is tender, 15 to 20 minutes. Drain any excess liquid and let cool briefly.
- Place a steamer insert into a saucepan and fill with water to just below the bottom of the steamer. Bring water to a boil. Add cauliflower, cover, and steam until tender, 2 to 6 minutes.
- Mix cooked quinoa, steamed cauliflower, carrots, Cheddar cheese, eggs, kale, flour, flax seeds, chia seeds, garlic, onion powder, salt, and pepper together in a bowl. Spoon mixture into the muffin cups and press down lightly.

- Bake in the preheated oven until edges are light brown, 10 to 12 minutes. Let cool in pan, about 5 minutes. Remove bites from pan and let cool, about 5 minutes more.

Nutrition Information

- Calories: 43 calories
- Total Fat: 2.2 g
- Cholesterol: 15 mg
- Sodium: 37 mg
- Total Carbohydrate: 3.9 g
- Protein: 2.1 g

41. Chicken Quinoa Stuffed Peppers

"These delicious cheese-topped stuffed red peppers get flavor, texture and fiber goodness from a tasty combination of quinoa, spinach and creamy mushroom soup. They're easy to prepare and packed with veggie goodness."

Serving: 4 | Prep: 20 m | Cook: 50 m | Ready in: 1 h 10 m

Ingredients

- 1 1/3 cups Swanson® Unsalted Chicken Stock
- 2/3 cup uncooked quinoa, rinsed
- 1 pound 98% fat-free ground chicken breast or 99% fat-free ground turkey breast
- 1 clove garlic, minced
- 1 medium onion, chopped
- 1 (10 ounce) package chopped frozen spinach, thawed and well drained
- 1 (10.5 ounce) can Campbell's® Healthy Request® Condensed Cream of Mushroom Soup
- 1/3 cup grated Parmesan cheese, divided
- 4 medium red bell peppers, cut in half lengthwise and seeded

Direction

- Set the oven to 350 degrees F.
- Heat the stock and quinoa in a 1-quart saucepan over high heat to a boil. Reduce the heat to low. Cover and cook for 13 minutes or until the quinoa is tender.
- Cook the chicken, garlic and onion in a 12-inch nonstick skillet over medium-high heat until the chicken is cooked through, stirring often to separate meat. Stir in the spinach, soup, quinoa and 3 tablespoons cheese.
- Place the pepper halves into an 11x8x2-inch baking dish. Spoon the chicken mixture into the pepper halves.
- Bake for 30 minutes or until hot. Sprinkle with the remaining cheese.
- Bake for 5 minutes or until the cheese is melted.

Nutrition Information

- Calories: 393 calories
- Total Fat: 9.2 g
- Cholesterol: 78 mg
- Sodium: 547 mg
- Total Carbohydrate: 38.2 g
- Protein: 38.6 g

42. Chicken and Quinoa Paella

"Traditional paella is made with rice This recipe replaces the rice with quinoa, which is very good at absorbing the flavor of whatever it cooks in. This recipe simplifies cooking paella by foregoing the paella pan and using a common baking pan, the perfect size for parties and potlucks. Garnish with lemon wedges."

Serving: 10 | Prep: 25 m | Cook: 1 h 10 m | Ready in: 1 h 35 m

Ingredients

- 6 cups chicken stock
- 2 bay leaves
- 3 teaspoons kosher salt, or more to taste, divided
- 2 teaspoons ground black pepper, divided
- 1 1/2 pounds skinless, boneless chicken breast halves, cut into 1 1/2-inch cubes
- 1 1/2 pounds tomatoes, halved

- 4 tablespoons olive oil, divided
- 2 teaspoons smoked paprika
- 1/2 cup onion strips, 1/4-inch thick
- 3 cloves garlic, minced
- 1/2 pound green beans, stem ends trimmed, halved
- 1 red bell pepper, cut into 1/4-inch strips
- 1 red bell pepper, cut into 1/4-inch strips
- 3 cups white quinoa
- 25 saffron threads
- 2 sprigs fresh rosemary, stemmed

Direction

- Preheat the oven to 375 degrees F (190 degrees C).
- Bring chicken stock and bay leaves to a boil in a large saucepan. Reduce heat and simmer while preparing the other ingredients. Taste stock; it should taste a little over-salted. Season with 1 to 2 teaspoons salt and 1 teaspoon black pepper as needed.
- Season chicken with salt and pepper.
- Squeeze out seeds from each tomato half over a sieve and into a bowl. Reserve the juice and discard the seeds. Grate the cut sides of the tomatoes over a bowl through the large holes of a box grater. Discard the skin. Combine the tomato juice and the grated pulp.
- Heat a large skillet over medium-high heat for 2 to 3 minutes and coat with 1 tablespoon olive oil. Add chicken in batches, in a single layer with space between pieces. Sauté until meat is mostly opaque, about 4 minutes; it will continue cooking in the oven. Place chicken in a 9x13-inch baking pan. Repeat with the remaining chicken, being careful not to burn the fats rendering in the skillet.
- Add 2 tablespoons olive oil to the same skillet. Add the tomato juice-pulp mixture. Cook, scraping up browned bits from the bottom of skillet, until juices are mostly evaporated, about 5 minutes. Add 2 teaspoons salt, 1 teaspoon black pepper, and paprika. Mix well. Add onions and garlic; sauté until is fragrant, about 3 minutes. Stir the mixture, called a sofrito, into the baking pan with the chicken.
- Heat the last tablespoon of olive oil in the hot skillet. Add green beans and sauté for 1 minute. Add bell peppers; sauté until green beans are crisp-tender, about 2 minutes more. Transfer mixture to the baking pan and stir well; mix in quinoa and saffron.
- Remove and discard bay leaves from stock and bring to a boil. Pour 1/2 into the baking pan. Mix carefully until well combined. Add remaining stock and stir carefully. Lay rosemary sprigs on top.
- Bake in the preheated oven until quinoa is tender yet firm to the bite, 35 to 45 minutes.

Nutrition Information

- Calories: 350 calories
- Total Fat: 10.8 g
- Cholesterol: 39 mg
- Sodium: 1030 mg
- Total Carbohydrate: 40.5 g
- Protein: 23.2 g

43. Chicken Chorizo on Quinoa with Peppers

"Delicious combination of chicken chorizo with quinoa. At my table the hotter the better!!! So don't be afraid to bring the hot sauce to the table to add some extra kick! Make a simple side dish to this recipe by combining your favorite jar of salsa with a cup or two of cooked, slightly cooled corn. Enjoy! :)"

Serving: 6 | Prep: 35 m | Cook: 40 m | Ready in: 1 h 15 m

Ingredients

- 2 tablespoons butter
- 1/2 onion, diced
- sea salt to taste
- 6 cups chicken stock
- 3 cups quinoa
- 2 tablespoons extra-virgin olive oil
- 6 (4 ounce) chicken chorizo sausage links
- 1 onion, cut into thin strips

- 4 cloves garlic, minced
- 2 teaspoons Spanish paprika
- 1 teaspoon ground cumin
- 2 red bell peppers, cut into thin strips
- 2 yellow bell peppers, cut into thin strips
- 2 poblano chile peppers, cut into thin strips
- 1 cup chicken stock
- sea salt and pepper to taste

Direction

- Melt the butter in a large pot over medium heat. Stir in the diced onion and sea salt to taste; cook and stir until the onion has caramelized to a deep brown, about 15 minutes. Once caramelized, pour in 6 cups of chicken stock and the quinoa; bring to a boil over high heat. Reduce heat to medium-low, cover, and simmer until the quinoa is tender, 20 to 25 minutes.
- Meanwhile, heat the olive oil in a large skillet over medium-high heat. Brown the sausages on all sides in the hot oil, then remove and cut into 1/2 inch thick slices. Return the sausage to the skillet, and continue cooking until browned on all sides and no longer pink in the center. Remove to drain on a paper towel lined plate, and keep warm.
- Reduce the heat to medium, and stir the sliced onion into the remaining oil in the skillet. Cook until the edges of the onions begin to turn a golden color, 3 to 5 minutes. Add the garlic, and cook 1 minute more. Season with the paprika and cumin, then stir in the red bell peppers, yellow bell peppers, poblano chile peppers, and 1 cup of chicken stock. Bring to a simmer, then cook until the peppers soften, and the mixture reduces and thickens, 10 to 15 minutes. Return the sausage to the skillet, season to taste with salt and pepper, and continue cooking until the sausage is hot. Serve over a bed of quinoa.

Nutrition Information

- Calories: 499 calories
- Total Fat: 17.7 g
- Cholesterol: 24 mg
- Sodium: 1214 mg
- Total Carbohydrate: 65.8 g
- Protein: 20.4 g

44. Chicken Quinoa

"If chicken soup and pilaf had a kid, I think it would be chicken quinoa. Quinoa is a very healthy ancient grain from South America; it's very filling! I think it's delicious. I used leftover roasted chicken to make this come together faster, but any kind of lean cooked meat can be used in this recipe. To make a vegetarian version, omit the meat and use vegetable stock instead of chicken."

Serving: 2 | Prep: 15 m | Cook: 30 m | Ready in: 45 m

Ingredients

- 1 tablespoon olive oil
- 1/4 cup diced onion
- 1/4 cup diced carrot
- 1/4 cup diced celery
- 1/4 cup diced green bell pepper
- 1 teaspoon minced garlic
- 1 cup chopped cooked chicken
- 1 tablespoon parsley flakes
- 1/2 cup quinoa
- 1 cup chicken broth
- salt and ground black pepper to taste

Direction

- Heat olive oil in a saucepan over medium heat. Cook and stir onion, carrot, celery, bell pepper, and garlic in hot oil until vegetables are tender, 5 to 7 minutes.
- Stir chicken and parsley into the vegetable mixture; cook and stir for about 1 minute. Add quinoa to the chicken mixture. Reduce heat to medium-low. Cook and stir until quinoa is toasted, about 2 minutes.
- Pour chicken broth over the quinoa mixture; bring to a boil. Reduce heat to medium low. Place a cover on the saucepan and cook mixture at a simmer until the quinoa is tender, about 15 minutes. Turn heat completely off

and allow mixture to sit covered another 5 minutes; season with salt and pepper. Fluff with a fork to serve.

Nutrition Information

- Calories: 377 calories
- Total Fat: 14.9 g
- Cholesterol: 55 mg
- Sodium: 553 mg
- Total Carbohydrate: 33.3 g
- Protein: 26.5 g

45. Chicken Quinoa Casserole

"I tried to figure out a casserole that I haven't seen before. Super good, super easy, and just the right amount of 'good-for-you' to cover up the guilt!"

Serving: 12 | Prep: 15 m | Cook: 45 m | Ready in: 1 h 5 m

Ingredients

- 1 serving cooking spray
- 2 cups vegetable broth
- 3 cloves garlic, minced
- 4 grinds salt
- 5 grinds black pepper
- 1 cup quinoa
- 1 rotisserie chicken - skin and bones removed, meat cut into bite-size pieces
- 2 tablespoons olive oil
- 3 cups clean fresh spinach, roughly chopped
- 1 cup carrot matchsticks
- 1/2 cup roasted red peppers, drained and chopped
- 1 1/2 (15 ounce) jars Alfredo sauce
- 1 teaspoon dried basil
- 2 tablespoons unsalted butter
- 3/4 cup panko bread crumbs
- 3/4 cup grated Parmesan cheese

Direction

- Preheat the oven to 375 degrees F (190 degrees C). Spray a casserole dish with cooking spray.
- Combine vegetable broth, garlic, salt, and pepper in a pot over medium-high heat and bring to a boil. Add quinoa, cover, reduce heat, and simmer until tender, about 15 minutes. Let stand 5 minutes.
- Heat olive oil in a skillet over medium-low heat. Add spinach, carrots, and red peppers and cook until barely tender, about 5 minutes.
- Mix chicken, cooked quinoa, cooked vegetables, Alfredo sauce, and basil together in a bowl. Pour into the prepared casserole dish, patting it down with a spoon.
- Melt butter in a small saucepan over medium heat and mix in bread crumbs until evenly coated. Remove from heat and stir in Parmesan cheese. Evenly distribute cheese crumbs over the top of the casserole.
- Bake in the preheated oven until cooked through and lightly browned on top, 25 to 30 minutes.

Nutrition Information

- Calories: 421 calories
- Total Fat: 29.4 g
- Cholesterol: 74 mg
- Sodium: 915 mg
- Total Carbohydrate: 19.7 g
- Protein: 21.7 g

46. Chicken Quinoa Salad

"I threw this recipe together based off a pasta salad I liked. I wanted something with quinoa to make it a little healthier. Very delicious!"

Serving: 6 | Prep: 15 m | Cook: 20 m | Ready in: 40 m

Ingredients

- 1 teaspoon extra-virgin olive oil, or to taste
- 1 cup quinoa, rinsed
- 2 cups chicken broth
- 15 fresh asparagus, cut into 1-inch pieces
- 2 cups chopped cooked chicken
- 12 grape tomatoes, quartered

- 1/4 cup finely chopped fresh basil
- 1/4 cup grated Parmesan cheese
- 1 clove garlic, minced
- 1/4 cup extra-virgin olive oil
- 1 teaspoon salt
- 1 teaspoon ground black pepper
- 1/4 teaspoon red pepper flakes

Direction

- Heat 1 teaspoon olive oil in a saucepan over medium heat, cook and stir quinoa until slightly toasted and water has evaporated from quinoa, 2 to 3 minutes. Add chicken broth and bring to a boil for 5 minutes. Cover saucepan, reduce heat to low, and simmer until quinoa is tender and has absorbed the broth, about 15 minutes. Remove saucepan from heat and let sit for 5 minutes; fluff with a fork.
- Mix quinoa, asparagus, chicken, tomatoes, basil, Parmesan cheese, and garlic together in a bowl. Drizzle 1/4 cup olive oil over salad and season with salt, pepper, and red pepper flakes; stir until evenly coated.

Nutrition Information

- Calories: 313 calories
- Total Fat: 16.5 g
- Cholesterol: 38 mg
- Sodium: 473 mg
- Total Carbohydrate: 22 g
- Protein: 19.4 g

47. Chicken Quinoa Salad with Apples and Mozzarella

"This is a variation on the popular farro chicken salad and is loaded with protein and healthy carbs."

Serving: 6 | Prep: 15 m | Cook: 20 m | Ready in: 55 m

Ingredients

- 2 cups water
- 1 cup uncooked quinoa
- 3 cups chopped cooked chicken
- 3 Granny Smith apples, cut into 1-inch slices
- 1 (8 ounce) package mozzarella cheese, cubed
- 2 tablespoons dried parsley
- 2 teaspoons dried thyme
- 1 teaspoon salt
- 1/2 teaspoon ground black pepper
- 1/4 cup raspberry vinaigrette dressing

Direction

- Bring water and quinoa to a boil in a saucepan. Reduce heat to medium-low, cover, and simmer until quinoa is tender, 15 to 20 minutes. Spread on a platter; let cool.
- Combine chicken, Granny Smith apples, mozzarella cheese, parsley, thyme, salt, and pepper in a large bowl. Mix in raspberry vinaigrette. Chill salad for 20 minutes.
- Fold quinoa into the salad. Refrigerate until serving.

Nutrition Information

- Calories: 400 calories
- Total Fat: 16.5 g
- Cholesterol: 78 mg
- Sodium: 813 mg
- Total Carbohydrate: 31.9 g
- Protein: 30.7 g

48. Chicken Quinoa Soup

"Quinoa is a tasty, protein-filled grain that makes a great addition to chicken soup! Add some carrots, celery, spinach, onions and bell peppers for amazing color and flavor. My husband loves this with multigrain crackers, but I think it's great as-is!"

Serving: 8 | Prep: 40 m | Cook: 53 m | Ready in: 1 h 33 m

Ingredients

- 3 cups water
- 1 cup quinoa
- 2 teaspoons olive oil, divided
- 5 skinless, boneless chicken breasts, cubed

- salt and ground black pepper to taste
- 1 yellow onion, chopped
- 1 cup chopped carrots
- 1 cup chopped celery
- 1/2 cup chopped red bell pepper
- 1/2 cup chopped yellow bell pepper
- 2 tablespoons chopped garlic
- 8 cups chicken broth
- 2 cups chopped spinach leaves
- 1/2 teaspoon dried marjoram
- 1/2 teaspoon dried oregano
- 1/2 teaspoon dried basil
- 1/2 teaspoon crushed bay leaf
- 1/3 cup cornstarch
- 1/4 cup cold water

Direction

- Bring 3 cups water and quinoa to a boil in a saucepan. Reduce heat to medium-low, cover, and simmer until quinoa is tender, 15 to 20 minutes.
- Heat 1 teaspoon olive oil in a Dutch oven over medium-high heat. Add chicken; season with salt and pepper. Cook and stir until chicken is no longer pink in the center, about 5 minutes. Transfer chicken to a plate.
- Heat remaining 1 teaspoon olive oil in the Dutch oven over medium heat. Add onion, carrots, celery, red bell pepper, yellow bell pepper, and garlic; cook and stir until soft, about 10 minutes.
- Pour chicken broth into the Dutch oven. Add spinach leaves, marjoram, oregano, basil, and bay leaf. Bring to a boil; reduce heat and simmer until flavors combine, about 10 minutes. Stir in cooked quinoa. Return chicken to the Dutch oven; cook until heated through, about 2 minutes.
- Dissolve cornstarch in 1/4 cup cold water in a small bowl. Pour slowly into the Dutch oven; cook, stirring occasionally, until soup thickens, about 1 minute.

Nutrition Information

- Calories: 214 calories
- Total Fat: 4.1 g
- Cholesterol: 37 mg
- Sodium: 90 mg
- Total Carbohydrate: 25.6 g
- Protein: 18.1 g

49. Chicken with Peas Quinoa

"Ever tried quinoa? It makes a nice substitute for rice or couscous, and this recipe is a delicious introduction to its fabulous taste and texture."

Serving: 4 | Prep: 10 m | Cook: 30 m | Ready in: 40 m

Ingredients

- 1 tablespoon olive oil
- 1 pound boneless, skinless chicken breast tenders
- 1 teaspoon smoked paprika
- 1 cup uncooked quinoa, rinsed
- 1 1/2 cups Swanson® Chicken Broth or Swanson® Chicken Stock
- 1 (24 ounce) jar Prego® Veggie Smart® Smooth Simple Italian Sauce
- 1 (10 ounce) package frozen peas, thawed

Direction

- Heat the oil in a 12-inch skillet over medium-high heat. Add the chicken and cook for 10 minutes or until well browned on both sides. Remove the chicken from the skillet, cover and keep warm.
- Add the paprika and quinoa to the skillet and stir to coat. Stir in the broth and sauce and heat to a boil. Reduce the heat to medium. Cover and cook for 15 minutes or until the quinoa is tender. Stir in the peas. Return the chicken to the skillet. Cook until the chicken is cooked through.

Nutrition Information

- Calories: 499 calories
- Total Fat: 11.3 g
- Cholesterol: 66 mg
- Sodium: 1079 mg

- Total Carbohydrate: 63.2 g
- Protein: 36.6 g

50. Chicken with Quinoa and Veggies

"A quick recipe that can be adjusted to include whatever vegetables you have on hand. It could probably be done well with shrimp also. You could easily try different vegetables. The times and amounts are variable depending upon how thick you slice your chicken and veggies, as well as how crisp you prefer the zucchini."

Serving: 4 | Prep: 30 m | Cook: 25 m | Ready in: 55 m

Ingredients

- 1 cup rinsed quinoa
- 2 cups chicken broth
- 2 tablespoons extra-virgin olive oil
- 2 garlic scapes, chopped
- 1 small onion, chopped
- 2 skinless, boneless chicken breast halves - cut into strips
- 2 tablespoons extra-virgin olive oil
- 1 zucchini, diced
- 1 tomato, diced
- 4 ounces crumbled feta cheese
- 8 fresh basil leaves
- 1 tablespoon lime juice

Direction

- Bring the quinoa and chicken broth to a boil in a saucepan; reduce heat to a simmer and cover the pan. Simmer until the broth is absorbed, the quinoa is fluffy, and the white line is visible in the grain, about 12 minutes.
- Heat 2 tablespoons of olive oil in a skillet; cook and stir the garlic scapes and onion until onion is translucent, about 5 minutes. Stir in the chicken breast strips and cook until the chicken is still slightly pink in the middle, about 5 more minutes. Remove the chicken meat and set aside. Pour 2 more tablespoons of olive oil in the skillet and cook and stir the zucchini and tomato until the zucchini is tender, 5 to 8 minutes. Return chicken to skillet and sprinkle with feta cheese, basil leaves, and lime juice. Cook until the chicken is fully cooked and hot, about 10 more minutes. Serve over hot quinoa.

Nutrition Information

- Calories: 453 calories
- Total Fat: 23.8 g
- Cholesterol: 61 mg
- Sodium: 841 mg
- Total Carbohydrate: 35.3 g
- Protein: 23.8 g

51. Chickpea and Quinoa Salad with Lemon and Tahini

"If you are looking for a balanced vegetarian meal that is easy to make but full of flavor, then I recommend this earthy, yet tangy chickpea and quinoa salad."

Serving: 4 | Prep: 10 m | Cook: 1 h 5 m | Ready in: 9 h 15 m

Ingredients

- 1/2 cup dry garbanzo beans (chickpeas)
- 1/2 cup uncooked quinoa, rinsed
- 1 cup water
- 1/4 cup chopped fresh parsley
- 1 shallot, chopped
- 1 clove garlic, minced
- 1/4 cup lemon juice
- 2 tablespoons tahini
- 1 tablespoon olive oil
- sea salt and ground black pepper to taste

Direction

- Place the garbanzo beans in a saucepan, and cover with several inches of water. Combine the quinoa with 1 cup of water in a small saucepan. Set both aside to soak overnight.

- The following day, pour the soaking water off of the garbanzo beans, and fill with fresh water. Bring to a boil over high heat, then reduce heat to medium-low, cover, and simmer until the garbanzo beans are tender, about 1 hour. Drain and set aside. Meanwhile, bring the quinoa to a boil over high heat in its soaking water. Reduce heat to low, and simmer until tender, about 10 minutes; set aside.
- Combine the drained garbanzo beans and quinoa in a mixing bowl with the parsley; set aside. In a separate bowl, whisk together the shallot, garlic, lemon juice, tahini, and olive oil. Season to taste with sea salt and pepper. Pour the dressing over the garbanzo bean mixture, and stir gently before serving.

Nutrition Information

- Calories: 259 calories
- Total Fat: 10.3 g
- Cholesterol: 0 mg
- Sodium: 101 mg
- Total Carbohydrate: 34.3 g
- Protein: 9.6 g

52. Chili with Quinoa

"My husband said this is the best chili yet! Plus it is so easy to make! To serve, put a small amount of pasta in a bowl and spoon in chili with quinoa. Add a dollop of sour cream (vegan or regular) and a sprinkle of chives for garnish. Enjoy!"

Serving: 10 | Prep: 20 m | Cook: 1 h 5 m | Ready in: 1 h 25 m

Ingredients

- 1 large onion, chopped
- 2 large cloves garlic, minced
- 2 (28 ounce) cans tomatoes, undrained
- 1 (28 ounce) can tomato sauce (such as Dei Fratelli®)
- 1 (15 ounce) can chili beans, drained and rinsed
- 1 (15 ounce) can kidney beans, drained and rinsed
- 3 tablespoons chili powder (such as Mexene®)
- 1 3/4 teaspoons ground cumin
- 1 1/2 teaspoons salt, or to taste
- 1 teaspoon white sugar
- 4 cups water, divided
- 1 cup quinoa

Direction

- Sauté onion and garlic in a stockpot over medium-high heat until softened, 5 to 10 minutes. Add canned tomatoes, tomato sauce, chili beans, kidney beans, chili powder, cumin, salt, and sugar; pour in 2 cups water and simmer until flavors blend, about 1 hour.
- Bring 2 cups water and quinoa to a boil in a saucepan. Reduce heat to medium-low, cover, and simmer until quinoa is tender and water has been absorbed, 15 to 20 minutes. Stir quinoa into chili.

Nutrition Information

- Calories: 198 calories
- Total Fat: 2.4 g
- Cholesterol: < 1 mg
- Sodium: 1295 mg
- Total Carbohydrate: 39.1 g
- Protein: 9.8 g

53. CiderGlazed Carrot and Quinoa Salad

This dish is a perfect side for roast chicken; or crumble feta on top for a vegetarian lunch. Quinoa freezes well, so cook a big batch, let cool, and freeze in resealable plastic bags until ready to use.

Serving: Makes 4 servings

Ingredients

- 1 cup quinoa, rinsed well in a fine-mesh sieve

- Kosher salt
- 1/2 small onion, chopped
- 1/4 cup olive oil plus more for baking sheet
- 2 tablespoons apple cider
- 2 tablespoons honey
- Freshly ground black pepper
- 3 medium carrots (about 1/2 pound), peeled, thinly sliced on a diagonal
- 1 tablespoon apple cider vinegar
- 2 teaspoons finely grated lemon zest
- 1 tablespoon fresh lemon juice
- 1/2 cup pickled beets, cut into matchsticks
- 2 tablespoons coarsely chopped fresh dill
- 1 head Bibb or butter lettuce, leaves torn

Direction

- Preheat oven to 450°F. Bring quinoa and 4 cups lightly salted water to a boil in a medium saucepan. Cover, reduce heat, and simmer until quinoa is tender, 10-15 minutes. Add onion; cook for 1 minute longer. Drain; return quinoa mixture to saucepan, cover, and let sit for 15 minutes. Fluff with a fork and transfer to a large bowl, let cool.
- Meanwhile, lightly coat a large rimmed baking sheet with oil. Whisk cider and honey in a large bowl to blend; season with salt and pepper. Add carrots and toss to coat. Transfer to prepared baking sheet and roast until tender, 15-20 minutes. Let cool.
- Whisk vinegar, lemon zest, and lemon juice in a small bowl. Gradually add 1/4 cup oil, whisking until dressing is blended. Season vinaigrette with salt and pepper. DO AHEAD: Quinoa, carrots, and vinaigrette can be made 6 hours ahead. Cover and chill separately.
- Add beets, dill, carrots, and half of vinaigrette to quinoa mixture and toss to coat. Add lettuce and remaining vinaigrette and toss to combine.

Nutrition Information

- Calories: 363
- Total Fat: 16 g (25%)
- Saturated Fat: 2 g (11%)
- Sodium: 510 mg (21%)
- Total Carbohydrate: 49 g (16%)
- Protein: 8 g (15%)
- Fiber: 6 g (24%)

54. Cilantro Lime Quinoa

"This is a delicious quinoa recipes that uses all the flavors of summer. It can be served warm or cold and is great on its own as a vegetarian dish or as a picnic side item."

Serving: 6 | Prep: 20 m | Cook: 25 m | Ready in: 45 m

Ingredients

- 1 tablespoon olive oil
- 2 cloves garlic, minced
- 1/2 red onion, diced
- 1 jalapeno pepper, diced
- 1/4 teaspoon salt
- 1 cup quinoa, rinsed and drained
- 1 1/2 cups low-sodium chicken broth
- 1 cup corn (optional)
- 1 mango, peeled and diced
- 1 avocado - peeled, pitted, and diced
- 1 1/2 tablespoons lime juice
- 2 tablespoons chopped fresh cilantro

Direction

- Heat olive oil in a saucepan over medium heat; cook and stir garlic until fragrant, about 1 minute. Add onion, jalapeno pepper, and salt; cook and stir until onion is tender, 5 to 10 minutes. Add quinoa and cook until slightly browned, 1 to 2 minutes. Pour in chicken broth and bring to a boil. Reduce heat to low and simmer until broth is absorbed, 15 to 20 minutes.
- Stir corn, mango, avocado, lime juice, and cilantro into quinoa mixture. Serve immediately or chill and serve cold.

Nutrition Information

- Calories: 234 calories
- Total Fat: 9.4 g
- Cholesterol: 1 mg
- Sodium: 135 mg

- Total Carbohydrate: 33.7 g
- Protein: 6.7 g

55. CinnaCoco Quinoa Bites

"A wonderfully delicious alternative to cookies, cakes, and cupcakes. Packed with nutrition and deliciously good for you!"

Serving: 24 | Prep: 15 m | Cook: 30 m | Ready in: 45 m

Ingredients

- 1 1/3 cups water
- 2/3 cup quinoa
- 1/4 cup shredded unsweetened coconut
- 1/4 cup brown sugar
- 2 tablespoons whole wheat flour
- 1/2 teaspoon ground cinnamon
- 1/4 teaspoon salt
- 2 large eggs, beaten

Direction

- Preheat oven to 350 degrees F (175 degrees C). Lightly grease 24 non-stick mini-muffin cups.
- Bring water and quinoa to a boil in a saucepan. Reduce heat to medium-low, cover, and simmer until quinoa is tender and water has been absorbed, 15 to 20 minutes.
- Stir coconut, brown sugar, whole wheat flour, cinnamon, and salt together in a bowl. Add quinoa and eggs to coconut mixture; stir until completely combined. Drop coconut mixture by the tablespoonful into prepared muffin cups.
- Bake in the preheated oven until slightly crisp and golden brown, 15 to 20 minutes.

Nutrition Information

- Calories: 41 calories
- Total Fat: 1.3 g
- Cholesterol: 16 mg
- Sodium: 32 mg
- Total Carbohydrate: 6 g
- Protein: 1.3 g

56. Coconut Quinoa

"A nice change from plain old grains. Quinoa has become a staple in our home because it only takes about 15 minutes to cook as opposed to 45 minutes for brown rice. I use canned coconut milk or coconut milk from the carton interchangeably. However, the coconut milk from the carton is sweetened, which my family likes but might not be right with some main dishes."

Serving: 6 | Prep: 10 m | Cook: 10 m | Ready in: 20 m

Ingredients

- 1 cup quinoa
- 2 cups coconut milk
- 2 tablespoons flaked coconut (optional)
- salt to taste

Direction

- Bring quinoa, coconut milk, and flaked coconut to a boil in a saucepan. Reduce heat to medium-low and simmer, stirring occasionally, until the quinoa is tender and the water has been absorbed, 10 to 15 minutes; season with salt.

Nutrition Information

- Calories: 266 calories
- Total Fat: 19 g
- Cholesterol: 0 mg
- Sodium: 12 mg
- Total Carbohydrate: 20.8 g
- Protein: 5.7 g

57. Coconut Quinoa with Harissa Roasted Sweet Potatoes

"The coconut milk and sweet potatoes help tame the heat from the harissa in this flavorful meal. If you use low-sodium chicken broth, be sure to add a little salt to the quinoa while it's cooking."

Serving: 4 | Prep: 15 m | Cook: 41 m | Ready in: 56 m

Ingredients

- 2 cups 1/2-inch diced sweet potatoes
- 2 tablespoons harissa
- 1/2 teaspoon smoked paprika
- 2 teaspoons oil
- 1 shallot, minced
- 1 tablespoon grated fresh ginger
- 1 clove garlic, smashed
- 1 cup quinoa
- 1 cup coconut milk
- 1 cup chicken broth
- 1 cup thinly sliced kale
- 1/2 lemon, juiced
- 2 ounces crumbled feta cheese
- 2 tablespoons minced cilantro

Direction

- Preheat oven to 400 degrees F (200 degrees C). Line a baking sheet with parchment paper.
- Toss sweet potatoes, harissa, and paprika together in a bowl until coated; spread onto the prepared baking sheet.
- Bake in the preheated oven for 10 minutes; stir sweet potatoes and continue baking until tender and lightly browned, 10 to 15 minutes more.
- Heat oil in a pot over medium heat; add shallot, ginger, and garlic. Cook and stir until fragrant, about 1 minute. Add quinoa, coconut milk, and chicken broth; bring to a boil. Reduce heat and simmer until quinoa is tender, about 15 minutes.
- Stir kale, lemon juice, and sweet potatoes into quinoa mixture. Top each serving with feta cheese and cilantro.

Nutrition Information

- Calories: 407 calories
- Total Fat: 20.4 g
- Cholesterol: 14 mg
- Sodium: 490 mg
- Total Carbohydrate: 47.1 g
- Protein: 11.1 g

58. Coconut Curry Lentil Stew Served over Quinoa

"This hardy, flavorful lentil stew is very nutritious and filling. Even my kids love it, which is surprising because they are picky. It is both vegan and gluten-free, so just about everyone can enjoy it. I like to spice mine up with garlic-chile sauce on the side. If you don't grow your own tomatoes, ripe ones can be hard to find. Ask your local produce grocer to set aside their damaged and overripe tomatoes for you when they restock and you can get them for a bargain."

Serving: 12 | Prep: 25 m | Cook: 35 m | Ready in: 1 h

Ingredients

- 2 cups quinoa
- 3 1/2 cups water
- 1 tablespoon salt
- 2 tablespoons coconut oil
- 1 small onion, chopped
- 6 cloves garlic, minced
- 5 large tomatoes, chopped
- 1 cup water
- 1 (14 ounce) can coconut milk
- 1 tablespoon molasses
- 1/4 cup coconut powder
- 1 (4 inch) cinnamon stick
- 3 tablespoons curry powder
- 2 tablespoons ground coriander
- 2 cups red lentils
- salt and pepper to taste
- 1 bunch fresh cilantro, chopped

Direction

- Soak the quinoa in a bowl filled with cold water for 5 minutes, then drain using a fine mesh strainer, and rinse with running water. Set the strainer aside so the quinoa can drain, then bring 3 1/2 cups of water and 1 tablespoon of salt to a boil in a saucepan. Stir in the quinoa, cover, and reduce the heat to medium-low. Simmer until the quinoa has absorbed the liquid and is tender, about 15 minutes. Set aside, and keep warm.
- Melt the coconut oil in a large saucepan over medium heat. Add the onion and garlic; cook and stir until the onion has softened and turned translucent, about 5 minutes. Stir in the tomatoes, and cook for 5 minutes more. Pour in the water and coconut milk, and add the molasses, coconut powder, cinnamon, curry powder, and ground coriander. Bring to a simmer over medium-high heat, then stir in the lentils, and cook until just tender, 10 to 15 minutes. Stir frequently as the lentils cook to keep them from sticking. Be careful not to overcook them, as they will quickly loose shape and become a paste.
- Once the lentils are done, season to taste with salt and pepper, and stir in the chopped cilantro. Serve the lentil stew over a bed of quinoa.

Nutrition Information

- Calories: 347 calories
- Total Fat: 13.5 g
- Cholesterol: 0 mg
- Sodium: 602 mg
- Total Carbohydrate: 45.5 g
- Protein: 14.4 g

59. Cold Chicken Quinoa Avocado Salad

"This is a summer-favorite of my family. It has a great fresh flavor and is so easy for a weeknight meal. The avocado is a fun alternative to a mayo dressing. Serve alone, on top of lettuce, or in a whole wheat pita."

Serving: 6 | Prep: 15 m | Cook: 15 m | Ready in: 1 h

Ingredients

- 1 cup water
- 1/2 cup red quinoa
- 2 avocados, peeled and mashed
- 2 tablespoons chopped fresh cilantro
- 1 tablespoon fresh lime juice
- salt and ground black pepper to taste
- 1 pound cubed cooked chicken, chilled
- 2 tomatoes, seeded and chopped
- 2 tablespoons chopped scallions

Direction

- Bring water and quinoa to a boil in a saucepan. Reduce heat to medium-low, cover, and simmer until quinoa is tender and water has been absorbed, 15 to 20 minutes. Cool quinoa to room temperature, about 30 minutes.
- Mix mashed avocado, cilantro, lime juice, salt, and pepper together in a bowl until dressing is smooth.
- Combine quinoa, chicken, tomatoes, and scallions in a bowl; add avocado dressing and toss to coat.

Nutrition Information

- Calories: 311 calories
- Total Fat: 16.5 g
- Cholesterol: 57 mg
- Sodium: 84 mg
- Total Carbohydrate: 17.7 g
- Protein: 24.6 g

60. Copycat First Watch Quinoa Power Bowl

"This is a copycat recipe of First Watch®'s Quinoa Power Bowl. I think you are really going to enjoy this protein-packed quinoa mixed with grilled chicken, lemon, feta, roasted tomatoes, and shredded carrots. The recipe is quite simple, and the dish is a complete meal all-in-one, so it takes the guesswork out of what side dishes to prepare to ensure a balanced meal of protein, whole grains, and fresh veggies."

Serving: 4 | Prep: 15 m | Cook: 35 m | Ready in: 55 m

Ingredients

- Quinoa:
- 2 cups chicken stock
- 1 cup quinoa, rinsed
- Lemon Dressing:
- 1 lemon, zested and juiced
- 3 tablespoons olive oil
- 1 teaspoon freshly cracked black pepper
- 1/4 teaspoon salt
- 2 cups finely chopped cooked chicken
- 1 1/2 cups water
- 1 (14 ounce) can diced tomatoes, drained
- 1 (4 ounce) package crumbled feta cheese
- 1/2 cup half-and-half
- 1/2 cup shredded carrots
- 1 tablespoon pesto sauce
- 1 teaspoon dried oregano

Direction

- Combine chicken stock and quinoa in a large pot over high heat; bring to a boil. Reduce heat to low and simmer, covered, until quinoa is tender, about 15 minutes. Remove from heat and let stand, covered, for 5 minutes.
- Whisk lemon zest, lemon juice, olive oil, pepper, and salt in a small bowl to make lemon dressing.
- Stir lemon dressing, chicken, water, diced tomatoes, feta cheese, half-and-half, carrots, pesto sauce, and oregano into the cooked quinoa. Cook over medium heat, stirring frequently, until thick and creamy, about 15 minutes. Spoon into individual bowls.

Nutrition Information

- Calories: 575 calories
- Total Fat: 33.2 g
- Cholesterol: 95 mg
- Sodium: 1206 mg
- Total Carbohydrate: 38.8 g
- Protein: 30.8 g

61. Cranberry and Cilantro Quinoa Salad

"I got this recipe from the restaurant my dad built. I love the unique way of cooking the quinoa and the great combinations of the flavors."

Serving: 6 | Prep: 10 m | Cook: 20 m | Ready in: 2 h 30 m

Ingredients

- 1 1/2 cups water
- 1 cup uncooked quinoa, rinsed
- 1/4 cup red bell pepper, chopped
- 1/4 cup yellow bell pepper, chopped
- 1 small red onion, finely chopped
- 1 1/2 teaspoons curry powder
- 1/4 cup chopped fresh cilantro
- 1 lime, juiced
- 1/4 cup toasted sliced almonds
- 1/2 cup minced carrots
- 1/2 cup dried cranberries
- salt and ground black pepper to taste

Direction

- Pour the water into a saucepan, and cover with a lid. Bring to a boil over high heat, then pour in the quinoa, recover, and continue to simmer over low heat until the water has been absorbed, 15 to 20 minutes. Scrape into a mixing bowl, and chill in the refrigerator until cold.
- Once cold, stir in the red bell pepper, yellow bell pepper, red onion, curry powder, cilantro, lime juice, sliced almonds, carrots, and

cranberries. Season to taste with salt and pepper. Chill before serving.

Nutrition Information

- Calories: 176 calories
- Total Fat: 3.9 g
- Cholesterol: 0 mg
- Sodium: 13 mg
- Total Carbohydrate: 31.6 g
- Protein: 5.4 g

62. Cranberry Apple Pecan Quinoa Salad

"A beautiful and light take on a fall salad. The tastes mix well together and it can be served hot or cold. I like to pair it with Dijon-crusted salmon!"

Serving: 6 | Prep: 10 m | Cook: 15 m | Ready in: 25 m

Ingredients

- 1 1/2 cups chicken broth
- 1 cup quinoa, rinsed
- Sauce:
- 3 tablespoons olive oil
- 1 1/2 tablespoons Dijon mustard
- 1 teaspoon maple syrup, or more to taste
- 1/4 teaspoon ground cinnamon
- salt and ground black pepper to taste
- 1 large crisp apple, chopped into small pieces
- 1 cup pecan pieces
- 1/2 cup dried cranberries
- 1/2 cup grated Parmesan cheese (optional)

Direction

- Stir chicken broth and quinoa together in a saucepan; bring to a boil, reduce heat to low, place cover on the saucepan, and cook until the broth is absorbed, about 10 minutes. Remove saucepan from heat and fluff with a fork.
- Whisk olive oil, Dijon mustard, maple syrup, and cinnamon together in a bowl; season with salt and pepper. Drizzle sauce over the quinoa; stir. Add apple pieces, pecan pieces, cranberries, and Parmesan cheese; stir. Return cover to the saucepan and let the mixture steam until the sauce warms and the apples soften slightly, 5 to 10 minutes.

Nutrition Information

- Calories: 372 calories
- Total Fat: 23.4 g
- Cholesterol: 6 mg
- Sodium: 198 mg
- Total Carbohydrate: 35.7 g
- Protein: 8.3 g

63. Cranberry Lentil and Quinoa Salad

"A healthy, protein-packed salad."

Serving: 12 | Prep: 15 m | Cook: 45 m | Ready in: 2 h

Ingredients

- Salad:
- 1 cup dried lentils
- 2 bay leaves, divided (optional)
- water to cover
- 2 cups water
- 1 cup quinoa
- Dressing:
- 3 tablespoons lemon juice
- 1 teaspoon honey
- 1 tablespoon white wine vinegar
- 1/4 teaspoon salt
- 3 tablespoons olive oil
- ground black pepper to taste
- 1/2 cup coarsely chopped walnuts, toasted
- 1/2 cup dried cranberries, or to taste
- 1/2 cup crumbled feta cheese
- 1 small green onion, finely chopped

Direction

- Place lentils and 1 bay leaf in a saucepan with enough water to cover and bring to a boil. Reduce heat to medium-low and simmer until lentils are tender, about 30 minutes; drain and discard bay leaf. Rinse with cold water until lentils cool and transfer to a large bowl.
- Bring 2 cups water, quinoa, and remaining bay leaf to a boil in a saucepan. Reduce heat to medium-low, cover, and simmer until quinoa is tender and water has been absorbed, 15 to 20 minutes. Rinse quinoa with cold water until cool, discarding bay leaf. Stir quinoa into lentils.
- Heat lemon juice in a microwave-safe bowl in a microwave until warm, about 30 seconds. Stir honey into juice until dissolved. Add vinegar and salt; whisk in olive oil and season with black pepper. Pour lemon juice mixture into lentils and quinoa.
- Mix walnuts, cranberries, feta cheese, and green onion into lentil and quinoa salad. Toss to coat. Refrigerate until chilled, about 1 hour.

Nutrition Information

- Calories: 205 calories
- Total Fat: 8.9 g
- Cholesterol: 6 mg
- Sodium: 123 mg
- Total Carbohydrate: 24.7 g
- Protein: 7.8 g

64. Cranberry Quinoa Salad with Broccoli

"This salad is delicious served hot or cold! It's vegan, gluten-free, and is pretty healthy!"

Serving: 4 | Prep: 10 m | Cook: 24 m | Ready in: 34 m

Ingredients

- 1 3/4 cups water
- 1 cup quinoa
- 3/4 cup dried cranberries
- 1 cup bite-size broccoli pieces
- Dressing:
- 2 tablespoons olive oil
- 1 tablespoon orange juice
- 1 tablespoon lime juice
- 1 clove garlic, minced
- 1/2 cup chopped walnuts

Direction

- Combine water and quinoa in a saucepan. Bring to a boil; reduce heat to medium-low and simmer until most of the water has been absorbed, about 8 minutes. Add cranberries; cook until plump and quinoa is tender, 4 to 5 minutes more. Transfer to a bowl.
- Place a steamer insert into a saucepan and fill with water to just below the bottom of the steamer. Bring water to a boil. Add broccoli, cover, and steam until tender, 2 to 5 minutes. Drain; fold into the quinoa mixture.
- Mix olive oil, orange juice, lime juice, and garlic together in a small bowl to make dressing. Pour over quinoa mixture; toss to combine. Sprinkle walnuts on top.

Nutrition Information

- Calories: 391 calories
- Total Fat: 19 g
- Cholesterol: 0 mg
- Sodium: 13 mg
- Total Carbohydrate: 50.3 g
- Protein: 9 g

65. Cream of Broccoli Soup with Quinoa

"Because of the broccoli, onion, sweet potato, and homemade vegetable stock, this is a healthy recipe. When combined with the protein-rich quinoa, it also filling and satisfying. It has become a staple on our menu. Garnish with broccoli, parsley, or dill."

Serving: 4 | Prep: 25 m | Cook: 45 m | Ready in: 1 h 10 m

Ingredients

- 2 cups water
- 1 cup quinoa, or more to taste
- 1 tablespoon vegetable oil
- 1 large onion, chopped
- 4 cups homemade vegetable stock
- 4 cups chopped broccoli
- 1 sweet potato, peeled and cut into 1-inch pieces
- salt to taste
- 1 pinch ground nutmeg, or to taste
- 1 pinch garam masala, or to taste
- 1 pinch ground pepper to taste
- Cashew Cream:
- 1/2 cup water (optional)
- 2 ounces raw cashews (optional)

Direction

- Bring 2 cups water and quinoa to a boil in a saucepan. Reduce heat to medium-low; cover and simmer until quinoa is tender, 15 to 20 minutes.
- Heat oil in a heavy 4-quart pot. Add onion; cook and stir until translucent, about 5 minutes. Stir in vegetable stock, broccoli, sweet potato, and salt. Bring soup to a boil; reduce heat and simmer until broccoli and sweet potato are very tender, 15 to 20 minutes.
- Remove soup from the heat. Puree with a hand-held immersion blender until smooth. Season with nutmeg, garam masala, and pepper.
- Combine 1/2 cup water and cashews in a high-speed blender; puree until smooth.
- Pour cashew mixture into the soup and bring to a boil.
- Place 1/3 cup cooked quinoa in the center of each serving bowl; ladle soup around quinoa.

Nutrition Information

- Calories: 405 calories
- Total Fat: 13.3 g
- Cholesterol: 0 mg
- Sodium: 579 mg
- Total Carbohydrate: 60.9 g
- Protein: 13.8 g

66. Creamy Quinoa Risotto

"Just as creamy and delicious as traditional risotto...but it's actually healthy!"

Serving: 4 | Prep: 10 m | Cook: 40 m | Ready in: 50 m

Ingredients

- 1 cup quinoa
- 5 cups chicken broth, or as needed
- 3 tablespoons unsalted butter
- 1 small yellow onion, chopped
- 2 cloves garlic, minced
- 1/2 cup dry white wine
- 1/2 cup freshly grated Parmesan cheese
- 1 tablespoon heavy whipping cream
- 1/4 teaspoon dried marjoram
- 1/4 teaspoon dried thyme
- salt and freshly cracked black pepper to taste

Direction

- Rinse quinoa twice and drain well.
- Pour chicken broth into a saucepan; bring to a boil.
- Melt butter in a separate saucepan over medium-high heat; sauté onion and garlic until onion is soft, about 5 minutes. Stir quinoa into onion mixture; cook, stirring frequently, until quinoa is toasted and coated in oil, about 3 minutes.

- Slowly pour wine over quinoa mixture; cook and stir until wine is absorbed, about 5 minutes. Ladle 1/2 cup chicken broth over quinoa mixture; cook, stirring frequently, until absorbed, 3 to 5 minutes. Continue ladling broth, 1/2 cup at a time, over quinoa mixture; cook, stirring frequently, until quinoa is tender and has burst, about 20 minutes. You may not use all the chicken broth.
- Mix Parmesan cheese and cream into quinoa mixture; season with marjoram, thyme, salt, and pepper. Add a splash of chicken broth to make quinoa more creamy, if desired.

Nutrition Information

- Calories: 324 calories
- Total Fat: 15.5 g
- Cholesterol: 37 mg
- Sodium: 199 mg
- Total Carbohydrate: 30.8 g
- Protein: 10.3 g

67. Crunchy Lemon Quinoa and Asparagus Bowl

"This is the perfect lunch or dinner recipe to help you get a great dose of veggies with added flavor and nutrients. Serve garnished with dried basil and parsley, more nutritional yeast, or another seasoning of your choice (such as Parmesan cheese)."

Serving: 4 | Prep: 15 m | Cook: 20 m | Ready in: 35 m

Ingredients

- 1 pound fresh asparagus, trimmed
- 2 teaspoons coconut oil
- 1/2 onion, diced
- 2 cloves garlic, minced
- 1 cup cooked red quinoa
- 1/2 cup low-sodium vegetable stock
- 1 tablespoon ground turmeric
- 1/2 cup nutritional yeast
- 1/2 large lemon, juiced

Direction

- Fill a saucepan halfway with water; bring to a boil. Add asparagus and cook uncovered until tender but still crispy, 2 to 3 minutes. Drain in a colander and rinse with cold water to stop the cooking process.
- Heat coconut oil in a large skillet over medium heat. Add the onion and garlic; cook until onion is translucent, about 5 minutes. Stir in cooked quinoa, vegetable stock, and turmeric; cook until flavors combine, 5 to 6 minutes. Stir in blanched asparagus, nutritional yeast, and lemon juice; cook and stir, 3 to 4 minutes.

Nutrition Information

- Calories: 166 calories
- Total Fat: 4.2 g
- Cholesterol: 0 mg
- Sodium: 37 mg
- Total Carbohydrate: 24.1 g
- Protein: 13 g

68. CrunchySweet Quinoa Couscous with Fresh Herbs

Herbaceous and packed with fiber and protein, this grain salad is a keeper.

Ingredients

- 1/4 cup dried chickpeas (or canned; see Cooks' Note:)
- 1 1" piece kombu
- sea salt
- 1 cup quinoa
- 1/2 cup raisins
- 1/2 cup toasted almonds, chopped
- 1/4 cup fresh flat-leaf parsley, chopped
- 1/2 cup fresh basil leaves, chopped
- 2 tbsp olive oil plus more
- 1/2 tsp Herbamare seasoning, ume vinegar, or sea salt

- squeeze of fresh lemon juice (optional)
- 1 tsp orange or lemon zest (optional)

Direction

- Cover chickpeas with 2" water and soak overnight (or see quick-soak tip on p. 35). Drain chickpeas and place in a medium pot; cover with 2"-3" of water. Bring to a rapid boil and skim any foam that rises to the surface. Add kombu and reduce heat to a simmer.
- Cook for 1-2 hours (very fresh chickpeas take longer to cook), adding water as needed. About 10 minutes before they're done, add 1/4 tsp salt. Drain and set aside.
- In another pot, cover quinoa with water and swirl with your hand to rinse. Drain. Add 2 cups fresh water and bring to a boil. Reduce heat to a simmer, cover, and cook for 25 minutes, or until all water is absorbed. Transfer quinoa to a large bowl to cool.
- After quinoa has cooled to slightly warmer than room temperature, add chickpeas, raisins, almonds, parsley, basil, 2 tbsp oil, and Herbamare, vinegar, or salt. Finish with a drizzle of oil and a splash of citrus juice or zest, if desired.
- Cooks' Note: s: To save time, skip the first two steps (and the kombu) and use drained and rinsed canned chickpeas in place of dried. Kombu is a type of edible kelp available at Japanese and health food stores.

Nutrition Information

- Calories: 212
- Total Fat: 10 g (15%)
- Saturated Fat: 1 g (5%)
- Sodium: 126 mg (5%)
- Total Carbohydrate: 27 g (9%)
- Protein: 7 g (13%)
- Fiber: 4 g (15%)

69. Curried Quinoa

"A light curry flavor makes delicious quinoa a great side dish for a multitude of main courses."

Serving: 2 | Prep: 5 m | Cook: 35 m | Ready in: 40 m

Ingredients

- 2 tablespoons olive oil, or as needed
- 1 small onion, diced
- 2 cloves garlic, minced
- 1 cup quinoa
- 2 cups chicken broth
- 1 tablespoon curry powder, or to taste
- 1 tablespoon ancho chile powder
- salt and pepper to taste

Direction

- Heat oil in a large skillet over medium heat. Add onion and garlic and cook and stir for 2 minutes; add quinoa and cook and stir until lightly toasted, about 5 minutes.
- Pour broth into the pan and bring to a boil. Reduce heat and add curry and chile powders; cover and simmer until tender, about 25 minutes. Season to taste with salt and pepper.

Nutrition Information

- Calories: 473 calories
- Total Fat: 19.8 g
- Cholesterol: 0 mg
- Sodium: 48 mg
- Total Carbohydrate: 62.8 g
- Protein: 13.5 g

70. Curried Quinoa Salad with Mango

"This easy recipe combines the pungent flavors of curry and mango for a filling and delicious dish that will have everyone going back for seconds!"

Serving: 4 | Prep: 10 m | Cook: 15 m | Ready in: 1 h 25 m

Ingredients

- 1 1/2 cups chicken stock
- 3/4 cup quinoa
- 1 1/2 teaspoons curry powder
- 1/4 teaspoon garlic powder
- 1/2 teaspoon salt
- 1/4 teaspoon black pepper
- 1 mango - peeled, seeded and diced
- 3 green onions, chopped

Direction

- Bring chicken stock, quinoa, curry powder, garlic powder, salt, and pepper to a boil in a saucepan over high heat. Reduce heat to medium-low, cover, and simmer until the quinoa is tender, 15 to 20 minutes. Once done, scrape the quinoa into a shallow dish and allow to cool to room temperature. Stir in the mango and green onions. Serve either at room temperature or cold.

Nutrition Information

- Calories: 162 calories
- Total Fat: 2.4 g
- Cholesterol: < 1 mg
- Sodium: 553 mg
- Total Carbohydrate: 31.1 g
- Protein: 5.3 g

71. Curried Quinoa with Red Lentils and Kale

"This is gluten-free, vegan, and dairy-free, if your omit the butter. It is a slightly sweet, savory dish with a kick of spice. Vegetarian comfort food. It's very modestly spicy for spicy food lovers, but very spicy for people who aren't accustomed to chiles."

Serving: 3 | Prep: 15 m | Cook: 35 m | Ready in: 50 m

Ingredients

- 2 cups water
- 1 cup vegetable broth
- 1/3 cup red lentils
- 1/4 cup finely chopped onion
- 1 jalapeno pepper, seeded and minced
- 3 cloves garlic, minced, or more to taste
- 1 cup rainbow quinoa
- 1 1/2 teaspoons ground cumin
- 1 teaspoon curry powder
- 1/2 teaspoon salt
- 1/2 teaspoon chili powder
- 1/2 teaspoon ground cinnamon
- 1/2 teaspoon ground black pepper
- 1/2 teaspoon ground coriander
- 1/4 teaspoon ground cardamom
- 1/4 teaspoon ground cloves
- 3 cups chopped kale
- 1/2 cup frozen peas
- 1 tablespoon unsalted butter, or more to taste (optional)

Direction

- Bring water and broth to a boil in a stockpot; add lentils, onion, jalapeno pepper, and garlic. Cover stockpot, reduce heat to medium, and simmer for 10 minutes.
- Mix quinoa, cumin, curry powder, salt, chili powder, cinnamon, black pepper, coriander, cardamom, and cloves into broth mixture; return to a boil. Cover stockpot, reduce heat to medium, and simmer until quinoa is tender, about 10 minutes more.
- Stir kale, peas, and butter into quinoa mixture and return to a boil. Cover stockpot, reduce

heat to medium, and cook until kale and peas are tender, about 10 minutes more.

Nutrition Information

- Calories: 404 calories
- Total Fat: 8.8 g
- Cholesterol: 10 mg
- Sodium: 616 mg
- Total Carbohydrate: 65.6 g
- Protein: 18.3 g

72. Curry Couscous and Quinoa Pilaf Vegetarian

"This couscous pilaf is very popular as a potluck dish (party size 15 to 20 people). Great for summer vegetables (change veg per season)."

Serving: 12 | Prep: 40 m | Cook: 25 m | Ready in: 9 h 20 m

Ingredients

- 4 cups vegetable stock
- 1 teaspoon olive oil
- 1 teaspoon salt
- 1 tablespoon turmeric powder
- 1 teaspoon curry powder
- 2 cups uncooked couscous
- 3 cups water
- 1 1/2 cups uncooked quinoa
- 1 tablespoon salted butter
- 2 tablespoons slivered almonds, or to taste (optional)
- 5 stalks celery, finely chopped
- 1 1/2 cups finely shredded carrots
- 1 cup drained garbanzo beans
- 1 cup chopped fresh parsley
- 1/2 cup raisins
- 3 green onions, finely sliced
- 1 tablespoon minced preserved lemon (optional)
- For the Dressing:
- 2/3 cup extra-virgin olive oil
- 2/3 cup apple cider vinegar
- 6 tablespoons honey
- 2 tablespoons turmeric powder
- 2 tablespoons curry powder, or more to taste
- 1 tablespoon dry vegetable soup mix
- 1 teaspoon salt, or to taste
- 1/2 teaspoon freshly ground black pepper

Direction

- Combine vegetable stock with 1 teaspoon olive oil and 1 teaspoon salt in a medium saucepan. Bring to a boil; add 1 teaspoon turmeric and 1 teaspoon curry powder. Stir in couscous and remove pan from heat. Cover and let sit until water is absorbed completely, about 15 minutes.
- Meanwhile, bring water to a boil in a pot and add quinoa. Bring to a simmer, stirring occasionally. Reduce heat to medium-low, cover, and simmer until water is absorbed, about 15 minutes. Cover and let stand for a few minutes if there is liquid left in the pot.
- Fluff couscous with a fork and place in a very large bowl. Mix quinoa into the bowl; allow to cool.
- Melt 1 tablespoon butter in a skillet over medium-high heat. Sauté almonds until toasted and golden brown, about 3 minutes. Let cool and add to the couscous and quinoa. Add celery, carrots, garbanzo beans, parsley, raisins, green onions, and preserved lemon. Stir to combine.
- Combine 2/3 cup olive oil, vinegar, honey, 2 tablespoons turmeric, 2 tablespoons curry powder, vegetable soup mix, 1 teaspoon salt, and pepper in a bowl. Whisk together. Toss dressing over the couscous mixture, a little at a time, stirring to combine. Cover with plastic wrap and refrigerate to let the flavors develop, 8 hours to overnight.

Nutrition Information

- Calories: 426 calories
- Total Fat: 16.8 g
- Cholesterol: 3 mg
- Sodium: 690 mg
- Total Carbohydrate: 60.4 g

- Protein: 9.2 g

73. Curry Quinoa and Couscous Salad

"This hearty recipe is good as a main dish or a side. I make this on the weekend so I have this all week."

Serving: 10 | Prep: 20 m | Cook: 25 m | Ready in: 55 m

Ingredients

- Salad:
- 2 cups water
- 1 cup quinoa
- 1 1/2 cups water
- 1 cup couscous
- 1 (15 ounce) can chickpeas, rinsed and drained
- 2 cups chopped tomatoes
- 2 red bell peppers, chopped
- 3 stalks celery, chopped
- 1 cup dried cranberries
- 1/2 cup chopped pecans
- 2 shallots, chopped
- 1/4 cup freshly chopped parsley (optional)
- 1 tablespoon chopped fresh cilantro, or to taste
- Dressing:
- 3 lemons, juiced
- 1/4 cup curry paste (such as Patak's®)
- 4 teaspoons soy sauce
- 2 teaspoons white sugar
- 2 teaspoons sesame oil
- 1 teaspoon ground cumin
- 1 teaspoon salt
- 1 cup olive oil

Direction

- Bring 2 cups water and quinoa to a boil in a saucepan. Reduce heat to medium-low, cover, and simmer until quinoa is tender, 15 to 20 minutes.
- Bring 1 1/2 cups water to a boil in a saucepan; remove from heat and stir couscous into the water. Cover saucepan and let stand until water is absorbed completely, about 10 minutes. Fluff couscous with a fork.
- Combine quinoa, couscous, chickpeas, tomatoes, red bell peppers, celery, cranberries, pecans, shallots, parsley, and cilantro.
- Combine lemon juice, curry paste, soy sauce, sugar, sesame oil, cumin, and salt in a blender; blend until smooth. Slowly pour olive oil into the blender while it is still running until dressing is emulsified. Pour dressing over quinoa-couscous mixture and toss to coat.

Nutrition Information

- Calories: 467 calories
- Total Fat: 28.2 g
- Cholesterol: 0 mg
- Sodium: 570 mg
- Total Carbohydrate: 48.2 g
- Protein: 7.6 g

74. Delicata Delish

"Delicious baked delicata squash is stuffed with and served over a fragrant mixture of quinoa, shallots, and pine nuts. This recipe is a great way to use the squash and shallots in your farm share delivery! We can't wait to try it with different seasonings and different types of squash. Two of us finished off the whole thing, but we think it ideally serves four."

Serving: 4 | Prep: 15 m | Cook: 30 m | Ready in: 45 m

Ingredients

- 1 large delicata squash, halved lengthwise and seeded
- 3 tablespoons butter, divided
- salt and pepper to taste
- 1 cup uncooked quinoa
- 2 cups water
- 2 shallots, chopped
- 1 clove garlic, minced
- 1/3 cup pine nuts

Direction

- Preheat oven to 350 degrees F (175 degrees C).

- Arrange the squash halves cut side up in a baking dish. Fill dish with about 1/4 inch water. Place 1 tablespoon butter on each half, and season halves with salt and pepper. Cover dish, and bake squash 30 minutes in the preheated oven, or until very tender.
- Place quinoa in a pot with 2 cups water. Bring to a boil. Reduce heat to low, cover, and simmer 15 minutes.
- Melt the remaining 1 tablespoon butter in a skillet over medium heat. Stir in shallots and garlic, and cook until tender. Stir in pine nuts, and cook until golden. Gently mix into the pot with the cooked quinoa.
- Cut the squash halves in half, and fill each quarter with the quinoa mixture. Serve each stuffed squash quarter on a bed of the remaining quinoa mixture.

Nutrition Information

- Calories: 376 calories
- Total Fat: 17.1 g
- Cholesterol: 23 mg
- Sodium: 75 mg
- Total Carbohydrate: 49 g
- Protein: 10.7 g

75. Diannes LemonFeta Quinoa Salad

"This fresh, colorful, Greek-inspired salad is perfect for summertime, either as a dinner side dish or a vegetarian lunch entree. This salad can be served immediately, or covered and refrigerated to serve later."

Serving: 6 | Prep: 15 m | Cook: 15 m | Ready in: 1 h

Ingredients

- 2 cups water
- 1 cup quinoa
- 1/2 teaspoon sea salt
- 2/3 cup halved grape tomatoes
- 1/2 cup crumbled feta cheese
- 1/4 cup roasted unsalted sunflower seeds
- 1/4 cup chopped fresh parsley
- 1 (2.25 ounce) can sliced black olives, drained
- 1 tablespoon minced shallot
- 3 tablespoons extra-virgin olive oil
- 3 tablespoons lemon juice
- 1 teaspoon Dijon mustard
- 1 teaspoon minced garlic
- 1/4 teaspoon sea salt
- 1/4 teaspoon fresh ground black pepper

Direction

- Bring water, quinoa, and 1/2 teaspoon sea salt to a boil in a saucepan. Reduce heat to medium-low, cover, and simmer until quinoa is tender and water has been absorbed, 15 to 20 minutes. Spread quinoa on a baking sheet and cool, about 30 minutes.
- Mix quinoa, tomatoes, feta cheese, sunflower seeds, parsley, olives, and shallot together in a large bowl.
- Whisk olive oil, lemon juice, mustard, garlic, 1/4 teaspoon sea salt, and pepper together in a bowl; pour over quinoa mixture and toss to coat.

Nutrition Information

- Calories: 231 calories
- Total Fat: 13.3 g
- Cholesterol: 11 mg
- Sodium: 479 mg
- Total Carbohydrate: 22 g
- Protein: 6.6 g

76. Easy Broccoli Quinoa Soup

"This kid-friendly soup is a tad sweet and, perhaps best of all, easy for little hands to spoon up without making a big mess."

Serving: 6 | Prep: 10 m | Cook: 20 m | Ready in: 30 m

Ingredients

- 1 tablespoon extra-virgin olive oil
- 1/2 onion, diced

- 2 cloves garlic, minced
- 2 cups broccoli florets
- 2 cups water
- 1 cup quinoa
- 2 cubes chicken bouillon
- 1 (12 fluid ounce) can fat-free evaporated milk
- 1 tablespoon all-purpose flour
- salt and ground black pepper to taste

Direction

- Heat olive oil in a skillet over medium heat. Cook and stir onion and garlic in hot oil until tender, about 5 minutes. Add broccoli, water, quinoa, and chicken bouillon cubes to the onion mixture; bring to a boil stirring to dissolve the bouillon cubes. Place a cover on the skillet, reduce heat to low, and simmer until quinoa is fluffy, 10 to 15 minutes.
- Stir evaporated milk and flour into the quinoa. Increase heat and bring the mixture to a boil; cook and stir until the mixture thickens, about 5 minutes. Season with salt and pepper to serve.

Nutrition Information

- Calories: 195 calories
- Total Fat: 4.2 g
- Cholesterol: 3 mg
- Sodium: 470 mg
- Total Carbohydrate: 29.9 g
- Protein: 9.6 g

77. Easy Quinoa Tabbouleh

"A refreshing twist on tabbouleh. Quinoa is used instead of bulgur, pomegranate in place of tomatoes and mint replaces cilantro. The pomegranate gives the salad an irresistible tangy crunch! Great side dish for a Mediterranean-style brunch of omelets, fresh bread, cheeses and freshly squeezed OJ."

Serving: 2 | Prep: 15 m | Cook: 15 m | Ready in: 45 m

Ingredients

- 1 cup water
- 1/2 cup quinoa
- 1 English cucumber, diced
- 1/2 onion, diced
- 3/4 cup pomegranate seeds
- 1/2 lemon, juiced
- 1 splash olive oil, or as needed
- 3 sprigs fresh mint, chopped
- salt and ground black pepper to taste

Direction

- Bring water and quinoa to a boil in a saucepan. Reduce heat to medium-low, cover, and simmer until quinoa is tender and water has been absorbed, 15 to 20 minutes. Cool to room temperature.
- Stir quinoa, cucumber, onion, and pomegranate seeds together in a bowl. Stir lemon juice, olive oil, mint, salt, and pepper into quinoa; toss to coat.

Nutrition Information

- Calories: 261 calories
- Total Fat: 5.4 g
- Cholesterol: 0 mg
- Sodium: 88 mg
- Total Carbohydrate: 46.8 g
- Protein: 8.8 g

78. Fall Salad with Quinoa Brussels Sprouts and Pomegranate

"This is a hearty fall salad with bright flavors from pistachios, pomegranate seeds, Dijon mustard, and honey."

Serving: 4 | Prep: 15 m | Cook: 40 m | Ready in: 55 m

Ingredients

- 1 tablespoon butter
- 1 1/2 cups quinoa, rinsed and drained
- 1 1/2 cups vegetable broth
- 3 cups roughly chopped Brussels sprouts
- 6 tablespoons olive oil, divided
- salt and ground black pepper to taste
- 1/3 cup white wine vinegar
- 1/4 cup honey
- 2 tablespoons Dijon mustard
- 1 clove garlic, minced
- 1 pinch herbes de Provence, or to taste
- 4 cups arugula
- 1 1/4 cups pomegranate seeds
- 1/3 cup roasted and salted shelled pistachios
- 1/2 cup crumbled goat cheese
- 4 slices multigrain bread, toasted

Direction

- Melt butter in a small saucepan over medium high heat. Add quinoa and sauté until it begins to brown and pop, 1 to 3 minutes. Add broth and cover. Reduce heat to low and simmer until all liquid is absorbed, about 25 minutes.
- Preheat the oven to 400 degrees F (200 degrees C). Line a baking sheet with parchment paper.
- While quinoa is cooking, place Brussels sprouts on the prepared baking sheet. Drizzle with 2 tablespoons olive oil and sprinkle with salt and pepper. Toss to coat.
- Roast Brussels sprouts in the preheated oven until browned and cooked through, but still firm, 15 to 20 minutes.
- Mix remaining olive oil, vinegar, honey, mustard, garlic, herbes de Provence, salt, and pepper together in a small bowl.
- Combine cooked quinoa, roasted Brussels sprouts, pistachios, and dressing in a large bowl. Add arugula, two-thirds of the pomegranate seeds, and two-thirds of the goat cheese and mix lightly.
- Portion salad into 4 bowls and garnish with remaining pomegranate seeds and goat cheese. Serve each with 1 slice toasted bread.

Nutrition Information

- Calories: 764 calories
- Total Fat: 38.3 g
- Cholesterol: 24 mg
- Sodium: 702 mg
- Total Carbohydrate: 91.4 g
- Protein: 20.8 g

79. Fresh Taco Salad with Creamy Avocado Lime Dressing

This taco salad is very different from the taco salads that my mom used to order at Mexican restaurants. They were the lightest option on the menu, but I always found myself wondering, how do those giant fried tortillas hold up to all the cheese and sour cream?

Here's my fresher, vegetarian version of those taco salads, which serves as a balanced, full meal in a bowl. Crisp romaine and peppery arugula tossed in a creamy, intentionally zippy avocado-lime dressing form the base. Chili-flavored quinoa and black beans make it plenty hearty, while tomatoes, radishes, and avocado lend some color and pops of flavor. The ode to my mom's taco salads wouldn't be complete without some crispy tortilla strips on top.

Serving: Makes 4 large salads

Ingredients

- 1 tablespoon extra-virgin olive oil
- 4 cloves garlic, pressed or minced
- 1 1/2 teaspoons chili powder
- 1 teaspoon ground cumin
- 1 tablespoon tomato paste
- 1/2 cup quinoa, rinsed
- 1 cup water
- 1 (15-ounce) can black beans, rinsed and drained, or 1 1/2 cups cooked black beans

- 1/4 teaspoon fine sea salt
- Freshly ground black pepper
- 1 1/2 teaspoons extra-virgin olive oil
- 3 corn tortillas, cut into 2-inch-long, 1/4-inch-wide strips
- Fine sea salt
- 1/4 cup lime juice (from about 2 limes)
- 1 tablespoon extra-virgin olive oil
- 1 tablespoon water
- 1/2 medium-large avocado, pitted
- 1/4 cup lightly packed fresh cilantro (some stems are okay)
- 1 small-medium jalapeño, seeded, deribbed, and roughly chopped
- 1 clove garlic, roughly chopped
- 1/4 teaspoon fine sea salt
- 1 small head romaine lettuce, chopped (or 5 ounces chopped romaine)
- 3 cups packed baby arugula (about 3 ounces)
- 1 cup thinly sliced grape or cherry tomatoes
- 1/3 cup thinly sliced and roughly chopped radishes (3 to 4), or chopped red onion
- 1/3 cup crumbled feta cheese (about 2 ounces)
- 1/2 medium-large avocado

Direction

- To make the taco filling: In a medium saucepan, warm the olive oil over medium heat until shimmering. Add the garlic, chili powder, and cumin. Cook until fragrant, stirring constantly, about 30 seconds. Add the tomato paste and sauté for another minute, stirring constantly. Add the rinsed quinoa and water, and stir to combine. Bring the mixture to a gentle boil, then cover the pot and reduce the heat as necessary to maintain a gentle simmer. Cook until the liquid is absorbed, 15 to 20 minutes (the quinoa might not be fluffy yet, but don't worry).
- Remove the pot from the heat and let it rest, still covered, for 5 minutes. Then, uncover and fluff the quinoa with a fork. Gently stir in the black beans and salt. Season to taste with pepper and additional salt, if necessary. Cover and set aside for a couple of minutes to warm up the beans.
- To make the tortilla strips: In a large skillet, warm the olive oil over medium heat until shimmering. Toss in the tortilla strips, sprinkle them with salt, and stir. Cook until the strips are crispy and turning golden, stirring occasionally, 5 to 10 minutes. Drain the tortilla strips on a plate covered with a piece of paper towel.
- To make the dressing: In a small food processor or blender, combine the lime juice, olive oil, and water. Using a spoon, scoop in the half avocado and add the cilantro, jalapeño, garlic, and salt. Process until the dressing is nice and smooth. The dressing should be zippy, but if it's unpleasantly tart or difficult to blend, dilute it with 1 to 2 tablespoons of water and blend again.
- To assemble the salads: Combine the romaine and arugula in a large bowl. Wait to dress the salad until you are ready to serve, as the greens wilt fairly quickly once dressed. (If you won't be consuming all 4 servings of this salad right away, portion off the greens you'd like to save for later, and dress only the greens you intend to eat now.)
- When you're ready, drizzle the mixture with just enough dressing to lightly coat the greens (you might have extra). Toss until the dressing is evenly distributed.
- Arrange the dressed greens in 4 individual salad bowls (or dinner plates, if your bowls are on the small side). Top each salad with taco filling, tomatoes, radishes, crispy tortilla strips, and feta. Slice the remaining avocado half into long strips and place a couple of strips on each salad. Serve immediately.
- If you have leftover dressing, press plastic wrap against the surface to prevent browning and store it in the refrigerator for later. Leftover tortilla strips tend to become unpalatably tough within a couple of hours, so you might want to skip those and add a few crushed tortilla chips to leftovers.
- Ingredient Note: If you're in a hurry, you can replace the crispy tortilla strips with a small handful of crumbled tortilla chips. Sprinkle them over the salads just before serving.

Nutrition Information

- Calories: 565
- Total Fat: 22 g (34%)
- Saturated Fat: 5 g (24%)
- Cholesterol: 13 mg (4%)
- Sodium: 1428 mg (60%)
- Total Carbohydrate: 75 g (25%)
- Protein: 23 g (47%)
- Fiber: 26 g (102%)

80. Fruity Curried Lentil Salad

"This recipe is very good. Serve warm for a main dish or cold for a side dish. In place of quinoa, you can also use the same amount of brown rice or bulghur wheat."

Serving: 4 | Prep: 15 m | Cook: 45 m | Ready in: 1 h

Ingredients

- 1 (8 ounce) can pineapple chunks, juice reserved
- 1/2 cup quinoa
- 1/2 cup lentils
- salt and ground black pepper to taste
- 2 teaspoons curry powder
- 1/2 cup unsweetened dried coconut
- 1/4 cup chopped pecans
- 1/4 cup finely diced red onion
- 1 tablespoon chopped fresh cilantro

Direction

- Pour the pineapple juice into a measuring pitcher, and add enough water to make 2 cups. Set the pineapple chunks aside. Pour the pineapple juice into a saucepan, and stir in the quinoa and lentils. Season with salt, black pepper, and curry powder. Bring to a boil over high heat, then reduce heat to medium-low, cover, and simmer until the lentils and quinoa have absorbed the water, about 30 minutes. Stir in the coconut, and simmer for 5 minutes more.
- Stir in the pineapple chunks, pecans, and onion; cook briefly to reheat. Sprinkle with cilantro to serve.

Nutrition Information

- Calories: 328 calories
- Total Fat: 14.1 g
- Cholesterol: 0 mg
- Sodium: 9 mg
- Total Carbohydrate: 42.1 g
- Protein: 11.1 g

81. Garbanzo Bean and Quinoa Salad

"This salad uses quinoa, which gives a nice texture and mild nutty flavor to the dish. Best served chilled, this salad is wonderful for picnics."

Serving: 8 | Prep: 15 m | Cook: 15 m | Ready in: 1 h 30 m

Ingredients

- 1 cup quinoa
- 2 cups water
- 1 (15 ounce) can garbanzo beans, drained
- 1/2 cup dried cranberries
- 1/2 cup golden raisins
- 1/3 cup sliced almonds
- 1/4 cup mint leaves, chopped
- 3/4 teaspoon ground coriander
- 1/4 teaspoon ground cumin
- 1 tablespoon extra-virgin olive oil
- salt and pepper to taste

Direction

- Bring the quinoa and water to a boil in a saucepan over high heat. Reduce heat to medium-low, cover, and simmer until the quinoa is tender, and the water has been absorbed, 15 to 20 minutes. Scrape the quinoa into a large bowl, and refrigerate until cold.

- Stir the garbanzo beans, cranberries, raisins, almonds, mint, coriander, cumin, and olive oil into the quinoa. Season to taste with salt and pepper.

Nutrition Information

- Calories: 212 calories
- Total Fat: 5.4 g
- Cholesterol: 0 mg
- Sodium: 112 mg
- Total Carbohydrate: 36.6 g
- Protein: 5.8 g

82. Garlic Cheese Quinoa

"This versatile dish can be served as a meal or side because its made with quinoa (keen-wah), a complete protein. This fabulous grain tends to pick up surrounding flavors and in this case, GARLIC and CHEEEEEEESE!"

Serving: 8 | Prep: 15 m | Cook: 45 m | Ready in: 1 h

Ingredients

- 3 cups water
- 1 1/2 cups quinoa
- 2 cloves garlic, minced
- 1/2 teaspoon onion powder
- cooking spray
- 1 cup milk
- 2 large eggs
- 3/4 cup shredded sharp Cheddar cheese
- 3/4 cup cubed processed cheese food (such as Velveeta®)
- salt and ground black pepper to taste
- 1/4 cup panko bread crumbs, or to taste

Direction

- Bring water, quinoa, garlic, and onion powder to a boil in a saucepan. Reduce heat to medium-low, cover, and simmer until quinoa is tender and water has been absorbed, about 15 minutes.
- Preheat oven to 350 degrees F (175 degrees C). Prepare a 9x13-inch baking dish with cooking spray.
- Whisk milk and eggs together in a large bowl. Stir Cheddar cheese and processed cheese food into quinoa mixture until cheeses begin to melt; season with salt and black pepper. Mix quinoa mixture into milk mixture. Transfer quinoa-milk mixture to the prepared baking dish; top with panko bread crumbs.
- Bake in the preheated oven until topping is lightly browned, 30 to 35 minutes.

Nutrition Information

- Calories: 238 calories
- Total Fat: 10 g
- Cholesterol: 67 mg
- Sodium: 218 mg
- Total Carbohydrate: 25.7 g
- Protein: 12.2 g

83. Garlic Kale Quinoa

"Great for a quick-but-healthy side dish. White cooking wine can be used instead of 1 tablespoon water at the end of cooking."

Serving: 2 | Prep: 10 m | Cook: 25 m | Ready in: 35 m

Ingredients

- 2/3 cup water
- 1/3 cup quinoa
- 1 tablespoon olive oil
- 1 cup chopped kale
- 1 clove garlic, minced
- salt and ground black pepper to taste
- 1/4 teaspoon sesame oil
- 1 tablespoon water, or as needed

Direction

- Bring 2/3 cup water and quinoa to a boil in a saucepan. Reduce heat to medium-low, cover, and simmer until quinoa is tender and water has been absorbed, 15 to 20 minutes.

- Heat olive oil in a skillet over medium heat; sauté kale and garlic in the hot oil until kale is wilted, about 5 minutes. Season with salt and pepper.
- Stir quinoa into kale mixture and add sesame oil; cook until flavors blend, about 5 more minutes. Add 1 tablespoon water to mixture to keep from sticking.

Nutrition Information

- Calories: 188 calories
- Total Fat: 9.3 g
- Cholesterol: 0 mg
- Sodium: 19 mg
- Total Carbohydrate: 22 g
- Protein: 5.2 g

84. Garlic Quinoa

"This is a quick and easy, basic quinoa recipe that we use in our house instead of rice as a great side."

Serving: 4 | Prep: 5 m | Cook: 20 m | Ready in: 30 m

Ingredients

- 1 tablespoon butter
- 1 tablespoon minced garlic
- 2 cups chicken broth
- 1 cup quinoa

Direction

- Melt butter in a saucepan over medium heat. Cook and stir garlic in melted butter until just browned, about 5 minutes.
- Pour chicken broth into the saucepan; add quinoa and stir. Bring the mixture to a boil, reduce heat to low, cover, and simmer until liquid is absorbed, about 15 minutes.
- Remove saucepan from heat and rest mixture 5 minutes before fluffing with a fork.

Nutrition Information

- Calories: 192 calories
- Total Fat: 5.7 g
- Cholesterol: 10 mg
- Sodium: 503 mg
- Total Carbohydrate: 28.5 g
- Protein: 6.7 g

85. Gingery Quinoa Stuffed Acorn Squash

"This hearty dish combines quinoa with apples, veggies, and loads of ginger in an acorn squash bowl that is perfect fare for those blustery fall and winter evenings."

Serving: 2 | Prep: 35 m | Cook: 50 m | Ready in: 1 h 25 m

Ingredients

- 1 acorn squash, halved and seeded
- 2/3 cup quinoa
- 1 1/3 cups water
- 1 1/2 teaspoons butter
- salt and pepper to taste
- 1 tablespoon extra-virgin olive oil
- 1/2 large onion, chopped
- 1/2 green bell pepper, chopped
- 2 stalks celery, chopped
- 1 apple, diced
- 3 cloves garlic, minced
- 1 (2 inch) piece fresh ginger, minced
- 1 tablespoon apple cider vinegar
- 1 tablespoon white sugar
- 1 teaspoon ground cinnamon
- 1/8 teaspoon ground nutmeg
- 1 dash crushed red pepper flakes
- 1/2 cup shredded mozzarella cheese

Direction

- Preheat oven to 425 degrees F (220 degrees C). Place the squash halves, cut-side up into a small baking dish, and bake until tender, about 45 minutes.
- Bring the quinoa and water to a boil in a saucepan over high heat. Reduce heat to medium-low, cover, and simmer until the

quinoa is tender, 20 to 25 minutes. When done, stir in the butter until melted, then season to taste with salt and pepper.
- Meanwhile, heat the olive oil in a skillet over medium heat. Stir in the onion, green pepper, and celery; cook and stir until the onion has softened and turned translucent, about 10 minutes. Stir in the apple, and continue cooking until the vegetables are tender, about 10 minutes more. Add the garlic and ginger, cook 2 minutes more, then stir in the vinegar, sugar, cinnamon, nutmeg, and red pepper flakes; season to taste with salt and pepper.
- When the squash is tender, scoop out some of the flesh, leaving the halves 1/2 inch thick. Roughly chop the acorn squash, and combine with the quinoa and apple mixture. Spoon the mixture back into the squash shells, and sprinkle with the mozzarella cheese. Return to the oven, and bake until the cheese has melted and is bubbly, about 5 minutes.

Nutrition Information

- Calories: 574 calories
- Total Fat: 18.5 g
- Cholesterol: 26 mg
- Sodium: 249 mg
- Total Carbohydrate: 88.9 g
- Protein: 18.5 g

- Crumble Topping:
- 3/4 cup brown sugar
- 1/2 cup butter, softened
- 1/2 cup rice flour
- 1/2 cup quinoa flakes
- 1/2 cup rice flakes

Direction

- Preheat oven to 350 degrees F (175 degrees C).
- Combine apples, 1/4 cup rice flour, white sugar, and cinnamon in a bowl; transfer to an 8-inch baking dish.
- Mix brown sugar, butter, 1/2 cup rice flour, quinoa flakes, and rice flakes in the same bowl used for apple mixture. Sprinkle crumble topping over apple mixture and pat down gently.
- Bake in the preheated oven until apples are tender and topping is slightly browned, 35 minutes.

Nutrition Information

- Calories: 420 calories
- Total Fat: 16.6 g
- Cholesterol: 41 mg
- Sodium: 116 mg
- Total Carbohydrate: 67 g
- Protein: 3.1 g

86. GlutenFree Apple Crisp

"A yummy gluten-free family favorite. Company prefer this adaptation to the regular crisp. Other fruits could easily be substituted for the apples."

Serving: 6 | Prep: 10 m | Cook: 35 m | Ready in: 45 m

Ingredients

- Apple Mix:
- 5 cups chopped apples
- 1/4 cup rice flour
- 3 tablespoons white sugar
- 1 teaspoon ground cinnamon

87. GlutenFree Moist Chocolate Cake

"This deliciously moist and fudgy chocolate cake is made with a gluten-free twist that nobody ever suspects: quinoa! I've also made a vegan option of this by using egg substitute and replacing the milk with almond milk. The taste and texture was identical to my non-vegan original! Either version stores well in a sealed container in the refrigerator for up to 1 week or in the freezer for up to 1 month. My favorite frosting for this cake is coconut cream cheese."

Serving: 10 | Prep: 15 m | Cook: 1 h | Ready in: 1 h 45 m

Ingredients

- 1 1/3 cups water
- 2/3 cup quinoa
- 3/4 cup butter, melted and cooled
- 1/3 cup milk
- 4 large eggs
- 1 teaspoon vanilla extract
- 1 1/2 cups white sugar
- 1 cup unsweetened cocoa powder
- 1 1/2 teaspoons baking powder
- 1/2 teaspoon baking soda
- 1/2 teaspoon salt

Direction

- Bring water and quinoa to a boil in a saucepan. Reduce heat to medium-low, cover, and simmer for 10 minutes. Turn off the heat and let sit until quinoa is tender and water is absorbed, about 10 minutes more. Fluff with a fork and cool to room temperature.
- Preheat oven to 350 degrees F (175 degrees C). Lightly grease two 8-inch cake pans and line the bottoms of the pans with parchment paper.
- Blend butter, milk, eggs, and vanilla extract in a blender until combined. Add 2 cups cooked quinoa and blend until smooth, scraping down the sides of the blender with a rubber spatula as necessary.
- Whisk sugar, cocoa powder, baking powder, baking soda, and salt together in a bowl. Add quinoa mixture into sugar mixture and whisk until batter is smooth. Pour batter into prepared cake pans.
- Bake in the preheated oven until a knife inserted into the center of the cakes comes out clean, 40 to 45 minutes. Cool completely in the pans before removing to a plate.

Nutrition Information

- Calories: 334 calories
- Total Fat: 17.8 g
- Cholesterol: 112 mg
- Sodium: 385 mg
- Total Carbohydrate: 42.7 g
- Protein: 6.2 g

88. GlutenFree Multigrain Bread

"This bread tastes like our favorite gluten-free multigrain. Has a better texture then any others we've tried and is good for you."

Serving: 10 | Prep: 20 m | Cook: 45 m | Ready in: 2 h 35 m

Ingredients

- 1 teaspoon butter, or as needed
- 3/4 cup brown rice flour
- 1/4 cup tapioca starch
- 1/4 cup potato starch
- 2 teaspoons active dry yeast
- 2 teaspoons guar gum
- 1 teaspoon salt
- 1 teaspoon baking powder
- 1/4 cup quinoa
- 1/4 cup sunflower seeds
- 1/4 cup toasted almonds, chopped
- 1/4 cup flax seeds
- 3/4 cup warm milk (115 degrees F or 46 degrees C)
- 2 eggs
- 2 egg whites
- 2 tablespoons molasses
- 2 tablespoons agave nectar
- 2 tablespoons olive oil
- 2 teaspoons apple cider vinegar
- 1 teaspoon sesame seeds (optional)

Direction

- Butter and flour a 9x5-inch loaf pan.
- Sift rice flour, tapioca starch, potato starch, yeast, guar gum, salt, and baking powder together in a bowl.
- Place quinoa, sunflower seeds, almonds, and flax seeds in a coffee grinder. Grind until very fine. Mix into the flour mixture.
- Combine milk, eggs, egg whites, molasses, agave nectar, olive oil, and vinegar in the bowl of a stand mixer fitted with the paddle attachment; beat on low until well blended. Pour in dry mixture slowly, beating on medium-high and pushing dough down with a spatula as necessary.
- Scoop dough into the prepared pan, spreading it evenly with a wet spatula. Sprinkle with sesame seeds. Fill a large bowl with boiling-hot water and place it in a microwave. Rest a cooling rack on top of the bowl. Place pan on top and cover the dough. Let dough rise until it reaches the top of the pan, about 1 hour 30 minutes.
- Preheat the oven to 350 degrees F (175 degrees C).
- Bake in the preheated oven until the top is golden and an instant-read thermometer inserted in the center reads 200 degrees F (93 degrees C), about 45 minutes. Let bread cool thoroughly before slicing with a serrated knife.

Nutrition Information

- Calories: 228 calories
- Total Fat: 10.6 g
- Cholesterol: 40 mg
- Sodium: 322 mg
- Total Carbohydrate: 28 g
- Protein: 6.7 g

89. Grain Bowl Soup

Like your favorite grain bowl in soup form, this warming, brothy dish is topped off with a bright and slightly sweet parsley-dill sauce.

Serving: 4 servings | Prep: 15 m | Cook: 45 m

Ingredients

- 1 lb. mixed wild mushrooms, cut into 1/4" slices
- 12 oz. mixed baby heirloom cherry tomatoes
- 2 shallots, thinly sliced
- 3/4 cup extra-virgin olive oil, divided
- 1 1/2 tsp. kosher salt, plus more
- 1/2 cup finely chopped dill (from about 2 bunches)
- 1/2 cup finely chopped parsley (from about 1 bunch)
- 1/4 cup fresh lemon juice
- 1 tsp. honey
- 1/4 tsp. crushed red pepper flakes
- 7 cups homemade beef or chicken bone stock or low-sodium bone broth
- 3 cups cooked grains, such as barley, quinoa, rice, farro, or spelt
- 1 large or 2 small bunches curly kale, stems removed, torn into pieces
- 4 garlic cloves, thinly sliced

Direction

- Arrange a rack in center of oven; preheat to 425°F. Toss mushrooms, tomatoes, shallots, 2 Tbsp. oil, and 1/2 tsp. salt on a rimmed baking sheet. Roast until mushrooms are golden brown and tomatoes are deflating, about 15 minutes.
- Whisk dill, parsley, lemon juice, honey, red pepper flakes, 1/2 cup oil, and 1/2 tsp. salt in a medium bowl; set aside.
- Meanwhile, bring stock to a boil in a large pot over medium-high heat. Add cooked grains and let simmer 5 minutes. Add mushroom mixture and let simmer 5 minutes more. Season with salt.
- While soup cooks, toss kale, garlic and remaining 2 Tbsp. oil and 1/2 tsp. salt on same

sheet you used to roast mushrooms, then arrange in a single layer. Roast until kale is wilted and crisped in places, about 4 minutes.
- Divide soup among bowls. Top with kale mixture and herbed oil.

Nutrition Information

- Calories: 1250
- Total Fat: 62 g (96%)
- Saturated Fat: 14 g (69%)
- Cholesterol: 80 mg (27%)
- Sodium: 1121 mg (47%)
- Total Carbohydrate: 125 g (42%)
- Protein: 50 g (100%)
- Fiber: 32 g (128%)

90. Grain Bowl With Spiced Squash Mushrooms and Curried Yogurt

No squash? No problem. This rice bowl — which was developed for our #cook90 initiative — can handle all sorts of roasted vegetables (and, for that matter, can be made with all kinds of grains). But the curried yogurt? That's crucial.

Serving: Serves 2 | Prep: 15 m | Cook: 1 h 10 m

Ingredients

- 1/2 cup red, white, or brown rice, quinoa, or barley
- Kosher salt
- 3 tablespoons olive oil
- 1/4 teaspoon freshly ground black pepper
- 1/4 teaspoon ground cinnamon
- 1 medium delicata squash (about 1 pound), halved lengthwise, or 1/2 acorn squash (about 1 pound), quartered, seeded, cut crosswise into 1/2"-thick slices
- 8 ounces cremini or button mushrooms, trimmed, sliced
- 1 small red onion, sliced 1/2" thick
- 1/2 cup Greek-style plain full or low-fat yogurt
- 1 1/2 teaspoons fresh lemon juice
- 1/4 teaspoon curry powder
- 2 cups baby greens, such as watercress or arugula
- Lemon wedges and cilantro leaves (for serving; optional)

Direction

- Preheat oven to 400°F. Cook grains with 1/2 tsp. salt according to package directions.
- Meanwhile, whisk oil, pepper, cinnamon, and 3/4 tsp. salt with a fork in a large bowl. Add squash, mushrooms, and onion and toss to coat. Spread on a rimmed baking sheet and roast, tossing once halfway through, until vegetables are lightly browned and fork-tender, 25–30 minutes.
- Mix yogurt, lemon juice, curry powder, and 1/8 tsp. salt in a medium bowl. Divide yogurt mixture between 2 bowls, swooshing it along the side of the bowl if desired. Top with rice, then vegetables and greens. Squeeze with lemon and top with cilantro, if desired.

Nutrition Information

- Calories: 526
- Total Fat: 23 g (36%)
- Saturated Fat: 4 g (19%)
- Cholesterol: 4 mg (1%)
- Sodium: 1262 mg (53%)
- Total Carbohydrate: 72 g (24%)
- Protein: 13 g (27%)
- Fiber: 7 g (29%)

91. Grape Lime and Quinoa Salad Surprise

"A great summer salad that's healthy and delicious. Throw in some cooked shrimp to make it into a meal."

Serving: 10 | Prep: 30 m | Ready in: 3 h 30 m

Ingredients

- 2 cups seedless red grapes, halved

- 1 cucumber, chopped
- 1/2 cup cooked quinoa, or more to taste
- 1/4 cup chopped fresh mint, or to taste
- 1/4 cup chopped fresh spinach, or more to taste
- 2/3 cup toasted slivered almonds
- 1 teaspoon salt
- 8 teaspoons grapeseed oil
- 8 teaspoons lime juice

Direction

- Toss grapes, cucumber, quinoa, mint, spinach, and almonds together in a large bowl; sprinkle salt over the top.
- Whisk grapeseed oil and lime juice together in a small bowl; pour over quinoa mixture and toss to coat. Refrigerate until flavors combine, at least 3 hours.

Nutrition Information

- Calories: 115 calories
- Total Fat: 7.7 g
- Cholesterol: 0 mg
- Sodium: 236 mg
- Total Carbohydrate: 10.5 g
- Protein: 2.4 g

92. Green Quinoa Tabbouleh

"We're heading straight into grilling season, and for me, tabbouleh is one of the all-time great cold side dishes, since it pairs so perfectly with all those highly-seasoned, smoky meats. Maybe it's the size of quinoa, or the less wheaty flavor, but for me this vibrant, bracing salad is significantly better with quinoa instead of the traditional bulgur wheat. Blanching the herbs keeps this fresh and green for several days."

Serving: 6 | Prep: 25 m | Cook: 20 m | Ready in: 3 h

Ingredients

- 6 cups water
- 2 large bunches curly parsley, stemmed
- 1 large bunch fresh mint, stemmed
- 1 bunch fresh tarragon, stemmed
- 2 cups white quinoa
- salt to taste
- 2 cloves garlic, or more to taste
- 2 lemons, halved, or more to taste
- 1/2 cup extra-virgin olive oil
- 1 pinch salt and freshly ground black pepper to taste
- cayenne pepper

Direction

- Bring water to a boil and prepare a bowl of iced water. Add 1/2 of the parsley, 1/2 of the mint, and 1/2 of the tarragon. Blanch herbs for 5 seconds, then scoop into the iced water. Let cool completely, about 2 minutes. Drain well and squeeze out the water.
- Rinse quinoa well. Sprinkle salt into the blanching water. Add the quinoa and simmer on medium heat until just barely tender, about 12 minutes.
- Meanwhile, chop the remaining herbs into small pieces.
- Add garlic to the blender with the blanched herbs. Squeeze in lemon juice and add olive oil. Blend starting on low speed, pulsing on and off, and finishing on high speed, until dressing is smooth and green.
- Remove quinoa from heat; place in a strainer set over a bowl and drain for 5 minutes, tossing occasionally. Transfer quinoa to a bowl. Season with salt, black pepper, and cayenne pepper. Let cool until it is between warm and room temperature, 5 to 10 minutes.
- Stir dressing into the quinoa. Continue cooling if salad is not yet at room temperature, 5 to 10 minutes more. Add the chopped herbs and mix to combine. Wrap bowl in plastic wrap and refrigerate until flavors meld, about 2 hours.
- Taste the salad and adjust seasoning as desired. Transfer salad to a serving bowl.

Nutrition Information

- Calories: 402 calories
- Total Fat: 22.6 g
- Cholesterol: 0 mg
- Sodium: 78 mg

- Total Carbohydrate: 43.4 g
- Protein: 9.8 g

93. Grilled Steak Vegetable and Quinoa Salad with Yogurt Tahini Dressing

Grilled fennel, tomatoes, and scallions and cumin-rubbed grilled steak turn this quinoa salad into a one-dish dinner you'll want to keep serving all summer long.

Serving: Serves 4 | Prep: 35 m | Cook: 45 m

Ingredients

- 3 tablespoons extra-virgin olive oil
- 2 tablespoons red wine vinegar
- 1 teaspoon honey
- 1/2 teaspoon kosher salt
- 2 cups cooked quinoa
- 1 cup cooked French lentils
- 1/2 cup coarsely chopped fresh dill
- 1 tablespoon finely chopped fresh oregano
- 1/2 cup plain Greek yogurt
- 1/4 cup fresh lemon juice
- 3 tablespoons tahini
- 2 tablespoons extra-virgin olive oil
- 1/2 teaspoon kosher salt
- 1 large fennel bulb, trimmed, sliced lengthwise into 1/4" planks, fronds reserved for serving
- 1 pint cherry tomatoes
- 12 scallions, roots trimmed (about 2 bunches)
- Olive oil (for brushing)
- 1 teaspoon kosher salt, divided, plus more
- 3/4 teaspoon freshly ground black pepper, divided, plus more
- 1/2 pound Halloumi cheese, sliced into 1/4" planks (optional)
- 1 pound flank or skirt steak
- 1/2 teaspoon ground cumin

Direction

- Make the quinoa salad: Whisk oil, vinegar, honey, and salt in a large bowl. Add quinoa, lentils, dill, and oregano and stir to combine. Set aside.
- Make the yogurt dressing: Whisk yogurt, lemon juice, tahini, oil, salt, and 1 Tbsp. water in a small bowl. Set aside.
- Grill the vegetables and steak and assemble the salad: Prepare a grill or grill pan for medium-high heat. Brush fennel, tomatoes, and scallions with oil and season with 1/2 tsp. salt and 1/4 tsp. pepper. Grill, turning occasionally, until tender and charred in spots, 10–15 minutes; let cool. If using Halloumi cheese, brush with oil and grill, turning occasionally, until charred and warmed through, about 2 minutes per side.
- Meanwhile, rub steak with cumin, remaining 1/2 tsp. salt, and remaining 1/2 tsp. pepper. Grill until medium-rare, 5–7 minutes per side for flank steak, about 2 minutes per side for skirt steak. Let rest, then thinly slice against the grain.
- Transfer quinoa salad to a large platter. Top with grilled vegetables and steak. Season with additional salt and pepper and top with fennel fronds. Serve immediately with yogurt dressing alongside.
- Do Ahead   The yogurt dressing can be chilled for up to 3 days.

Nutrition Information

- Calories: 858
- Total Fat: 49 g (75%)
- Saturated Fat: 11 g (57%)
- Cholesterol: 78 mg (26%)
- Sodium: 1069 mg (45%)
- Total Carbohydrate: 65 g (22%)
- Protein: 45 g (91%)
- Fiber: 12 g (48%)

94. Guacamole Style Quinoa

"My husband and I are following the guidelines of the Virgin Diet (no gluten, soy, eggs, dairy, peanuts, corn, or sugar) and wanted to experiment with some new ways to eat quinoa. We love guacamole, and decided to transfer the ingredients into this healthy and flavorful quinoa dish."

Serving: 6 | Prep: 10 m | Cook: 20 m | Ready in: 1 h 30 m

Ingredients

- 1 teaspoon olive oil
- 1/2 sweet onion, diced
- 2 cloves garlic, minced, or more to taste
- 1 cup quinoa
- 1 lime, juiced
- 1 3/4 cups chicken stock, or as needed
- 6 tablespoons chopped fresh cilantro
- 6 grape tomatoes, quartered
- 1 avocado, cubed
- 1 jalapeno pepper, diced (optional)

Direction

- Heat olive oil in a saucepan over medium heat; cook and stir onion and garlic in the hot oil until slightly browned, about 5 minutes. Stir quinoa into onion mixture and cook until quinoa is lightly browned, about 30 seconds.
- Squeeze lime juice into a 2-cup measuring cup; pour in enough chicken stock to make 2 cups liquid. Pour chicken stock mixture over quinoa and bring to a boil. Reduce heat, cover saucepan, and simmer until liquid is absorbed and quinoa is tender, about 15 minutes. Remove saucepan from heat and chill in the refrigerator, about 1 hour.
- Fold cilantro, tomatoes, avocado, and jalapeno pepper into quinoa mixture. Return quinoa to refrigerator for flavors to blend or serve immediately.

Nutrition Information

- Calories: 204 calories
- Total Fat: 8 g
- Cholesterol: < 1 mg
- Sodium: 213 mg
- Total Carbohydrate: 29.4 g
- Protein: 6.5 g

95. Healthy After School Granola Bars

"I'll usually make a huge batch of these and freeze them, then grab one for a healthy snack."

Serving: 32 | Prep: 15 m | Cook: 25 m | Ready in: 1 h

Ingredients

- 2 1/2 cups oats
- 1 1/2 cups quinoa
- 1 cup slivered almonds
- 1/3 cup chia seeds
- 1 cup crunchy peanut butter
- 1/2 cup honey
- 1/4 cup coconut oil, warmed
- 1/2 cup flaxseed meal
- 1 teaspoon salt
- 2 cups dark chocolate chips

Direction

- Preheat oven to 350 degrees F (175 degrees C). Spread oats, quinoa, almonds, and chia seeds on a baking sheet.
- Toast in the preheated oven, stirring halfway through, until golden brown, about 15 minutes.
- Mix peanut butter, honey, and coconut oil together in a bowl until thoroughly combined. Mix in oat mixture, flaxseed meal, and salt until well combined. Press granola mixture into a 12x18-inch baking pan.
- Bake in the preheated oven until bars set, about 5 minutes. Remove from oven; sprinkle with chocolate chips. Bake until chocolate is just melted, about 5 minutes. Spread melted chocolate evenly over bars with a rubber spatula.
- Place in the freezer until chocolate is firm, about 20 minutes; cut into bars.

Nutrition Information

- Calories: 223 calories
- Total Fat: 12.7 g
- Cholesterol: 0 mg
- Sodium: 117 mg
- Total Carbohydrate: 24.6 g
- Protein: 5.8 g

96. Healthy Quinoa Salad

"My go-to recipe for my side for the week! Love it, and it always turns out perfect!"

Serving: 8 | Prep: 20 m | Cook: 20 m | Ready in: 40 m

Ingredients

- 4 cups water
- 1 (12 ounce) box quinoa
- 3 carrots, chopped
- 1 cup corn
- 1 cup peas
- 1 cup chopped broccoli florets
- 1/4 cup extra-virgin olive oil
- 1/4 cup lemon juice
- 1 teaspoon chili powder
- 1/4 teaspoon cayenne pepper

Direction

- Bring water and quinoa to a boil in a saucepan. Reduce heat to medium-low, cover, and simmer until quinoa is tender and water has been absorbed, 15 to 20 minutes.
- Place a steamer insert into a saucepan and fill with water to just below the bottom of the steamer. Bring water to a boil. Add carrots, corn, peas, and broccoli to steamer; cover, and steam until tender, 5 to 10 minutes.
- Mix quinoa and vegetable mixture together in a bowl.
- Whisk olive oil, lemon juice, chili powder, and cayenne pepper together in a bowl; pour over quinoa mixture and toss to coat.

Nutrition Information

- Calories: 266 calories
- Total Fat: 9.9 g
- Cholesterol: 0 mg
- Sodium: 50 mg
- Total Carbohydrate: 37.6 g
- Protein: 8.1 g

97. Hearty Multigrain Bread

"This bread is a solid textured loaf appropriate for sandwiches, spreads or eating with a meal. It has two kinds of grains and three kinds of seeds in it. It is solid and hardy; yet light and sweet."

Serving: 12 | Prep: 5 m | Cook: 2 h 55 m | Ready in: 3 h

Ingredients

- 3/4 cup water
- 1 tablespoon butter, softened
- 1 teaspoon salt
- 2 tablespoons sunflower seeds
- 1 tablespoon sesame seeds
- 1 tablespoon flax seeds
- 1 tablespoon millet
- 1 tablespoon quinoa
- 1 cup bread flour
- 1 cup whole wheat flour
- 1 tablespoon dry milk powder
- 1/4 cup packed brown sugar
- 1 1/2 tablespoons bread machine yeast

Direction

- Place ingredients in the pan of the bread machine in the order recommended by the manufacturer. Select cycle; press Start.

Nutrition Information

- Calories: 124 calories
- Total Fat: 2.3 g
- Cholesterol: 3 mg
- Sodium: 207 mg
- Total Carbohydrate: 22.6 g

- Protein: 4.1 g

98. HighProtein Quinoa Breakfast Bowl

"This is my new favorite breakfast and snack, easy to prepare when I need to stop those sweet cravings and have a good source of protein. Great breakfast for my husband who has gout."

Serving: 1 | Prep: 5 m | Cook: 20 m | Ready in: 40 m

Ingredients

- 1/2 cup water
- 1/4 cup multi-colored quinoa
- 1/2 cup reduced-sodium cottage cheese
- 1/2 banana, sliced
- 1 tablespoon fresh blueberries
- 1 teaspoon chia seeds
- 1 pinch ground cinnamon

Direction

- Bring water and quinoa to a boil in a saucepan. Reduce heat to medium-low, cover, and simmer until quinoa is tender, 15 to 20 minutes. Let cool briefly.
- Combine 1/2 cup quinoa and cottage cheese in a bowl. Accessorize with banana, blueberries, chia seeds, and cinnamon. Mix up and serve.

Nutrition Information

- Calories: 313 calories
- Total Fat: 4.7 g
- Cholesterol: 4 mg
- Sodium: 22 mg
- Total Carbohydrate: 47.9 g
- Protein: 21.1 g

99. HighProtein Vegan StirFry

"A delicious, high-protein vegan recipe with tofu, sweet potato, and quinoa that can be tweaked depending on what you have on hand. Feel free to throw in a few handfuls of your favorite veggies, or replace the tofu with tempeh or another veggie protein. Carnivores could use chicken, salmon, or beef, or serve as a side with grilled meat. Or add scrambled egg for a delicious breakfast stir-fry! Serve chilled for a yummy summer salad."

Serving: 2 | Prep: 20 m | Cook: 35 m | Ready in: 1 h 30 m

Ingredients

- 1/2 (12 ounce) package extra-firm tofu
- 1/4 cup reduced-sodium soy sauce
- 1 tablespoon agave nectar
- 1 tablespoon Dijon mustard
- 1/2 teaspoon ground ginger
- 1/4 teaspoon sesame oil
- 1 pinch cayenne powder, or to taste
- 1 cup water
- 1/2 cup uncooked quinoa
- 1 sweet potato, peeled and cubed, or more to taste
- 1 onion, chopped
- 2 tablespoons peanut oil

Direction

- Layer 2 folded dish towels on a cutting board and place tofu on top. Place 2 more folded dish towels and a heavy book on top. Press tofu for 5 to 10 minutes or longer. Cut into bite-sized cubes.
- Heat a large nonstick pan over medium heat. Add tofu and dry-fry until golden on 1 side, about 5 minutes. Flip and cook until golden on the other side, about 5 minutes more.
- While tofu is frying, whisk soy sauce, agave nectar, Dijon mustard, ginger, sesame oil, and cayenne pepper together in a bowl. Stir in the fried tofu, coating thoroughly in the marinade. Cover the bowl and refrigerate about 30 minutes or longer.
- Combine water and quinoa in a small saucepan and bring to a boil. Reduce heat to medium and simmer until quinoa is fluffy and

water has been absorbed, 13 to 15 minutes. Monitor the quinoa while it cooks; add extra water if necessary.
- While quinoa is cooking, place sweet potatoes in a small saucepan and cover with 1 or 2 inches of water. Bring to a boil and cook for 3 minutes. Drain.
- Combine cooked quinoa, tofu and marinade, cooked sweet potatoes, onion, and peanut oil in a large frying pan over medium-high heat. Cook, stirring constantly, until onion is soft, 3 to 4 minutes.

Nutrition Information

- Calories: 503 calories
- Total Fat: 20.9 g
- Cholesterol: 0 mg
- Sodium: 1302 mg
- Total Carbohydrate: 65.2 g
- Protein: 16.8 g

100. Instant Pot Chicken Quinoa Tortilla Soup

"This wonderful Instant Pot® chicken tortilla soup is such a delicious, quick, and easy dinner option that you will put together in no time!"

Serving: 4 | Prep: 20 m | Cook: 18 m | Ready in: 43 m

Ingredients

- 5 cups chicken stock
- 1 (14.5 ounce) can canned diced tomatoes with their juice
- 1 onion, diced
- 2 cloves garlic, minced
- 1 1/2 pounds boneless chicken breasts
- 2 teaspoons chili powder
- 2 teaspoons ground cumin
- 1 teaspoon paprika
- 1 teaspoon salt
- 1/2 teaspoon ground black pepper
- 2 cups frozen corn kernels
- 1/2 cup shredded cabbage
- 1 cup cooked quinoa
- 1 tablespoon lemon juice
- 1 (8 ounce) package tortilla chips
- 1 tablespoon fresh cilantro

Direction

- Turn on a multi-functional pressure cooker (such as Instant Pot(R)). Add chicken stock, tomatoes, onions, and garlic to the pot. Place chicken breasts on top and sprinkle with chili powder, cumin, paprika, salt, and pepper. Add corn and cabbage on top; do not stir. Close and lock the lid. Select high pressure according to manufacturer's instructions; set timer for 8 minutes. Allow 10 to 15 minutes for pressure to build.
- Release pressure carefully using the quick-release method according to manufacturer's instructions, about 5 minutes. Unlock and remove lid. Remove chicken from pot and place in a plate; shred with 2 forks. Put chicken back into the pot with cooked quinoa, lemon juice, and tortilla chips. Sprinkle with chopped cilantro.

Nutrition Information

- Calories: 647 calories
- Total Fat: 19.8 g
- Cholesterol: 89 mg
- Sodium: 1920 mg
- Total Carbohydrate: 77.7 g
- Protein: 44.8 g

101. Instant Pot Mexican Quinoa

"Mexican quinoa flavored with cumin, smoked paprika, and chili powder. This easy 1-pot meal is made in the Instant Pot® and is the perfect meal for those busy days. Vegan and gluten free! Top with guacamole, salsa, or some sour cream."

Serving: 4 | Prep: 15 m | Cook: 15 m | Ready in: 40 m

Ingredients

- 1 tablespoon olive oil
- 1 small onion, chopped
- 1 jalapeno pepper, minced, or to taste
- 3 cloves garlic, chopped
- 1 (15 ounce) can black beans, drained and rinsed
- 1 (14.5 ounce) can fire-roasted diced tomatoes
- 3/4 cup corn kernels
- 3/4 teaspoon salt, or to taste
- 1/2 teaspoon ground cumin
- 1/2 teaspoon smoked paprika
- 1/4 teaspoon chili powder
- 1/8 teaspoon black pepper
- 1 cup dry quinoa
- 1 cup vegetable broth, or as needed
- 2 tablespoons chopped cilantro, or to taste
- 1 lime, juiced
- 1 avocado, diced

Direction

- Turn on a multi-functional pressure cooker (such as Instant Pot(R)) and select Sauté function. Add oil, onion, jalapeno pepper, and garlic. Sauté until onion is softened, about 2 minutes. Add black beans, tomatoes, and corn; mix well. Season with salt, cumin, paprika, chili powder, and black pepper. Add quinoa and toss until well combined. Pour in broth and mix.
- Close and lock the lid; set valve to the sealing position. Select high pressure according to manufacturer's instructions; set timer for 1 minute. Allow 10 to 15 minutes for pressure to build.
- Release pressure using the natural-release method according to manufacturer's instructions, 10 to 40 minutes. Open the pot and fluff quinoa using a fork. Add cilantro and lime juice. Stir in avocado.

Nutrition Information

- Calories: 442 calories
- Total Fat: 14.2 g
- Cholesterol: 0 mg
- Sodium: 1245 mg
- Total Carbohydrate: 66 g
- Protein: 16 g

102. Instant Pot Vegan Quinoa and Kale Minestrone Soup

"Everyone's favorite vegan minestrone soup can be done in minutes in your Instant Pot®. Simple, rich, and flavorful with the addition of quinoa and kale."

Serving: 8 | Prep: 15 m | Cook: 45 m | Ready in: 1 h 15 m

Ingredients

- 1 (15 ounce) can cannellini beans, drained and rinsed
- 1 (15 ounce) can kidney beans, drained and rinsed
- 6 cups vegetable broth
- 3/4 cup quinoa
- 1 yellow onion, chopped
- 1 zucchini, diced
- 2 stalks celery, chopped
- 2 carrots, diced
- 1 cup chopped kale
- 2 cloves garlic, minced
- 1/2 teaspoon salt
- 1/2 teaspoon dried oregano
- 1/2 teaspoon dried rosemary

Direction

- Combine cannellini beans, kidney beans, vegetable broth, quinoa, onion, zucchini, celery, carrots, kale, garlic, salt, oregano, and rosemary in a multi-functional pressure cooker (such as Instant Pot(R)). Close and lock the lid.

- Select high pressure according to manufacturer's instructions; set timer for 35 minutes. Allow 10 to 15 minutes for pressure to build.
- Release pressure using the natural-release method according to manufacturer's instructions, about 10 minutes. Complete releasing pressure carefully using the quick-release method according to manufacturer's instructions, about 5 minutes. Unlock and remove the lid.

Nutrition Information

- Calories: 186 calories
- Total Fat: 1.9 g
- Cholesterol: 0 mg
- Sodium: 729 mg
- Total Carbohydrate: 33.8 g
- Protein: 8.5 g

103. Italian Quinoa Salad

"I created this recipe when I ran out of pasta and needed to make a quick salad for a potluck. This versatile recipe has become one of our favorites for taking to picnics and for eating after a workout. Eat immediately or refrigerate 2 hours to overnight for best flavor. Quinoa really soaks up the dressing, so you may want to add more to taste after the refrigeration period."

Serving: 6 | Prep: 15 m | Cook: 15 m | Ready in: 1 h

Ingredients

- 4 cups water
- 2 cups quinoa
- 1 tablespoon chicken bouillon granules (optional)
- 2 tomatoes, diced
- 1 large cucumber, diced
- 1/2 cup crumbled feta cheese
- 1/4 cup finely chopped red onion
- 3/4 cup Italian salad dressing

Direction

- Bring water, quinoa, and chicken bouillon to a boil in a saucepan. Reduce heat to medium-low, cover, and simmer until quinoa is tender and water has been absorbed, 15 to 20 minutes. Remove saucepan from heat and cool quinoa to room temperature, about 30 minutes.
- Mix quinoa, tomatoes, cucumber, feta cheese, and red onion together in a bowl. Pour Italian dressing over quinoa mixture and stir to coat.

Nutrition Information

- Calories: 369 calories
- Total Fat: 16.5 g
- Cholesterol: 19 mg
- Sodium: 919 mg
- Total Carbohydrate: 44.4 g
- Protein: 12 g

104. ItalianStyle QuinoaStuffed Sole

"Delicate sole is wrapped around spiced quinoa for a tender and filling dish."

Serving: 2 | Prep: 20 m | Cook: 23 m | Ready in: 1 h 3 m

Ingredients

- 1/4 cup quinoa
- 1/2 cup water
- 1 tablespoon chopped fresh parsley
- 1 tablespoon chopped fresh basil
- 1 teaspoon lemon zest
- 4 (2 ounce) sole fillets
- 2 tablespoons grated Parmesan cheese
- 4 lemon slices
- ground black pepper
- 2 tablespoons red wine vinegar
- 1/2 cup water

Direction

- Stir together the quinoa, 1/2 cup water, parsley, basil, and lemon zest in a small saucepan over high heat. Bring to a boil, then reduce heat to medium-low, cover, and simmer until the quinoa is tender, about 20 minutes. Pour into a mixing bowl, fold in the Parmesan cheese, and allow the mixture to cool.
- Preheat the oven's broiler and set the oven rack at about 6 inches from the heat source. Lightly grease a small baking dish.
- Spoon a quarter of the quinoa mixture onto one end of each sole fillet. Fold the other side of the sole overtop, sprinkle with black pepper, and place a lemon slice on top. Place the sole into the prepared baking dish, and add the vinegar and remaining water.
- Broil in the preheated oven until the sole flakes easily with a fork, and the flesh is opaque, 3 to 4 minutes.

Nutrition Information

- Calories: 215 calories
- Total Fat: 4.2 g
- Cholesterol: 59 mg
- Sodium: 175 mg
- Total Carbohydrate: 18.4 g
- Protein: 26.8 g

105. Jans Brown Rice and Quinoa Cheesy Rice Balls

"Fun twist on fried mozzarella sticks using rice. Makes a delicious appetizer or snack. Great way to use up leftover rice!"

Serving: 24 | Prep: 10 m | Cook: 15 m | Ready in: 25 m

Ingredients

- 1 (6 ounce) box UNCLE BEN'S® Brown Rice Quinoa Roasted Red Pepper
- 3 large eggs, divided
- 1/2 cup shredded mozzarella cheese
- 1/4 cup grated Parmesan cheese
- 1/2 teaspoon garlic powder
- 1/8 teaspoon ground black pepper
- 1/2 cup all-purpose flour
- 1 cup bread crumbs, or more if needed
- salt to taste
- 4 cups vegetable oil for frying
- 1 cup prepared marinara sauce

Direction

- Cook rice according to package directions. Allow to cool until comfortable to handle.
- Stir in one egg, mozzarella cheese, Parmesan cheese, garlic powder, and black pepper. Mix until well blended.
- Place flour in a small bowl. Beat 2 eggs in a second bowl. Place bread crumbs in a third bowl.
- Divide rice mixture into 24 equal portions about the size of a golf ball. Roll each portion into a ball. Roll rice ball in flour. Place on baking sheet lined with parchment paper. (Mix will be sticky.)
- Dip each rice ball into the egg wash. Dredge in bread crumbs, and place rice balls back on baking sheet. Refrigerate 15 minutes.
- Give each rice ball another quick roll in your hands to tighten up and smooth out the surface.
- Heat oil to 375 degrees F in a large sauce pan.
- Cook rice balls in the hot oil in batches, about 4 per batch. Gently stir with spoon. Cook until rice balls are golden brown, about 2 to 3 minutes.
- Drain on paper-towel-lined plate or baking sheet. Salt lightly.
- Serve hot with heated marinara sauce.

Nutrition Information

- Calories: 112 calories
- Total Fat: 5.7 g
- Cholesterol: 26 mg
- Sodium: 182 mg
- Total Carbohydrate: 11.8 g
- Protein: 3.5 g

106. Jicama-Lime Salad

"I threw this together one afternoon after having purchased a jicama and some limes. It turned out to be a nice, fresh, and unexpectedly tasty healthy salad! I knew that jicama is often prepared with lime, but throw in the coconut and pineapple; delicious!"

Serving: 6 | Prep: 20 m | Cook: 20 m | Ready in: 1 h 25 m

Ingredients

- 2 cups water
- 1 cup quinoa, rinsed and drained
- 1/4 teaspoon salt
- 1 large jicama, peeled and diced
- 1 cup sweetened shredded coconut
- 1 cup diced pineapple
- 3/4 cup golden raisins
- 3/4 cup diced sweet onion
- 2 limes, zested and juiced
- 1/4 cup chopped fresh cilantro
- 1/2 jalapeno pepper, chopped
- salt and ground black pepper to taste

Direction

- Bring water and quinoa to a boil in a saucepan. Stir 1/4 teaspoon salt into the water and return water to a rolling boil. Reduce heat to low, cover the saucepan, and cook until the moisture is absorbed completely, about 15 minutes. Remove pan from heat and let pan sit covered for 5 minutes more.
- Spread quinoa in a thin later on a platter and refrigerate to cool completely, at least 15 minutes.
- Mix jicama, coconut, pineapple, raisins, sweet onion, lime zest, lime juice, cilantro, and jalapeno pepper together in a large bowl; add cooled quinoa and toss. Season salad with salt and black pepper.
- Cover bowl with plastic wrap and refrigerate until salad is completely chilled, about 30 minutes.

Nutrition Information

- Calories: 325 calories
- Total Fat: 5.5 g
- Cholesterol: 0 mg
- Sodium: 149 mg
- Total Carbohydrate: 65.3 g
- Protein: 7 g

107. Kale and Quinoa Patties with Herb Dipping Sauce

"I needed a recipe to use up leftover quinoa and lentils. This is what I came up with using what I had on hand. Very versatile, quick, and easy."

Serving: 6 | Prep: 25 m | Cook: 21 m | Ready in: 46 m

Ingredients

- Patties:
- 2 tablespoons olive oil, divided
- 1/2 onion, finely chopped
- 1 clove garlic, finely chopped
- 1 1/2 cups stemmed and chopped kale
- 1 1/4 cups cooked quinoa
- 1/2 cup crumbled feta cheese
- 1/2 cup Italian bread crumbs
- 1/4 cup cooked lentils
- 2 eggs, beaten
- 1 tablespoon chopped parsley
- salt and ground black pepper to taste
- Sauce:
- 3 tablespoons mayonnaise
- 6 fresh basil leaves, chopped
- 1 tablespoon chopped parsley
- 2 teaspoons dried dill weed
- 1 teaspoon lemon juice
- salt and ground black pepper to taste

Direction

- Heat 1 tablespoon oil in a large cast iron skillet over medium heat. Cook onion and garlic, stirring frequently, until translucent, about 4

minutes. Add kale; cook until wilted, 4 to 5 minutes.
- Place quinoa, feta cheese, bread crumbs, lentils, eggs, 1 tablespoon parsley, salt, and pepper in a large bowl. Mix to fully combine. Mix in the kale mixture. Form into patties by hand.
- Heat the remaining 1 tablespoon oil in a skillet over medium heat. Cook the patties, covered, until golden brown, about 5 minutes per side.
- Set oven rack about 6 inches from the heat source and preheat the oven's broiler. Transfer the skillet to the oven; broil the patties until top is crispy, 3 to 5 minutes.
- Combine mayonnaise, basil, 1 tablespoon parsley, dill, lemon juice, salt, and pepper in bowl to make the sauce. Dollop onto the patties and serve.

Nutrition Information
- Calories: 282 calories
- Total Fat: 17.7 g
- Cholesterol: 83 mg
- Sodium: 531 mg
- Total Carbohydrate: 21.2 g
- Protein: 10.7 g

108. Kale and Quinoa Salad

"Delicious and nutritious! This salad is sure to please the crowd! And with so many options to mix and match to your tastes, you can't go wrong. You can play with the kale-to-quinoa ratio to make this your own. Use alternative nuts and dried fruit to customize to your own taste buds."

Serving: 6 | Prep: 5 m | Cook: 15 m | Ready in: 55 m

Ingredients
- 2 cups water
- 1 cup quinoa
- 10 leaves kale, cut into small pieces
- 3 tablespoons olive oil
- 2 tablespoons lemon juice
- 1 teaspoon Dijon mustard
- 1 large garlic clove, minced
- 1 teaspoon fresh cracked black pepper
- 1/2 teaspoon ground sea salt
- 1 cup pecans
- 1 cup currants
- 3/4 cup crumbled feta cheese

Direction
- Bring water to a boil in a saucepan. Stir quinoa into the boiling water, reduce heat to medium-low, place cover on the saucepan, and cook until water absorbs into the quinoa, about 12 minutes. Remove saucepan from heat and let rest covered for 5 minutes. Remove cover and allow quinoa to cool completely.
- Put kale in a large mixing bowl.
- Whisk olive oil, lemon juice, Dijon mustard, garlic, pepper, and salt together in a bowl until oil emulsifies into the mixture; drizzle over kale. Add cooled quinoa, pecans, currants, and feta cheese to the dressed kale and toss to incorporate.

Nutrition Information
- Calories: 439 calories
- Total Fat: 27 g
- Cholesterol: 17 mg
- Sodium: 397 mg
- Total Carbohydrate: 43.9 g
- Protein: 10.7 g

109. Kale Carrot and Sunflower Seed Salad

"This super simple salad is packed with goodies to give you energy and stay full!"

Serving: 1 | Prep: 15 m | Ready in: 15 m

Ingredients
- 1/2 lemon, juiced
- 1 tablespoon olive oil
- 1 teaspoon apple cider vinegar
- 1/2 teaspoon nutritional yeast
- 1 pinch dried oregano

- 1 pinch dried basil
- 2 carrots, shaved into strips using a vegetable peeler
- 1 1/2 cups chopped kale
- 1/3 cup cooked quinoa
- 1/3 cup sunflower seeds

Direction

- Whisk lemon juice, olive oil, apple cider vinegar, nutritional yeast, oregano, and basil together in a large bowl. Add carrots, kale, quinoa, and sunflower seeds; toss to combine.

Nutrition Information

- Calories: 594 calories
- Total Fat: 40.6 g
- Cholesterol: 0 mg
- Sodium: 153 mg
- Total Carbohydrate: 48 g
- Protein: 18.4 g

110. Kale Quinoa and Avocado Salad with Lemon Dijon Vinaigrette

"Steaming the kale removes some of the bitterness. The salad dressing ties all the flavors together. A quartet of super foods (kale, quinoa, avocado, and olive oil) make this a healthy meal!"

Serving: 4 | Prep: 25 m | Cook: 15 m | Ready in: 40 m

Ingredients

- Salad
- 2/3 cup quinoa
- 1 1/3 cups water
- 1 bunch kale, torn into bite-sized pieces
- 1/2 avocado - peeled, pitted, and diced
- 1/2 cup chopped cucumber
- 1/3 cup chopped red bell pepper
- 2 tablespoons chopped red onion
- 1 tablespoon crumbled feta cheese
- Dressing
- 1/4 cup olive oil
- 2 tablespoons lemon juice
- 1 1/2 tablespoons Dijon mustard
- 3/4 teaspoon sea salt
- 1/4 teaspoon ground black pepper

Direction

- Bring the quinoa and 1 1/3 cup water to a boil in a saucepan. Reduce heat to medium-low, cover, and simmer until the quinoa is tender, and the water has been absorbed, about 15 to 20 minutes. Set aside to cool.
- Place kale in a steamer basket over 1 inch of boiling water in a saucepan. Cover saucepan with a lid and steam kale until hot, about 45 seconds; transfer to a large plate. Top kale with quinoa, avocado, cucumber, bell pepper, red onion, and feta cheese.
- Whisk olive oil, lemon juice, Dijon mustard, sea salt, and black pepper together in a bowl until the oil emulsifies into the dressing; pour over the salad.

Nutrition Information

- Calories: 342 calories
- Total Fat: 20.3 g
- Cholesterol: 2 mg
- Sodium: 552 mg
- Total Carbohydrate: 35.4 g
- Protein: 8.9 g

111. Kale Quinoa Salad

"This recipe was born of my desire to incorporate quinoa into my diet. I absolutely love the taste of it. This yields a large salad and could be halved if necessary."

Serving: 2 | Prep: 15 m | Cook: 20 m | Ready in: 40 m

Ingredients

- 1/2 cup water
- 1/4 cup quinoa
- 4 leaves kale, chopped, or more to taste

- 1/2 avocado - peeled, pitted, and cut into cubes
- 1/2 tomato, cut into cubes
- 1/4 cucumber, peeled and cut into cubes
- 1/4 cup crumbled feta cheese
- 2 tablespoons Italian-style salad dressing

Direction

- Bring water and quinoa to a boil in a saucepan. Reduce heat to medium-low, cover, and simmer until quinoa is tender, 15 to 20 minutes. Drain water and run quinoa under cold water to cool.
- Place a steamer insert into a saucepan and fill with water to just below the bottom of the steamer. Bring water to a boil. Add kale, cover, and steam until tender, 2 to 3 minutes. Place chopped kale in a bowl and refrigerate until chilled, 3 to 5 minutes.
- Mix avocado, tomato, and cucumber together in a bowl; add quinoa and kale. Sprinkle feta cheese over quinoa mixture; add Italian dressing and stir.

Nutrition Information

- Calories: 313 calories
- Total Fat: 19.9 g
- Cholesterol: 28 mg
- Sodium: 620 mg
- Total Carbohydrate: 26.6 g
- Protein: 10.3 g

112. Kale Tabbouleh with Quinoa

"I got this recipe from a good friend. I absolutely love it.

It is a refreshing and surprisingly healthy salad. You can have it as a side dish, or, for a heartier meal, throw some grilled chicken on it and enjoy! The salad can be eaten right away or kept in the fridge for up to three days. If you make it in advance, toss the salad again before serving to redistribute the juices."

Serving: 6 | Prep: 15 m | Cook: 15 m | Ready in: 30 m

Ingredients

- 1/2 cup water
- 1/4 cup quinoa
- 1 bunch curly leaf parsley
- 1/2 bunch curly leaf kale
- 1 pint grape tomatoes, halved
- 1/2 English cucumber, diced
- 1 shallot, minced
- 1/4 cup fresh lemon juice
- 2 tablespoons extra-virgin olive oil, or more to taste
- salt to taste

Direction

- Bring water and quinoa to a boil in a small saucepan. Reduce heat to medium-low, cover, and simmer until quinoa is tender and water has been absorbed, 15 to 20 minutes.
- Starting at the leafy top, cut parsley and kale perpendicular to the stems in 1/2- or 1/4-inch cuts until you reach the point where there's nothing left but stems. Discard stems. Chop the pile of greens on your board with a knife or cleaver until the pieces of parsley and kale are no larger than 1/4 inch. It should be pretty fine, but you don't want it to turn into a paste. Transfer parsley and kale to a large mixing bowl. Toss quinoa, grape tomatoes, cucumber, and shallot with the parsley and kale.
- Whisk lemon juice, olive oil, and salt together in a small bowl; drizzle over the salad and toss to coat.

Nutrition Information

- Calories: 111 calories

- Total Fat: 5.5 g
- Cholesterol: 0 mg
- Sodium: 29 mg
- Total Carbohydrate: 14.3 g
- Protein: 3.4 g

113. Leek Tomato Quinoa

This recipe is an accompaniment for Grilled Beef Tenderloin with Roasted Garlic Sauce .

Serving: Makes about 2 3/4 cups

Ingredients

- 1 1/2 cups quinoa*
- 2 cups water
- 1/2 teaspoon salt
- 1 tablespoon butter
- 2 cups finely chopped leeks (white and pale green parts only)
- 1/4 cup low-salt chicken broth
- 3 tablespoons olive oil
- 2 medium-size yellow tomatoes, seeded, chopped
- 3 tablespoons chopped green onions
- 3 tablespoons chopped fresh basil
- 1 tablespoon fresh lemon juice

Direction

- Place quinoa in strainer. Rinse under cold running water until water runs clear; drain. Mix quinoa, 2 cups water, and salt in heavy medium saucepan. Bring to boil. Reduce heat to medium-low, cover, and simmer until quinoa is just tender and almost all water is absorbed, about 20 minutes. Drain. Set aside. (Quinoa can be made 1 day ahead. Cool, then cover; chill.)
- Melt butter in large nonstick skillet over medium heat. Add leeks; sauté until beginning to soften, about 5 minutes. Add broth. Cover; simmer until leeks are tender, about 5 minutes. Add quinoa and oil; stir until heated through, about 5 minutes. Stir in tomatoes, onions, basil, and lemon juice. Season with salt and pepper.
- *A tiny, bead-shaped, ivory-colored grain available at natural foods stores.

Nutrition Information

- Calories: 265
- Total Fat: 12 g (18%)
- Saturated Fat: 3 g (13%)
- Cholesterol: 5 mg (2%)
- Sodium: 225 mg (9%)
- Total Carbohydrate: 34 g (11%)
- Protein: 7 g (15%)
- Fiber: 4 g (16%)

114. Lemon Herb Quinoa

"A light yet flavorful quinoa dish that goes great with fish or chicken! I invented it on-the-fly one day when I couldn't find quite what I was looking for. For a stronger flavor, add extra lemon juice and herbs. For a more al dente quinoa, remove the lid half way through the cooking time and continue to cook uncovered until most of the water is absorbed."

Serving: 6 | Prep: 10 m | Cook: 20 m | Ready in: 35 m

Ingredients

- 2 cups water
- 1 cup quinoa
- 1 lemon, juiced and zested
- 1 tablespoon chopped fresh parsley
- 1 tablespoon chopped fresh basil
- 1 teaspoon minced garlic
- 1 teaspoon roasted red pepper and garlic seasoning blend

Direction

- Stir water, quinoa, lemon juice, lemon zest, parsley, basil, garlic, and seasoning blend together in a saucepan. Bring to a boil; reduce heat to medium-low, cover, and simmer until quinoa is tender and water is absorbed, about 20 minutes. Let rest, covered, for 5 minutes; fluff with a fork.

Nutrition Information

- Calories: 109 calories
- Total Fat: 1.8 g
- Cholesterol: 0 mg
- Sodium: 82 mg
- Total Carbohydrate: 20.5 g
- Protein: 4.3 g

115. LemonBasil Quinoa Salad

"Found this and thought I would share since quinoa seems to be becoming so popular. This make-ahead salad (served warm or room temperature) is great for outdoor parties since it won't spoil in the sun."

Serving: 4 | Prep: 15 m | Cook: 15 m | Ready in: 30 m

Ingredients

- 2 cups low-sodium chicken broth
- 1 cup quinoa
- 1 large lemon, zested and juiced
- 1/2 cup roasted red peppers, drained and diced
- 1/4 cup dried cranberries
- 2 tablespoons minced red onion
- 2 tablespoons chopped fresh basil

Direction

- Bring chicken broth and quinoa to a boil in a saucepan. Reduce heat to medium-low, cover, and simmer until quinoa is tender and broth has been absorbed, 15 to 20 minutes.
- Stir quinoa, lemon zest, and lemon juice together in a bowl. Add red peppers, cranberries, onion, and basil to quinoa; toss to combine.

Nutrition Information

- Calories: 205 calories
- Total Fat: 3 g
- Cholesterol: 2 mg
- Sodium: 157 mg
- Total Carbohydrate: 38.8 g
- Protein: 8.4 g

116. LemonScented Quinoa

Don't let the much-touted health benefits of this fluffy grain put you off— it also happens to be absolutely delicious. The light, lemony taste of this version makes it a great accompaniment to a whole host of dishes, and it pairs particularly well with the Spicy Calamari with Bacon and Scallions.

Serving: Makes 4 (side dish) servings | Prep: 10 m | Cook: 35 m

Ingredients

- 1 cup quinoa
- 1 1/2 tablespoons olive oil
- 1 teaspoon grated lemon zest
- 2 teaspoons fresh lemon juice

Direction

- Wash quinoa in 3 changes of cold water in a bowl, draining in a sieve each time.
- Cook quinoa in a medium pot of boiling salted water (1 tablespoon salt for 2 quarts water), uncovered, until almost tender, about 15 minutes. Drain in sieve, then set sieve over same pot above 1 inch of simmering water (water should not touch bottom of sieve). Cover quinoa with a folded kitchen towel, then cover sieve with a lid (don't worry if lid doesn't fit tightly) and steam over simmering water until tender, fluffy, and dry, about 10 minutes. Remove pot from heat and remove lid. Let stand, still covered with towel, 5 minutes.
- Transfer quinoa to a bowl and stir in oil, zest, lemon juice, and 1/4 teaspoon salt.

Nutrition Information

- Calories: 202
- Total Fat: 8 g (12%)
- Saturated Fat: 1 g (5%)
- Sodium: 2 mg (0%)

- Total Carbohydrate: 28 g (9%)
- Protein: 6 g (12%)
- Fiber: 3 g (12%)

- Sodium: 74 mg
- Total Carbohydrate: 21.4 g
- Protein: 5.9 g

117. Lemony Quinoa

"Quinoa is a high-protein, good-for-you grain. It can be substituted for couscous and makes a lovely side dish. This recipe is a crunchy, lemony, healthy dish that can be used as a side or as a light meal."

Serving: 6 | Prep: 15 m | Cook: 10 m | Ready in: 25 m

Ingredients

- 1/4 cup pine nuts
- 1 cup quinoa
- 2 cups water
- sea salt to taste
- 1/4 cup fresh lemon juice
- 2 stalks celery, chopped
- 1/4 red onion, chopped
- 1/4 teaspoon cayenne pepper
- 1/2 teaspoon ground cumin
- 1 bunch fresh parsley, chopped

Direction

- Toast the pine nuts briefly in a dry skillet over medium heat. This will take about 5 minutes, and stir constantly as they will burn easily. Set aside to cool.
- In a saucepan, combine the quinoa, water and salt. Bring to a boil, then reduce heat to medium and cook until quinoa is tender and water has been absorbed, about 10 minutes. Cool slightly, then fluff with a fork.
- Transfer the quinoa to a serving bowl and stir in the pine nuts, lemon juice, celery, onion, cayenne pepper, cumin and parsley. Adjust salt and pepper if needed before serving.

Nutrition Information

- Calories: 147 calories
- Total Fat: 4.8 g
- Cholesterol: 0 mg

118. Lemony Quinoa with Chickpeas and Huckleberries

"There are not nearly enough huckleberries on this website, so here is one for the huckleberry lovers out there. Blueberries could also be substituted. Can be served hot or at room temperature."

Serving: 6 | Prep: 10 m | Cook: 30 m | Ready in: 40 m

Ingredients

- 2 cups water
- 1 cup quinoa, rinsed and drained
- 1/4 cup sunflower seed kernels
- 1 (15 ounce) can chickpeas (garbanzo beans), drained and rinsed
- 1 cup huckleberries
- 1 carrot, grated finely
- 1/4 onion, diced
- 1/4 cup fresh lemon juice
- 1 teaspoon lemon zest
- salt and ground black pepper to taste

Direction

- Bring water and quinoa to a boil in a saucepan. Reduce heat to medium-low, cover, and simmer until quinoa is soft and water has been absorbed, about 25 minutes.
- Heat a small skillet over medium heat; toast sunflower kernels in hot skillet until fragrant, 3 to 5 minutes.
- Transfer quinoa to a large bowl and fluff with a fork; add sunflower kernels, chickpeas, huckleberries, carrot, onion, lemon juice, and lemon zest. Gently stir the salad until thoroughly mixed; season with salt and pepper.

Nutrition Information

- Calories: 220 calories

- Total Fat: 5.5 g
- Cholesterol: 0 mg
- Sodium: 154 mg
- Total Carbohydrate: 36.5 g
- Protein: 8 g

119. Little Quinoa Patties

goat cheese, garlic, herbs

Anytime I have leftover cooked quinoa, I make these little patties. They're good hot or cold and are well suited to fighting afternoon hunger pangs. It's a bit of a stretch, but they could be described as a (very) distant cousin of arancini, Italy's beloved deep-fried risotto balls. In contrast, these are pan-fried in a touch of oil, and smushed flat in the pan to get as much surface browning and crust as possible. I'm including my basic version, but often times I'll add a handful of very finely chopped this-or-that: broccoli, asparagus, or cauliflower, depending on the season. They're great on their own, slathered with ripe avocado or drizzled with hot sauce.

Serving: Makes 12 little patties

Ingredients

- 2 1/2 cups/12 oz/340 g cooked quinoa, at room temperature
- 4 large eggs, beaten
- 1/2 teaspoon fine-grain sea salt
- 1/3 cup/.5 oz /15 g finely chopped fresh chives
- 1 yellow or white onion, finely chopped
- 1/3 cup/.5 oz/15 g freshly grated Parmesan or Gruyère cheese
- 3 cloves garlic, finely chopped
- 1 cup/3.5 oz /100 g whole grain bread crumbs, plus more if needed
- Water, if needed
- 1 tablespoon extra-virgin olive oil or clarified butter

Direction

- Combine the quinoa, eggs, and salt in a medium bowl. Stir in the chives, onion, cheese, and garlic. Add the bread crumbs, stir, and let sit for a few minutes so the crumbs can absorb some of the moisture. At this point, you should have a mixture you can easily form into twelve 1-inch/2.5cm thick patties. I err on the very moist side because it makes for a not-overly-dry patty, but you can add more bread crumbs, a bit at a time, to firm up the mixture, if need be. Conversely, a bit more beaten egg or water can be used to moisten the mixture.
- Heat the oil in a large, heavy skillet over medium-low heat, add 6 patties, if they'll fit with some room between each, cover, and cook for 7 to 10 minutes, until the bottoms are deeply browned. Turn up the heat if there is no browning after 10 minutes and continue to cook until the patties are browned. Carefully flip the patties with a spatula and cook the second sides for 7 minutes, or until golden. Remove from the skillet and cool on a wire rack while you cook the remaining patties. Alternatively, the quinoa mixture keeps nicely in the refrigerator for a few days; you can cook patties to order, if you prefer.
- To cook quinoa: Combine 2 cups/12 oz/340 g of well-rinsed uncooked quinoa with 3 cups / 700 ml water and 1/2 teaspoon fine-grain sea salt in a medium saucepan. Bring to a boil, cover, decrease the heat, and simmer for 25 to 30 minutes, until the quinoa is tender and you can see the little quinoa curlicues.

Nutrition Information

- Calories: 111
- Total Fat: 4 g (6%)
- Saturated Fat: 1 g (5%)
- Cholesterol: 63 mg (21%)
- Sodium: 158 mg (7%)
- Total Carbohydrate: 13 g (4%)
- Protein: 5 g (10%)
- Fiber: 1 g (6%)

120. LowCarb Turkey Quinoa Lasagna

"I made this because I needed a low-carb meal. This is delicious and satisfying. Serve hot, topped with Parmesan cheese if you like."

Serving: 12 | Prep: 20 m | Cook: 1 h 20 m | Ready in: 1 h 40 m

Ingredients

- 1/4 cup olive oil, divided
- 2 eggplants, peeled and sliced 1/8-inch thick
- 3 cloves garlic, minced
- 1 pound ground turkey
- 1 small yellow onion, chopped
- 1 cup quinoa
- salt and ground black pepper to taste
- 1 (24 ounce) jar spaghetti sauce (such as Hunt's®)
- 1 (16 ounce) package shredded mozzarella cheese
- 1 (16 ounce) package shredded Cheddar-Monterey Jack cheese blend
- 1 tablespoon Parmesan cheese (optional)

Direction

- Heat 1 tablespoon oil in a large skillet over medium-high heat. Fry eggplant slices a single layer at a time, replenishing oil between batches, until golden brown and soft, about 1 minute per side.
- Preheat oven to 350 degrees F (175 degrees C).
- Heat remaining 1 tablespoon olive oil in the skillet over medium heat. Add garlic; cook and stir until fragrant, about 1 minute. Add turkey and onion; cook and stir until turkey is crumbled and no longer pink, about 5 minutes. Stir in quinoa and season with salt and pepper. Pour in spaghetti sauce; cook until sauce is bubbly, 5 to 10 minutes.
- Spread a layer of sauce in the bottom of a 9x13-inch baking pan. Top with even layers of eggplant slices and Cheddar-Monterey Jack cheese. Repeat layering sauce, eggplant, and cheese, ending with sauce on top. Spread mozzarella cheese evenly on top. Cover with aluminum foil.
- Bake in the preheated oven until cheese is melted and bubbly, about 45 minutes. Uncover and continue baking until top is golden, about 15 minutes more.

Nutrition Information

- Calories: 465 calories
- Total Fat: 27.7 g
- Cholesterol: 90 mg
- Sodium: 755 mg
- Total Carbohydrate: 25.3 g
- Protein: 29.6 g

121. LTF DTox Mediterranean Chicken Quinoa Salad

"D.TOX-friendly quinoa veggie salad with chicken. Serve warm or cold over a bed of baby spinach."

Serving: 6 | Prep: 20 m | Cook: 20 m | Ready in: 40 m

Ingredients

- 2 cups water
- 1 clove garlic, diced
- 1 cup uncooked quinoa
- 2 large cooked chicken breasts, cut into bite-sized pieces
- 1 large green bell pepper, diced
- 1 large red onion, diced
- 1/2 cup chopped Kalamata olives
- 1/4 cup chopped fresh parsley
- 1/4 cup chopped fresh chives
- 1/2 teaspoon salt
- 1/3 cup fresh lemon juice
- 1/4 cup olive oil
- 1 tablespoon balsamic vinegar

Direction

- Combine water and garlic in a pot over high heat. Bring to a boil. Stir in quinoa; reduce heat to medium-low. Cover and simmer until

quinoa is tender and water has been absorbed, 15 to 20 minutes.
- Scrape quinoa into a large bowl. Stir in chicken, green bell pepper, red onion, olives, parsley, chives, and salt.
- Mix lemon juice, olive oil, and vinegar together in a separate bowl. Drizzle dressing over the quinoa mixture; stir until salad is evenly mixed.

Nutrition Information

- Calories: 373 calories
- Total Fat: 19.2 g
- Cholesterol: 55 mg
- Sodium: 431 mg
- Total Carbohydrate: 24.8 g
- Protein: 25 g

122. Make-Ahead Spinach Salad in a Jar

"Prep these salads once and eat for the week! Make sure to firmly pack the spinach into each jar and they will stay fresh all week. Use extra spinach if necessary. A great use for leftover quinoa!"

Serving: 5 | Prep: 20 m | Cook: 20 m | Ready in: 40 m

Ingredients

- 5 (16 oz) pint jars
- 2 cups water
- 1 cup quinoa
- Dressing:
- 3 tablespoons fresh squeezed orange juice
- 1 tablespoon white wine vinegar
- 1/4 teaspoon grated orange zest
- 1/4 teaspoon salt
- 1/4 teaspoon curry powder
- 1/8 teaspoon black pepper
- 1/4 cup light olive oil
- Salad:
- 2/3 cup dried cherries
- 1/2 cup crumbled goat cheese
- 5 cups tightly packed fresh spinach
- 5 tablespoons chopped walnuts

Direction

- Bring water and quinoa to a boil in a saucepan. Reduce heat to medium-low, cover, and simmer until quinoa is tender, 15 to 20 minutes. Allow to cool.
- Whisk orange juice, vinegar, orange zest, salt, curry powder, and pepper together in a small bowl. Slowly drizzle in olive oil, whisking continuously until well blended.
- Line up 5 pint jars in an assembly line fashion.
- Place 1 1/2 tablespoons of dressing into the bottom of each jar. Place 1/2 cup cooked quinoa into each jar, and top with 2 tablespoons cherries. Add 1 1/2 tablespoons goat cheese on top of the cherries. Top with 1 cup of spinach per jar and pack down tightly to remove air pockets; jars should be filled to the top. Finish each jar with 1 tablespoon walnuts. Cover jars and refrigerate until ready to eat.

Nutrition Information

- Calories: 396 calories
- Total Fat: 22.4 g
- Cholesterol: 11 mg
- Sodium: 217 mg
- Total Carbohydrate: 39.2 g
- Protein: 11 g

123. Mango Quinoa Salad

"This dish is as healthy as it is colorful!"

Serving: 12 | Prep: 30 m | Cook: 12 m | Ready in: 42 m

Ingredients

- 2 cups water
- 1 teaspoon salt
- 1 cup quinoa
- 3 mangoes, peeled and chopped
- 1 cup chopped cucumber
- 1/2 cup diced red bell pepper
- 1/3 cup chopped green onions

- 2 cups packed fresh baby spinach
- Dressing:
- 1/4 cup Mazola® Corn Oil
- 2 tablespoons white wine vinegar
- 1 tablespoon mango chutney
- 1/4 teaspoon Spice Islands® Fine Grind Black Pepper
- 1 1/2 teaspoons Spice Islands® Curry Powder
- 1/4 teaspoon Spice Islands® Ground Mustard
- 1/4 teaspoon Spice Islands® Ground Ginger

Direction

- Heat water and salt in a medium saucepan; bring to boil. Add quinoa and cook until tender but still firm to bite, stirring occasionally, about 12 minutes. Remove from heat and let rest for 5 minutes. Transfer to medium bowl. Add mango, cucumber, red pepper and onion to quinoa. Mix well.
- To make dressing: Blend oil, vinegar, chutney, black pepper, curry, mustard and ginger in a food processor. Add 1/4 cup dressing to quinoa mixture. Stir to coat. Spoon quinoa salad over spinach OR mix spinach with quinoa mixture. Drizzle with remaining dressing. Chill if desired.

Nutrition Information

- Calories: 126 calories
- Total Fat: 5.8 g
- Cholesterol: 0 mg
- Sodium: 202 mg
- Total Carbohydrate: 17.5 g
- Protein: 2.6 g

124. Mediterranean Quinoa

"This colorful quinoa dish is easy to cook, and my toddler loves it!"

Serving: 4 | Prep: 20 m | Cook: 25 m | Ready in: 45 m

Ingredients

- 2 tablespoons vegetable oil
- 2 onions, chopped
- 1 green bell pepper, seeded and chopped
- 1 red bell pepper, seeded and chopped
- 1 yellow bell pepper, seeded and chopped
- 2 cloves garlic, crushed
- 3/4 cup uncooked quinoa
- 4 cups vegetable broth or stock
- 1 tablespoon tomato puree
- 3 tomatoes - peeled, seeded and chopped
- Italian seasoning to taste

Direction

- Heat the oil in a large skillet over medium-high heat. Add the onions and red, green and yellow peppers; cook and stir for about 5 minutes. Add the garlic, and cook for about 2 more minutes. Stir in the quinoa, vegetable stock, and tomato puree.
- Return to a boil, then cover and simmer over low heat for 20 minutes, or until quinoa grains are soft. Stir in the diced tomatoes and season with Italian seasoning. Cook until heated through, then serve.

Nutrition Information

- Calories: 276 calories
- Total Fat: 9.8 g
- Cholesterol: 0 mg
- Sodium: 487 mg
- Total Carbohydrate: 40.8 g
- Protein: 8.1 g

125. Mediterranean Quinoa Salad

"If you are looking for a super healthy dish that has robust flavor and leaves your guests feeling full without guilt, this is a great accompaniment to any meal or can stand on its own as a vegetarian dish. It is vegetarian, gluten- and dairy-free."

Serving: 6 | Prep: 30 m | Cook: 1 h 20 m | Ready in: 5 h 50 m

Ingredients

- 1 eggplant, cut in half
- 1 small yellow onion, finely chopped
- 3 cups water
- 1 1/2 cups quinoa
- 3 large heirloom tomatoes, sliced
- 1/2 cup finely chopped fresh basil
- 1 lemon, juiced
- 1/2 teaspoon sea salt

Direction

- Preheat oven to 425 degrees F (220 degrees C). Grease a pie pan; place eggplant in pie pan. Sprinkle onion on top and around eggplant.
- Bake in the preheated oven until eggplant is soft and browned, about 1 hour.
- Bring water to a boil in a 2-quart pot. Stir in quinoa; reduce heat. Simmer, uncovered, until water is absorbed, about 15 minutes.
- Combine heirloom tomatoes, basil, lemon juice, and sea salt in a large bowl. Stir in the warm quinoa, a little at a time, until salad is combined.
- Scoop out warm eggplant, in chunks, from the skin with a spoon; discard skin. Stir eggplant chunks and onion into salad. Cover with plastic wrap.
- Place salad into the refrigerator; chill until flavors combine, about 4 hours.

Nutrition Information

- Calories: 204 calories
- Total Fat: 3 g
- Cholesterol: 0 mg
- Sodium: 160 mg
- Total Carbohydrate: 39.1 g
- Protein: 8.2 g

126. Mediterranean Quinoa Salad with Shrimp

"This is a variation of one of my favorites, cold whole grains, raw vegetables, feta, olives, and balsamic vinegar. This is a simple dish that is healthy and delicious!"

Serving: 10 | Prep: 30 m | Ready in: 45 m

Ingredients

- 1 cup cooked shrimp
- 1 lemon, juiced
- salt and ground black pepper to taste
- 1 pint grape tomatoes
- 1 cup cooked quinoa
- 3/4 English cucumber, chopped
- 1/2 yellow bell pepper, chopped
- 1/2 green bell pepper, chopped
- 1/2 cup kalamata olives, chopped
- 1/4 red onion, chopped
- 1/4 cup crumbled feta cheese
- 1/4 cup olive oil
- 2 tablespoons balsamic vinegar
- 1 teaspoon oregano

Direction

- Toss shrimp with lemon juice, salt, and black pepper in a bowl; set aside to marinate, about 15 minutes.
- Mix tomatoes, quinoa, cucumber, yellow bell pepper, green bell pepper, kalamata olives, red onion, and feta cheese together in a large bowl.
- Whisk together olive oil, vinegar, and oregano in a separate bowl; add to vegetable and quinoa mixture and toss well to combine.
- Top quinoa mixture with marinated shrimp to serve.

Nutrition Information

- Calories: 134 calories

- Total Fat: 9.2 g
- Cholesterol: 31 mg
- Sodium: 229 mg
- Total Carbohydrate: 9 g
- Protein: 5.1 g

127. Mexican Quinoa

"As a healthier alternative to Mexican or Spanish rice, this version uses gluten-free quinoa instead of rice for its additional protein and fiber and great taste. However, it still has all the great flavor and spices of your usual Mexican or Spanish rice dish."

Serving: 4 | Prep: 20 m | Cook: 20 m | Ready in: 40 m

Ingredients

- 1 tablespoon olive oil
- 1 cup quinoa, rinsed
- 1 small onion, chopped
- 2 cloves garlic, minced
- 1 jalapeno pepper, seeded and chopped (optional)
- 1 (10 ounce) can diced tomatoes with green chile peppers (such as RO*TEL®)
- 1 envelope gluten-free taco seasoning mix
- 2 cups low-sodium chicken broth
- 1/4 cup chopped fresh cilantro

Direction

- Heat olive oil in a large skillet over medium heat; cook and stir quinoa and onion in the hot oil until onion is translucent, about 5 minutes. Add garlic and jalapeno pepper to quinoa mixture and cook until garlic is fragrant and slightly softened, 1 or 2 more minutes.
- Mix undrained can of diced tomatoes with green chiles, taco seasoning mix, and chicken broth into quinoa mixture. Bring to a boil, reduce heat to medium-low, and simmer until liquid has been absorbed, 15 to 20 minutes. Stir in cilantro.

Nutrition Information

- Calories: 244 calories
- Total Fat: 6.1 g
- Cholesterol: 2 mg
- Sodium: 986 mg
- Total Carbohydrate: 38.1 g
- Protein: 8.1 g

128. Mexican Quinoa Salad

"A delicious, fresh Mexican dish with a little kick!"

Serving: 4 | Prep: 30 m | Ready in: 30 m

Ingredients

- Salad:
- 1 (15 ounce) can black beans, drained and rinsed
- 1 1/2 cups cooked quinoa
- 1 cup frozen corn
- 1 red bell pepper, diced
- 1/2 cup chopped green onion
- 1/2 cup finely chopped cilantro, plus more for garnish
- 1 teaspoon minced garlic
- Dressing:
- 1/2 cup olive oil
- 1 lime, juiced
- 2 tablespoons honey
- 6 pickled jalapeno pepper slices, chopped
- 1/4 teaspoon dry mustard
- 1/4 teaspoon paprika

Direction

- Stir black beans, quinoa, corn, red bell pepper, green onion, cilantro, and garlic together in a large bowl.
- Whisk olive oil, lime juice, honey, jalapeno, mustard, and paprika together in a bowl until dressing is smooth and creamy. Pour dressing over quinoa mixture and toss to coat. Garnish with cilantro.

Nutrition Information

- Calories: 507 calories
- Total Fat: 29.2 g
- Cholesterol: 0 mg
- Sodium: 447 mg
- Total Carbohydrate: 53.8 g
- Protein: 11.6 g

129. MexiQuinoa Chicken Casserole

"Spicy, half-healthy casserole; would be great with ground beef too."

Serving: 5 | Prep: 20 m | Cook: 35 m | Ready in: 55 m

Ingredients

- 2 cups chicken broth
- 1 cup quinoa
- 2 tablespoons olive oil, divided
- 3 skinless, boneless chicken breast halves, cut into bite-size pieces
- 1 onion, chopped
- 1 green bell pepper, chopped
- 1 jalapeno pepper, chopped
- 1 (15 ounce) can black beans, rinsed and drained
- 1 1/2 cups salsa
- 1 (6 ounce) can tomato paste
- 2 teaspoons garlic salt
- 1 teaspoon ground cumin
- 1 teaspoon chili powder
- 1 teaspoon ground black pepper
- 1 teaspoon dried oregano
- 1/4 cup sour cream (optional)
- 1/4 cup shredded Cheddar cheese (optional)

Direction

- Bring chicken broth and quinoa to a boil in a saucepan. Reduce heat to medium-low, cover, and simmer until quinoa is tender and water has been absorbed, 15 to 20 minutes.
- Heat 1 tablespoon oil in a skillet; cook and stir chicken until no longer pink in the center, about 10 minutes.
- Heat 1 tablespoon oil in a separate large skillet over medium heat; cook and stir onion, green bell pepper, and jalapeno pepper until tender, 5 to 10 minutes. Mix quinoa, chicken, black beans, salsa, tomato paste, garlic salt, cumin, chili powder, black pepper, and oregano into onion mixture; cook, stirring occasionally, until casserole is heated through and thickened, 5 to 10 minutes. Top casserole with sour cream and Cheddar cheese.

Nutrition Information

- Calories: 458 calories
- Total Fat: 14.4 g
- Cholesterol: 52 mg
- Sodium: 2256 mg
- Total Carbohydrate: 54.8 g
- Protein: 29.9 g

130. Micheles Thai Chicken Soup

"This is a delicious, substantial soup. I have substituted quinoa for rice in the traditional recipe to make it a bit healthier. I hope you like it!"

Serving: 6 | Prep: 20 m | Cook: 45 m | Ready in: 1 h 5 m

Ingredients

- 1 tablespoon vegetable oil
- 1 (10 ounce) package coarsely chopped fresh mushrooms
- 1/2 cup finely chopped onion
- 5 skinless, boneless chicken thighs, diced
- 6 cups chicken stock, or more as needed
- 1 (13.5 ounce) can coconut milk
- 1 cup quinoa, rinsed
- 1/2 cup half-and-half, or more as needed
- 2 tablespoons tomato paste
- 2 tablespoons lemongrass paste (such as Gourmet Garden™)
- 2 teaspoons red curry paste

- 1 1/2 teaspoons sambal oelek (Indonesian red chile paste)
- 1 teaspoon fish sauce
- 1 teaspoon Worcestershire sauce
- 1/2 roasted red pepper, chopped
- 1 tablespoon water
- 1 tablespoon cornstarch

Direction

- Heat oil in a large pot over medium heat. Add mushrooms and onion; cook and stir until mushrooms brown and onion is soft, about 5 minutes. Add chicken thighs; cook and stir until no longer pink in the center, 5 to 8 minutes.
- Pour chicken stock, coconut milk, quinoa, and half-and-half into the pot. Stir in tomato paste, lemongrass paste, red curry paste, sambal, fish sauce, and Worcestershire sauce. Simmer until flavors combine, about 30 minutes. Stir in roasted red pepper.
- Mix water and cornstarch together in a small bowl until no lumps remain. Pour into the pot; stir soup until slightly thickened, about 5 minutes.

Nutrition Information

- Calories: 450 calories
- Total Fat: 28.3 g
- Cholesterol: 66 mg
- Sodium: 901 mg
- Total Carbohydrate: 29.8 g
- Protein: 25.2 g

131. Mini Baked Quinoa Patties

"These baked quinoa patties make a perfect protein-packed finger food for toddlers; just break them into small pieces! Freeze extras and defrost when needed! Don't keep in the fridge for more than about 3 days."

Serving: 18 | Prep: 15 m | Cook: 35 m | Ready in: 50 m

Ingredients

- 3 cups water
- 1 cup quinoa
- olive oil cooking spray
- 1 cup frozen chopped spinach, thawed and drained
- 1 cup dry bread crumbs
- 4 eggs, whisked
- 1/3 cup shredded Colby cheese

Direction

- Bring water and quinoa to a boil in a saucepan. Reduce heat to medium-low, cover, and simmer until quinoa is tender and water has been absorbed, 15 to 20 minutes.
- Preheat oven to 400 degrees F (200 degrees C). Spray a baking sheet with olive oil cooking spray.
- Stir quinoa, spinach, bread crumbs, eggs, and Colby cheese together in a bowl. Drop spoonfuls of the quinoa mixture onto the prepared baking sheets and press to desired thickness.
- Bake in the preheated oven until the bottoms of the patties are golden, about 15 minutes. Flip patties and bake until golden, about 5 minutes more.

Nutrition Information

- Calories: 85 calories
- Total Fat: 2.7 g
- Cholesterol: 43 mg
- Sodium: 80 mg
- Total Carbohydrate: 10.9 g
- Protein: 4.3 g

132. Miso Stew

Packed with sea vegetables such as arame and kombu (both loaded with beneficial minerals), this recipe from Alexandra Jamieson, vegan chef and girlfriend of Super Size Me's Morgan Spurlock, is as good for you as it gets. Adding the miso after the stew is cooked ensures the preservation of its healthful microorganisms.

Serving: Makes 2 main-course servings | Prep: 30 m | Cook: 30 m

Ingredients

- 2 tablespoons arame*
- 4 1/2 cups water (preferably filtered)
- 1/3 cup quinoa** (1 3/4 oz)
- 1 (1-inch) piece kombu* (kelp)
- 1/2 medium onion, cut into 3/4-inch pieces
- 2 teaspoons extra-virgin olive oil
- 2 garlic cloves, thinly sliced
- 1/2 lb firm tofu, cut crosswise into 6 slices and each slice quartered
- 1/2 carrot, halved lengthwise, then cut crosswise into 1/4-inch-thick slices
- 5 fresh shiitake mushrooms, stems discarded and caps thinly sliced
- 2 to 3 tablespoons white miso*** (also called shiro miso; not sweet, preferably white rice and soy miso)
- 1 cup very thinly sliced bok choy or Napa cabbage
- 1 teaspoon tamari**** (wheat-free sauce from refined soy), or to taste
- 1 scallion, thinly sliced
- 1/2 teaspoon dulse flakes*****

Direction

- Soak arame in 1 cup filtered water in a small bowl and set aside.
- Wash quinoa in 3 changes of cold water in a bowl, draining quinoa in a sieve each time, then put quinoa in a 2- to 3-quart saucepan with kombu and 1 cup filtered water. Simmer, uncovered, until quinoa is just tender, about 20 minutes. Drain in a sieve.
- About 10 minutes before quinoa is done, cook onion in oil in a 3- to 4-quart heavy saucepan over moderate heat, stirring frequently, until it begins to brown, about 5 minutes, then add garlic and cook, stirring, 30 seconds.
- Add tofu, carrot, shiitakes, and remaining 2 1/2 cups filtered water and simmer, covered, until carrot is just tender, about 5 minutes. Remove kombu from quinoa and discard. Stir quinoa into stew, then remove from heat.
- Put miso in a small bowl and add 1/4 cup stew liquid, whisking until miso is incorporated, then stir mixture into stew. Drain and rinse arame and add to stew along with bok choy and tamari, stirring to combine.
- Divide stew between 2 bowls and sprinkle with scallion and dulse flakes.
- *Available at Asian markets, natural foods stores, and edenfoods.com.
- **Available at specialty foods shops, natural foods stores, and ethnicgrocer.com.
- ***Available at Asian markets, natural foods stores, and Uwajimaya (800-889-1928).
- ****Available at natural foods stores.
- *****Available at Asian markets, natural foods stores, and seaveg.com.

133. Molasses Almond Quinoa Vegan Cookies

"Quinoa, a super grain, in a cookie! Molasses and almonds add extra nutrition to these tasty treats. Enjoy!"

Serving: 23 | Prep: 15 m | Cook: 32 m | Ready in: 57 m

Ingredients

- 2 cups water
- 1 cup quinoa
- 1 cup warm water
- 3 tablespoons flax seeds
- 1 cup spelt flour
- 1 cup amaranth flour
- 1 cup chopped raw almonds
- 1 teaspoon baking powder
- 1 teaspoon salt
- 1/2 cup agave nectar

- 1/2 cup crystallized sugar cane juice (such as Sucanat®)
- 1/4 cup molasses
- 2 teaspoons almond extract
- 1 teaspoon vanilla extract

Direction

- Bring 2 cups water and quinoa to a boil in a saucepan. Reduce heat to medium-low, cover, and simmer until quinoa is tender, about 20 minutes.
- Preheat oven to 350 degrees F (175 degrees C). Line a baking sheet with parchment paper.
- Blend 1 cup warm water and flax seeds in a blender until seeds are broken down; let sit until flax mixture is thickened, about 10 minutes.
- Mix 2 cup cooked quinoa, spelt flour, amaranth flour, almonds, baking powder, and salt together in a bowl.
- Combine agave nectar, crystallized sugar cane juice, molasses, almond extract, and vanilla extract with flax mixture and blend on high speed until smooth. Mix flax mixture with flour mixture until dough is thoroughly mixed.
- Spoon dough onto the prepared baking sheet.
- Bake in the preheated oven until cookies are lightly browned around the edges, 12 to 15 minutes.

Nutrition Information

- Calories: 146 calories
- Total Fat: 3.7 g
- Cholesterol: 0 mg
- Sodium: 126 mg
- Total Carbohydrate: 25.6 g
- Protein: 3.6 g

134. Moms Quinoa Burgers

"I made these with leftover quinoa and some vegetables I had in the fridge. Super easy! Great on a multigrain bun with some tomatoes, spinach, and your favorite spread!

My 2 1/2-year-old said, I love it Mommy! If necessary, while frying, flatten the burgers with the back of your spatula (but don't make them too thin)."

Serving: 6 | Prep: 30 m | Cook: 36 m | Ready in: 1 h 31 m

Ingredients

- 1 1/2 cups water
- 3/4 cup dry quinoa
- 2 tablespoons olive oil, divided
- 1/4 cup chopped onion
- 2 tablespoons chopped celery
- 1/2 cup chopped zucchini
- 1/4 cup chopped yellow bell pepper
- 1/4 cup chopped red bell pepper
- 1 teaspoon finely chopped garlic
- 3 tablespoons whole wheat flour, or more if needed
- 1 egg
- salt and ground black pepper to taste
- cayenne pepper (optional)
- 1/2 cup shredded mozzarella cheese

Direction

- Bring water and quinoa to a boil in a saucepan. Reduce heat to medium-low, cover, and simmer until quinoa is tender, 15 to 20 minutes. Set aside to cool slightly, about 15 minutes.
- Heat 1 tablespoon olive oil in a skillet over medium-high heat. Add onion and celery; sauté for 1 minute. Add zucchini, yellow bell pepper, and red bell pepper; sauté until tender, 5 to 7 minutes more. Set aside to cool, about 10 minutes.
- Mix quinoa, zucchini-pepper mixture, and garlic together in a bowl. Stir in flour; stir in egg. Season with salt, pepper, and cayenne. Mix in mozzarella cheese. Form into about 6 equal-size patties; place on a plate.

- Heat 1 tablespoon oil in a skillet over medium heat. Fry patties until heated through and browned, 5 minutes per side.

Nutrition Information

- Calories: 176 calories
- Total Fat: 8.3 g
- Cholesterol: 37 mg
- Sodium: 103 mg
- Total Carbohydrate: 18.7 g
- Protein: 7.2 g

135. Moroccan Quinoa Salad

"While searching for something to whip together for dinner, and as a way to use up a bunch of fresh herbs I had on hand, I came up with this recipe and was extremely pleased with the results! I've made it several times since and my family loves it! Very light and flavorful! Enjoy as is or serve along with grilled chicken."

Serving: 6 | Prep: 30 m | Cook: 30 m | Ready in: 1 h 45 m

Ingredients

- 3 tablespoons olive oil
- 5 cloves garlic, minced
- 3 shallots, diced
- 1 1/2 teaspoons ground cumin
- 1 1/2 teaspoons ground ginger
- 1 1/2 teaspoons ground cinnamon
- 4 cups chicken broth
- 2 cups red quinoa
- 1 1/4 cups raisins
- 2 cups hot water
- lemon, juiced
- 1 (29 ounce) can garbanzo beans, drained
- 2 carrots, shredded
- 1/3 cup chopped fresh parsley
- 1/3 cup chopped fresh basil
- 1/3 cup chopped fresh mint

Direction

- Heat the olive oil in a skillet over medium heat. Stir in the garlic and shallots; cook and stir until the shallots have softened and turned translucent, about 5 minutes. Stir in the cumin, ginger, and cinnamon. Cook until fragrant, about 1 minute more. Add the chicken broth and quinoa, and bring to a boil, then reduce heat to low. Cover and cook until the quinoa is tender and the liquid has been absorbed, about 20 minutes.
- Meanwhile, place raisins in a bowl and cover with hot water. Soak until the raisins soften and plump up, about 15 minutes. Drain and set aside.
- Fluff the quinoa with a fork and stir in the lemon juice. Remove from heat and allow to cool to room temperature. Stir in the garbanzo beans, raisins, carrots, parsley, basil, and mint. Serve at room temperature or chilled.

Nutrition Information

- Calories: 575 calories
- Total Fat: 12.3 g
- Cholesterol: 0 mg
- Sodium: 441 mg
- Total Carbohydrate: 104.9 g
- Protein: 17.4 g

136. Mushroom Meatballs

"My recipe today is a meaty substitute made of mushrooms (it is also vegan and vegetarian), but the end result is as savory and satisfying as a beef meatball!"

Serving: 4 | Prep: 30 m | Cook: 15 m | Ready in: 45 m

Ingredients

- 2 (8 ounce) packages cremini mushrooms, chopped
- 1 1/2 cups cooked quinoa
- 1 cup cooked lentils
- 1 white onion, chopped
- 3 cloves garlic, chopped
- 1/4 cup nutritional yeast
- 1/4 cup almond meal
- 1/4 cup flax seeds
- 1 1/2 teaspoons Worcestershire sauce

- 1 pinch dried sage
- 1 pinch dried oregano
- 1 pinch dried basil
- 1 pinch dried rosemary
- 1 pinch dried thyme
- 1 pinch dried mint
- 1 pinch ground cayenne pepper

Direction

- Preheat oven to 350 degrees F (175 degrees C). Grease a baking sheet.
- Place mushrooms, quinoa, lentils, onion, and garlic in a food processor or blender; pulse until coarsely combined.
- Sprinkle nutritional yeast, almond meal, flax seeds, Worcestershire sauce, sage, oregano, basil, rosemary, thyme, mint, and cayenne pepper into the food processor. Blend until mixture is combined but still slightly choppy.
- Shape mixture into balls and arrange on the baking sheet.
- Bake in the preheated oven until darkened and slightly crispy on the outside but moist on the inside, about 15 minutes.

Nutrition Information

- Calories: 302 calories
- Total Fat: 10 g
- Cholesterol: 0 mg
- Sodium: 42 mg
- Total Carbohydrate: 39.5 g
- Protein: 18.8 g

137. Mystic Mushroom and Quinoa Chowder

"A tasty soup with mushrooms and quinoa; great as a first course or a wonderful accompaniment to a salad or sandwich for a meal."

Serving: 6 | Prep: 10 m | Cook: 30 m | Ready in: 40 m

Ingredients

- 1/2 cup quinoa
- 2 tablespoons butter
- 1 medium onion, diced
- 1 (8 ounce) package button mushrooms, chopped
- 2 tablespoons molasses
- 3 cups chicken stock
- 1 tablespoon butter
- 2/3 cup chopped fresh shiitake mushrooms
- 1 cup heavy cream
- salt and pepper to taste
- 1/3 cup creme fraiche
- chopped fresh chives

Direction

- Toast quinoa in a dry, heavy skillet over medium heat until fragrant.
- In a large saucepan or stockpot, melt 2 tablespoons butter over medium-high heat. Stir in onions, and cook until caramelized, about 6 to 8 minutes. Stir in quinoa, mushrooms, and molasses; cook until mushrooms release their liquid, adding a little chicken stock if necessary to facilitate cooking. Add remaining chicken stock, and bring to a boil; reduce heat to low, and let simmer for 18 to 20 minutes, or until quinoa is cooked.
- Meanwhile, melt 1 tablespoon butter in a skillet over medium heat. Cook shiitake mushrooms in butter until softened; set aside.
- Puree soup in a food processor or blender, and return to saucepan. Stir in cream, and heat (DO NOT BOIL). Season with salt and pepper to taste. Garnish with creme fraiche, shiitake mushrooms, and chives.

Nutrition Information

- Calories: 340 calories
- Total Fat: 26.8 g
- Cholesterol: 90 mg
- Sodium: 938 mg
- Total Carbohydrate: 20.9 g
- Protein: 6.2 g

138. New Years Soup

"Black-eyed peas for luck, and collard greens for money - this New Year's soup is healthy, tasty, and bound to bring a great year!"

Serving: 4 | Prep: 15 m | Cook: 1 h | Ready in: 1 h 15 m

Ingredients

- 1 tablespoon extra-virgin olive oil
- 2 cloves garlic, crushed
- 1 small onion, chopped
- 2 carrots, peeled and sliced
- 3 leaves collard greens, coarsely chopped
- 1 (14.5 ounce) can vegetable broth
- 1 (15 ounce) can black-eyed peas, rinsed and drained
- 1/2 cup quinoa
- 1 cup water
- 1 tablespoon cider vinegar, or to taste
- salt and ground black pepper to taste

Direction

- Heat olive oil in a soup pot over medium heat; cook and stir garlic until it begins to brown, about 3 minutes. Add onion and carrots. Cook and stir until carrots begin to brown and onion becomes translucent, 7 to 8 minutes. Cook and stir collard greens into onion mixture until wilted, about 5 minutes.
- Pour vegetable broth and black-eyed peas into vegetables, bring to a boil, and reduce heat to low. Cover and simmer soup until vegetables are softened, 20 to 25 minutes.
- While soup is simmering, mix quinoa and water in a saucepan, bring to a boil, and reduce heat to low. Cover and simmer until the water has absorbed into the quinoa, about 10 minutes. Stir cooked quinoa into soup and simmer until collard greens are tender, about 10 more minutes. Stir cider vinegar into soup to taste and season with salt and black pepper.

Nutrition Information

- Calories: 232 calories
- Total Fat: 5.6 g
- Cholesterol: 0 mg
- Sodium: 556 mg
- Total Carbohydrate: 36.6 g
- Protein: 9.5 g

139. NoBake Quinoa Bars

"Delicious and nutritious bars with quinoa."

Serving: 12 | Prep: 10 m | Cook: 20 m | Ready in: 1 h

Ingredients

- 1 1/2 cups water
- 3/4 cup quinoa
- 1 cup pitted dates
- 1 cup old-fashioned oats
- 2/3 cup dried cranberries
- 1/2 cup maple syrup
- 1 tablespoon ground cinnamon

Direction

- Bring water and quinoa to a boil in a saucepan. Reduce heat to medium-low, cover, and simmer until quinoa is tender, 15 to 20 minutes. Uncover, fluff with a fork, and let cool completely, about 30 minutes.
- Combine dates, oats, cranberries, and maple syrup in a food processor. Blend until a sticky paste forms.
- Mix 2 cups cooled quinoa, date mixture, and cinnamon together in a bowl.
- Line a small baking pan with parchment paper. Press mixture firmly into the pan. Cut into bars.

Nutrition Information

- Calories: 155 calories
- Total Fat: 1.2 g
- Cholesterol: 0 mg
- Sodium: 3 mg
- Total Carbohydrate: 35.3 g
- Protein: 2.7 g

140. NoBake Quinoa Protein Bars

"These are protein and whole grain packed, with just enough sweetness. They are perfect for a quick snack that will help you power through the next part of your day! Bars can be stored in the freezer for a quick grab-n-go breakfast! See Note: s for other variations."

Serving: 24 | Prep: 30 m | Ready in: 1 h 30 m

Ingredients

- 3 cups cooked quinoa, cooled
- 1 1/2 cups pitted dates
- 1/2 cup honey
- 1/2 cup unsweetened applesauce, or as needed
- 1/2 cup shredded coconut
- 1/2 cup sunflower seeds
- 2 tablespoons coconut oil
- 1 tablespoon vanilla extract
- 4 cups ground oats, or as needed, divided
- 1/2 cup ground flax seed
- 3 tablespoons protein powder
- 2 tablespoons sesame seeds
- 2 tablespoons chia seeds
- 1/2 teaspoon salt

Direction

- Line a 9x13-inch baking pan with parchment paper.
- Blend quinoa, dates, honey, applesauce, coconut, sunflower seeds, coconut oil, and vanilla together in a food processor until smooth. Add enough of the oats to fill the processor bowl and blend until combined.
- Stir the quinoa mixture with the remaining oats, flax seed, protein powder, sesame seeds, chia seeds, and salt in a large bowl until mixture is able to hold its shape without sticking to your hands. Press mixture firmly into prepared baking pan and refrigerate until chilled, at least 1 hour.

Nutrition Information

- Calories: 245 calories
- Total Fat: 6.9 g
- Cholesterol: 0 mg
- Sodium: 64 mg
- Total Carbohydrate: 40.4 g
- Protein: 7.1 g

141. Nothing Id Rather Eat Quinoa Patties

"What a treat! You will never miss hamburger meat again. This is real food that you can feel good about and that tastes so delicious and in addition is packed with the healthiest ingredients. These burgers do not need a bun so you will save some calories there. I made this in my quest to satisfy my Chase and her difficult palate and it is a winner. Keep the batter ready to go in your refrigerator."

Serving: 24 | Prep: 20 m | Cook: 41 m | Ready in: 1 h 6 m

Ingredients

- 5 cups water
- 2 1/2 cups quinoa
- 1 tablespoon olive oil
- 2 onions, chopped
- salt to taste
- 2 large sweet potatoes
- 4 eggs
- 1/2 cup tahini
- 1/2 cup kefir
- 1/2 cup ground flax seeds
- 1/2 cup grated Parmesan cheese, or more to taste
- 1/4 cup sesame seeds
- 1/4 cup sunflower seeds
- 1/4 cup coarsely chopped pumpkin seeds, or more to taste
- 1 tablespoon soy sauce
- 1 tablespoon all-purpose vegetable seasoning
- 1 tablespoon raw apple cider vinegar (such as Bragg®)
- salt and ground black pepper to taste
- 3/4 cup frozen corn kernels, thawed
- 1/2 cup spelt flour, or more as needed
- 2 tablespoons butter
- 24 thin slices Cheddar cheese

Direction

- Bring water and quinoa to a boil in a saucepan. Reduce heat to medium-low, cover, and simmer until quinoa is soft, 15 to 20 minutes.
- Heat olive oil in a large skillet over medium heat. Add onions and salt; cook and stir until tender, 5 to 8 minutes.
- Place sweet potatoes on a microwave-safe plate; prick all over with a fork. Cook on high, turning once, until tender, 8 to 10 minutes. Cool until easily handled, about 5 minutes.
- Peel sweet potatoes and place flesh in a bowl. Add eggs, tahini, kefir, flax seeds, Parmesan cheese, sesame seeds, sunflower seeds, pumpkin seeds, soy sauce, vegetable seasoning, vinegar, salt, and pepper; beat with an electric mixer until well blended. Stir in quinoa, onions, and corn.
- Stir enough spelt flour into the sweet potato mixture until it barely holds together.
- Melt 1/4 teaspoon butter on a griddle over medium heat. Spoon a burger-sized patty onto the hot griddle and cook until browned, about 4 minutes. Flip; add 1 slice Cheddar cheese. Cover patty with a frying pan and cook until cheese is melted, about 4 minutes more. Repeat with remaining butter, sweet potato mixture, and Cheddar cheese.

Nutrition Information

- Calories: 279 calories
- Total Fat: 14.7 g
- Cholesterol: 50 mg
- Sodium: 245 mg
- Total Carbohydrate: 27 g
- Protein: 11.6 g

142. Oat and Quinoa Breakfast Cake

"This is a family favorite. It makes weekday mornings a cinch! Who doesn't want cake for breakfast? Serve chilled, with Greek yogurt and a drizzle of honey."

Serving: 10 | Prep: 20 m | Cook: 1 h | Ready in: 1 h 50 m

Ingredients

- Crust:
- 1 cup almond flour
- 1 tablespoon coconut oil
- 2 tablespoons cold water, or as needed
- Filling:
- 3 eggs
- 2 cups vanilla soy milk
- 1 cup milk
- 2/3 cup maple syrup
- 1/3 cup hemp powder
- 1 tablespoon ground cinnamon
- 1/4 teaspoon ground nutmeg
- 2 apples, peeled and diced
- 1 1/2 cups rolled oats, divided
- 1 cup uncooked quinoa
- 1/3 cup chopped pecans
- 1/4 cup raisins
- 1/4 cup flax seeds
- 1 banana, thinly sliced

Direction

- Preheat oven to 350 degrees F (175 degrees C). Lightly grease a 9x13-inch baking dish.
- Mix almond flour and coconut oil together in a bowl. Add enough water to form a thick dough. Press into the bottom of the baking dish to form a crust.
- Beat eggs in a large bowl until smooth. Add soy milk, milk, maple syrup, hemp powder, cinnamon, and nutmeg; beat until combined. Stir apples, 1 1/4 cup oats, quinoa, pecans, raisins, and flax seeds into the batter.
- Spread banana slices over crust. Pour batter evenly over banana slices. Sprinkle remaining 1/4 cup oats on top.
- Bake in the preheated oven until cake is mostly set but retains some moisture, about 1

hour. Let cool to room temperature, about 30 minutes. Cover and chill before serving.

Nutrition Information

- Calories: 407 calories
- Total Fat: 17.2 g
- Cholesterol: 58 mg
- Sodium: 60 mg
- Total Carbohydrate: 52.5 g
- Protein: 14.1 g

143. OMG Quinoa Patties

"I use all organic ingredients. These quinoa patties are OMG good!"

Serving: 14 | Prep: 15 m | Cook: 25 m | Ready in: 40 m

Ingredients

- 2 cups low-sodium vegetable broth
- 2 cups quinoa
- 2 cups water
- 3 tablespoons olive oil, or more as needed, divided
- 1 white onion, chopped
- 1 zucchini, grated
- 1 large carrot, grated
- garlic powder, or more to taste
- salt and ground black pepper to taste
- 4 large eggs, lightly beaten
- 1/2 cup oat groats, ground into a powder

Direction

- Bring vegetable broth, water, and quinoa to a boil in a saucepan. Reduce heat to medium-low, cover, and simmer until quinoa is tender and broth has been absorbed, 15 to 20 minutes. Spread quinoa onto a large platter to cool.
- Heat 1 tablespoon olive oil in a large skillet over medium heat. Cook and stir onion, zucchini, and carrot in hot oil until the onion is translucent, 3 to 5 minutes; transfer to a plate to cool.
- Mix cooled vegetables with 3 cups of the cooled quinoa in a large bowl; season with garlic powder, salt, and black pepper. Pour eggs and ground oats into the bowl; stir until the mixture comes together. Divide mixture into 14 portions and shape into patties.
- Heat 2 tablespoons olive oil in a large skillet over medium heat. Fry patties in hot oil until browned, about 2 minutes per side. Use more oil between batches as needed.

Nutrition Information

- Calories: 166 calories
- Total Fat: 6.2 g
- Cholesterol: 53 mg
- Sodium: 67 mg
- Total Carbohydrate: 21.8 g
- Protein: 6.2 g

144. One Skillet Mexican Quinoa

"With a large family, I love these one skillet dishes where, for at least 15 minutes, I can 'set it and forget it!' And the kids love it! Serve it for Cinco de Mayo or any night of the week!"

Serving: 4 | Prep: 15 m | Cook: 25 m | Ready in: 40 m

Ingredients

- 1 tablespoon olive oil
- 1 jalapeno pepper, chopped
- 2 cloves garlic, chopped
- 1 (15 ounce) can black beans, rinsed and drained
- 1 (14.5 ounce) can fire-roasted diced tomatoes
- 1 cup yellow corn
- 1 cup quinoa
- 1 cup chicken broth
- 1 tablespoon red pepper flakes
- 1 1/2 teaspoons chili powder
- 1/2 teaspoon cumin
- 1 pinch kosher salt and ground black pepper to taste
- 1 avocado - peeled, pitted, and diced

- 1 lime, juiced
- 2 tablespoons chopped fresh cilantro

Direction

- Heat oil in a large skillet over medium-high heat. Sauté jalapeno pepper and garlic in hot oil until fragrant, about 1 minute.
- Stir black beans, tomatoes, yellow corn, quinoa, and chicken broth into skillet; season with red pepper flakes, chili powder, cumin, salt, and black pepper. Bring to a boil, cover the skillet with a lid, reduce heat to low, and simmer until quinoa is tender and liquid is mostly absorbed, about 20 minutes. Stir avocado, lime juice, and cilantro into quinoa until combined.

Nutrition Information

- Calories: 449 calories
- Total Fat: 14.9 g
- Cholesterol: 1 mg
- Sodium: 1048 mg
- Total Carbohydrate: 67 g
- Protein: 16.5 g

- 1/4 lime, juiced

Direction

- Heat oil in a saucepan over medium-high heat. Sauté jalapeno peppers and garlic in hot oil until fragrant, about 1 minute.
- Pour vegetable broth into the saucepan. Stir black beans, tomatoes, quinoa, corn, and salt into the broth. Bring to a boil, reduce heat to low, and simmer, covered, until the liquid is fully absorbed into the quinoa, 20 to 25 minutes.
- Fluff quinoa with a fork. Stir in cilantro and lime juice.

Nutrition Information

- Calories: 232 calories
- Total Fat: 3.9 g
- Cholesterol: 0 mg
- Sodium: 638 mg
- Total Carbohydrate: 39.8 g
- Protein: 10.1 g

145. One-Pan Mexican Quinoa

"Super-healthy and super-tasty quinoa with a Mexican kick."

Serving: 6 | Prep: 15 m | Cook: 25 m | Ready in: 40 m

Ingredients

- 2 teaspoons olive oil
- 3 jalapeno peppers, seeded and finely chopped
- 2 cloves garlic, minced
- 1 1/4 cups vegetable broth
- 1 (15 ounce) can black beans, drained and rinsed
- 1 (14.5 ounce) can diced tomatoes with juice
- 1 cup quinoa
- 1 cup frozen corn kernels
- 1/2 teaspoon kosher salt
- 1/3 cup chopped fresh cilantro

146. One-Skillet Quinoa and Chicken Dinner

"Fast and easy chicken dish recipe good for meal preppers."

Serving: 4 | Prep: 15 m | Cook: 25 m | Ready in: 40 m

Ingredients

- 1 tablespoon olive oil
- 1 cup red onion, chopped
- 1 pound skinless, boneless chicken
- 1 cup frozen mixed vegetables
- 2 cloves garlic, minced
- 1/2 teaspoon salt
- 1/2 teaspoon black pepper
- 12 ounces crushed tomatoes
- 1 cup water
- 1 cup quinoa
- 2 tablespoons cilantro, or to taste

- 6 ounces shredded fat-free Cheddar cheese (such as Kraft®)

Direction

- Heat oil in a large ovenproof skillet over medium-high heat. Add onion and cook until tender, about 2 minutes. Add chicken, frozen vegetables, and garlic. Sprinkle with salt and pepper. Cook, stirring occasionally, until browned, 6 to 8 minutes.
- Pour tomatoes and water into the skillet with the chicken; bring to a boil. Stir in quinoa and cilantro. Cook until quinoa is tender and most of the liquid has evaporated, about 15 minutes; the dish should look thick and saucy. Spread an even layer of Cheddar cheese on top.
- Set an oven rack about 6 inches from the heat source and preheat the oven's broiler.
- Place skillet into oven and melt Cheddar cheese under the broiler until bubbly and golden, 2 to 3 minutes; be sure to watch carefully to prevent burning.

Nutrition Information

- Calories: 434 calories
- Total Fat: 8.8 g
- Cholesterol: 63 mg
- Sodium: 807 mg
- Total Carbohydrate: 45 g
- Protein: 43.4 g

147. Pad Thai Quinoa Bowl

"This recipe uses quinoa which is gluten-free, high in protein and fiber, and has a nice nutty flavor. But you can always substitute for either rice or noodles.
Take out the chicken and add extra edamame and you have a great vegetarian meal instead. Or add shrimp if you like.
A seriously good, versatile recipe!"

Serving: 8 | Prep: 30 m | Cook: 30 m | Ready in: 1 h

Ingredients

- 4 cups low-sodium chicken broth
- 2 cups quinoa, rinsed and drained
- 1 tablespoon coconut oil, divided
- 1 large boneless, skinless chicken breast, cut into thin strips
- 3/4 cup shredded cabbage
- 1/2 cup edamame
- 1/4 cup diced broccoli stems
- 2 carrots, cut into matchsticks
- 2 green onions, chopped
- 3 eggs
- 1 teaspoon sesame oil
- Thai peanut sauce:
- 1/4 cup natural peanut butter
- 1/4 cup reduced-sodium soy sauce
- 3 tablespoons rice vinegar
- 2 tablespoons chili garlic sauce
- 2 tablespoons chopped fresh ginger
- 3 cloves garlic, minced
- 1 teaspoon sesame oil
- 1/2 cup salted peanuts, chopped
- 3 tablespoons chopped fresh cilantro

Direction

- Bring chicken broth and quinoa to a boil in a saucepan. Reduce heat to medium-low, cover, and simmer until quinoa is tender, 15 to 20 minutes. Set aside.
- Heat 1 1/2 teaspoons coconut oil in a wok or large skillet over medium-high heat. Add chicken; stir until cooked through; about 5 minutes. Remove chicken from wok. Heat remaining 1 1/2 teaspoons coconut oil. Add cabbage, edamame, broccoli, carrot, and green onions and sauté until vegetables soften slightly, 2 to 3 minutes.
- Whisk eggs with sesame oil in a small bowl. Push vegetables to the sides of the wok to make a well in the center; pour eggs in and stir to scramble, about 3 minutes.
- Combine peanut butter, soy sauce, rice vinegar, chili garlic sauce, ginger, garlic, and sesame oil together in a small bowl. Pour Thai peanut sauce over vegetable and egg mixture in the wok.
- Return chicken to the wok and add quinoa; mix well to combine. Stir in chopped peanuts and cilantro and serve.

Nutrition Information

- Calories: 393 calories
- Total Fat: 17.9 g
- Cholesterol: 38 mg
- Sodium: 651 mg
- Total Carbohydrate: 37.3 g
- Protein: 23 g

148. Pantry Curried Quinoa with Garbanzo Beans and Roasted Peppers

"This salad is easy to put together if you have a well-stocked pantry. Eat as a side dish with dinner and the leftovers make a great lunch!"

Serving: 4 | Prep: 10 m | Cook: 25 m | Ready in: 45 m

Ingredients

- 1/2 cup raisins
- 1 cup warm water
- 1 tablespoon olive oil
- 1 small red onion, diced
- 1 clove garlic, minced
- 1 1/2 teaspoons curry powder
- 1/2 teaspoon ground cumin
- 1/2 teaspoon dried cilantro
- 1/4 teaspoon ground ginger
- 2 cups vegetable broth
- 1 (15 ounce) can garbanzo beans, drained
- 1 cup quinoa
- 1/2 cup diced roasted red peppers
- 1/4 cup toasted almonds
- salt to taste

Direction

- Soak raisins in 1 cup warm water in a bowl while you complete remaining steps.
- Heat olive oil in large saucepan over medium heat. Cook and stir onion and garlic until onion has softened and turned translucent, about 5 minutes. Stir in curry powder, cumin, cilantro, and ginger and cook until fragrant, about 30 seconds.
- Stir in vegetable broth, garbanzo beans, and quinoa. Bring to a boil, then reduce heat to medium-low heat, cover, and simmer until quinoa is tender, about 20 minutes.
- Drain raisins. Lightly toss quinoa mixture with raisins, roasted red peppers, and toasted almonds. Season with salt.

Nutrition Information

- Calories: 415 calories
- Total Fat: 11.8 g
- Cholesterol: 0 mg
- Sodium: 842 mg
- Total Carbohydrate: 67.1 g
- Protein: 12.9 g

149. Parsley Walnut Pesto Quinoa Salad

"A seriously amazing and fresh salad; the epitome of healthy and nutrition-packed. I served this over fresh baby kale with balsamic dressing on the side for those that want a more robust flavor. This is amazing with the addition of garlic! Serve cold or at room temperature."

Serving: 4 | Prep: 20 m | Cook: 20 m | Ready in: 1 h

Ingredients

- 1 cup water
- 1/2 cup quinoa
- 2 cups broccoli florets
- 1 cup fresh parsley
- 1/4 cup walnuts
- 2 tablespoons olive oil, or more as needed
- 1 cup diced tomato
- 1 cup diced baby cucumber
- 1/4 cup sliced leeks
- 1/4 cup crumbled blue cheese, or more to taste
- sea salt to taste

Direction

- Bring water and quinoa to a boil in a saucepan. Reduce heat to medium-low, cover, and simmer until quinoa is tender and water is absorbed, 15 to 20 minutes. Cool to room temperature.
- Place a steamer insert into a saucepan and fill with water to just below the bottom of the steamer. Bring water to a boil. Add broccoli, cover the saucepan, and steam until broccoli is tender, 2 to 4 minutes. Cool to room temperature.
- Puree parsley, walnuts, and olive oil together in a blender or food processor until sauce is smooth.
- Stir quinoa, broccoli, tomato, cucumber, and leeks together in a large bowl. Pour parsley sauce over quinoa mixture and toss to coat completely. Sprinkle blue cheese over the top and season with sea salt.

Nutrition Information

- Calories: 254 calories
- Total Fat: 15.8 g
- Cholesterol: 6 mg
- Sodium: 228 mg
- Total Carbohydrate: 22.6 g
- Protein: 8.4 g

150. Perfectly Crunchy Granola

"For those who love crunchy granola and want to know just what's in it! Be prepared to fall in love with this stuff! Serve it with fruit and yogurt or pour a little milk over it as your new favorite cereal. Store in an airtight container."

Serving: 40 | Prep: 15 m | Cook: 40 m | Ready in: 55 m

Ingredients

- 1 1/2 cups brown sugar
- 1/2 cup water
- 1/4 cup honey
- 1/4 cup coconut oil
- 1 tablespoon vanilla extract
- salt to taste
- 3 cups rolled oats
- 3 cups quick-cooking oats
- 2 cups chopped almonds
- 1 1/2 cups puffed quinoa
- 1/4 cup chia seeds
- 1/4 cup shredded coconut

Direction

- Preheat oven to 275 degrees F (135 degrees C). Line 2 baking sheets with parchment paper.
- Combine brown sugar, water, and honey in a large microwave-safe bowl. Microwave on high until sugar is completely dissolved, about 5 minutes. Stir in coconut oil, vanilla, and salt.
- Mix rolled oats, quick-cooking oats, almonds, puffed quinoa, chia seeds, and shredded coconut together in a large bowl. Pour in sugar mixture and mix thoroughly until granola is combined and starting to clump together.
- Spread granola mixture no more than 3/4-inch high on prepared baking sheets.
- Bake in the preheated oven until golden and crunchy, 35 to 45 minutes. Allow to cool completely.

Nutrition Information

- Calories: 140 calories
- Total Fat: 5.5 g
- Cholesterol: 0 mg
- Sodium: 8 mg
- Total Carbohydrate: 20.3 g
- Protein: 3.5 g

151. Pesto Quinoa

"I got this recipe from a friend who was living in Ecuador. Quinoa was a staple of her diet there; it is a great source of protein."

Serving: 4 | Prep: 5 m | Cook: 20 m | Ready in: 25 m

Ingredients

- 1 cup quinoa, rinsed and drained
- 2 cups chicken broth

- 2 tablespoons basil pesto
- 1 tomato, diced
- salt and pepper to taste

Direction

- Bring the quinoa and chicken broth to a boil in a saucepan; cover, reduce heat to low, and simmer until the moisture is completely absorbed, about 15 minutes. Remove from heat; stir the pesto through the quinoa. Fold the tomato into the mixture. Season with salt and pepper to serve.

Nutrition Information

- Calories: 198 calories
- Total Fat: 6.1 g
- Cholesterol: 2 mg
- Sodium: 70 mg
- Total Carbohydrate: 28.7 g
- Protein: 7.3 g

152. Pineapple Fried Quinoa

"Like pineapple fried rice, but with the ancient grain quinoa. Simple to make and bursting with Asian flavors! Always nice with fresh pineapple, but canned or frozen work well, too."

Serving: 4 | Prep: 15 m | Cook: 40 m | Ready in: 55 m

Ingredients

- 1 cup uncooked quinoa
- 2 cups chicken broth
- 1 cup water
- 3 eggs
- 1 tablespoon peanut oil
- 2 tablespoons chili oil
- 5 cloves garlic, pressed or minced
- 1 bunch green onions
- 3/4 cup diced pineapple
- 1 tablespoon chopped fresh cilantro
- 1/4 cup soy sauce
- 1/2 teaspoon red pepper flakes, or to taste

Direction

- Rinse quinoa until water runs clear. Bring the quinoa, chicken broth and water to a boil in a saucepan over high heat. Reduce heat to medium-low, cover, and simmer until the quinoa is tender, and the liquid has been absorbed, about 15 to 20 minutes.
- Beat the eggs in a bowl. Heat a skillet over medium heat. Cook and stir eggs until scrambled. Remove eggs from the skillet and set aside. Heat peanut oil and chili oil over medium-low heat. Cook and stir garlic for 2 minutes, then stir in green onions to heat through. Stir in pineapple and cilantro, then add the cooked quinoa. Toss with scrambled eggs, soy sauce, and red pepper flakes until thoroughly heated.

Nutrition Information

- Calories: 337 calories
- Total Fat: 15.4 g
- Cholesterol: 140 mg
- Sodium: 969 mg
- Total Carbohydrate: 38.4 g
- Protein: 13.2 g

153. Pomegranate Steak with Quinoa

"Strip steak is marinated in pomegranate juice, balsamic vinegar and herbs and served with quinoa and more pomegranates for garnish. This is one colorful dish."

Serving: 4 | Ready in: 50 m

Ingredients

- 2 (8 ounce) beef Strip Steaks, boneless, 3/4-inch thick
- 2 ounces goat cheese, crumbled
- Pomegranate seeds (optional)
- Marinade Sauce:
- 1 cup pomegranate juice
- 1/4 cup balsamic vinegar

- 2 tablespoons minced fresh rosemary
- 2 tablespoons minced fresh thyme
- 2 tablespoons olive oil
- 3 cloves garlic, minced
- 2 teaspoons Dijon-style mustard
- 1/2 teaspoon ground black pepper
- Quinoa:
- 1 cup uncooked quinoa
- 2 cups vegetable or beef broth
- 1 cup thinly sliced fresh baby spinach
- 1/2 cup pomegranate seeds or sweetened dried cranberries
- 1/4 cup chopped toasted walnuts (optional)

Direction

- Combine Marinade Sauce ingredients in medium bowl. Reserve 3/4 cup for basting sauce. Place beef steaks and remaining marinade in food-safe plastic bag; turn steaks to coat. Close bag securely and marinate in refrigerator 15 minutes to 2 hours.
- Meanwhile, prepare basting sauce. Pour reserved 3/4 cup marinade into small saucepan; bring to a boil. Reduce heat; cook 15 to 20 minutes or until reduced by half and slightly thickened, stirring occasionally. Set aside.
- Cook quinoa in broth in medium saucepan according to package directions. Stir in spinach, pomegranate seeds and walnuts. Keep warm.
- Remove steaks from marinade; discard marinade. Place steaks on grid over medium, ash-covered coals. Grill, covered, 7 to 10 minutes (over medium heat on preheated gas grill, times remain the same) for medium rare (145 degrees F) to medium (160 degrees F) doneness, turning occasionally and basting with sauce.
- Carve steaks into slices; season with salt, as desired. Place quinoa on serving platter; top with cheese. Arrange beef around quinoa. Garnish with pomegranate seeds, if desired.

Nutrition Information

- Calories: 626 calories
- Total Fat: 25.4 g
- Cholesterol: 60 mg
- Sodium: 420 mg
- Total Carbohydrate: 71.4 g
- Protein: 31.2 g

154. Pork Fried Quinoa

"These tiny quinoa seeds really are sponges for flavor.

I was really surprised how decadent and satisfying this seemed, and with only a tablespoon of vegetable oil and a handful of very lean smoked ham."

Serving: 4 | Prep: 15 m | Cook: 25 m | Ready in: 45 m

Ingredients

- 1 cup quinoa
- 1 1/2 cups cold water
- salt to taste
- 1 tablespoon vegetable oil
- 1 cup cubed fully cooked ham
- 1/2 cup diced red bell pepper
- 1/2 cup chopped green onion, white and green parts separated
- 3 cloves garlic, minced
- 1 tablespoon rice vinegar
- 1 tablespoon soy sauce, or to taste
- 1 teaspoon chile-garlic sauce (such as Sriracha®), or more to taste (optional)
- 1 teaspoon sesame seeds, or to taste (optional)

Direction

- Rinse quinoa in cold water for about 1 minute and drain well.
- Place in a saucepan and cover with 1 1/2 cup cold water and salt. Bring to a boil and reduce heat to low. Simmer, covered, until quinoa is tender, about 15 minutes. Remove from heat and let sit for 5 minutes.
- Fluff quinoa with a fork and set aside.
- Heat vegetable oil in a large skillet over medium heat. Cook and stir ham, red bell pepper, and the white parts of the green onion

until the ham begins to brown, about 5 minutes. Set chopped green onion tops aside. Add garlic, remove from heat, and stir until garlic becomes aromatic, 1 or 2 minutes.
- Stir in quinoa and return to stove over medium-low heat. Cook and stir until warmed through, 2 to 3 minutes. Remove from heat and add vinegar, soy sauce, chile-garlic sauce, and sesame seeds. Garnish with reserved green onion tops.

Nutrition Information

- Calories: 287 calories
- Total Fat: 12.6 g
- Cholesterol: 19 mg
- Sodium: 730 mg
- Total Carbohydrate: 30.3 g
- Protein: 12.8 g

155. Power Salad Bowl

"This hearty, power salad bowl is loaded with quinoa, beans, and egg for a vegetarian meal with great sources of protein."

Serving: 1 | Prep: 20 m | Ready in: 20 m

Ingredients

- 1 cup finely chopped kale
- 1/2 cup cooked quinoa
- 1/2 cup garbanzo beans
- 1/2 red bell pepper, chopped
- 1 carrot, grated
- 1 hard-boiled egg, chopped
- Dressing:
- 1/2 lemon, juiced
- 1 tablespoon olive oil
- 1 tablespoon chopped fresh parsley
- 1 teaspoon Dijon mustard
- 1/2 teaspoon maple syrup, or to taste
- salt and ground black pepper to taste

Direction

- Arrange kale, quinoa, garbanzo beans, red bell pepper, carrot, and egg in a bowl.
- Whisk lemon juice, olive oil, parsley, mustard, maple syrup, salt, and pepper together in a small bowl until dressing is well mixed. Pour dressing over salad.

Nutrition Information

- Calories: 554 calories
- Total Fat: 22.9 g
- Cholesterol: 212 mg
- Sodium: 785 mg
- Total Carbohydrate: 72.5 g
- Protein: 20.4 g

156. ProteinPacked Spicy Vegan Quinoa with Edamame

"I adapted this from a turkey burger recipe when I went vegan. It is also gluten-free if you use gluten-free soy sauce. I use it as a post-workout meal, as it is delicious, satisfying and relatively high in plant-based protein. Enjoy!"

Serving: 8 | Prep: 15 m | Cook: 30 m | Ready in: 45 m

Ingredients

- 3 1/2 cups water
- 2 cups quinoa, rinsed
- 4 teaspoons vegetable bouillon (such as Better Than Bouillon®)
- 2 1/2 cups frozen shelled edamame (green soybeans)
- 1 tablespoon olive oil
- 2 sweet onions, chopped
- 2 bell peppers, chopped
- 2 tablespoons minced fresh ginger
- 6 cloves garlic, minced
- 1/4 cup reduced-sodium soy sauce
- 2 tablespoons chopped fresh cilantro
- 1 tablespoon hot chile paste (such as sambal oelek), or to taste (optional)

Direction

- Bring water, quinoa, and vegetable bouillon to a boil in a large pot; stir in edamame, cover, and simmer until quinoa is tender, 15 to 20 minutes.
- Heat olive oil in a large skillet over medium heat; cook and stir onions and bell peppers until onions are translucent, about 5 minutes. Add ginger and garlic; cook and stir until fragrant, about 2 minutes. Remove from heat; stir in soy sauce, cilantro, and chile paste.
- Stir onion mixture into quinoa mixture; simmer, stirring occasionally, until excess broth has been absorbed, about 5 minutes.

Nutrition Information

- Calories: 323 calories
- Total Fat: 10.1 g
- Cholesterol: 0 mg
- Sodium: 305 mg
- Total Carbohydrate: 43.8 g
- Protein: 17.6 g

157. Pumpkin Quinoa Muffins

"Moist and delicious, I came up with this recipe for my young vegetarian daughter because it is high in protein, fiber, vitamins, and good fats. It has been a hit with everybody who's tried it. Makes a great breakfast, after-school snack, or addition to a kids lunch. These muffins will be moist in the middle."

Serving: 24 | Prep: 15 m | Cook: 35 m | Ready in: 1 h 5 m

Ingredients

- 1 1/4 cups quinoa
- 2 cups pumpkin puree
- 1 1/2 cups milk
- 1/2 cup water
- 1/2 cup whole wheat flour
- 1/2 cup flaxseed meal
- 1 egg
- 1/4 cup honey
- 1/4 cup coconut oil
- 2 tablespoons walnut oil
- 2 tablespoons chia seeds
- 2 teaspoons ground cinnamon
- 1 teaspoon baking powder
- 1 teaspoon ground ginger
- 1/2 teaspoon salt

Direction

- Preheat oven to 375 degrees F (190 degrees C). Line 24 muffin cups with paper muffin liners.
- Spread quinoa onto a baking sheet and toast in preheating oven until lightly browned, about 5 minutes.
- Pour toasted quinoa into a blender and pulse until the quinoa has the consistency of cornmeal.
- Stir ground quinoa, pumpkin puree, milk, water, whole wheat flour, flaxseed meal, egg, honey, coconut oil, walnut oil, chia seeds, cinnamon, baking powder, ground ginger, and salt together in a large mixing bowl until smooth. Rest mixture until chia seeds and flaxseed meal absorb some moisture and soften, about 15 minutes.
- Ladle batter into prepared muffin cups to about 3/4 full.
- Bake in the preheated oven until golden and the tops spring back when lightly pressed, 30 to 40 minutes.

Nutrition Information

- Calories: 116 calories
- Total Fat: 5.8 g
- Cholesterol: 9 mg
- Sodium: 129 mg
- Total Carbohydrate: 14 g
- Protein: 3.1 g

158. Puree of Green Things Soup with Quinoa and Pepper Relish

"I threw this together one night, using leftover green veggies from the fridge. Broccoli is the main flavor, complemented by a topping of quinoa and pan-grilled red pepper with lime juice. This can easily be made vegetarian by using vegetable broth instead of chicken broth."

Serving: 6 | Prep: 30 m | Cook: 30 m | Ready in: 1 h

Ingredients

- For the Soup:
- 2/3 cup quinoa
- 1 1/3 cups water
- 2 tablespoons extra virgin olive oil
- 1 yellow onion, diced
- 2 parsnips, peeled and cubed
- 3 stalks celery, chopped
- 2 pounds broccoli florets
- salt to taste
- 1/4 cup water
- 5 green onions, sliced
- 1/2 head romaine lettuce, washed and chopped
- 12 ounces baby spinach leaves
- 4 cloves garlic, minced
- 4 cups chicken broth
- For the Garnish:
- 2 red bell peppers, seeded and cut into quarters
- 2 shallots, halved lengthwise
- 2 teaspoons olive oil
- 1 lime, juiced
- ground black pepper

Direction

- Bring the quinoa and 1 1/3 cups water to a boil in a saucepan over high heat. Reduce heat to medium-low, cover, and simmer until the quinoa is tender, and the water has been absorbed, about 15 to 20 minutes.
- Meanwhile, heat 2 tablespoons of extra virgin olive oil in a large soup pot over medium heat. Stir in the onion, parsnips, and celery; cook and stir until the onion has softened and turned translucent, about 5 minutes. Stir in the broccoli, season with salt, and cook a few minutes until the broccoli darkens and begins to soften. Pour in 1/4 cup of water, and continue cooking until the broccoli is just cooked through. Once tender, stir in the green onions, lettuce, spinach, garlic, and chicken broth. Bring to a boil over high heat, then reduce heat to medium-low, and simmer until all of the vegetables are soft, about 15 minutes.
- While the soup is simmering, prepare the garnish by heating a cast iron grill pan over medium-high heat. Toss the bell peppers and shallot halves with 2 teaspoons of olive oil, and sprinkle with salt. Place into the hot grill pan, and cook until slightly blackened and tender, turning once. Remove from the pan, and chop. Stir the chopped pepper mixture together with the lime juice in a small bowl. Season to taste with black pepper, and set aside.
- Pour the soup into a blender, filling the pitcher no more than halfway full. Hold down the lid of the blender with a folded kitchen towel, and carefully start the blender, using a few quick pulses to get the soup moving before leaving it on to puree. Puree in batches until smooth and pour into a clean pot. Alternately, you can use a stick blender and puree the soup right in the cooking pot.
- To serve: ladle soup into bowl. Top with a small scoop of quinoa and the red pepper relish.

Nutrition Information

- Calories: 282 calories
- Total Fat: 8.5 g
- Cholesterol: 0 mg
- Sodium: 128 mg
- Total Carbohydrate: 45.7 g
- Protein: 11.3 g

159. Quick Coconut Curry Bowls

"This easy recipe makes a tasty dinner or a meal plan of 4 portions to refrigerate and reheat throughout the week. Other than the toppings, the prep requires no chopping."

Serving: 4 | Prep: 10 m | Cook: 20 m | Ready in: 30 m

Ingredients

- 1 cup uncooked quinoa
- 1 (15 ounce) can garbanzo beans, rinsed and drained
- 1 (14 ounce) can light coconut milk
- 1/4 cup water
- 2 tablespoons Thai red curry paste, or more to taste
- 1 (14.5 ounce) can Del Monte® Cut Green Beans or Sweet Peas, well drained
- 1 (14.5 ounce) can Del Monte® Sliced Carrots, well drained
- Lime wedges
- Topping Options:
- Cilantro or basil
- Chopped peanuts
- Chopped green onions
- Sriracha chile sauce

Direction

- Rinse quinoa and combine with garbanzo beans, coconut milk, water and curry paste in a medium saucepan; stir well. Bring to a boil over high heat. Reduce heat to low; cover and simmer 20 minutes.
- Uncover and top quinoa with green beans and carrots (do not stir). Cover and let stand 5 to 10 minutes until most of liquid is absorbed.
- Stir gently and serve with lime juice and choice of toppings. Or, portion evenly into 4 microwaveable storage containers and refrigerate. Reheat in microwave, loosely covered, about 2 minutes or until hot. Top as desired.

Nutrition Information

- Calories: 391 calories
- Total Fat: 16.8 g
- Cholesterol: 0 mg
- Sodium: 1113 mg
- Total Carbohydrate: 57 g
- Protein: 14.1 g

160. Quinoa Almond Pilaf

"High-protein side dish with plenty of flavor and crunch. Rinsing the quinoa three times will help to eliminate any bitterness."

Serving: 3 | Prep: 20 m | Cook: 25 m | Ready in: 45 m

Ingredients

- 1/2 cup quinoa, rinsed and drained
- 1 cup cold water
- 1/4 teaspoon salt
- 3 tablespoons olive oil
- 1 celery rib, chopped
- 1 small onion, chopped
- 1 carrot, chopped
- 1 clove garlic, minced
- 8 almonds, coarsely chopped
- 1 small tomato, seeded and chopped
- 2 tablespoons raisins
- 1/8 teaspoon salt
- 1/8 teaspoon ground black pepper
- 1/8 teaspoon dried thyme
- 1/8 teaspoon dried oregano
- 1 pinch coarse sea salt

Direction

- Combine quinoa, cold water, and salt in a saucepan; bring to a boil, reduce heat to medium-low, place a cover on the saucepan, and cook until the liquid is fully absorbed, about 15 minutes.
- Heat olive oil in a skillet over medium heat. Cook and stir celery, onion, carrot, and garlic in the hot oil until the onion is translucent, 5 to 7 minutes. Stir almonds, tomato, raisins, salt, pepper, thyme, and oregano into the vegetable mixture; cook and stir 1 minute more.

- Fluff the quinoa with a fork and stir into the mixture in the skillet; cook and stir until evenly mixed and hot, about 30 seconds.
- Divide between 3 plates; sprinkle the top of each portion with a scattering of a few coarse sea salt granules for a surprising crunch of salty goodness.

Nutrition Information

- Calories: 303 calories
- Total Fat: 17.1 g
- Cholesterol: 0 mg
- Sodium: 506 mg
- Total Carbohydrate: 33 g
- Protein: 6.2 g

161. Quinoa and Black Bean Chili

"Vegetarian chili with quinoa. Sprinkle cheese on top to serve."

Serving: 10 | Prep: 30 m | Cook: 30 m | Ready in: 1 h

Ingredients

- 1 cup uncooked quinoa, rinsed
- 2 cups water
- 1 tablespoon vegetable oil
- 1 onion, chopped
- 4 cloves garlic, chopped
- 1 tablespoon chili powder
- 1 tablespoon ground cumin
- 1 (28 ounce) can crushed tomatoes
- 2 (19 ounce) cans black beans, rinsed and drained
- 1 green bell pepper, chopped
- 1 red bell pepper, chopped
- 1 zucchini, chopped
- 1 jalapeno pepper, seeded and minced
- 1 tablespoon minced chipotle peppers in adobo sauce
- 1 teaspoon dried oregano
- salt and ground black pepper to taste
- 1 cup frozen corn
- 1/4 cup chopped fresh cilantro

Direction

- Bring the quinoa and water to a boil in a saucepan over high heat. Reduce heat to medium-low, cover, and simmer until the quinoa is tender, and the water has been absorbed, about 15 to 20 minutes; set aside.
- Meanwhile, heat the vegetable oil in a large pot over medium heat. Stir in the onion, and cook until the onion softens and turns translucent, about 5 minutes. Add the garlic, chili powder, and cumin; cook and stir 1 minute to release the flavors. Stir in the tomatoes, black beans, green bell pepper, red bell pepper, zucchini, jalapeno pepper, chipotle pepper, and oregano. Season to taste with salt and pepper. Bring to a simmer over high heat, then reduce heat to medium-low, cover, and simmer 20 minutes.
- After 20 minutes, stir in the reserved quinoa and corn. Cook to reheat the corn for 5 minutes. Remove from the heat, and stir in the cilantro to serve.

Nutrition Information

- Calories: 233 calories
- Total Fat: 3.5 g
- Cholesterol: 0 mg
- Sodium: 540 mg
- Total Carbohydrate: 42 g
- Protein: 11.5 g

162. Quinoa and Black Bean Chili from GOYA

"Enjoy a healthful, vegetarian meal packed with protein and flavor! In this hearty recipe, GOYA® Low Sodium Black Beans are cooked with onions, a medley of spices, rich tomato sauce, bell peppers and a hint of smoky chipotle. Once ready, the chili is mixed with GOYA® Organic Quinoa and corn, and garnished with fresh cilantro sprigs for an extra touch of flavor. This chili is good, and good for you, too!"

Serving: 6 | Prep: 20 m | Ready in: 40 m

Ingredients

- 1 cup GOYA® Organic Quinoa
- 1 tablespoon GOYA® Extra Virgin Olive Oil
- 1 large onion, chopped
- 1 tablespoon GOYA® Minced Garlic
- 1 tablespoon chili powder
- 1 tablespoon GOYA® Ground Cumin
- 1 teaspoon GOYA® Oregano Leaves
- 1 (8 ounce) can GOYA® Tomato Sauce
- 2 (15.5 ounce) cans GOYA® Low Sodium Black Beans, drained and rinsed
- 1/2 large green bell pepper, seeded and diced
- 1/2 large red bell pepper, seeded and diced
- 1 tablespoon GOYA® Chipotle Peppers, in Adobo Sauce, finely chopped
- 1 (15.5 ounce) can GOYA® Corn Kernels, drained and rinsed
- Fresh cilantro

Direction

- In a medium pot, bring quinoa, 1 1/2 cups water and 1/2 of olive oil to a boil. Reduce heat, cover and let simmer for 20 minutes, until water is absorbed and quinoa is tender. Set aside.
- Meanwhile, in a large pot, heat remaining olive oil on medium-high heat. Add onion and garlic, and cook until translucent, about 5 minutes. Add chili powder, cumin and oregano, and stir for about 1 minute. Stir in tomato sauce, black beans, green and red peppers, chipotle peppers and 1 cup water. Bring to a boil; then reduce heat, cover and simmer for 20 minutes.
- After 20 minutes, stir in reserved quinoa and corn. Cook for another 5 minutes. Serve and top with fresh cilantro sprigs.

Nutrition Information

- Calories: 126 calories
- Total Fat: 2 g
- Cholesterol: 0 mg
- Sodium: 17 mg
- Total Carbohydrate: 22.7 g
- Protein: 4.7 g

163. Quinoa and Black Bean Salad

"Scoop this salad onto a bed of fresh spinach."

Serving: 4 | Prep: 25 m | Ready in: 25 m

Ingredients

- 2 cups cooked quinoa
- 1 1/2 cups cooked black beans
- 2 stalks celery, diced
- 1/4 cup chopped red onion
- 2 tablespoons chopped preserved lemon
- 2 tablespoons extra-virgin olive oil
- 1/2 orange, zested and juiced
- 1 teaspoon apple cider vinegar
- 1/2 teaspoon agave nectar
- 1/2 teaspoon salt
- 1 pinch ground black pepper
- 1 pinch ground coriander

Direction

- Mix quinoa, black beans, celery, onion, and preserved lemon together in a large bowl.
- Mix olive oil, 2 tablespoons orange juice, zest, apple cider vinegar, agave, salt, pepper, and coriander together in a small bowl. Pour over quinoa mixture. Toss gently to coat.

Nutrition Information

- Calories: 277 calories
- Total Fat: 8.9 g

- Cholesterol: 0 mg
- Sodium: 1065 mg
- Total Carbohydrate: 39.8 g
- Protein: 10 g

164. Quinoa and Black Beans

"Very flavorful alternative to black beans and rice. Quinoa is a nutty grain from South America."

Serving: 10 | Prep: 15 m | Cook: 35 m | Ready in: 50 m

Ingredients

- 1 teaspoon vegetable oil
- 1 onion, chopped
- 3 cloves garlic, chopped
- 3/4 cup quinoa
- 1 1/2 cups vegetable broth
- 1 teaspoon ground cumin
- 1/4 teaspoon cayenne pepper
- salt and ground black pepper to taste
- 1 cup frozen corn kernels
- 2 (15 ounce) cans black beans, rinsed and drained
- 1/2 cup chopped fresh cilantro

Direction

- Heat oil in a saucepan over medium heat; cook and stir onion and garlic until lightly browned, about 10 minutes.
- Mix quinoa into onion mixture and cover with vegetable broth; season with cumin, cayenne pepper, salt, and pepper. Bring the mixture to a boil. Cover, reduce heat, and simmer until quinoa is tender and broth is absorbed, about 20 minutes.
- Stir frozen corn into the saucepan, and continue to simmer until heated through, about 5 minutes; mix in the black beans and cilantro.

Nutrition Information

- Calories: 153 calories
- Total Fat: 1.7 g

- Cholesterol: 0 mg
- Sodium: 517 mg
- Total Carbohydrate: 27.8 g
- Protein: 7.7 g

165. Quinoa and Broccoli Brunch Cups

"Eggs and cream mixed with broccoli florets, cooked quinoa, and Cheddar cheese and baked in muffins cups make a perfect brunch offering."

Serving: 6 | Prep: 15 m | Cook: 20 m | Ready in: 35 m

Ingredients

- 1 tablespoon butter, softened
- 4 large eggs
- 3 tablespoons heavy cream
- 1 cup cooked truRoots® Accents® Organic Sprouted Quinoa Trio
- 3/4 cup shredded sharp Cheddar cheese
- 1/2 cup chopped fresh broccoli florets
- 2 tablespoons minced green onion
- 1/2 teaspoon garlic salt

Direction

- Heat oven to 375 degrees F. Coat 6 muffin cups generously with butter.
- Beat eggs and cream in medium bowl. Stir in quinoa, cheese, broccoli, onion and garlic salt. Divide mixture evenly into prepared muffin cups.
- Bake 19 to 21 minutes or until golden brown. Let stand 5 minutes before removing from pan.

Nutrition Information

- Calories: 263 calories
- Total Fat: 15.7 g
- Cholesterol: 157 mg
- Sodium: 331 mg
- Total Carbohydrate: 19.4 g
- Protein: 12.2 g

- Protein: 2.3 g

166. Quinoa and Dill Flatbread

"A great way to use quinoa! It can be used as a crust or flatbread, made into a main dish, side dish, or appetizer! This is one that works well and can be easily changed with the herbs you have on hand or in your garden. We are starting clean-eating this week and tweaked some recipes. This can also be used as a pizza crust, topped with hummus, bruschetta, pesto, or even egg/tofu salad. It's great for any gluten-free, dairy-free, vegan, or vegetarian diet."

Serving: 16 | Prep: 10 m | Cook: 20 m | Ready in: 30 m

Ingredients

- cooking spray
- 1 1/2 cups quinoa
- 2 cups water, or more as needed
- 1/4 cup olive oil
- 2 tablespoons chopped fresh dill
- 1 tablespoon chopped fresh rosemary
- 1/2 teaspoon salt
- 1 pinch ground black pepper

Direction

- Preheat oven to 350 degrees F (175 degrees C). Lightly grease two 9-inch round pans with cooking spray.
- Pulse quinoa in a food processor until ground into flour, 3 to 5 minutes.
- Combine quinoa flour, water, olive oil, dill, rosemary, salt, and pepper in a bowl. Whisk, adding more water if needed, until combined. Divide dough evenly between the prepared cake pans.
- Bake in the preheated oven until tops are golden, about 20 minutes. Cut into wedges.

Nutrition Information

- Calories: 89 calories
- Total Fat: 4.4 g
- Cholesterol: 0 mg
- Sodium: 75 mg
- Total Carbohydrate: 10.3 g

167. Quinoa and GrilledPepper Salad

Quinoa, an ancient grain eaten by the Incas, is naturally coated with a bitter-tasting substance called saponin. But once the residue is rinsed away, you have a versatile, nutty-tasting grain that makes a fine alternative to rice and barley.
For convenience, grill the bell peppers in this dish at the same time as the vegetables and beef for the main-course kebabs.

| Prep: 15 m | Cook: 35 m

Ingredients

- 1 1/4 cups quinoa
- 3 yellow and/or orange bell peppers, quartered
- 2 teaspoons extra-virgin olive oil
- 1 teaspoon fresh lime juice
- 1 teaspoon soy sauce
- 1/2 teaspoon ground cumin
- 1/4 cup chopped fresh cilantro
- 3 scallions, chopped

Direction

- Prepare grill for cooking.
- Wash quinoa in at least 5 changes of water, rubbing grains and letting them settle before pouring off water, until water runs clear. Drain in a large sieve. Add quinoa to a saucepan of boiling salted water and cook 10 minutes. Drain in sieve and rinse under cold water.
- Set sieve over a saucepan with 1 1/2 inches boiling water (sieve should not touch water) and steam quinoa, covered with a kitchen towel and lid, until fluffy and dry, about 10 minutes. (Check water level in pan occasionally, adding water if necessary.) Spread quinoa on a baking sheet to cool.

- While quinoa is cooking, grill bell peppers on a well-oiled rack set 5 to 6 inches over glowing coals until slightly softened, about 4 minutes on each side Cut bell peppers crosswise into thin strips.
- Whisk together oil, lime juice, soy sauce, and cumin in a large bowl and stir in quinoa, bell peppers, cilantro, scallions, and salt and pepper to taste.
- Cooks' Note: You can make quinoa salad 1 day ahead and chill, covered. Bring to room temperature before serving.
- If you prefer, grill bell peppers in a hot well-seasoned ridged grill pan over moderate heat. Each serving about 166 calories and 4 grams fat
- Nutritional analysis provided by Gourmet

168. Quinoa and Honey Mustard Chicken Slow Cooker Meal

"This goes into the cooker quickly, with no precooking and chicken straight from the freezer. I like to put it in before we leave for church so I can come home to a nice meal. Serve with a green salad and some steamed veggies."

Serving: 4 | Prep: 10 m | Cook: 3 h | Ready in: 3 h 15 m

Ingredients

- 1 cup quinoa
- hot water to cover
- 3 tablespoons nutritional yeast flakes
- 1 tablespoon chopped chives
- 1 1/2 teaspoons sea salt, or to taste
- 1 teaspoon onion powder
- 1/4 teaspoon dill weed
- 1/8 teaspoon ground turmeric
- 1 3/4 cups water
- 1 tablespoon butter
- 1 teaspoon red wine vinegar
- 3 tablespoons spicy brown mustard
- 1 tablespoon honey
- 4 frozen skinless, boneless chicken breast halves

Direction

- Soak quinoa in a bowl with enough hot water to cover for 5 minutes; drain.
- Mix yeast flakes, chives, sea salt, onion powder, dill, and turmeric together in a bowl. Stir drained quinoa, yeast flake mixture, 1 3/4 cup water, butter, and vinegar together in a slow cooker.
- Place chicken breasts on top of quinoa mixture; season lightly with salt. Combine mustard and honey in a bowl; spoon over chicken breasts.
- Cook on High for 3 hours.

Nutrition Information

- Calories: 344 calories
- Total Fat: 8.7 g
- Cholesterol: 66 mg
- Sodium: 884 mg
- Total Carbohydrate: 34.7 g
- Protein: 31.8 g

169. Quinoa and Lentil Salad

"A salad made with a superfood! It's light, fresh, and packed with flavor. Not to mention, it's easy to make. You can sub honey for the agave nectar."

Serving: 4 | Prep: 20 m | Cook: 20 m | Ready in: 40 m

Ingredients

- 1 1/2 cups quinoa
- 3 cups water
- 1/2 cup dry lentils
- 2 cups water
- 2 tablespoons rice vinegar
- 2 tablespoons olive oil
- 1 teaspoon lemon juice
- 1 teaspoon agave nectar
- sea salt and ground black pepper to taste
- 1 small carrot, chopped
- 1/2 cucumber, chopped
- 2 green onions, chopped

- 1/2 yellow bell pepper, chopped

Direction

- Bring the quinoa and 6 cups water to a boil in a large pot. Reduce heat to medium-low, cover, and simmer until the quinoa is tender and the water has been absorbed, 15 to 20 minutes. Run under cold water to cool; drain. Pour into a large bowl.
- Meanwhile, bring the lentils and 2 cups water to a boil in a separate saucepan. Reduce heat to medium-low, cover, and simmer until the lentils are tender, 15 to 20 minutes. Run under cold water to cool; drain any excess moisture.
- Whisk the rice vinegar, olive oil, lemon juice, and agave nectar together in a bowl until well incorporated. Season with sea salt and black pepper. Pour the dressing over the quinoa and stir to coat evenly. Add the lentils, carrot, cucumber, green onions, and yellow bell pepper; stir until evenly mixed. Serve immediately.

Nutrition Information

- Calories: 379 calories
- Total Fat: 10.8 g
- Cholesterol: 0 mg
- Sodium: 114 mg
- Total Carbohydrate: 57.3 g
- Protein: 14.4 g

170. Quinoa and Pepper Pilaf

"Protein-packed quinoa is toasted, then cooked until tender with sweet peppers and garlic for a hearty side dish. You can serve this wholesome grain dish hot, at room temperature or even chilled--perfect for any season!"

Serving: 4 | Prep: 20 m | Ready in: 50 m

Ingredients

- 1 tablespoon olive oil
- 1 shallot, minced
- 2 cloves garlic, minced
- 1 medium red bell pepper, diced
- 1 medium yellow bell pepper, diced
- 1 cup uncooked quinoa, rinsed
- 2 cups Swanson® Certified Organic Vegetable Broth or Swanson® Vegetable Broth
- 2 tablespoons chopped fresh parsley

Direction

- Heat the oil in a 2-quart saucepan over medium-high heat. Add the shallot and garlic and cook for 2 minutes, stirring occasionally. Add the peppers and quinoa and cook for 2 minutes, stirring occasionally.
- Stir in the broth and heat to a boil. Reduce the heat to low. Cover and cook for 20 minutes or until the quinoa is tender and the liquid is absorbed. Stir in the parsley. Season, if desired.

Nutrition Information

- Calories: 223 calories
- Total Fat: 6.1 g
- Cholesterol: 0 mg
- Sodium: 272 mg
- Total Carbohydrate: 35.2 g
- Protein: 7.1 g

171. Quinoa and Red Lentil Burgers

Quinoa and red lentils cook in the same amount of time, right in the same saucepan, making these burgers super convenient.

Serving: Makes 8 burgers

Ingredients

- 1 cup uncooked quinoa, rinsed in a fine sieve
- 1/2 cup dried red lentils
- 1 tablespoon salt-free all-purpose seasoning blend
- 1/4 cup quick-cooking oats or quinoa flakes
- 3 scallions, white and green parts, thinly sliced
- 2 teaspoons good-quality curry powder
- 1 teaspoon ground cumin

- 1 teaspoon sweet or smoked paprika
- 1/4 to 1/2 cup minced fresh cilantro or parsley
- Crushed red pepper flakes or sriracha to taste
- Salt and freshly ground pepper to taste
- 1 tablespoon extra-virgin olive oil (optional)
- Whole-grain buns, pitas, or English muffins (optional)

Direction

- Preheat the oven to 425°F.
- Combine the quinoa, lentils, seasoning blend, and oats in a medium saucepan with 3 1/2 cups water. Bring to a rapid simmer; then add the scallions, curry powder, cumin, and paprika as the water is heating up.
- Simmer gently until the water is absorbed and the quinoa and lentils are done, about 15 minutes. Stir in the cilantro, then season with red pepper flakes, salt, and pepper. Stir in the olive oil if desired for a little added richness.
- Line a baking sheet with parchment paper. Coat the inside of a round 1/2-cup measuring cup (like the one in the photo on the facing page) with a little olive oil. Grab a level scoop of the quinoa mixture; invert it onto the parchment, and give the bottom a sharp tap to release it. Using the bottom of the measuring cup, flatten the quinoa mixture into a 1/2-inch-thick patty. Repeat with the remaining quinoa mixture; you should wind up with 8 patties.
- If you don't have a round 1/2-cup measuring cup, you can improvise by using any sort of 1/2-cup measure and shaping the mounds into burgers once they're on the parchment paper.
- Bake for 15 minutes, then carefully flip each burger and bake an additional 15 minutes, or until golden and firm on each side. Remove from the oven and serve the burgers on their own or with the bread of your choice.
- Serving Suggestions: These burgers are tasty enough to stand on their own, but consider any two or three of the following embellishments—whether or not you're serving them on bread:
- Lettuce leaves, baby spinach or arugula, or baby kale (raw or barely wilted)
- Roasted red peppers
- Sliced tomatoes
- Sliced red onions
- Green sprouts
- Peeled and sliced avocado
- Tartar sauce, or ketchup and mustard Per Burger: Calories: 130; Total fat: 1g; Protein: 6g; Carbohydrates: 24g; Fiber: 3g; Sodium: 20mg

172. Quinoa and Spinach Pilaf

"Great with any meat."

Serving: 4 | Prep: 10 m | Cook: 25 m | Ready in: 35 m

Ingredients

- 1 tablespoon unsalted butter
- 1 small yellow onion, finely chopped
- 1 clove garlic, minced
- 1 cup quinoa
- 1 1/4 cups water
- 5 (5 ounce) packages baby spinach
- 1 tablespoon grated lemon zest
- salt and ground black pepper to taste

Direction

- Melt butter in a large saucepan over medium heat; cook and stir onion and garlic until onion is softened, about 4 minutes. Add quinoa to onion mixture; cook and stir for about 1 minute more.
- Pour water over quinoa mixture; bring to a boil. Reduce heat to medium, cover saucepan, and simmer until quinoa is tender and water is absorbed, about 20 minutes.
- Stir spinach and lemon zest into quinoa mixture; season with salt and pepper.

Nutrition Information

- Calories: 231 calories
- Total Fat: 6.2 g

- Cholesterol: 8 mg
- Sodium: 146 mg
- Total Carbohydrate: 35.8 g
- Protein: 11.4 g

173. Quinoa and SteelCut Oats Crunchy Granola

"The best of healthy fats and carbs. Eat it plain or sprinkled in your yogurt. Once you start you can't stop!"

Serving: 16 | Prep: 10 m | Cook: 30 m | Ready in: 1 h 10 m

Ingredients

- 1/2 cup quinoa
- 1/2 cup steel-cut oats
- 1/2 cup slivered almonds
- 1/2 cup sweetened dried cranberries (such as Craisins®) (optional)
- 1/2 cup raw sunflower seeds
- 1/2 cup raw pumpkin seeds
- 1/2 cup unsweetened coconut flakes
- 1/4 cup chia seeds
- 1/4 cup flax seeds
- 2 tablespoons unsweetened cocoa powder (optional)
- 1 tablespoon ground cinnamon, or more to taste (optional)
- 1/3 cup honey (optional)
- 1/4 cup coconut oil
- 2 tablespoons vanilla extract
- 2 packets stevia powder

Direction

- Preheat oven to 300 degrees F (150 degrees C). Line a baking sheet with parchment paper.
- Mix quinoa, steel-cut oats, almonds, cranberries, sunflower seeds, pumpkin seeds, coconut flakes, chia seeds, flax seeds, cocoa powder, and cinnamon together in a large bowl.
- Combine honey, coconut oil, vanilla extract, and stevia in a microwave-safe bowl. Heat in the microwave until melted together, 30 seconds to 1 minute.
- Pour honey mixture over the quinoa mixture; mix well to combine. Spread in an even layer on the baking sheet.
- Bake in the preheated oven until golden brown, about 30 minutes. Let cool completely before breaking into pieces, about 30 minutes.

Nutrition Information

- Calories: 206 calories
- Total Fat: 12 g
- Cholesterol: 0 mg
- Sodium: 4 mg
- Total Carbohydrate: 21.6 g
- Protein: 4.5 g

174. Quinoa and Sweet Potato Bakes

Make these gluten-free quinoa and sweet potato "muffins" ahead for a quick breakfast or energizing mid-day snack.

Serving: Makes 6

Ingredients

- 2 sweet potatoes (kumara) (800 grams), peeled and chopped into 3/4-inch cubes
- 2 tablespoons extra virgin olive oil, plus extra for drizzling
- 1 teaspoon sea salt flakes
- 2 cups (340 grams) cooked quinoa, preferabbly black, plus extra for sprinkling
- 2 tablespoons linseeds (flaxseeds)
- 2 tablespoons store-bought caramelized onion
- 1 3/4 cups (420 grams) fresh ricotta
- 1 1/2 cups (120 grams) finely grated Parmesan
- 2 tablespoons thyme leaves
- 2 eggs
- Cracked black pepper
- 150 grams goat cheese, sliced
- 6 sprigs thyme, extra

Direction

- Preheat oven to 400°F (200°C). Lightly grease 6 [3/4-cup-capacity (180ml)] Texas muffin tins, line with non-stick baking paper and set aside. Place the sweet potato, oil, and salt on a baking tray lined with baking paper and toss to combine. Roast for 20 to 25 minutes or until golden brown. Allow to cool slightly and transfer to a large bowl. Add the quinoa, linseeds, onion, ricotta, Parmesan, thyme, eggs and pepper and mix until just combined. Spoon into the prepared tins and top with the goat's cheese and extra thyme. Sprinkle with the extra quinoa, drizzle with extra oil and bake for 30 to 35 minutes or until golden. Serve warm.
- Cooks' Note: Black or red varieties of quinoa are available in supermarkets and greengrocers. Mostly selected for their color, they can vary slightly from regular white quinoa in texture when cooked, but all three are essentially interchangeable. 1 cup cooked black or red quinoa is 170g.

Nutrition Information

- Calories: 459
- Total Fat: 28 g (43%)
- Saturated Fat: 14 g (71%)
- Cholesterol: 114 mg (38%)
- Sodium: 574 mg (24%)
- Total Carbohydrate: 27 g (9%)
- Protein: 26 g (51%)
- Fiber: 5 g (19%)

175. Quinoa and Turkey Stuffed Tomatoes

"A quick dinner that's super healthy!"

Serving: 4 | Prep: 10 m | Cook: 30 m | Ready in: 40 m

Ingredients

- 4 large tomatoes
- 1 tablespoon olive oil
- 2 zucchini, chopped
- 1/2 cup chopped green bell pepper
- 2 cloves garlic, minced
- 1 teaspoon salt
- 1 pound ground turkey
- 2 cups cooked quinoa
- 1 (8 ounce) can tomato sauce, divided

Direction

- Preheat oven to 350 degrees F (175 degrees C).
- Cut the tops off each tomato and scoop out a small amount of the insides. Discard tops and insides.
- Heat olive oil in a skillet over medium heat; cook and stir zucchini, green bell pepper, garlic, and salt until tender, about 10 minutes. Add ground turkey; cook and stir until turkey is browned and crumbly, 5 to 7 minutes. Stir quinoa and 1/2 of the tomato sauce into the ground turkey mixture.
- Arrange tomatoes in a baking dish. Fill each tomato with turkey-quinoa mixture. Pour remaining tomato sauce over each stuffed tomato. Pour a 1/2 inch of water into the bottom of the baking dish.
- Bake in the preheated oven until tomatoes are tender, about 15 minutes.

Nutrition Information

- Calories: 369 calories
- Total Fat: 14.3 g
- Cholesterol: 84 mg
- Sodium: 961 mg
- Total Carbohydrate: 32.9 g
- Protein: 29.8 g

176. Quinoa Asparagus and Feta Salad

"A perfect spring, summer, or anytime salad. Loaded with protein and fiber, but so delicious you would never guess how healthy it is! If you are making the salad ahead of time, add the dressing just before serving to keep the asparagus an attractive bright green. Leftovers keep well for a couple of days."

Serving: 6 | Prep: 15 m | Cook: 15 m | Ready in: 35 m

Ingredients

- Salad:
- 1 1/2 cups water
- 3/4 cup quinoa
- 1/4 teaspoon salt
- 1 bunch fresh asparagus, trimmed and cut into 1 1/2-inch pieces
- 4 ounces crumbled feta cheese
- 1/3 cup toasted slivered almonds
- 2 green onions, thinly sliced, or to taste
- 2 tablespoons chopped fresh parsley
- 1 teaspoon chopped fresh thyme
- 1 lemon, zested
- Dressing:
- 1/4 cup lemon juice
- 2 tablespoons olive oil
- 1 tablespoon honey
- 1 clove garlic, minced
- 1 1/2 teaspoons Dijon mustard
- freshly ground black pepper to taste

Direction

- Pour water into a saucepan and bring to a boil; add quinoa and salt, stir, cover saucepan with a lid, and reduce heat to low. Simmer mixture until quinoa is tender, 10 to 15 minutes. Remove saucepan from heat, let quinoa rest for 5 minutes, and transfer quinoa to a bowl to cool.
- Bring a large pot of lightly salted water to a boil. Add asparagus and cook uncovered until tender but still crisp, 2 to 3 minutes; drain in a colander and immediately immerse asparagus in ice water for several minutes until cold to stop the cooking process. Drain.
- Stir asparagus, feta cheese, almonds, green onions, parsley, thyme, and lemon zest into quinoa.
- Whisk lemon juice, olive oil, honey, garlic, Dijon mustard, and black pepper together in a bowl until dressing is smooth. Pour dressing over quinoa mixture and stir gently to combine.

Nutrition Information

- Calories: 238 calories
- Total Fat: 13 g
- Cholesterol: 17 mg
- Sodium: 346 mg
- Total Carbohydrate: 23.4 g
- Protein: 8.9 g

177. Quinoa Bean and Ground Turkey Chili

"Ground turkey chili with quinoa is great for chili dogs, nachos, or just in a bowl."

Serving: 8 | Prep: 15 m | Cook: 51 m | Ready in: 1 h 6 m

Ingredients

- 1 tablespoon ghee
- 1 pound ground turkey
- 1 large onion, chopped
- 5 cloves garlic, minced
- 1/4 teaspoon ground black pepper
- 1 (15 ounce) can diced tomatoes
- 1 (6 ounce) can tomato paste
- 2 stalks celery, chopped
- 2 tablespoons chili powder, or more to taste
- 1 tablespoon Worcestershire sauce
- 1 tablespoon ground cumin
- 1 teaspoon dried oregano
- 1/8 teaspoon garlic powder
- 1/8 teaspoon onion powder
- Himalayan pink salt to taste
- 4 cups vegetable broth

- 1 (15 ounce) can black beans, drained and rinsed
- 1 (15 ounce) can kidney beans, drained and rinsed
- 1 cup tri-colored quinoa

Direction

- Heat ghee in a Dutch oven over medium heat. Add turkey, onion, garlic, and black pepper. Cook and stir until turkey is browned, about 6 minutes. Drain and discard fat.
- Stir tomatoes, tomato paste, celery, chili powder, Worcestershire sauce, cumin, oregano, garlic powder, onion powder, and salt into the turkey mixture. Add broth, black beans, and kidney beans; stir to combine. Add quinoa; bring to a boil. Reduce heat to low and simmer until quinoa is tender, about 40 minutes.

Nutrition Information

- Calories: 335 calories
- Total Fat: 8.4 g
- Cholesterol: 46 mg
- Sodium: 889 mg
- Total Carbohydrate: 43.5 g
- Protein: 22.9 g

178. Quinoa Beet and Arugula Salad

"Quinoa has a light, fluffy texture when cooked, and can be used as an alternative to white rice or couscous in most dishes. The arugula has a rich peppery taste, and has an exceptionally strong flavor for a leafy green which goes well with the slightly nutty flavor of the quinoa."

Serving: 6 | Prep: 15 m | Cook: 20 m | Ready in: 1 h 35 m

Ingredients

- 1/2 pound beets, peeled and sliced
- 1 cup red quinoa
- 2 cups water
- 1/2 cup olive oil
- 1/2 cup red wine vinegar
- 1 1/2 teaspoons white sugar
- 1 clove garlic, crushed
- 1 teaspoon salt
- 1/4 teaspoon ground black pepper
- 2 green onions, sliced
- 3 ounces arugula, chopped
- 5 ounces goat cheese, crumbled

Direction

- Place a steamer insert into a saucepan, and fill with water to just below the bottom of the steamer. Cover pan and bring the water to a boil. Add beets, cover pan, and steam until just tender, 7 to 10 minutes. Set aside.
- Bring quinoa and 2 cups water a saucepan over high heat. Reduce the heat to medium-low, cover, and simmer until the quinoa is tender and the liquid has been absorbed, about 15 minutes.
- While the quinoa is cooking, whisk olive oil, red wine vinegar, sugar, garlic, salt, and black pepper together in a large bowl.
- Remove quinoa from heat, then immediately add half of the vinegar dressing while fluffing the quinoa with a fork; reserve remaining dressing. Cover and refrigerate quinoa until cool, at least 1 hour.
- Stir green onions, arugula, goat cheese, beets, and remaining dressing into cooled quinoa mixture. Toss lightly before serving.

Nutrition Information

- Calories: 379 calories
- Total Fat: 26.9 g
- Cholesterol: 19 mg
- Sodium: 552 mg
- Total Carbohydrate: 25.6 g
- Protein: 9.9 g

179. Quinoa Biryani

"A delicious take on the traditional Indian biryani."

Serving: 4 | Prep: 35 m | Cook: 45 m | Ready in: 1 h 20 m

Ingredients

- 1 tablespoon vegetable oil
- 1 cup quinoa, rinsed and drained
- 2 cloves garlic, minced
- 1 teaspoon minced fresh ginger root
- 2 cinnamon sticks
- 1 teaspoon ground turmeric
- 1 pod cardamom
- 3 whole cloves
- 3 cups water
- 1 cup peeled, diced potato
- 1 cup chopped carrots
- 1 cup cauliflower florets
- 1 cup broccoli florets
- 1 cup fresh green beans, cut into 1-inch pieces
- 1/2 cup fresh or frozen peas
- 1 tablespoon butter
- 1 onion, sliced into rings
- 2 tablespoons cashew pieces
- 1/4 cup chopped fresh cilantro

Direction

- Heat vegetable oil in a large skillet over medium heat. Stir in quinoa and allow to toast briefly. Stir in the garlic, ginger, cinnamon sticks, turmeric, cardamom, and cloves. Cook and stir until the spices are fragrant, about 2 minutes. Pour in the water. Increase the heat to high and bring to a boil; add potatoes, carrots, and cauliflower. Recover, then reduce heat to low and cover and simmer for 10 minutes.
- Stir in the broccoli and green beans, then replace cover and simmer until the quinoa is tender and the water has been absorbed, about 10 minutes. Stir in the green peas, and cook until heated through, about 5 minutes. Remove from heat and discard cinnamon sticks and cloves.
- Heat the butter in a skillet over medium heat. Stir in onion; cook and stir until the onion is golden, about 8 minutes. Mix in the cashew pieces, stirring constantly until lightly toasted. Transfer quinoa and vegetables to a large platter or bowl. Top with the onion/cashew mixture and chopped cilantro.

Nutrition Information

- Calories: 334 calories
- Total Fat: 11.2 g
- Cholesterol: 8 mg
- Sodium: 129 mg
- Total Carbohydrate: 50.3 g
- Protein: 10.6 g

180. Quinoa Black Bean Burgers

"These vegetarian burgers are delicious! Your carnivorous friends will be impressed. My favorite way to serve is on a whole-wheat bun with garlic-lemon mayonnaise, fresh raw spinach, sliced tomato, and caramelized onions!"

Serving: 5 | Prep: 15 m | Cook: 20 m | Ready in: 35 m

Ingredients

- 1 (15 ounce) can black beans, rinsed and drained
- 1/4 cup quinoa
- 1/2 cup water
- 1/2 cup bread crumbs
- 1/4 cup minced yellow bell pepper
- 2 tablespoons minced onion
- 1 large clove garlic, minced
- 1 1/2 teaspoons ground cumin
- 1/2 teaspoon salt
- 1 teaspoon hot pepper sauce (such as Frank's RedHot®)
- 1 egg
- 3 tablespoons olive oil

Direction

- Bring the quinoa and water to a boil in a saucepan. Reduce heat to medium-low, cover,

and simmer until the quinoa is tender and the water has been absorbed, about 15 to 20 minutes.
- Roughly mash the black beans with a fork leaving some whole black beans in a paste-like mixture.
- Mix the quinoa, bread crumbs, bell pepper, onion, garlic, cumin, salt, hot pepper sauce, and egg into the black beans using your hands.
- Form the black bean mixture into 5 patties.
- Heat the olive oil in a large skillet.
- Cook the patties in the hot oil until heated through, 2 to 3 minutes per side.

Nutrition Information

- Calories: 245 calories
- Total Fat: 10.6 g
- Cholesterol: 37 mg
- Sodium: 679 mg
- Total Carbohydrate: 28.9 g
- Protein: 9.3 g

181. Quinoa Black Bean Tacos Vegan

"A hearty vegan main dish for carnivores and herbivores alike (and everyone between). Great topped with guacamole or avocados, hot sauce, sour cream, cheese, or vegan dairy alternatives."

Serving: 8 | Prep: 15 m | Cook: 25 m | Ready in: 40 m

Ingredients

- 1 teaspoon olive oil
- 1 onion, chopped
- 2 (8 ounce) cans tomato sauce
- 1 1/2 cups water
- 1/2 cup quinoa
- 1 (1 ounce) envelope taco seasoning mix
- 2 (14.5 ounce) cans black beans, rinsed and drained
- 24 corn tortillas

Direction

- Heat olive oil in a saucepan over medium heat; cook and stir onion until translucent, 5 to 10 minutes. Add tomato sauce, water, quinoa, and taco seasoning; bring to a boil. Reduce heat, cover saucepan, and simmer until quinoa is tender, about 15 minutes. Add black beans and simmer until heated through, about 5 minutes more. Serve quinoa-black bean filling in tortillas.

Nutrition Information

- Calories: 339 calories
- Total Fat: 3.9 g
- Cholesterol: 0 mg
- Sodium: 985 mg
- Total Carbohydrate: 65.4 g
- Protein: 13 g

182. Quinoa Bowl

"Simple dish that is very healthy, vegetarian, and can be a side or main course. Great to make and pack as a lunch for a few days after."

Serving: 6 | Prep: 15 m | Cook: 30 m | Ready in: 1 h

Ingredients

- 1 tablespoon extra-virgin olive oil, or as needed
- 3 sweet potatoes, cut into 1/2-inch pieces, or more to taste
- salt to taste
- 1 large yellow onion, chopped
- 1 clove garlic, chopped
- 1 cup asparagus, or more to taste
- 4 cups water
- 2 cups quinoa
- 1 cup cashews

Direction

- Heat olive oil in a skillet over medium-high heat. Add sweet potatoes and salt; stir to coat

sweet potatoes with oil and sauté until tender yet firm to the bite, about 10 minutes. Transfer sweet potatoes to a plate and season with more salt.
- Sauté onion and garlic in the same skillet until softened, 4 to 5 minutes.
- Place a steamer insert into a saucepan and fill with water to just below the bottom of the steamer. Bring water to a boil. Add asparagus, cover, and steam until tender, about 4 minutes. Cut asparagus into 1/2-inch pieces.
- Bring water and quinoa to a boil in a saucepan. Reduce heat to medium-low, cover, and simmer until quinoa is tender and water has been absorbed, 10 to 15 minutes.
- Toss sweet potatoes, onion-garlic mixture, asparagus, and quinoa together in a bowl; cool to room temperature. Add cashews and top with more olive oil and salt.

Nutrition Information

- Calories: 473 calories
- Total Fat: 16.4 g
- Cholesterol: 0 mg
- Sodium: 218 mg
- Total Carbohydrate: 70 g
- Protein: 14.1 g

183. Quinoa Breakfast Cereal

"A nice change from the usual bowl of oatmeal, this is jam-packed with nutrients and energy! Serve warm with milk. If sweetness is desired, add a splash of maple syrup or honey. Add quinoa to your breakfast repertoire with this easy hot cereal recipe made with apricots, almonds, flax seeds, and warm spices."

Serving: 4 | Prep: 5 m | Cook: 16 m | Ready in: 21 m

Ingredients

- 2 cups water
- 1 cup quinoa, rinsed
- 1/2 cup chopped dried apricots
- 1/2 cup slivered almonds
- 1/3 cup flax seeds
- 1 teaspoon ground cinnamon
- 1/2 teaspoon ground nutmeg

Direction

- Combine water and quinoa in a saucepan over medium heat; bring to a boil. Reduce heat and simmer until most of the water has been absorbed, 8 to 12 minutes. Stir in apricots, almonds, flax seeds, cinnamon, and nutmeg; cook until quinoa is tender, 2 to 3 minutes more.

Nutrition Information

- Calories: 350 calories
- Total Fat: 15.1 g
- Cholesterol: 0 mg
- Sodium: 13 mg
- Total Carbohydrate: 44.5 g
- Protein: 11.8 g

184. Quinoa Broccoli Casserole

"This is vegetarian comfort super-food. Warm, gooey, and delicious. Serve with a green salad and sliced fruit."

Serving: 6 | Prep: 10 m | Cook: 40 m | Ready in: 1 h 20 m

Ingredients

- 1 cup quinoa
- 2 cups water
- 1 teaspoon olive oil
- 1 teaspoon salt
- 2 cups chopped broccoli
- 1 (10 ounce) can low-sodium cream of mushroom soup
- 1 cup shredded Cheddar cheese
- 1/2 cup French-fried onions
- 1/2 cup light sour cream
- 1 teaspoon lemon pepper
- salt and ground black pepper to taste
- 1/2 cup French-fried onions

Direction

- Place quinoa in a bowl; pour in enough water to cover. Soak for 30 minutes. Drain and rinse several times.
- Bring quinoa, water, olive oil, and 1 teaspoon salt to a boil in a saucepan. Reduce heat to medium-low, cover, and simmer until quinoa is tender and the water has been absorbed, about 20 minutes.
- Preheat oven to 350 degrees F (175 degrees C). Grease an 8-inch square baking dish.
- Place a steamer insert into a saucepan and fill with water to just below the bottom of the steamer. Bring water to a boil. Add broccoli, cover, and steam until tender, 2 to 4 minutes.
- Stir broccoli, cream of mushroom soup, Cheddar cheese, 1/2 cup French-fried onions, sour cream, and lemon pepper into cooked quinoa; season with salt and black pepper to taste. Spoon quinoa mixture into the prepared baking dish.
- Bake in the preheated oven until heated through, 10 minutes. Sprinkle with 1/2 cup French-fried onions and bake until topping is lightly browned, about 5 more minutes.

Nutrition Information

- Calories: 494 calories
- Total Fat: 32.1 g
- Cholesterol: 31 mg
- Sodium: 938 mg
- Total Carbohydrate: 39.8 g
- Protein: 10.3 g

185. Quinoa Brown Rice Sushi

Benefits: Heart + Metabolism

My mother innovated constantly to satisfy her two sons' demanding palates, so she adapted quinoa with brown rice to make one of our all-time favorite foods: sushi. Once called "Inca Gold" due to its stamina-building properties, quinoa contains all the essential amino acids, rendering it a complete protein food. Its high manganese content supplies the body's production of superoxide dismutase, an enzyme that protects against free radical damage to your energy factory. Consider this an energizing longevity recipe!

Serving: Serves 4

Ingredients

- 1 cup sticky brown rice
- 1/2 cup quinoa
- 8 ounces baked bean curd/tofu, cut into long thin strips
- 4 to 5 carrots cut into matchsticks
- 4 nori seaweed sheets
- 2 pickled cucumbers (low sodium), cut into matchsticks
- 2 avocados, peeled, pitted, and sliced
- Cilantro sprigs, for garnish
- Pickled ginger, for garnish

Direction

- Place the rice, quinoa, and 3 cups water into a rice cooker and cook according to the manufacturer's instructions. (You can also cook the rice and quinoa in 3 cups water in a pressure cooker for 15 minutes).
- Bring a saucepan of water to a boil and cook the carrots until softened, about 30 seconds. Drain and rinse them under cold water.
- Unroll a bamboo sushi mat on a work surface and put a sheet of nori on it Wet your hands and divide the rice into 4 equal portions. Divide one portion into 4 small, firm balls and press them evenly onto the nori, covering the entire sheet with a thin layer of grains. Evenly spread one-quarter of the bean curd, one quarter of the carrots, one-quarter of the cucumbers, and one quarter of the avocado in the center of the rice. Using the mat as a guide, roll the topped nori tightly and evenly into a

sushi roll, wetting the edges of the nori sheet with water if necessary, so it sticks together at the seam. Repeat three more times with the remaining nori, rice, and vegetables.
- Slice the rolls into 1 1/2-inch-thick pieces with a sharp, wet knife and transfer them to a serving platter. Garnish with cilantro and pickled ginger.
- Quinoa originated in the Andean region of South America, where it has been a highly valued food for thousands of years. It is usually identified as a grain, but actually it is the seed of the Chenopodium quinoa plant, and is related to beets and chard. Quinoa is a great source of magnesium, which is beneficial for blood pressure, heart health, and energy production. It is remarkable for its high amount of protein, which is unusually complete for a plant source in that it includes all nine essential amino acids. Quinoa is a good food to eat for balancing blood sugar; where other refined, low-protein grains contain high amounts of starch that can upset the blood sugar balance, quinoa helps keep blood sugar levels steady.

Nutrition Information

- Calories: 502
- Total Fat: 20 g (31%)
- Saturated Fat: 3 g (16%)
- Sodium: 68 mg (3%)
- Total Carbohydrate: 72 g (24%)
- Protein: 15 g (30%)
- Fiber: 13 g (52%)

186. Quinoa Burgers

"The perfect size to fit the new sandwich rounds that are sprouting up on the market. Also great to add chopped mushrooms or a handful of grated carrots."

Serving: 9 | Prep: 15 m | Cook: 20 m | Ready in: 35 m

Ingredients

- 2 1/2 cups cooked quinoa (at room temperature)
- 4 eggs, beaten
- 1 sweet yellow onion, finely chopped
- 1/3 cup freshly grated Parmesan cheese
- 3 cloves garlic, finely chopped
- 1/2 teaspoon fine sea salt
- 1 cup whole-grain bread crumbs
- 1 teaspoon butter, or as needed

Direction

- Mix quinoa, eggs, yellow onion, Parmesan cheese, garlic, and sea salt in a bowl; add bread crumbs and stir. Form into 9 small patties.
- Melt butter in a flat skillet over-medium high heat. Cook the patties in the hot butter until crispy, 8 to 10 minutes per side.

Nutrition Information

- Calories: 169 calories
- Total Fat: 5.2 g
- Cholesterol: 86 mg
- Sodium: 270 mg
- Total Carbohydrate: 22.4 g
- Protein: 8.1 g

187. Quinoa Cakes with Eggplant Tomato Ragù and Smoked Mozzarella

Food editor Lillian Chou, who is also gourmet's resident runner of marathons, swears by quinoa: "I have so much more energy if I eat it before a race!" And transforming this power grain into crisp cakes topped with a substantial rustic sauce and gooey softened mozzarella creates another compelling reason to love it – it just tastes so good.

Serving: Makes 4 servings | Prep: 45 m | Cook: 1.25 h

Ingredients

- 1 1/2 cups water
- 1 cup quinoa
- 1 large egg, lightly beaten
- 4 to 5 tablespoons olive oil, divided
- 1 1/2 pounds eggplant, cut into 1/2-inch cubes
- 1 small onion, finely chopped
- 2 teaspoons finely chopped garlic
- 1/2 teaspoon dried oregano
- 3 tablespoons olive oil
- 1 cup grape or cherry tomatoes, halved
- 1/2 cup drained bottled roasted red peppers, rinsed and chopped
- 3/4 cup water
- 1 tablespoon chopped flat-leaf parsley
- 1/4 pound smoked mozzarella, diced (1 cup)

Direction

- Make quinoa cakes: Bring water and 1/2 teaspoon salt to a boil in a heavy medium saucepan.
- Meanwhile, wash quinoa in 3 changes of water in a bowl, then drain well in a fine-mesh sieve.
- Stir quinoa into boiling water and return to a boil, then simmer, covered, until quinoa is dry and water is absorbed, 20 to 30 minutes. Remove from heat and let stand, covered, 5 minutes. Transfer to a large bowl and cool, stirring occasionally, 10 minutes, then stir in egg.
- Line a baking sheet with plastic wrap and lightly brush with oil. Lightly oil a 1-cup dry-ingredient measure. Pack enough quinoa into measure with a rubber spatula to fill it two-thirds full. (If spatula becomes sticky, dip in water.) Unmold onto baking sheet and gently pat quinoa into a 4-inch-wide patty with spatula. Make 3 more quinoa cakes, brushing measure with oil each time. Chill cakes, uncovered, at least 15 minutes.
- Make topping while quinoa cooks and chills: Toss eggplant with 1 teaspoon salt in a colander and drain 30 minutes. Squeeze handfuls of eggplant to extract liquid, then pat dry.
- Cook eggplant, onion, garlic, oregano, and 1/4 teaspoon each of salt and pepper in oil in a 12-inch heavy skillet over medium heat, covered, stirring occasionally, until softened, about 5 minutes. Stir in tomatoes, roasted peppers, and water and simmer, covered, stirring occasionally, until eggplant is very tender and mixture is thick (if dry, thin with a little water), about 10 minutes.
- Cook quinoa cakes: Heat 2 tablespoons oil in a 12-inch nonstick skillet over medium heat until it shimmers. Carefully add quinoa cakes and cook, turning once carefully and adding remaining 2 to 3 tablespoons oil, until crisp and golden, 8 to 10 minutes total (pat cakes to reshape with cleaned rubber spatula while cooking if necessary). Transfer to plates.
- To serve: Return eggplant ragù to a simmer and stir in parsley and half of mozzarella, then simmer, stirring, until cheese just begins to soften, about 30 seconds. Spoon over quinoa cakes, then sprinkle with remaining mozzarella.
- Cooks' Note: Quinoa cakes can be formed 1 day ahead and chilled, covered.
- Eggplant-tomato ragù, without parsley and mozzarella, can be made 1 day ahead and chilled, covered.

Nutrition Information

- Calories: 547
- Total Fat: 36 g (55%)
- Saturated Fat: 8 g (40%)

- Cholesterol: 69 mg (23%)
- Sodium: 209 mg (9%)
- Total Carbohydrate: 43 g (14%)
- Protein: 16 g (33%)
- Fiber: 9 g (37%)

188. Quinoa Chard Pilaf

"This simple vegan dish combines the distinctive, nutty flavor of quinoa with chard, mushrooms, and lentils. Try using rainbow chard for a colorful effect!"

Serving: 8 | Prep: 20 m | Cook: 20 m | Ready in: 40 m

Ingredients

- 1 tablespoon olive oil
- 1 onion, diced
- 3 cloves garlic, minced
- 2 cups uncooked quinoa, rinsed
- 1 cup canned lentils, rinsed
- 8 ounces fresh mushrooms, chopped
- 1 quart vegetable broth
- 1 bunch Swiss chard, stems removed

Direction

- Heat the oil in a large pot over medium heat. Stir in the onion and garlic, and sauté 5 minutes, until onion is tender. Mix in quinoa, lentils, and mushrooms. Pour in the broth. Cover, and cook 20 minutes.
- Remove the pot from heat. Shred chard, and gently mix into the pot. Cover, and allow to sit 5 minutes, or until chard is wilted.

Nutrition Information

- Calories: 224 calories
- Total Fat: 4.7 g
- Cholesterol: 0 mg
- Sodium: 323 mg
- Total Carbohydrate: 36.6 g
- Protein: 9.6 g

189. Quinoa Chicken

"This is incredibly easy, delicious and spicy! Taste-test approved by a very picky 3-year-old."

Serving: 6 | Prep: 10 m | Cook: 40 m | Ready in: 50 m

Ingredients

- 2 cups chicken broth
- 1 cup quinoa
- 2 teaspoons vegetable oil, or as needed
- 1/2 onion, chopped
- 2 cloves garlic, or to taste, minced
- 1 1/2 pounds ground chicken
- 1 1/2 (10 ounce) cans diced tomatoes with green chile peppers (such as RO*TEL®)

Direction

- Bring chicken broth and quinoa to a boil in a saucepan. Reduce heat to medium-low, cover, and simmer until quinoa is tender and water has been absorbed, 15 to 20 minutes.
- Heat vegetable oil in a large skillet over medium-high heat. Sauté onion and garlic in hot oil until onion is translucent, 5 to 7 minutes. Add ground chicken and break into small pieces while cooking until completely browned, 7 to 10 minutes.
- Stir cooked quinoa and diced tomatoes into the chicken mixture; bring to a simmer and cook long enough for the flavors to meld, about 10 minutes more.

Nutrition Information

- Calories: 280 calories
- Total Fat: 7.1 g
- Cholesterol: 71 mg
- Sodium: 663 mg
- Total Carbohydrate: 22.6 g
- Protein: 30.4 g

190. Quinoa Chicken Sausage and White Bean Stew

"Wholesome and heartwarming! Serve with freshly grated Parmesan cheese and some good fresh bread."

Serving: 6 | Prep: 10 m | Cook: 30 m | Ready in: 40 m

Ingredients

- 1 (12 ounce) package good-quality precooked chicken sausages
- 2 tablespoons olive oil, divided
- 1 small yellow onion, finely chopped
- 1 (8 ounce) package sliced fresh mushrooms
- 1 teaspoon dried thyme
- 1 teaspoon smoked paprika
- 1 teaspoon salt
- 1 pinch cayenne pepper
- ground black pepper to taste
- 2 (32 fluid ounce) containers chicken stock
- 1 (16 ounce) can cannellini beans, drained
- 1 (16 ounce) can diced tomatoes
- 1 (10 ounce) package frozen chopped spinach, thawed and drained
- 1 cup quinoa

Direction

- Remove the casings from the chicken sausages. Slice in half lengthwise, then crosswise into half-moons. Heat 1 tablespoon olive oil in a large sauté pan and sauté chicken sausage until well browned, about 5 minutes. Remove from the pan.
- Heat remaining oil in the same pan. Sauté onion, mushrooms, thyme, paprika, salt, cayenne, and pepper until mushrooms are well browned, about 5 minutes. Remove from heat.
- Heat chicken stock in a large stockpot. Add cannellini beans, tomatoes, spinach, and quinoa. Simmer until quinoa is tender, about 15 minutes. Add the sausage and mushroom mixture. Simmer until heated through, about 5 minutes. Serve in soup bowls.

Nutrition Information

- Calories: 333 calories
- Total Fat: 11.8 g
- Cholesterol: 44 mg
- Sodium: 1903 mg
- Total Carbohydrate: 38.5 g
- Protein: 19.4 g

191. Quinoa Chili

"A super delicious chili which can be made vegetarian by excluding the ground beef. With its unique texture and sweet savory flavor with a hint of spice, this recipe will have your friends asking for seconds!"

Serving: 8 | Prep: 30 m | Cook: 35 m | Ready in: 1 h 5 m

Ingredients

- 1 cup uncooked quinoa, rinsed
- 2 cups water
- 1 pound extra lean ground beef
- 1 tablespoon olive oil
- 1 onion, chopped
- 4 cloves garlic, minced
- 1 jalapeno pepper, seeded and minced
- 1 tablespoon chili powder
- 1 tablespoon ground cumin
- 1 (28 ounce) can crushed tomatoes
- 2 (19 ounce) cans black beans, rinsed and drained
- 1 green bell pepper, chopped
- 1 red bell pepper, chopped
- 1 zucchini, chopped (optional)
- 1 teaspoon dried oregano leaves
- 1 teaspoon dried parsley
- salt and ground black pepper to taste
- 1 cup frozen corn kernels, thawed
- 1/4 cup chopped fresh cilantro

Direction

- Bring the quinoa and water to a boil in a saucepan over high heat. Reduce heat to medium-low, cover, and simmer until the quinoa is tender, and the water has been absorbed, about 15 to 20 minutes.

- Heat a large skillet over medium-high heat and stir in the ground beef. Cook and stir until the beef is crumbly, evenly browned, and no longer pink. Drain and discard any excess grease; set beef aside.
- Heat the olive oil in a large pot over medium heat. Stir in the onion, garlic, and jalapeno pepper; cook and stir until the onion has softened and turned translucent, about 5 minutes. Season with chili powder and cumin; cook 1 minute more to release the flavor of the spices. Stir in the tomatoes, black beans, green bell pepper, red bell pepper, zucchini, oregano, and parsley. Season to taste with salt and black pepper. Simmer until the bell peppers are tender, about 20 minutes.
- Once the red and green peppers are tender, stir in the quinoa, beef, and corn kernels. Return to a simmer, and cook 5 minutes to reheat. Stir in the cilantro to serve.

Nutrition Information

- Calories: 412 calories
- Total Fat: 11.5 g
- Cholesterol: 45 mg
- Sodium: 705 mg
- Total Carbohydrate: 52.8 g
- Protein: 27.5 g

192. Quinoa Chocolate Treats

"A delicious yet nutrient-rich treat. Rich in protein and vitamins, this sweet chocolate treat is something everyone feels good about eating and making!"

Serving: 5 | Prep: 5 m | Cook: 10 m | Ready in: 45 m

Ingredients

- 2 cups chocolate chips
- 2 teaspoons ground cinnamon
- 1/2 cup brown sugar
- 1/2 cup butter
- 3 drops peppermint extract
- 3 cups uncooked quinoa, rinsed
- 1 cup marshmallows

Direction

- Grease a baking tray.
- Heat the chocolate chips, cinnamon, brown sugar, butter, and peppermint extract together in a large saucepan over low heat; cook and stir until the mixture forms a smooth liquid. Fold the quinoa and marshmallows into the chocolate mixture until evenly distributed; immediately spread into the prepared tray. Allow to cool completely before cutting into triangles to serve.

Nutrition Information

- Calories: 1009 calories
- Total Fat: 44.8 g
- Cholesterol: 49 mg
- Sodium: 158 mg
- Total Carbohydrate: 138.6 g
- Protein: 17.7 g

193. Quinoa Chorizo

"Vegan chorizo substitute made with quinoa. Works well in chili, tacos, tofu scrambles, burritos or any recipe calling for chorizo."

Serving: 6 | Prep: 20 m | Cook: 30 m | Ready in: 1 h

Ingredients

- 1 cup quinoa, rinsed and drained
- 1 3/4 cups vegetable broth
- 2 tablespoons vegetable oil
- 1/2 large onion, chopped
- 3 cloves garlic, thinly sliced
- 1 tomato, seeded and chopped
- 3 tablespoons annatto paste (achiote)
- 2 tablespoons cider vinegar
- 1 teaspoon smoked paprika
- 1 teaspoon dried oregano
- 1/2 teaspoon ground cumin
- 1 dried chipotle chile pepper
- kosher salt, to taste

Direction

- Preheat oven to 350 degrees F (175 degrees C).
- Cover quinoa with vegetable broth in an oven-proof saucepan. Bring to a boil. Cover the saucepan with aluminum foil.
- Bake in preheated oven until quinoa is dry and fluffy, about 15 minutes. Keep covered.
- Heat a skillet over medium heat. Pour in vegetable oil. Cook and stir onion and garlic until soft, about 5 minutes. Stir in tomatoes, annatto paste, vinegar, paprika, oregano, cumin, and chipotle pepper. Cook until mixture is thick and stew-like, 10 to 15 minutes.
- Toss the mixture with the baked quinoa. Let cool, about 10 minutes. Season with salt.

Nutrition Information

- Calories: 171 calories
- Total Fat: 6.6 g
- Cholesterol: 0 mg
- Sodium: 211 mg
- Total Carbohydrate: 23.4 g
- Protein: 4.9 g

194. Quinoa Couscous and Farro Salad with Summer Vegetables

"This light and delicious salad is packed with protein, vitamins, and fiber. I tried this while visiting a resort in Marco Island and could not wait to recreate it myself. This salad is the perfect dish for a light lunch or a side dish at dinner. Your vegetarian friends will thank you for serving this at any dinner party or BBQ."

Serving: 8 | Prep: 20 m | Cook: 30 m | Ready in: 2 h 50 m

Ingredients

- 6 1/2 cups water, divided
- 1 cup red quinoa
- 1 cup pearl (Israeli) couscous
- 1 cup farro
- 1 cucumber, seeded and chopped
- 1/2 red onion, chopped
- 1 orange bell pepper, seeded and chopped
- 1 yellow squash, seeded and chopped
- 1/2 cup extra-virgin olive oil
- 1 lemon, juiced
- 1/2 teaspoon kosher salt
- 1 (6 ounce) container crumbled feta cheese

Direction

- Bring 2 cups water and quinoa to a boil in a saucepan. Reduce heat to medium-low, cover, and simmer until quinoa is tender and water has been absorbed, 15 to 20 minutes.
- Bring 1 1/2 cup water and couscous to a boil in a separate saucepan. Reduce heat to medium-low, cover, and simmer until couscous is tender yet firm to the bite, about 10 minutes.
- Bring 3 cups water and farro to a boil in a separate saucepan. Reduce heat to medium-low, cover, and simmer until farro is tender and water has been absorbed, about 25 minutes.
- Combine quinoa, couscous, farro, cucumber, red onion, orange bell pepper, and yellow squash together in a bowl
- Whisk olive oil, lemon juice, and salt together in a bowl. Pour dressing over grain-vegetable mixture; toss to coat. Sprinkle feta cheese over salad. Refrigerate until chilled, at least 2 hours.

Nutrition Information

- Calories: 424 calories
- Total Fat: 20.9 g
- Cholesterol: 19 mg
- Sodium: 370 mg
- Total Carbohydrate: 50.3 g
- Protein: 11.6 g

195. Quinoa Crab Salad

"Great and healthy salad for lunch or dinner! Imitation crab is okay for this recipe. It's best if made the night before."

Serving: 10 | Prep: 15 m | Cook: 15 m | Ready in: 1 h

Ingredients

- 1 1/3 cups water
- 2/3 cup quinoa
- 1 pound finely chopped cooked crabmeat
- 1 cup diced cucumber
- 1 cup sliced grape tomatoes
- 1 cup fat-free feta cheese, crumbled
- 1/2 cup Greek salad dressing
- 2 tablespoons lemon juice
- 2 tablespoons balsamic vinegar, or more to taste

Direction

- Bring water and quinoa to a boil in a saucepan. Reduce heat to medium-low, cover, and simmer until quinoa is tender and water has been absorbed, 15 to 20 minutes. Cool quinoa completely.
- Mix crabmeat, cucumber, tomatoes, and feta cheese together in a large bowl; add quinoa and stir. Whisk Greek salad dressing, lemon juice, and balsamic vinegar together in a separate bowl; drizzle over the quinoa mixture and stir to coat.

Nutrition Information

- Calories: 185 calories
- Total Fat: 8.4 g
- Cholesterol: 43 mg
- Sodium: 597 mg
- Total Carbohydrate: 11 g
- Protein: 17.3 g

196. Quinoa Dijon and Swiss Burger

"Great dish for gluten free and vegetarian diet. Loaded with protein."

Serving: 2 | Prep: 10 m | Cook: 10 m | Ready in: 20 m

Ingredients

- 1 1/2 cups cooked quinoa
- 2 tablespoons Dijon mustard
- 1 egg, beaten
- 1 clove garlic, minced
- 2 grinds fresh black pepper
- 1/2 cup chickpea (garbanzo bean) flour, or as needed
- 2 teaspoons vegetable oil, or as needed
- 2 slices Swiss cheese

Direction

- Mix quinoa, mustard, egg, garlic, and black pepper together in a bowl; add enough chickpea flour to hold mixture together to form 2 patties.
- Heat oil in a skillet over medium heat; cook patties in the hot oil until browned and cooked through, about 4 minutes per side. Add a Swiss cheese slice to each patty and warm until cheese melts, 2 to 3 minutes.

Nutrition Information

- Calories: 455 calories
- Total Fat: 19.1 g
- Cholesterol: 119 mg
- Sodium: 475 mg
- Total Carbohydrate: 48.8 g
- Protein: 21.7 g

197. Quinoa Fried Rice

"Great side dish and substitute for fried rice."

Serving: 6 | Prep: 15 m | Cook: 30 m | Ready in: 8 h 50 m

Ingredients

- Quinoa:
- 1 1/2 cups water
- 1 cup quinoa
- salt to taste
- Sauce:
- 2 1/2 tablespoons soy sauce
- 1 1/2 tablespoons teriyaki sauce
- 3/4 teaspoon sesame oil
- Fried Quinoa:
- 1 tablespoon olive oil, divided
- 2 carrots, peeled and chopped
- 1/4 onion, chopped
- 3 scallions, chopped, divided
- 3 cloves garlic, minced
- 1/2 teaspoon minced fresh ginger
- 2 eggs, beaten
- 1/2 cup frozen peas

Direction

- Bring water and quinoa to a boil in a saucepan; season with salt. Reduce heat to medium-low, cover, and simmer until quinoa is tender and water has been absorbed, 15 to 20 minutes. Remove saucepan from heat and let sit for 5 minutes; fluff quinoa with a fork. Refrigerate until cool, 8 hours to overnight.
- Mix soy sauce, teriyaki sauce, and sesame oil together in a bowl until sauce is evenly mixed.
- Heat 1 1/2 teaspoons oil in a large skillet over high heat; sauté carrots and onion for 2 minutes. Add 2 scallions, garlic, and ginger; sauté until fragrant, about 2 minutes more. Add the remaining 1 1/2 teaspoons oil and quinoa; cook until heated through, about 2 minutes.
- Stir sauce into quinoa mixture; cook and stir until evenly coated, about 2 minutes.
- Make well in the center of the quinoa mixture. Pour eggs into the well; cook and stir until eggs are scrambled and cooked through, 2 to 3 minutes. Add peas and cook until heated through, 2 to 3 minutes. Add remaining scallion.

Nutrition Information

- Calories: 189 calories
- Total Fat: 6.4 g
- Cholesterol: 62 mg
- Sodium: 607 mg
- Total Carbohydrate: 25.5 g
- Protein: 8 g

198. Quinoa Grape and Prune Salad

"This quinoa salad is loaded with flavor, perfect for a great lunch or healthy side dish!"

Serving: 6 | Prep: 15 m | Cook: 15 m | Ready in: 1 h 30 m

Ingredients

- Salad:
- 2 cups water
- 1 cup quinoa
- 1 cup halved red grapes
- 1/2 cup Sunsweet® D'Noir™ Prunes, chopped
- 1/2 cup thinly sliced celery
- 1/2 cup sliced green onion
- 1/2 cup chopped toasted walnuts
- Dressing:
- 1/3 cup extra-virgin olive oil
- 1/4 cup red wine vinegar
- 1 tablespoon honey
- 1/2 teaspoon salt, or to taste
- 1 clove garlic, minced
- Freshly ground black pepper to taste

Direction

- Rinse quinoa in a fine mesh strainer; drain well. Bring water and quinoa to a boil in a medium saucepan; reduce heat and simmer,

covered, for 12 minutes. Let stand for 10 minutes, then fluff with a fork and let cool.
- Place in a large bowl with remaining salad ingredients. Whisk together all dressing ingredients and pour over salad; toss well to coat. Cover and chill for at least 1 hour.

Nutrition Information

- Calories: 351 calories
- Total Fat: 20.7 g
- Cholesterol: 0 mg
- Sodium: 208 mg
- Total Carbohydrate: 37.1 g
- Protein: 6.3 g

199. Quinoa GreekInspired Salad

"I love pesto, and quinoa is so good for you. So why not mix them and all the amazingness! Bacon is not necessary; chicken would work, or you could go with no meat at all. Serve hot or cold."

Serving: 4 | Prep: 10 m | Cook: 15 m | Ready in: 25 m

Ingredients

- 1 cup chicken broth
- 1/2 cup quinoa
- 2 tablespoons pesto
- 1 roma tomatoes, diced
- 2 ounces crumbled feta cheese
- 4 slices cooked bacon, crumbled (optional)

Direction

- Bring broth and quinoa to a boil in a saucepan. Reduce heat to medium-low, cover, and simmer until quinoa is tender and broth has been absorbed, 15 to 20 minutes. Transfer quinoa to a bowl and fluff with a fork.
- Stir pesto, tomatoes, feta cheese, and bacon into the quinoa.

Nutrition Information

- Calories: 210 calories
- Total Fat: 11.8 g
- Cholesterol: 26 mg
- Sodium: 667 mg
- Total Carbohydrate: 15.7 g
- Protein: 10.1 g

200. Quinoa High Protein Muffins

"No-flour muffins, packed with protein."

Serving: 12 | Prep: 15 m | Cook: 37 m | Ready in: 52 m

Ingredients

- 1 teaspoon coconut oil, or as needed
- 2/3 cup light coconut milk
- 1/2 cup quinoa
- 1 pinch salt
- 2 tablespoons coconut oil (optional)
- 2 tablespoons honey
- 5 large eggs
- 1/3 cup shredded unsweetened coconut (optional)
- 1 teaspoon vanilla extract, or to taste
- 1/3 cup almonds
- 1/4 cup chopped pitted dates
- 1/4 cup chia seeds
- 1/4 cup walnuts
- 1/4 cup ground flax seeds
- 1 large carrot, roughly chopped
- 1 apple, peeled and roughly chopped

Direction

- Preheat oven to 350 degrees F (175 degrees C). Grease a muffin tin with 1 teaspoon coconut oil.
- Bring coconut milk, quinoa, and pinch of salt to a boil in a saucepan. Reduce heat to medium-low, cover, and simmer until quinoa is tender and milk is absorbed, 20 to 25 minutes. Remove from heat and cool.
- Combine 2 tablespoons coconut oil and honey in a large microwave-safe bowl; heat in microwave until melted and smooth, 20 to 30 seconds. Beat eggs, shredded coconut, and

vanilla extract into honey mixture until well combined. Stir cooled quinoa into mixture until well mixed.
- Place dates, chia seeds, walnuts, and ground flax in a food processor; pulse until roughly chopped. Stir into quinoa batter.
- Place carrot and apple in food processor and pulse until evenly chopped; stir into quinoa batter. Sprinkle a pinch of salt over batter and stir well. Divide batter into the muffin cups, filling almost full.
- Bake in the preheated oven until the tops are golden brown and puffed and a toothpick inserted in the middle comes out clean, 12 to 15 minutes.

Nutrition Information

- Calories: 201 calories
- Total Fat: 13.5 g
- Cholesterol: 78 mg
- Sodium: 51 mg
- Total Carbohydrate: 15.8 g
- Protein: 6.1 g

201. Quinoa Jambalaya

"Move over Zatarain's® this is healthier and tastier."

Serving: 6 | Prep: 10 m | Cook: 30 m | Ready in: 40 m

Ingredients

- 1 tablespoon vegetable oil, or as needed
- 1 pound kielbasa (Polish) sausage, halved lengthwise and sliced
- 1/2 sweet onion (such as Vidalia®), diced
- 6 miniature multi-colored sweet peppers, diced
- 1 teaspoon dried oregano
- 1 teaspoon dried thyme
- 1/2 teaspoon cayenne pepper
- 1/4 teaspoon celery salt
- 1 pinch red pepper flakes
- 1 cup quinoa
- 2 cups chicken broth
- 1/2 cup marinara sauce

Direction

- Heat oil in a large skillet over medium heat; cook and stir sausage until browned, about 5 minutes. Add onion to sausage; cook and stir until slightly browned, about 5 minutes. Stir sweet pepper, oregano, thyme, cayenne pepper, celery salt, and red pepper flakes into sausage mixture; cook and stir until fragrant, 1 to 2 minutes
- Mix quinoa into sausage mixture; cook and stir until quinoa is slightly toasted, about 1 minute. Pour broth and marinara sauce over quinoa mixture. Cover skillet and simmer until quinoa is tender, about 15 minutes.

Nutrition Information

- Calories: 420 calories
- Total Fat: 27.8 g
- Cholesterol: 56 mg
- Sodium: 1091 mg
- Total Carbohydrate: 26.1 g
- Protein: 14.7 g

202. Quinoa Lasagna

"Easy, healthier lasagna recipe."

Serving: 12 | Prep: 10 m | Cook: 55 m | Ready in: 1 h 5 m

Ingredients

- 1/4 cup olive oil
- 1 cup minced onion
- 2 cloves garlic, minced
- 1 pound ground beef
- 2 (8 ounce) cans tomato sauce
- 1 (14.5 ounce) can whole peeled tomatoes, chopped
- 2 teaspoons dried oregano
- 1 teaspoon salt
- 3 cups cooked quinoa, divided
- 1 (8 ounce) container ricotta cheese
- 4 ounces shredded mozzarella cheese

- 4 ounces grated Parmesan cheese

Direction

- Preheat oven to 350 degrees F (175 degrees C).
- Heat olive oil in a large skillet over medium heat. Add onion and garlic; cook and stir until golden brown, about 5 minutes. Add beef; cook and stir until browned, about 5 minutes. Stir in tomato sauce, chopped tomatoes, oregano, and salt. Simmer sauce until flavors combine, about 10 minutes.
- Spread 1/4 of the sauce in the bottom of a 9x13-inch baking dish. Top with a 1/3 of the quinoa. Drop spoonfuls of ricotta on top of quinoa, and sprinkle 1/3 of the mozzarella cheese and Parmesan cheese on top. Repeat layers twice more, ending with sauce and Parmesan cheese on top.
- Bake lasagna in the preheated oven until sauce is bubbly and top is golden, about 35 minutes.

Nutrition Information

- Calories: 276 calories
- Total Fat: 15.8 g
- Cholesterol: 44 mg
- Sodium: 690 mg
- Total Carbohydrate: 16.3 g
- Protein: 17.5 g

203. Quinoa Lime and ChiliCrumbed Snapper With Sweet Potato Wedges

This dish is a regular on my weeknight dinner roster – it's delicious! Using quinoa instead of a regular breadcrumbs, and sweet potato wedges instead of regular, means it's better for you, too.

Serving: 4 Servings

Ingredients

- 1 teaspoon ground cumin
- 2 teaspoons chili flakes
- 1 teaspoon sea salt, plus more for sprinkling
- 1 1/2 pounds sweet potatoes, cut into wedges
- Cracked black pepper
- 2 tablespoons extra-virgin olive oil
- 2 cups quinoa flakes
- 1 tablespoon finely grated lime zest
- 2 eggs
- 4 (5 1/4-ounce) snapper fillets
- 1/2 cup flat-leaf parsley leaves, finely chopped
- Mayonnaise and lime wedges, to serve

Direction

- Preheat oven to 425°F. Place the cumin, 1/2 teaspoon of the chili flakes and 1 teaspoon of the salt in a bowl and mix to combine. Place the sweet potatoes on a rimmed baking sheet and sprinkle with half the salt mixture, pepper and 1 tablespoon of the oil. Roast, turning halfway, for 20 minutes or until golden.
- Place the quinoa, lime zest, remaining chili flakes, salt and pepper in a bowl and mix to combine. Place the eggs in a bowl and whisk to combine.
- Heat the remaining oil in a large non-stick frying pan over medium heat. Dip the fish into the egg and press into the quinoa mixture to coat. Cook for 2–3 minutes on each side or until golden and cooked through. Serve the fish and potatoes with the remaining salt mixture, the parsley, mayonnaise and lime wedges.

Nutrition Information

- Calories: 717
- Total Fat: 16 g (25%)
- Saturated Fat: 3 g (14%)
- Cholesterol: 135 mg (45%)
- Sodium: 700 mg (29%)
- Total Carbohydrate: 94 g (31%)
- Protein: 49 g (97%)
- Fiber: 13 g (51%)

204. Quinoa Milk

"A nutrient-packed alternative to milk. I use EVOO and a pinch of salt here but you can season to taste adding honey, cinnamon, vanilla, or any flavor you really love!"

Serving: 4 | Prep: 15 m | Cook: 25 m | Ready in: 8 h 40 m

Ingredients

- 1 cup quinoa
- 4 cups water
- 1 tablespoon extra-virgin olive oil, or to taste
- salt to taste

Direction

- Soak quinoa in a bowl with water to cover until it starts to germinate and you see the grain tails, 8 to 10 hours.
- Wash quinoa through a strainer. Pour quinoa into a pot and add 4 cups water. Bring to a boil. Reduce heat to low and simmer until tender, 20 to 30 minutes. Let cool briefly.
- Pour quinoa and water into a blender; add olive oil and salt. Cover and hold lid down with a potholder; pulse a few times before leaving on to blend, about 1 minute. Let cool until safe to handle, and strain through a cheesecloth for an even better texture.

Nutrition Information

- Calories: 187 calories
- Total Fat: 6 g
- Cholesterol: 0 mg
- Sodium: 48 mg
- Total Carbohydrate: 27.3 g
- Protein: 6 g

205. Quinoa Mushroom Risotto

"Delicious way to enjoy healthy, protein-packed quinoa!"

Serving: 4 | Prep: 20 m | Cook: 30 m | Ready in: 50 m

Ingredients

- 2 cups water
- 1 cup quinoa
- 1 tablespoon coconut oil
- 1 teaspoon chicken bouillon granules
- 2 tablespoons coconut oil
- 4 cups sliced crimini ('baby bella') mushrooms
- 1/2 large yellow onion, thinly sliced
- 1 large red bell pepper, seeded and thinly sliced
- salt to taste
- 1/4 cup red wine
- 2 tablespoons soy sauce
- 1/4 cup grated Parmesan cheese, or to taste (optional)

Direction

- Mix water, quinoa, 1 tablespoon coconut oil, and chicken bouillon granules in a saucepan; bring to a boil, reduce heat to medium-low, and simmer until white threads appear on the quinoa grains, about 15 minutes.
- Melt 2 tablespoons coconut oil in a skillet over medium-high heat. Sauté mushrooms, onion, and red bell pepper in hot oil until softened, 5 to 7 minutes; season with salt.
- Stir red wine and soy sauce into the vegetable mixture; bring to a simmer, reduce heat to medium-low, and cook until the liquid is reduced, about 10 minutes.
- Mix quinoa and vegetables in a large serving bowl; top with Parmesan cheese.

Nutrition Information

- Calories: 338 calories
- Total Fat: 14.7 g
- Cholesterol: 4 mg
- Sodium: 705 mg
- Total Carbohydrate: 35.9 g
- Protein: 13.4 g

206. Quinoa Peanut White Bean Soup

"An easy, nutritious way to use quinoa. Hearty and perfect for a cold day."

Serving: 6 | Prep: 25 m | Cook: 35 m | Ready in: 1 h

Ingredients

- 2 teaspoons canola oil
- 3/4 cup chopped onion
- 1 jalapeno pepper, seeded and chopped
- 3 cloves garlic, minced
- 2 (15 ounce) cans white beans, drained
- 5 carrots, sliced
- 1/2 cup quinoa
- 6 cups vegetable broth
- 1 (10 ounce) can diced tomatoes and green chiles (such as RO*TEL®)
- 1/4 cup soy sauce
- 1/2 cup chopped red bell pepper
- 1/2 cup peanut butter
- 1/4 cup chopped cilantro, or to taste
- 1 tablespoon hot pepper sauce (such as Tabasco®)
- 1 lime, cut into wedges
- freshly ground black pepper to taste

Direction

- Heat oil in a large pot over medium heat. Cook and stir onion and jalapeno pepper in the hot oil until softened, 4 to 5 minutes. Stir in garlic; cook until fragrant, about 30 seconds. Stir in white beans, carrots, and quinoa.
- Pour vegetable broth, diced tomatoes, and soy sauce into the pot; bring to a boil. Reduce heat and simmer, covered, until carrots and quinoa are tender, about 20 minutes. Add red bell pepper; cook until softened, about 5 minutes. Stir in peanut butter until dissolved into the broth, about 1 minute.
- Garnish soup with cilantro, hot sauce, lime juice, and black pepper.

Nutrition Information

- Calories: 437 calories
- Total Fat: 14.4 g
- Cholesterol: 0 mg
- Sodium: 1414 mg
- Total Carbohydrate: 60 g
- Protein: 20.8 g

207. Quinoa Pilaf

"A delicious and easy quinoa recipe. Serve with a salad and crusty bread for a complete meal."

Serving: 4 | Prep: 10 m | Cook: 25 m | Ready in: 35 m

Ingredients

- 1 tablespoon vegetable oil
- 1/2 cup chopped onion
- 2 carrots, chopped
- 1 cup quinoa, rinsed
- 2 cups vegetable broth
- 3/4 cup chopped walnuts
- 1/4 cup chopped fresh parsley

Direction

- Heat oil in a saucepan over medium-high heat. Cook onion in oil for 5 minutes, or until translucent. Add carrot, and cook 3 minutes more. Stir in quinoa and vegetable broth, and bring to a boil. Reduce to a simmer, cover, and cook 15 to 20 minutes, or until quinoa is tender and fluffy.
- In a bowl, toss quinoa together with walnuts and parsley. Serve hot or at room temperature.

Nutrition Information

- Calories: 365 calories
- Total Fat: 20.9 g
- Cholesterol: 0 mg
- Sodium: 260 mg
- Total Carbohydrate: 36.9 g
- Protein: 10.1 g

208. Quinoa Pilaf With Mushrooms

"Quinoa is not a grain, but a seed."

Serving: 4 | Prep: 15 m | Cook: 35 m | Ready in: 1 h

Ingredients

- 1 tablespoon olive oil
- 1 small shallot, chopped
- 1/2 cup thinly sliced cremini mushrooms
- 1 1/2 cups quinoa, rinsed and drained
- 1/2 teaspoon fresh thyme leaves
- 1 bay leaf
- 1 1/2 teaspoons kosher salt
- freshly ground black pepper to taste
- 3 cups vegetable stock

Direction

- Heat a large saucepan over medium heat and swirl olive oil around the inside of the pan to coat. Cook shallot in the hot oil until translucent, about 3 minutes; stir in cremini mushrooms, cooking and stirring until mushrooms are browned, 8 to 10 minutes. Stir quinoa, thyme, bay leaf, kosher salt, and black pepper into mushroom mixture. Cook, stirring often, until quinoa gives off a slightly toasted fragrance, about 5 minutes.
- Pour vegetable stock into quinoa mixture (stock may spatter a bit); stir to combine. Bring to a full boil, reduce heat to low, and cover pan; simmer until liquid is absorbed, about 15 minutes. Remove from heat and fluff quinoa pilaf with a fork; cover pan and let pilaf stand 10 more minutes to steam dry.

Nutrition Information

- Calories: 290 calories
- Total Fat: 7.4 g
- Cholesterol: 0 mg
- Sodium: 1084 mg
- Total Carbohydrate: 45.4 g
- Protein: 9.9 g

209. Quinoa Pilaf with Shredded Chicken

"Make a simple pilaf a quick meal by adding shredded chicken."

Serving: 4 | Prep: 15 m | Cook: 30 m | Ready in: 45 m

Ingredients

- 2 tablespoons coconut oil
- 1 small onion, diced
- 1 stalk celery, diced
- 3 carrots, diced
- 1 cup quinoa
- 2 cups chicken broth
- 1 tablespoon Italian seasoning
- 1 teaspoon chopped fresh sage
- 1 cup shredded cooked chicken meat
- salt and black pepper to taste

Direction

- Heat the coconut oil in a saucepan over medium heat. Cook and stir the onion, celery, and carrots in the hot oil until tender, about 7 minutes. Add the quinoa, chicken broth, Italian seasoning, and sage. Bring to a boil over high heat; reduce heat to medium-low, cover, and simmer until the liquid has been absorbed and the quinoa is tender, about 20 minutes. Stir in the chicken meat; season with salt and pepper.

Nutrition Information

- Calories: 312 calories
- Total Fat: 12.4 g
- Cholesterol: 26 mg
- Sodium: 64 mg
- Total Carbohydrate: 34.3 g
- Protein: 16.4 g

210. Quinoa Pilaf with Veggies and Chickpeas

"Delicious gluten-free side or main dish!"

Serving: 8 | Prep: 15 m | Cook: 30 m | Ready in: 45 m

Ingredients

- 4 cups chicken stock
- 2 cups quinoa
- 2 tablespoons olive oil
- 1 pound asparagus, chopped
- 2 green bell peppers, chopped
- 1 red onion, chopped
- 1 (14.5 ounce) can chickpeas, drained and rinsed
- 2 tablespoons balsamic vinegar
- 1 tablespoon lemon juice
- salt and ground black pepper to taste
- 1 tablespoon balsamic vinegar, or more to taste (optional)

Direction

- Combine chicken stock and quinoa in a saucepan and bring to a boil. Reduce heat to medium-low, cover, and simmer until quinoa is tender, about 15 minutes. Remove from heat.
- Heat olive oil in a large skillet over medium heat until shimmering. Add asparagus, bell peppers, and onion; cook and stir until softened, about 6 minutes. Stir in chickpeas. Pour in 2 tablespoons balsamic vinegar and cook until reduced, about 4 minutes. Add lemon juice, salt, and black pepper. Stir in cooked quinoa. Drizzle 1 tablespoon balsamic vinegar over pilaf before serving.

Nutrition Information

- Calories: 282 calories
- Total Fat: 6.9 g
- Cholesterol: 2 mg
- Sodium: 659 mg
- Total Carbohydrate: 45.3 g
- Protein: 10.7 g

211. Quinoa Pilau

"Inspired by traditional rice pilau of southern India, this addictive recipe is time-efficient with practice. Once tasted, it is impossible to get enough. Enjoy!"

Serving: 4 | Prep: 10 m | Cook: 20 m | Ready in: 1 h

Ingredients

- 2 cups water
- 1/2 teaspoon sea salt
- 1 cup quinoa
- 3 tablespoons olive oil
- 1 onion, finely chopped
- 1 (2 inch) piece fresh ginger, finely chopped
- 1/2 teaspoon ground cinnamon
- 1/2 teaspoon ground cloves
- 2 tablespoons finely chopped fresh mint
- 2 tablespoons finely chopped fresh cilantro
- sea salt and ground black pepper to taste
- 1 teaspoon chopped blanched almonds, or more to taste (optional)

Direction

- Bring water, 1/2 teaspoon sea salt, and quinoa to a boil in a saucepan; cook until quinoa has absorbed all the water, 15 to 20 minutes.
- Heat olive oil in a large skillet over medium heat; cook and stir onion and ginger until onion is lightly browned, 10 to 12 minutes. Add cinnamon and cloves; stir to coat. Stir in cooked quinoa.
- Remove skillet from heat; stir in mint and cilantro. Season with sea salt and black pepper. Allow mixture to cool; fluff with fork before serving. Garnish with blanched almonds.

Nutrition Information

- Calories: 262 calories
- Total Fat: 13.1 g
- Cholesterol: 0 mg
- Sodium: 316 mg
- Total Carbohydrate: 30.5 g
- Protein: 6.2 g

212. Quinoa Pudding

"Quinoa is a high-protein grain native to South America. You can find it in most health food stores and some grocery stores. This is a simple, delicious vegan recipe full of plump raisins, and sweetened with apple juice. Serve with berries, sliced bananas and maple syrup."

Serving: 6 | Prep: 5 m | Cook: 35 m | Ready in: 40 m

Ingredients

- 1 cup quinoa
- 2 cups water
- 2 cups apple juice
- 1 cup raisins
- 2 tablespoons lemon juice
- 1 teaspoon ground cinnamon, or to taste
- salt to taste
- 2 teaspoons vanilla extract

Direction

- Place quinoa in a sieve and rinse thoroughly. Allow to drain, then place quinoa in a medium saucepan with water. Bring to a boil over high heat. Cover pan with lid, lower heat, and allow to simmer until all water is absorbed and quinoa is tender, about 15 minutes.
- Mix in apple juice, raisins, lemon juice, cinnamon, and salt. Cover pan and allow to simmer for 15 minutes longer. Stir in vanilla extract. Serve warm.

Nutrition Information

- Calories: 202 calories
- Total Fat: 1.9 g
- Cholesterol: 0 mg
- Sodium: 8 mg
- Total Carbohydrate: 42.6 g
- Protein: 4.4 g

213. Quinoa Raisin Breakfast Bites

"These protein-packed, dairy-free quinoa raisin muffin bites have no refined sugar. A perfect low-calorie anytime snack. Store in an airtight container in the refrigerator for up to 1 week."

Serving: 12 | Prep: 10 m | Cook: 25 m | Ready in: 55 m

Ingredients

- cooking spray
- 1 cup cooked quinoa
- 1 cup gluten-free oat flour
- 1/2 cup unsweetened vanilla-flavored almond milk
- 1/4 cup maple syrup
- 1/4 cup raisins
- 1 egg white
- 1 teaspoon vanilla extract
- 1/4 teaspoon ground cinnamon
- 1 pinch sea salt

Direction

- Preheat oven to 350 degrees F (175 degrees C). Grease a muffin tin with cooking spray.
- Mix cooked quinoa, oat flour, almond milk, maple syrup, raisins, egg white, vanilla extract, cinnamon, and salt together in a large bowl.
- Fill each muffin cup to the top with quinoa mixture.
- Bake in the preheated oven until golden brown, about 25 minutes. Cool muffins completely in the tin, about 20 minutes, before removing.

Nutrition Information

- Calories: 83 calories
- Total Fat: 1.2 g
- Cholesterol: 0 mg
- Sodium: 40 mg
- Total Carbohydrate: 16.5 g
- Protein: 2.1 g

214. Quinoa Risotto with Mushrooms and Thyme

Serving: Makes 4 main-course or 6 side-dish servings | Prep: 25 m | Cook: 25 m

Ingredients

- 1 cup quinoa, rinsed
- 1 tablespoon olive oil
- 1 1/2 cups chopped onion
- 1 garlic clove, pressed
- 1 8-ounce package sliced crimini (baby bella) mushrooms
- 6 ounces fresh shiitake mushrooms, stemmed, sliced
- 3 teaspoons chopped fresh thyme, divided
- 1 cup dry white wine
- Grated Parmesan cheese

Direction

- Bring 2 cups salted water to boil in medium saucepan. Add quinoa, reduce heat to medium-low, cover, and simmer until tender and water is absorbed, about 13 minutes.
- Meanwhile, heat oil in large skillet over medium-high heat. Add onion and sauté until onion begins to brown, 5 minutes. Add garlic; stir 30 seconds. Add mushrooms and thyme. Sautee; until mushrooms are tender, 6 minutes. Add wine; stir until wine is reduced and liquid is syrupy, 2 minutes.
- Mix quinoa into mushroom mixture; season with salt and pepper. Pass cheese separately.
- Per serving: 320.1 kcal calories, 32.1 % calories from fat, 11.4 g fat, 2.3 g saturated fat, 10.0 mg cholesterol, 38.3 g carbohydrates, 13.1 g dietary fiber, 6.2 g total sugars, 25.2 g net carbohydrates, 16.8 g protein
- Nutritional analysis provided by Bon Appétit

215. Quinoa Salad

Serving: Makes 1 serving

Ingredients

- 1/4 cup quinoa
- 1/4 chopped red pepper
- 1/4 cup shelled edamame
- 1/8 diced onion
- 1/8 cup dried tart cherries
- 2 tbsp olive oil
- 2 tbsp white wine vinegar
- 1 tsp Dijon mustard
- Pinch sugar
- Salt and pepper to taste
- 2 tbsp sunflower seeds, shelled

Direction

- Cook quinoa, cool and toss with red pepper, edamame, onion, and dried tart cherries.
- For white wine vinaigrette dressing, whisk together olive oil, white wine vinegar, Dijon mustard, and sugar. Add salt and pepper. Mix 2 tbsp dressing (or more to taste) into salad and sprinkle with 2 tbsp shelled sunflower seeds.

Nutrition Information

- Calories: 637
- Total Fat: 41 g (63%)
- Saturated Fat: 5 g (26%)
- Sodium: 528 mg (22%)
- Total Carbohydrate: 55 g (18%)
- Protein: 15 g (30%)
- Fiber: 8 g (33%)

216. Quinoa Salad Vegan

"Quinoa with fruit and nuts. Very filling. Best served on the day you make it."

Serving: 6 | Prep: 15 m | Cook: 25 m | Ready in: 4 h 40 m

Ingredients

- 2 cups apple juice
- 1 cup quinoa, rinsed
- Dressing:
- 1/3 cup agave nectar
- 1/4 cup safflower oil
- 1 tablespoon poppy seeds
- 1 teaspoon prepared yellow mustard
- 1 Fuji apple, chopped
- 3/4 cup dried cranberries
- 3/4 cup chopped cashews
- 1/4 cup diced sweet onion
- 1/2 teaspoon salt

Direction

- Combine apple juice and quinoa in a saucepan. Bring to a boil; reduce heat and simmer, partially covered, until quinoa is tender, about 20 minutes. Drain excess water and transfer to a large bowl.
- Whisk agave nectar, safflower oil, poppy seeds, and mustard together in a small bowl to make dressing.
- Chill quinoa and dressing in the refrigerator, at least 4 hours.
- Fold apple, cranberries, cashews, onion, and salt into chilled quinoa. Add dressing; mix well to combine.

Nutrition Information

- Calories: 443 calories
- Total Fat: 19.5 g
- Cholesterol: 0 mg
- Sodium: 318 mg
- Total Carbohydrate: 64.2 g
- Protein: 7.1 g

217. Quinoa Salad with Beets Blue Cheese and Nutty Herb Vinaigrette

This is one of those ingredient combinations that, like the Little Black Dress, always seems to be in style, and it's no wonder: earthy, sweet beets, sharp and creamy blue cheese, and bitter greens simply go together beautifully. Skillet-Toasted Quinoa provides additional texture and protein. Like Chimichurri, this vinaigrette s flavors grow more robust if allowed to sit at room temperature for at least 1 day.

Serving: 4 Servings

Ingredients

- 1 garlic clove
- 1/3 cup (1 1/2 ounces/45 grams) walnuts, toasted
- 1 cup (2 ounces/60 grams) watercress with stems
- 2 tablepoons red wine vinegar
- 1 teaspoon Dijon mustard
- Finely grated zest of 1 orange
- 6 tablepoons extra-virgin olive oil
- Salt and freshly ground black pepper
- 3 cups (18 ounces/540 grams) Skillet-Toasted Quinoa
- 8 ounces/225 grams cooked red or golden beets, cut into slices or wedges
- 2 ounces/60 grams Stilton cheese, crumbled
- Salt and freshly ground black pepper

Direction

- For the vinaigrette: Finely chop the garlic. Add the walnuts to the cutting board on top of the garlic and chop them finely. Transfer the garlic-walnut mixture to a medium bowl. Finely chop the watercress and add it to the bowl. Add the vinegar, mustard, and orange zest and whisk to combine. While whisking, drizzle in the olive oil. Adjust the seasoning with salt and pepper.
- For the salad: Divide the quinoa evenly among 4 plates. Top each quinoa mound with an equal amount of beets. Sprinkle the beets with cheese, whisk the

dressing to recombine, and dress each salad with 2 to 3 tablespoons of vinaigrette. Serve immediately.

Nutrition Information

- Calories: 817
- Total Fat: 39 g (60%)
- Saturated Fat: 7 g (35%)
- Cholesterol: 11 mg (4%)
- Sodium: 668 mg (28%)
- Total Carbohydrate: 95 g (32%)
- Protein: 24 g (49%)
- Fiber: 13 g (50%)

218. Quinoa Salad with Dried Fruit and Nuts

"This is an unusual and tasty high-protein grain salad. Quinoa is a grain that has almost no flavor, but the spices add zest. It's well worth trying, I make it often since discovering quinoa at my health food store."

Serving: 10 | Prep: 20 m | Cook: 20 m | Ready in: 2 h

Ingredients

- 1 1/2 cups quinoa
- 1/4 teaspoon salt
- 3 1/2 cups water
- 1 bunch green onions, chopped
- 3/4 cup chopped celery
- 1/2 cup raisins
- 1 pinch cayenne pepper
- 1 tablespoon vegetable oil
- 1 tablespoon distilled white vinegar
- 2 tablespoons lemon juice
- 2 tablespoons sesame oil
- 1/3 cup chopped fresh cilantro
- 3/4 cup chopped pecans

Direction

- Bring the quinoa, salt, and water to a boil in a saucepan. Reduce heat to medium-low, cover, and simmer until the quinoa is tender, 20 to 25 minutes. Once done, scrape into a large bowl, and allow to cool for 20 minutes. Stir in the green onions, celery, raisins, cayenne pepper, vegetable oil, vinegar, lemon juice, and sesame oil. Allow to stand at room temperature for 1 hour to allow the flavors to blend. Stir in the cilantro and pecans before serving.

Nutrition Information

- Calories: 221 calories
- Total Fat: 11.6 g
- Cholesterol: 0 mg
- Sodium: 72 mg
- Total Carbohydrate: 26.3 g
- Protein: 5.1 g

219. Quinoa Salad with Grapefruit Avocado and Arugula

"Intriguing combination of quinoa, arugula, dried cranberries, avocado and grapefruit with a spicy dressing make this a snazzy side dish or lovely summer lunch main dish."

Serving: 4 | Prep: 15 m | Cook: 20 m | Ready in: 1 h

Ingredients

- 1 cup quinoa
- 4 cups water
- 1/4 teaspoon salt
- 1/4 cup dried cranberries
- 1/4 cup fresh lime juice
- 1/4 cup olive oil
- 2 teaspoons honey
- 2 cloves garlic, minced
- 1 teaspoon minced serrano pepper
- 1/4 cup chopped fresh mint
- 1/4 cup minced cilantro
- 1 shallot, minced
- 1/2 cup arugula
- 1 pinch salt and black pepper to taste
- 4 cups baby arugula leaves, washed and dried
- 1 avocado - peeled, pitted and diced
- 1/2 grapefruit, peeled and sectioned

Direction

- In a dry skillet over medium heat, toast the quinoa until it has a nutty aroma. Remove from heat, rinse and drain in a fine mesh strainer. Bring water to a boil in a saucepan, add salt, and slowly add toasted quinoa. Cook until tender and the outer rings appear on the grains, 15 to 20 minutes. Strain through a fine mesh colander. Place in a large bowl to cool.
- In a small bowl, combine cranberries, lime juice, olive oil, honey, garlic, serrano pepper, mint, cilantro, shallot, and arugula. Stir into the cooled quinoa and add salt and freshly ground pepper to taste. Place 1 cup of baby arugula on each salad plate. Top with quinoa mixture, avocado, and grapefruit.

Nutrition Information

- Calories: 427 calories
- Total Fat: 23.7 g
- Cholesterol: 0 mg
- Sodium: 168 mg
- Total Carbohydrate: 49.5 g
- Protein: 8.4 g

220. Quinoa Salad with Mint Almonds and Cranberries

"Are you tired of eating your leftover Thanksgiving meal? If you are, try this recipe. It is healthy and delicious. The combination of the minty mint and the sweet cranberries are so refreshing, just like a dip in the pool."

Serving: 4 | Prep: 25 m | Cook: 15 m | Ready in: 40 m

Ingredients

- 2 cups chicken broth
- 1 cup quinoa
- 3 tablespoons olive oil
- 1/2 cup coarsely chopped mint leaves
- 1/2 cup dry-roasted almonds, unsalted
- 1/2 cup dried cranberries
- 1 cup coarsely chopped kale
- 1/2 cup sliced carrots
- 1/2 cup sliced celery
- 1 scallion, thinly sliced
- 18 grape tomatoes, halved
- 1 lemon, juiced
- 1/2 teaspoon lemon zest
- salt and ground black pepper to taste

Direction

- Bring the chicken broth to a boil in a saucepan over high heat. Add quinoa, reduce heat to medium-low, cover, and simmer until the quinoa is tender and the liquid has been absorbed, about 13 minutes. Stir in olive oil; fluff quinoa with a fork. Set aside to cool slightly.
- Stir mint, almonds, dried cranberries, kale, carrots, celery, scallion, grape tomatoes, lemon juice, and lemon zest. Season to taste with salt and ground black pepper.

Nutrition Information

- Calories: 436 calories
- Total Fat: 22.4 g
- Cholesterol: 2 mg
- Sodium: 527 mg
- Total Carbohydrate: 51.6 g
- Protein: 11.6 g

221. Quinoa Salad with Roasted Yams

"This is an all-time favorite of my friends and family! Add some roasted beets and Romanesco broccoli if desired."

Serving: 5 | Prep: 20 m | Cook: 35 m | Ready in: 1 h 10 m

Ingredients

- 1 1/2 cups diced yams
- 3 cups water
- 2 cups quinoa, soaked and rinsed

- 4 Persian cucumbers - peeled, trimmed, and cut into 1/4-inch cubes
- 1 cup chopped Italian parsley
- 1/4 cup extra-virgin olive oil
- 1/4 cup 1/4-inch cubed onion
- 1 lemon, juiced
- 2 tablespoons red wine vinegar
- salt and ground black pepper to taste
- 5 endive spears to garnish (optional)

Direction

- Preheat oven to 350 degrees F (175 degrees C). Line a baking sheet with aluminum foil; add yams.
- Bake in the preheated oven until yams are tender and wrinkled at the edges, about 20 minutes. Cool to room temperature, about 15 minutes.
- Bring water to a boil in a large saucepan. Add quinoa, stirring once; return to boil. Cook uncovered until water is absorbed, 10 to 12 minutes. Strain, shaking the sieve well to remove all moisture. Transfer to a mixing bowl.
- Stir cucumbers, yams, parsley, olive oil, onion, lemon juice, red wine vinegar, salt, and pepper into the quinoa. Garnish with endive spears.

Nutrition Information

- Calories: 453 calories
- Total Fat: 15.8 g
- Cholesterol: 0 mg
- Sodium: 57 mg
- Total Carbohydrate: 69 g
- Protein: 12.6 g

222. Quinoa Salad with Winter Veggies and Buffalo Chicken Sausage

"This hearty grain salad with browned sausage, carrots, and butternut squash is tossed with quinoa for a delicious all-in-one meal."

Serving: 8

Ingredients

- 3/4 cup uncooked quinoa
- 1 1/4 cups low-sodium chicken broth
- 3 tablespoons olive oil
- 6 links Dietz Watson Buffalo Chicken Sausage, cut into chunks
- 1 medium onion, diced
- 2 cups butternut squash, cut into 1/2-inch cubes
- 1 cup shredded carrot
- 2 tablespoons fresh lemon juice
- 1/2 teaspoon ground cumin
- 1/4 teaspoon salt
- 1/4 teaspoon freshly ground black pepper
- 1 medium red bell pepper, diced
- 1/4 cup fresh flat-leaf parsley, chopped

Direction

- Put the quinoa and chicken broth in a medium saucepan and bring to a boil. Reduce heat to low, cover and simmer until the liquid is absorbed, 12 to 15 minutes. Fluff with a fork.
- While quinoa cooks, heat 1 tablespoon of the oil in a large skillet over medium-high heat. Add the sausage and cook, stirring occasionally, until browned, about 5 minutes. Transfer sausage to a plate.
- Add another tablespoon oil to pan, then add the onion and cook until softened, about 3 minutes. Add the squash and carrots and cook about 5 minutes, until the vegetables are tender-firm.
- In a large bowl, whisk together the lemon juice, remaining oil, cumin, salt and black pepper. Add quinoa, sausage, squash-carrot and onion mixture and mix. Chill in the

refrigerator at least 30 minutes or up to two days. When ready to serve, stir in the parsley.

Nutrition Information

- Calories: 223 calories
- Total Fat: 11.5 g
- Cholesterol: 31 mg
- Sodium: 547 mg
- Total Carbohydrate: 18.5 g
- Protein: 13.4 g

223. Quinoa Side Dish

"Quinoa is a great alternative to rice - it's lighter, and cooks in about half the time."

Serving: 4 | Prep: 15 m | Cook: 20 m | Ready in: 35 m

Ingredients

- 1 tablespoon butter
- 1 cup uncooked quinoa
- 2 cups vegetable broth
- 2 teaspoons chopped garlic
- 2 tablespoons chopped fresh parsley
- 1/2 tablespoon chopped fresh thyme
- 1/4 teaspoon salt
- 1 small onion, finely chopped
- 1 dash fresh lemon juice (optional)

Direction

- Melt butter in a saucepan over medium heat. Add the quinoa, and toast, stirring occasionally, until lightly browned, about 5 minutes. Stir in broth, and bring to a boil. Reduce to a simmer, cover, and cook for 15 minutes, or until quinoa is tender.
- In a bowl, toss quinoa together with garlic, parsley, thyme, salt, and onion. Sprinkle with lemon juice, and serve.

Nutrition Information

- Calories: 207 calories
- Total Fat: 5.8 g
- Cholesterol: 8 mg
- Sodium: 400 mg
- Total Carbohydrate: 32 g
- Protein: 6.9 g

224. Quinoa Squash Muffins

"Protein and texture from the quinoa, sweet pockets from the squash and raisins. You can use any squash, cooked or shredded for these muffins. Enjoy."

Serving: 18 | Prep: 15 m | Cook: 45 m | Ready in: 1 h

Ingredients

- 1 cup water
- 1/2 cup uncooked quinoa, rinsed and drained
- 1 1/2 cups all-purpose flour
- 1 cup whole wheat flour
- 1/2 teaspoon salt
- 1 1/2 teaspoons ground cinnamon
- 1 1/2 teaspoons baking powder
- 1 teaspoon baking soda
- 1 pinch ground cloves (optional)
- 1 pinch ground nutmeg (optional)
- 1 pinch ground allspice (optional)
- 1 pinch ground ginger (optional)
- 1 pinch cayenne pepper (optional)
- 1 1/2 cups shredded squash
- 1 1/2 cups plain yogurt
- 1/2 cup brown sugar
- 1/2 cup raisins
- 1/2 cup chopped walnuts
- 2 eggs
- 1 teaspoon vanilla extract

Direction

- Bring water and quinoa to a boil in a saucepan. Reduce heat to medium-low, cover, and simmer until quinoa is tender and water is absorbed, 15 to 20 minutes.
- Preheat oven to 375 degrees F (190 degrees C). Grease 18 muffin cups or line with paper muffin liners.

- Mix all-purpose flour, whole wheat flour, cinnamon, baking powder, baking soda, cloves, nutmeg, allspice, ground ginger, and cayenne pepper together in a bowl.
- Stir squash, yogurt, brown sugar, raisins, walnuts, eggs, and vanilla together in a large bowl. Add flour mixture to squash mixture; stir. Spoon batter into prepared muffin cups.
- Bake in the preheated oven until golden brown, 30 minutes.

Nutrition Information

- Calories: 161 calories
- Total Fat: 3.6 g
- Cholesterol: 22 mg
- Sodium: 202 mg
- Total Carbohydrate: 28.1 g
- Protein: 5.2 g

225. Quinoa Stuffed Peppers

"This vegetarian dish is so filling, and I love it because its incredibly versatile. You can add whatever spices and vegetables you like!"

Serving: 6 | Prep: 30 m | Cook: 50 m | Ready in: 1 h 20 m

Ingredients

- 1 cup quinoa, rinsed and drained
- 2 cups water
- 2 tablespoons olive oil
- 1 small onion, diced
- 2 cloves garlic, minced
- 1 zucchini, diced
- 1 small eggplant, diced
- 1 tomato, diced
- 1 cup tomato sauce
- salt and ground black pepper to taste
- 6 bell peppers, tops cut off and seeded
- 1 cup shredded mozzarella cheese, or more to taste

Direction

- Preheat oven to 350 degrees F (175 degrees C). Line a deep baking dish with aluminum foil.
- Mix quinoa and water together in a saucepan; bring to a boil. Cover, reduce heat, and simmer until quinoa is tender and water is absorbed, about 15 minutes.
- Heat olive oil in a large skillet over medium heat; cook and stir onion and garlic until fragrant and slightly translucent, 5 to 7 minutes. Add zucchini, eggplant, and tomato; cook until slightly tender, 3 to 5 minutes. Stir tomato sauce into vegetable mixture; cover and simmer until vegetables have softened, about 10 more minutes.
- Stir quinoa into vegetable mixture. Season with salt and pepper. Fill bell peppers with quinoa-vegetable mixture. Place peppers in prepared baking dish. Cover dish with aluminum foil.
- Bake in the preheated oven until bell peppers are slightly tender, about 18 minutes. Remove aluminum foil cover; sprinkle peppers with mozzarella cheese. Bake until cheese is bubbling and melted, about 5 more minutes.

Nutrition Information

- Calories: 251 calories
- Total Fat: 9.6 g
- Cholesterol: 12 mg
- Sodium: 347 mg
- Total Carbohydrate: 32.4 g
- Protein: 11.1 g

226. Quinoa Stuffed Pork Tenderloin

"I've been searching for stuffing recipes that don't use bread as I try and avoid gluten. This quinoa stuffing was my own solution. The sweetness of the apple and raisins in this dish plays nicely with baked yams. Hopefully there are others who will enjoy it as much as I did."

Serving: 4 | Prep: 40 m | Cook: 55 m | Ready in: 1 h 45 m

Ingredients

- 1/4 cup uncooked quinoa
- 1/2 cup water
- 2 tablespoons olive oil
- 1/2 onion, chopped
- 2 cloves garlic, chopped
- 1 small apples - peeled, cored and chopped
- 1/4 cup raisins
- 2 tablespoons pine nuts
- 4 mushrooms, chopped
- 2 tablespoons white wine
- 1 (1 pound) pork tenderloin
- 1 pinch ground cinnamon
- 1 pinch garam masala, or to taste
- salt and ground black pepper to taste

Direction

- Bring the quinoa and water to a boil in a saucepan over medium-high heat. Reduce heat to low, cover, and simmer until the quinoa is tender, and the water has been absorbed, about 15 minutes.
- Heat the olive oil in a skillet over medium heat. Cook and stir the onion, garlic, apples, raisins, pine nuts, and mushrooms until the onion has softened and turned translucent, about 8 minutes. Stir in the white wine, and cook another minute until the liquid has evaporated. Combine the apple mixture and quinoa until evenly mixed; set aside.
- Preheat an oven to 425 degrees F (220 degrees C).
- Cut the pork tenderloin from one side through the middle horizontally to within one-half inch of the other side. Open the two sides and spread them out like an open book. Place between two sheets of heavy plastic (resealable freezer bags work well) on a solid, level surface. Firmly pound the tenderloin with the smooth side of a meat mallet to a thickness of 1/2 inch.
- Season the tenderloin on both sides with cinnamon, garam masala, salt, and black pepper. Spoon the quinoa filling onto the tenderloin, then roll up and secure with kitchen twine or toothpicks. Place onto a roasting pan.
- Roast in the preheated oven until the pork is no longer pink in the center, about 35 minutes. An instant-read thermometer inserted into the center of the filling should read 145 degrees F (63 degrees C). Cover with aluminum foil, and let rest for 10 minutes before slicing.

Nutrition Information

- Calories: 282 calories
- Total Fat: 12.5 g
- Cholesterol: 49 mg
- Sodium: 44 mg
- Total Carbohydrate: 21.2 g
- Protein: 21.2 g

227. Quinoa Stuffing

"Quinoa is a fluffy, slightly crunchy, high-protein, gluten-free alternative grain native to South America. This can be used to stuff a turkey or served as a side dish."

Serving: 8 | Prep: 25 m | Cook: 20 m | Ready in: 45 m

Ingredients

- 4 cups vegetable stock
- 2 cups quinoa
- 1/4 cup olive oil
- 1 butternut squash - peeled, seeded, and diced
- 2 small zucchinis, cut into 1-inch cubes
- 1 bunch green onions, chopped
- 1 cup diced dried apricots
- 1 cup dried cranberries

- 1 cup chopped fresh parsley
- 1 lime, juiced, or to taste

Direction

- Bring vegetable stock to a boil in a saucepan, reduce heat to low, and stir in quinoa. Cover pan and simmer until quinoa absorbs the liquid, 10 to 15 minutes. Remove from heat.
- Heat olive oil in a large skillet over medium heat. Cook and stir butternut squash and zucchinis in the hot oil until slightly browned, about 10 minutes. Stir quinoa into the vegetables and gently mix green onions, apricots, cranberries, and parsley into the stuffing. Drizzle with lime juice to taste.

Nutrition Information

- Calories: 387 calories
- Total Fat: 9.8 g
- Cholesterol: 0 mg
- Sodium: 258 mg
- Total Carbohydrate: 70.7 g
- Protein: 9.1 g

228. Quinoa Summer Salad

"If you are looking for something different and distinct to bring to a summer barbeque, you have found the perfect recipe. Gluten-free, dairy-free, and vegetarian. The lack of allergy-inducing ingredients does not reflect the intense sensory-flavor experience you and your guests will enjoy."

Serving: 8 | Prep: 15 m | Cook: 15 m | Ready in: 4 h 30 m

Ingredients

- 4 cups water
- 1 cup white quinoa
- 1 cup red quinoa
- 1 1/2 large red onions, chopped
- 1 red bell pepper, chopped
- 1 yellow bell pepper, chopped
- 1 teaspoon sea salt
- 12 grinds black pepper from a grinder
- 1/4 cup olive oil
- 2 limes, juiced
- 2 tablespoons chopped fresh cilantro

Direction

- Bring water to a boil in a pot; add white quinoa and red quinoa. Reduce heat, cover, and simmer until water is absorbed, 15 minutes. Set quinoa aside to cool while you complete the remaining steps.
- Combine red onions, red bell pepper, yellow bell pepper, sea salt, and black pepper together in a bowl. Stir in white and red quinoa.
- Whisk olive oil and lime juice together in a separate bowl; pour over quinoa mixture. Stir to coat. Add cilantro and stir to incorporate. Cover salad and refrigerate for flavors to blend, at least 4 hours.

Nutrition Information

- Calories: 239 calories
- Total Fat: 9.5 g
- Cholesterol: 0 mg
- Sodium: 236 mg
- Total Carbohydrate: 32.9 g
- Protein: 6.4 g

229. Quinoa Summer Salad with Feta

"This a great healthy side dish or a quick lunch, if you have more than one serving."

Serving: 4 | Prep: 15 m | Cook: 15 m | Ready in: 1 h

Ingredients

- 2 cups water
- 1 cup quinoa
- 1 (4 ounce) package feta cheese, crumbled
- 1 small cucumber, thinly sliced
- 1 roma (plum) tomato, diced
- 1 tablespoon lemon juice

- 1 tablespoon cider vinegar
- 1 tablespoon olive oil
- 1 teaspoon dried dill weed
- 1 teaspoon salt
- 1 teaspoon ground black pepper

Direction

- Bring water and quinoa to a boil in a saucepan. Reduce heat to medium-low, cover, and simmer until quinoa is tender and water has been absorbed, 15 to 20 minutes. Refrigerate quinoa in a large bowl until cool, about 30 minutes.
- Stir feta cheese, cucumber, tomato, lemon juice, vinegar, olive oil, dill weed, salt, and black pepper into quinoa.

Nutrition Information

- Calories: 270 calories
- Total Fat: 11.9 g
- Cholesterol: 25 mg
- Sodium: 912 mg
- Total Carbohydrate: 30.8 g
- Protein: 10.1 g

230. Quinoa Tabbouleh

"This tabouli recipe is different. Instead of using bulgur like traditional tabouli, this recipe uses quinoa. It is a grain that is available at health food stores. It looks and tastes better than bulgur. My husband and I both love this and neither of us is vegetarian. It's a great meal for a hot summer day. The longer it sits the better it tastes."

Serving: 4 | Prep: 15 m | Cook: 15 m | Ready in: 30 m

Ingredients

- 2 cups water
- 1 cup quinoa
- 1 pinch salt
- 1/4 cup olive oil
- 1/2 teaspoon sea salt
- 1/4 cup lemon juice
- 3 tomatoes, diced
- 1 cucumber, diced
- 2 bunches green onions, diced
- 2 carrots, grated
- 1 cup fresh parsley, chopped

Direction

- In a saucepan bring water to a boil. Add quinoa and a pinch of salt. Reduce heat to low, cover and simmer for 15 minutes. Allow to cool to room temperature; fluff with a fork.
- Meanwhile, in a large bowl, combine olive oil, sea salt, lemon juice, tomatoes, cucumber, green onions, carrots and parsley. Stir in cooled quinoa.

Nutrition Information

- Calories: 354 calories
- Total Fat: 16.6 g
- Cholesterol: 0 mg
- Sodium: 286 mg
- Total Carbohydrate: 45.7 g
- Protein: 9.6 g

231. Quinoa Tabbouleh Salad

"Cool, refreshing vegetarian salad. Great for picnics! You can substitute water for the vegetable broth, if desired."

Serving: 12 | Prep: 25 m | Cook: 15 m | Ready in: 1 h 40 m

Ingredients

- 2 cups vegetable broth
- 1 cup quinoa
- 1 cucumber, chopped
- 2 tomatoes, chopped
- 1/2 cup fresh parsley, chopped
- 2 green onions, chopped
- 2 tablespoons chopped fresh mint
- 2 cloves garlic, minced
- 1/4 cup olive oil
- 1/4 cup lemon juice
- 1/2 teaspoon salt, or to taste

Direction

- Bring broth and quinoa to a boil in a saucepan. Reduce heat to medium-low, cover, and simmer until quinoa is tender and water has been absorbed, about 15 minutes.
- Combine cucumber, tomatoes, parsley, green onions, mint, and garlic in a large bowl. Add quinoa, olive oil, lemon juice, and salt to cucumber mixture; toss to combine. Cover the bowl with plastic wrap and refrigerate until flavors combine, at least 1 hour.

Nutrition Information

- Calories: 107 calories
- Total Fat: 5.5 g
- Cholesterol: 0 mg
- Sodium: 178 mg
- Total Carbohydrate: 12.3 g
- Protein: 2.6 g

232. Quinoa Tabbouleh Salad GlutenFree

"A refreshing twist on tabbouleh. This is my go-to recipe for so many occasions; potlucks, salads and lunches on the go. Every time I take it somewhere, someone asks for the recipe."

Serving: 4 | Prep: 25 m | Cook: 15 m | Ready in: 1 h

Ingredients

- 1 cup water
- 2/3 cup quinoa
- 5 carrots, diced
- 1/3 cup currants
- 1/4 cup chopped fresh mint
- 1/4 cup chopped fresh parsley
- 1/4 cup green onions, chopped
- 1/2 cup olive oil
- 1/4 cup lime juice
- 1 teaspoon agave nectar
- 1/2 teaspoon ground cumin
- 1/2 teaspoon salt

Direction

- Bring water and quinoa to a boil in a saucepan. Reduce heat to medium-low, cover, and simmer until quinoa is tender and water has been absorbed, about 15 minutes. Remove from heat and let quinoa rest, covered, for 5 minutes. Uncover the saucepan and cool to room temperature.
- Stir quinoa, carrots, currants, mint, parsley, and green onions together in a bowl.
- Combine olive oil, lime juice, agave nectar, cumin, and salt in a jar; seal the jar with a lid and shake vigorously until dressing is well-blended. Pour dressing over quinoa mixture and toss to coat. Cover the bowl with plastic wrap and refrigerate until flavors blend, at least 30 minutes.

Nutrition Information

- Calories: 422 calories
- Total Fat: 29.1 g
- Cholesterol: 0 mg
- Sodium: 352 mg
- Total Carbohydrate: 37.9 g
- Protein: 5.6 g

233. Quinoa Tuna Casserole

"My father is on a low-carb diet, but I love tuna casserole so I decided to try to make it with quinoa. This is also kind of a recipe for quinoa risotto as that is how I cooked the quinoa."

Serving: 15 | Prep: 15 m | Cook: 1 h 5 m | Ready in: 1 h 20 m

Ingredients

- 1 tablespoon olive oil
- 2 cups sliced fresh mushrooms
- 2 onions, sliced
- 2 tablespoons butter
- 2 cups quinoa
- 6 cups chicken stock
- salt to taste

- 1 (5 ounce) can tuna, drained
- ground black pepper to taste
- 1/4 cup butter
- 1 egg
- 2 tablespoons all-purpose flour
- 1/4 cup bread crumbs, or as needed

Direction

- Preheat oven to 325 degrees F (165 degrees C).
- Heat olive oil in a large skillet over medium heat. Cook and stir mushrooms and onion in hot oil until softened, about 5 minutes. Remove from heat and set aside.
- Melt 2 tablespoons of butter in a stockpot over medium heat. Cook quinoa in melted butter until lightly brown. Pour enough stock to just cover the quinoa. Allow the liquid to reduce to half. Continue this process until quinoa is soft and all stock is absorbed, about 30 minutes. Season with salt throughout process.
- Stir mushrooms, onion, and tuna through the quinoa; season with black pepper. Stir 1/4 cup butter, the egg, and flour into the quinoa mixture; transfer to a casserole dish and top with bread crumbs to cover.
- Bake until the top is golden brown and the center is hot, about 30 minutes.

Nutrition Information

- Calories: 176 calories
- Total Fat: 7.7 g
- Cholesterol: 27 mg
- Sodium: 332 mg
- Total Carbohydrate: 20.3 g
- Protein: 7 g

234. Quinoa Tuna Salad

"This high-protein dish makes a great side to any main course, or even a complete meal."

Serving: 6 | Prep: 20 m | Cook: 15 m | Ready in: 2 h 35 m

Ingredients

- 1/4 cup quinoa
- 1/2 cup water
- 1 (15 ounce) can garbanzo beans, drained and rinsed
- 1 (15 ounce) can black olives, drained and sliced
- 1 (14.5 ounce) can whole kernel corn, drained
- 2 (5 ounce) cans tuna, drained
- 1 cup chopped fresh spinach
- 1 cup diced fresh tomatoes
- 2 tablespoons olive oil, or more if needed
- 2 tablespoons chopped fresh cilantro, or more to taste

Direction

- Bring quinoa and water to a boil in a saucepan. Reduce heat to medium-low, cover, and simmer until the quinoa is tender and the water has been absorbed, about 15 to 20 minutes. Set aside to cool.
- Combine garbanzo beans, black olives, corn, tuna, spinach, tomatoes, olive oil, and cilantro in a large bowl; stir to coat. Stir in quinoa. Refrigerate salad to allow flavors to blend, 2 hours to overnight. Serve chilled.

Nutrition Information

- Calories: 311 calories
- Total Fat: 14 g
- Cholesterol: 13 mg
- Sodium: 981 mg
- Total Carbohydrate: 33.5 g
- Protein: 16.7 g

235. Quinoa Turkey Stuffing

"Quinoa, a delicious and nutritious whole grain, is used to make a light and tasty turkey stuffing. I prefer to bake this stuffing in the bird, but it can be baked separately in another baking dish and basted with the turkey juice."

Serving: 8 | Prep: 20 m | Cook: 4 h | Ready in: 4 h 20 m

Ingredients

- 1 cup quinoa, rinsed
- 2 cups water
- 1 onion, chopped
- 1 pound fresh mushrooms, sliced
- 2 apples - peeled, cored, and chopped
- 1/4 cup pine nuts
- 1/3 cup raisins
- 2 cloves garlic, minced
- 1 teaspoon salt
- 1/4 teaspoon ground black pepper
- 2 teaspoons poultry seasoning

Direction

- Place the quinoa and water in a large, microwave-safe bowl; cover. Cook on HIGH for 20 minutes.
- Stir the onion, mushrooms, apples, pine nuts, raisins, garlic, salt, pepper, and poultry seasoning in with the quinoa.
- Pack lightly into uncooked turkey. Roast turkey as directed.

Nutrition Information

- Calories: 164 calories
- Total Fat: 3.8 g
- Cholesterol: 0 mg
- Sodium: 299 mg
- Total Carbohydrate: 28.8 g
- Protein: 6.4 g

236. Quinoa Vegetable Medley

"I came up with this recipe with items I had on hand. It turned out pretty tasty, so I thought I'd share it."

Serving: 4 | Prep: 25 m | Cook: 35 m | Ready in: 1 h

Ingredients

- 1 tablespoon olive oil, or more if needed
- 1 sweet onion (such as Vidalia®), chopped
- 3 cloves garlic, minced, or to taste
- 1 cup quinoa, rinsed
- 1 1/4 cups vegetable broth
- 1 small zucchini, chopped
- 1 cup mushrooms, sliced
- 2 stalks celery, chopped
- 1 teaspoon ground black pepper
- 1/2 teaspoon sea salt
- 1 cup baby spinach leaves
- 1 (15 ounce) can garbanzo beans, drained and rinsed

Direction

- Heat olive oil in a large saucepan over medium heat; cook and stir the onion until translucent, about 5 minutes, then stir in garlic and quinoa. Reduce heat to medium-low; cook and stir the mixture until the quinoa becomes light brown in color and has a toasted fragrance, 5 to 7 minutes. Slowly pour in the stock, stirring constantly. Bring the mixture back to a boil over medium heat, and stir in the zucchini, mushrooms, and celery; season to taste with salt and black pepper. Reduce heat to medium-low, and allow the mixture to simmer, stirring occasionally, until the vegetables are tender, about 15 minutes. Stir in the baby spinach and garbanzo beans, and simmer until quinoa is tender, 10 to 15 more minutes.

Nutrition Information

- Calories: 314 calories
- Total Fat: 7.2 g
- Cholesterol: 0 mg
- Sodium: 603 mg
- Total Carbohydrate: 51.9 g

- Protein: 11.8 g

237. Quinoa Vegetable Salad

"This is a wonderful dish--light and very tasty! My four kids (ages 2-7) ate it up and asked for more!"

Serving: 12 | Prep: 20 m | Cook: 25 m | Ready in: 1 h 30 m

Ingredients

- 1 teaspoon canola oil
- 1 tablespoon minced garlic
- 1/4 cup diced (yellow or purple) onion
- 2 1/2 cups water
- 2 teaspoons salt, or to taste
- 1/4 teaspoon ground black pepper
- 2 cups quinoa
- 3/4 cup diced fresh tomato
- 3/4 cup diced carrots
- 1/2 cup diced yellow bell pepper
- 1/2 cup diced cucumber
- 1/2 cup frozen corn kernels, thawed
- 1/4 cup diced red onion
- 1 1/2 tablespoons chopped fresh cilantro
- 1 tablespoon chopped fresh mint
- 1 teaspoon salt
- 1/4 teaspoon ground black pepper
- 2 tablespoons olive oil
- 3 tablespoons balsamic vinegar

Direction

- Heat the canola oil in a saucepan over medium heat. Cook and stir the garlic and 1/4 cup onion in the hot oil until the onion has softened and turned translucent, about 5 minutes. Pour in the water, 2 teaspoons salt, and 1/4 teaspoon black pepper and bring to a boil; stir the quinoa into the mixture, reduce heat to medium-low, and cover. Simmer until the quinoa is tender, about 20 minutes. Drain any remaining water from the quinoa with a mesh strainer and transfer to a large mixing bowl. Refrigerate until cold.
- Stir the tomato, carrots, bell pepper, cucumber, corn, and 1/4 cup red onion into the chilled quinoa. Season with cilantro, mint, 1 teaspoon salt, and 1/4 teaspoon black pepper. Drizzle the olive oil and balsamic vinegar over the salad; gently stir until evenly mixed.

Nutrition Information

- Calories: 148 calories
- Total Fat: 4.5 g
- Cholesterol: 0 mg
- Sodium: 592 mg
- Total Carbohydrate: 22.9 g
- Protein: 4.6 g

238. Quinoa Vegetable Soup

"I had never heard of quinoa until I went to Peru and discovered a delicious, traditional soup. There are a lot of ingredients, but it is worth the work!"

Serving: 6 | Prep: 35 m | Cook: 25 m | Ready in: 1 h

Ingredients

- 1 tablespoon vegetable oil
- 2/3 cup quinoa
- 1 carrot, diced
- 1 stalk celery, diced
- 1/2 onion, finely chopped
- 1/2 green bell pepper, seeded and chopped
- 2 cloves garlic, crushed
- 2 (15 ounce) cans chicken broth
- 3 1/2 cups water
- 2 large tomatoes, finely chopped
- 1/4 head cabbage, chopped
- salt and pepper to taste
- 1/4 cup chopped fresh parsley, for garnish

Direction

- Heat the vegetable oil in a large pot on medium-high heat. Stir in the quinoa, carrot, celery, onion, bell pepper, and garlic. Cook for a few minutes, until lightly browned, stirring frequently.

- Pour in the chicken broth, water, tomatoes, and cabbage. Increase heat to high and bring to a boil. Reduce heat to medium and simmer until the quinoa and vegetables are tender, about 10 minutes. Season to taste with salt and pepper. Garnish with parsley before servings.

Nutrition Information

- Calories: 133 calories
- Total Fat: 4 g
- Cholesterol: 4 mg
- Sodium: 893 mg
- Total Carbohydrate: 20.1 g
- Protein: 4.9 g

239. Quinoa Veggie Salad with Zesty Vinaigrette

"Quinoa with various veggies and a zesty (and easy) vinaigrette that makes a wonderful salad dressing for any salad. I used one English cucumber instead of 2 normal cucumbers because we prefer the taste. Cook the quinoa with the water as you would normal rice (works in a rice cooker as well)."

Serving: 24 | Prep: 10 m | Cook: 20 m | Ready in: 1 h 30 m

Ingredients

- 4 cups quinoa
- 4 cups water
- 1/4 cup red wine vinegar
- 2 teaspoons salt
- 1 teaspoon ground black pepper
- 1 teaspoon lemon juice
- 4 teaspoons Dijon mustard
- 1 cup canola oil
- 2 cucumbers, peeled and chopped
- 1 green bell pepper, chopped
- 1/2 red onion, chopped
- 2 tomatoes, chopped
- 1 (15 ounce) can black olives, chopped

Direction

- Bring the quinoa and water to a boil in a saucepan. Reduce heat to medium-low, cover, and simmer until the quinoa is tender and the water has been absorbed, about 15 to 20 minutes. Scrape the cooked quinoa into a large bowl and refrigerate until cold, about 1 hour.
- Place the vinegar, salt, pepper, lemon juice, and mustard into a blender. Drizzle in the oil while blending at high speed until the dressing is thick.
- Add the cucumbers, bell pepper, red onion, tomato, and olives to the bowl with the quinoa. Pour the dressing overtop and gently fold until evenly mixed.

Nutrition Information

- Calories: 215 calories
- Total Fat: 13 g
- Cholesterol: 0 mg
- Sodium: 371 mg
- Total Carbohydrate: 21.2 g
- Protein: 4.4 g

240. Quinoa with Asian Flavors

"Quinoa is the ultimate super food. Cook it like rice in a rice cooker or on the stove with chicken broth, soy sauce, green onions, ginger, and garlic, and you have a delicious and healthy side dish. It goes great with chicken, fish, and seafood."

Serving: 4 | Prep: 5 m | Cook: 35 m | Ready in: 40 m

Ingredients

- 1 tablespoon extra-virgin olive oil
- 1 cup quinoa
- 2 cups chicken broth
- 2 tablespoons soy sauce
- 1 tablespoon minced fresh ginger root
- 1 clove garlic, minced
- 2 green onions, chopped

Direction

- Heat olive oil in a saucepan over medium heat. Stir in quinoa and allow to toast for 2 to 3 minutes, then add chicken broth, soy sauce, ginger and garlic. Increase heat and bring to a boil. Cover and reduce heat to low. Simmer until all liquid has been absorbed, 25 to 30 minutes. Fluff quinoa with fork and top with green onions before serving.

Nutrition Information

- Calories: 196 calories
- Total Fat: 6 g
- Cholesterol: 0 mg
- Sodium: 455 mg
- Total Carbohydrate: 28.9 g
- Protein: 6.7 g

241. Quinoa with Butternut Squash Chicken and Goat Cheese

"This recipe is a recreation of a fabulous lunch I had at a favorite restaurant in the Milwaukee, WI area. My teenagers and husband loved it too! Serve warm or cold with balsamic vinaigrette."

Serving: 6 | Prep: 15 m | Cook: 30 m | Ready in: 45 m

Ingredients

- 2 large boneless, skinless chicken breasts
- water to cover
- 1 1/2 cups quinoa
- 1 tablespoon chicken bouillon granules
- 2 tablespoons butter
- 1 cup chopped pecans
- 1 small butternut squash, peeled and cut into 1/2-inch dice
- 1 cup sweetened dried cranberries (such as Craisins®)
- 1 (5.5 ounce) package crumbled goat cheese
- 2 tablespoons fresh parsley, or more to taste
- salt and ground black pepper to taste

Direction

- Place chicken breasts in a saucepan; add water and bring to a boil. Lower heat to medium and simmer just until chicken breasts are no longer pink in the middle, 5 to 8 minutes. Remove chicken breasts and set aside to cool, reserving water.
- Measure 3 cups from reserved water and discard any remaining. Pour the 3 cups water back into saucepan. Add quinoa and bouillon; return to a boil. Reduce heat to medium-low, cover, and simmer until water is absorbed and quinoa is tender, 15 to 20 minutes.
- Melt butter in a large skillet over medium-high heat. Add pecans and toss until fragrant and one shade darker, about 5 minutes. Remove pecans and set aside. Add butternut squash and 2 tablespoons water to the same skillet; cook and stir until just tender, adding more water if needed, 4 to 5 minutes.
- Chop chicken breasts into 1/2-inch pieces.
- Combine cooked quinoa, chicken, squash, and pecans in a bowl. Stir in cranberries, goat cheese, and parsley; season with salt and pepper.

Nutrition Information

- Calories: 631 calories
- Total Fat: 29.1 g
- Cholesterol: 70 mg
- Sodium: 420 mg
- Total Carbohydrate: 66.9 g
- Protein: 29.9 g

242. Quinoa with Carrots and Raisins

"A sweet and spicy quinoa dish that's perfect for fall. Works well as either a main or side dish."

Serving: 6 | Prep: 10 m | Cook: 25 m | Ready in: 40 m

Ingredients

- 1/4 cup olive oil
- 1 yellow onion, diced
- 2 carrots, grated
- 1 1/4 cups raisins
- 1 tablespoon pumpkin pie spice
- 1 1/2 cups quinoa
- 3/4 cup chopped cilantro
- 1 1/2 cups orange juice
- 1 1/2 cups water
- 1/4 cup chopped walnuts (optional)

Direction

- Heat olive oil in a large saucepan over medium heat. Cook and stir onion, carrots, raisins, and pumpkin pie spice until onion becomes golden, about 5 minutes. Stir in quinoa and cilantro and allow to toast for a few minutes. Pour orange juice and water in and stir well, bringing to a boil. Reduce heat cook until all the liquid is absorbed, about 15 minutes. Remove from heat and let stand for 5 minutes, then add walnuts. Fluff with a fork and serve.

Nutrition Information

- Calories: 420 calories
- Total Fat: 15.3 g
- Cholesterol: 0 mg
- Sodium: 26 mg
- Total Carbohydrate: 66.1 g
- Protein: 8.8 g

243. Quinoa with Chicken Asparagus and Red Peppers

"I wanted to make a quick and light recipe using quinoa, and I had some asparagus and red peppers in the fridge -- who knew that the combination could taste so good!"

Serving: 4 | Prep: 15 m | Cook: 30 m | Ready in: 45 m

Ingredients

- 1 cup quinoa
- 2 cups chicken broth
- 1 tablespoon vegetable oil
- 3 skinless, boneless chicken breast halves, cut into 1-inch pieces
- 8 spears fresh asparagus, trimmed and cut into 1-inch pieces
- 1/2 red bell pepper, chopped

Direction

- Stir quinoa and chicken broth together in a saucepan and bring to a boil. Reduce heat to medium-low and simmer until the quinoa has absorbed the chicken broth, about 15 minutes.
- Heat vegetable oil in a large skillet over medium heat and cook and stir the chicken breast pieces in the hot oil until no longer pink inside, about 5 minutes. Stir asparagus and red bell pepper into the skillet and cook and stir until barely tender, about 3 more minutes.
- Lightly mix cooked quinoa into the chicken and vegetables until thoroughly combined, heat for 1 to 2 minutes, and serve.

Nutrition Information

- Calories: 291 calories
- Total Fat: 8 g
- Cholesterol: 48 mg
- Sodium: 527 mg
- Total Carbohydrate: 29.4 g
- Protein: 24.1 g

244. Quinoa with Chickpeas and Tomatoes

"This delicious recipe was presented to me by a vegan friend. The lime juice gives the quinoa a fresh flavor that can't be beat!"

Serving: 6 | Prep: 20 m | Cook: 20 m | Ready in: 40 m

Ingredients

- 1 cup quinoa
- 1/8 teaspoon salt
- 1 3/4 cups water
- 1 cup canned garbanzo beans (chickpeas), drained
- 1 tomato, chopped
- 1 clove garlic, minced
- 3 tablespoons lime juice
- 4 teaspoons olive oil
- 1/2 teaspoon ground cumin
- 1 pinch salt and pepper to taste
- 1/2 teaspoon chopped fresh parsley

Direction

- Place the quinoa in a fine mesh strainer, and rinse under cold, running water until the water no longer foams. Bring the quinoa, salt, and water to a boil in a saucepan. Reduce heat to medium-low, cover, and simmer until the quinoa is tender, 20 to 25 minutes.
- Once done, stir in the garbanzo beans, tomatoes, garlic, lime juice, and olive oil. Season with cumin, salt, and pepper. Sprinkle with chopped fresh parsley to serve.

Nutrition Information

- Calories: 185 calories
- Total Fat: 5.4 g
- Cholesterol: 0 mg
- Sodium: 176 mg
- Total Carbohydrate: 28.8 g
- Protein: 6 g

245. Quinoa with Feta Walnuts and Dried Cranberries

"Fast and easy to make, this can be used as a main dish, side dish, or even a snack. Please use the 'real deal' Greek feta; it will add so much more flavor!"

Serving: 6 | Prep: 15 m | Cook: 15 m | Ready in: 30 m

Ingredients

- 2 cups low-sodium chicken broth
- 1 cup quinoa
- 1/2 cup chopped walnuts
- 1/2 cup dried cranberries
- 1/3 cup crumbled feta cheese

Direction

- Bring chicken broth and quinoa to a boil in a saucepan. Reduce heat to low, cover, and simmer until quinoa is tender and broth has been absorbed, 15 to 20 minutes. Transfer quinoa to a bowl.
- Stir walnuts and cranberries through the quinoa; add feta cheese and gently stir.

Nutrition Information

- Calories: 243 calories
- Total Fat: 11.4 g
- Cholesterol: 14 mg
- Sodium: 195 mg
- Total Carbohydrate: 28.6 g
- Protein: 8.6 g

246. Quinoa with Ground Turkey

"This was a dish I threw together last minute that was a success! My husband and kids loved it and will be a dish we have often. The cheese really complements the dish and should not be left out."

Serving: 6 | Prep: 15 m | Cook: 35 m | Ready in: 50 m

Ingredients

- 1 1/2 cups water
- 1 cup quinoa

- 2 tablespoons olive oil
- 1/2 onion, chopped
- 1 red bell pepper, chopped
- 1 pinch Himalayan salt to taste
- 1 1/4 pounds ground turkey
- 1 pinch freshly ground black pepper to taste
- 4 cloves garlic, minced
- 1 teaspoon minced fresh sage
- 1 teaspoon minced fresh rosemary
- 1/2 cup grated Mizithra cheese

Direction

- Bring water and quinoa to a boil in a saucepan. Reduce heat to medium-low, cover, and simmer until quinoa is tender and water has been absorbed, 15 to 20 minutes.
- Heat olive oil in a skillet over medium heat. Cook and stir onion and red bell pepper in the hot oil until tender and starting to brown, about 10 minutes; season with salt.
- Generously season ground turkey with salt and pepper; add to onion mixture and increase temperature to medium-high. Cook and stir turkey mixture until almost browned and crumbly, 5 to 7 minutes; drain excess grease and reduce heat to medium-low. Add garlic, sage, and rosemary to turkey mixture; cook and stir until fragrant and turkey is browned, 2 to 3 minutes more.
- Mix quinoa into turkey mixture and cook until quinoa is heated through, 2 to 3 minutes. Add Mizithra cheese to quinoa and turkey and remove skillet from heat; season with salt and pepper.

Nutrition Information

- Calories: 330 calories
- Total Fat: 15.1 g
- Cholesterol: 77 mg
- Sodium: 303 mg
- Total Carbohydrate: 32.6 g
- Protein: 24.6 g

247. Quinoa with Mango and Curried Yogurt

Serving: Makes 6 side-dish servings

Ingredients

- 1/3 cup plain yogurt
- 1 tablespoon fresh lime juice
- 2 teaspoons curry powder
- 1 teaspoon finely grated peeled fresh ginger
- 3/4 teaspoon salt
- 1/4 teaspoon black pepper
- 2 tablespoons vegetable or peanut oil
- 1 1/3 cups quinoa (7 1/2 ounce)*
- 1 pound firm-ripe mango, peeled, pitted, and cut into 1/2-inch chunks (2 cups)
- 1 red bell pepper, cut into 1/4-inch dice
- 1 fresh jalapeño chile, seeded (if desired for less heat) and minced
- 1/3 cup chopped fresh mint
- 1/2 cup salted roasted peanuts (2 1/2 ounces), chopped

Direction

- Whisk together yogurt, lime juice, curry powder, ginger, salt, and pepper in a large bowl. Add oil in a slow stream, whisking until combined.
- Rinse quinoa in a bowl using 5 changes of water, rubbing grains and letting them settle before pouring off water (if quinoa does not settle, drain in a large sieve after each rinsing).
- Cook quinoa in a 4- to 5-quart pot of boiling salted water 10 minutes. Drain in a large sieve and rinse under cold running water.
- Set sieve with quinoa over a saucepan containing 1 1/2 inches boiling water (sieve should not touch water) and steam quinoa, covered with a kitchen towel and lid, until fluffy and dry, 10 to 12 minutes. Toss quinoa with curried yogurt and remaining ingredients in a large bowl. Serve warm or at room temperature.
- *Available at specialty foods shops, natural foods stores, and ethnicgrocer.com (866-438-4642).

Nutrition Information

- Calories: 172
- Total Fat: 11 g (17%)
- Saturated Fat: 2 g (9%)
- Cholesterol: 2 mg (1%)
- Sodium: 302 mg (13%)
- Total Carbohydrate: 16 g (5%)
- Protein: 5 g (9%)
- Fiber: 3 g (13%)

248. Quinoa with Moroccan Winter Squash and Carrot Stew

A gorgeous, satisfying vegetarian main course that's easy to make. Quinoa requires no pre-soaking, so it's as simple to do as rice.

Serving: Makes 4 to 6 servings

Ingredients

- 2 tablespoons olive oil
- 1 cup chopped onion
- 3 garlic cloves, chopped
- 2 teaspoons Hungarian sweet paprika
- 1 teaspoon salt
- 1/2 teaspoon ground black pepper
- 1/2 teaspoon ground coriander
- 1/2 teaspoon ground cumin
- 1/2 teaspoon turmeric
- 1/2 teaspoon ground ginger
- 1/2 teaspoon cayenne pepper
- Pinch of saffron
- 1 cup water
- 1 14 1/2-ounce can diced tomatoes, drained
- 2 tablespoons fresh lemon juice
- 3 cups 1-inch cubes peeled butternut squash (from 1 1/2-pound squash)
- 2 cups 3/4-inch cubes peeled carrots
- 1 cup quinoa*
- 1 tablespoon butter
- 1 tablespoon olive oil
- 1/2 cup finely chopped onion
- 1/4 cup finely chopped peeled carrot
- 2 garlic cloves, minced
- 1/2 teaspoon salt
- 1/2 teaspoon turmeric
- 2 cups water
- 1/2 cup chopped fresh cilantro, divided
- 2 teaspoons chopped fresh mint, divided

Direction

- For stew: Heat oil in large saucepan over medium heat. Add onion; sauté until soft, stirring often, about 5 minutes. Add garlic; stir 1 minute. Mix in paprika and next 8 ingredients. Add 1 cup water, tomatoes, and lemon juice. Bring to boil. Add squash and carrots. Cover and simmer over medium-low heat until vegetables are tender, stirring occasionally, about 20 minutes. Season with salt and pepper. (Can be prepared 1 day ahead. Cover and chill.)
- For quinoa: Rinse quinoa; drain. Melt butter with oil in large saucepan over medium heat. Add onion and carrot. Cover; cook until vegetables begin to brown, stirring often, about 10 minutes. Add garlic, salt, and turmeric; sauté 1 minute. Add quinoa; stir 1 minute. Add 2 cups water. Bring to boil; reduce heat to medium-low. Cover; simmer until liquid is absorbed and quinoa is tender, about 15 minutes.
- Rewarm stew. Stir in half of cilantro and half of mint. Spoon quinoa onto platter, forming well in center. Spoon stew into well. Sprinkle remaining herbs over.
- *A grain with a delicate flavor and a texture similar to couscous; available at natural foods stores.
- Per serving: 271 calories, 11 g fat (2 g saturated), 5 mg cholesterol, 645 mg sodium, 40 g carbohydrates, 7 g fiber, 7 g protein
- Nutritional analysis provided by Nutrition Data
- See Nutrition Data's complete analysis of this recipe ›

249. Quinoa with Mushrooms

"Quinoa is a healthy grain that can be substituted in most recipes for rice or couscous. I recently experimented with quinoa and made this dish which my husband and I both love. This easy-to-make and tasty side dish is similar to a pilaf."

Serving: 6 | Prep: 20 m | Cook: 20 m | Ready in: 40 m

Ingredients

- 1 tablespoon olive oil
- 1 (8 ounce) package mushrooms, chopped
- 1 onion, chopped
- 1 clove garlic, minced
- 1 tablespoon butter
- 1 1/2 cups quinoa, rinsed
- 3 cups chicken broth
- 1/3 cup grated Parmesan cheese

Direction

- Heat the oil in a skillet over medium heat. Cook and stir the mushrooms, onion, and garlic in the hot oil until browned, about 5 minutes; set aside.
- Melt the butter in a pot over medium-high heat. Add the quinoa to the melted butter and let it brown, about 3 minutes. Pour the chicken broth over the quinoa; bring to a boil. Cover and reduce heat to low; simmer 10 minutes. Stir in the sautéed mushroom mixture and cook another 2 minutes. Sprinkle with Parmesan cheese to serve.

Nutrition Information

- Calories: 233 calories
- Total Fat: 8.5 g
- Cholesterol: 10 mg
- Sodium: 103 mg
- Total Carbohydrate: 30.6 g
- Protein: 9.5 g

250. Quinoa with Peas

"A delicious side dish that goes with just about anything."

Serving: 6 | Prep: 10 m | Cook: 20 m | Ready in: 30 m

Ingredients

- 1 tablespoon butter
- 1 cup uncooked quinoa
- 2 cups chicken broth
- 1/4 cup chopped onion
- 1 clove garlic, minced
- 1 teaspoon chopped fresh thyme
- 1/2 teaspoon black pepper
- 3/4 cup frozen peas
- 1/2 cup grated Pecorino Romano cheese (such as Locatelli®), divided
- 2 tablespoons chopped fresh parsley

Direction

- Melt the butter in a saucepan over medium heat. Stir in the quinoa, and cook 2 minutes until toasted. Pour in the chicken broth, onion, garlic, thyme, and black pepper. Cover, and let come to a boil. Once boiling, stir in the frozen peas. Recover, reduce heat to medium-low, and continue simmering until the quinoa is tender and has absorbed the chicken stock, 15 to 20 minutes.
- Stir in half of the Pecorino Romano cheese and the parsley until evenly mixed. Scoop the quinoa into a serving dish, and sprinkle with the remaining Pecorino Romano cheese to serve.

Nutrition Information

- Calories: 157 calories
- Total Fat: 4.7 g
- Cholesterol: 8 mg
- Sodium: 97 mg
- Total Carbohydrate: 21.8 g
- Protein: 6.5 g

251. Quinoa with Salmon and Swiss Chard

"Quinoa is a high flavor, high protein grain made popular by the Incas, then rediscovered by NASA. Need I say any more?"

Serving: 4 | Prep: 15 m | Cook: 45 m | Ready in: 1 h

Ingredients

- 2 tablespoons olive oil
- 1 onion, diced
- 2 cloves garlic, minced
- 1 cup uncooked quinoa
- 2 cups vegetable broth
- 3/4 pound salmon fillets
- 1 cup white wine
- 1/2 cup water, or more as needed to cover
- 1 tablespoon olive oil
- 2 cloves garlic, minced
- 1 bunch Swiss chard, stems and tough ribs removed, leaves cut into 1/2-inch-wide ribbons
- 2 tablespoons lemon juice
- salt to taste
- 1 pinch ground black pepper

Direction

- Heat 2 tablespoons olive oil in a saucepan over medium heat. Cook and stir onion and 2 cloves garlic until fragrant, about 2 minutes.
- Stir quinoa into onion mixture until lightly toasted, about 5 minutes.
- Pour vegetable broth into quinoa mixture. Bring to a boil, then cover and reduce heat to low. Simmer until quinoa is tender, about 20 minutes.
- Meanwhile, heat salmon, white wine, and water in a saucepan over medium heat. Simmer until salmon is cooked through and easily flaked with a fork, 10 to 12 minutes; drain.
- Transfer salmon to a plate and flake fish meat; discard skin and set salmon aside.
- Heat 1 tablespoon olive oil in a skillet over medium heat. Cook and stir 2 cloves garlic until fragrant, about 1 minute.
- Stir Swiss chard and lemon juice into garlic until Swiss chard begins to soften, about 2 minutes; remove from heat.
- Gently fold flaked salmon and chard into the cooked quinoa. Season with salt and black pepper.

Nutrition Information

- Calories: 471 calories
- Total Fat: 18 g
- Cholesterol: 38 mg
- Sodium: 402 mg
- Total Carbohydrate: 40.1 g
- Protein: 26.2 g

252. Quinoa with Sweet Potato and Mushrooms

"Sweet Potato, onion, mushrooms, and chopped pecans are served over a bed of quinoa. This dish is perfect as a warm meal or side dish during cold weather."

Serving: 4 | Prep: 25 m | Cook: 30 m | Ready in: 55 m

Ingredients

- 1/3 cup quinoa
- 1 cup water
- 1 pinch salt
- 1 tablespoon olive oil
- 1 teaspoon minced garlic
- 1 small sweet onion, chopped
- 1 cup crimini mushrooms, sliced
- 1 small sweet potato, peeled and diced
- 1/4 teaspoon cayenne pepper
- salt and pepper to taste
- 1/4 cup chopped, toasted pecans

Direction

- Stir the quinoa in a saucepan over medium heat until it begins to take on a toasty aroma, about 5 minutes. Pour in the water, and add pinch of salt. Bring to a boil, then reduce heat

to medium-low, cover, and simmer until the quinoa is tender, about 20 minutes.
- Meanwhile, heat the olive oil in a large skillet over medium heat. Stir in the garlic and onion, and cook until the onion has softened and turned translucent, about 5 minutes. Add the mushrooms, sweet potatoes, and cayenne pepper; season to taste with salt and pepper. Cover the skillet, reduce heat to medium-low, and cook until the sweet potato is soft, about 20 minutes, stirring occasionally. Pour a splash of water into the skillet if needed to keep the vegetables from burning. Spoon the vegetable mixture over a bed of quinoa, and sprinkle with chopped pecans to serve.

Nutrition Information

- Calories: 173 calories
- Total Fat: 9.2 g
- Cholesterol: 0 mg
- Sodium: 108 mg
- Total Carbohydrate: 19.3 g
- Protein: 4.4 g

253. Quinoa with Sweet Potatoes and Broccoli

"The flavors of the broccoli and sweet potatoes compliment each other wonderfully in this recipe! I wasn't sure if steaming the sweet potatoes was necessary or not. It might be okay to skip that step. However, I wasn't sure if they would get tender enough by just cooking them in oil, so I went ahead and did it and it turned out great!"

Serving: 5 | Prep: 10 m | Cook: 20 m | Ready in: 30 m

Ingredients

- 1 cup quinoa
- 2 cups water
- 1 large sweet potato, peeled and cut into 1/4-inch cubes
- 2 tablespoons canola oil
- 1 onion, chopped
- 2 cups frozen chopped broccoli, thawed
- 1 tablespoon garlic powder
- 1/2 cup whole almonds
- 1 tablespoon soy sauce, or to taste (optional)

Direction

- Bring the quinoa and water to a boil in a saucepan over high heat. Reduce heat to medium-low, cover, and simmer until the quinoa is tender and the water has been absorbed, about 15 to 20 minutes.
- Meanwhile, place the diced sweet potatoes into a saucepan, and pour in 1/4-inch of water. Cover, and bring to a simmer over medium-high heat. Steam until the sweet potatoes are just slightly tender, about 10 minutes. While the potatoes are steaming, heat the canola oil in a skillet over medium-high heat. Cook and stir the onion and broccoli until the onion is tender, about 10 minutes.
- Once the potatoes have finished steaming, add them to the broccoli mixture, and season with garlic powder. Continue cooking until the potatoes have cooked to your desired degree of doneness, about 5 minutes. Stir the broccoli mixture together with the cooked quinoa and almonds. Season to taste with soy sauce if desired to serve.

Nutrition Information

- Calories: 376 calories
- Total Fat: 15.1 g
- Cholesterol: 0 mg
- Sodium: 252 mg
- Total Carbohydrate: 51.6 g
- Protein: 12 g

254. Quinoa with Veggies

"I love quinoa and I wanted to make something that was flavorful and filling. The vegetables can be changed to your liking!"

Serving: 4 | Prep: 10 m | Cook: 20 m | Ready in: 30 m

Ingredients

- 1 cup quinoa
- 3 cups water
- 1 pinch salt
- 3 tablespoons olive oil
- 3 cloves garlic, minced
- 1 red bell pepper, chopped
- 1/2 cup corn kernels
- 1/2 teaspoon cumin
- 1 teaspoon dried oregano
- salt and pepper to taste
- 2 green onions, chopped

Direction

- Bring the quinoa, water, and 1 pinch of salt to a boil in a saucepan. Reduce heat to medium-low, cover, and simmer until the quinoa is tender, about 20 minutes. Once done, drain a mesh strainer, and set aside.
- Meanwhile, heat the olive oil in a saucepan over medium heat. Stir in the garlic, and cook until the garlic softens and the aroma mellows, about 2 minutes. Add the red pepper, and corn; continue cooking until the pepper softens, about 5 minutes. Season with cumin, oregano, salt, and pepper, and cook for 1 minute more, then stir in the cooked quinoa and green onions. Serve hot or cold.

Nutrition Information

- Calories: 280 calories
- Total Fat: 13.1 g
- Cholesterol: 0 mg
- Sodium: 14 mg
- Total Carbohydrate: 34.4 g
- Protein: 7.3 g

255. Quinoa Zucchini Protein Muffins

"Healthy breakfast. Modified from quinoa squash muffins. You can add raisins or nuts."

Serving: 22 | Prep: 20 m | Cook: 30 m | Ready in: 50 m

Ingredients

- 2 1/2 cups whole wheat pastry flour
- 1/2 cup brown sugar
- 1 1/2 teaspoons ground cinnamon
- 1 1/2 teaspoons baking powder
- 1 teaspoon baking soda
- 1/2 teaspoon salt
- 1/8 teaspoon ground cloves
- 1/8 teaspoon ground allspice
- 1/8 teaspoon ground ginger
- 1/8 teaspoon ground nutmeg
- 1 1/2 cups nonfat Greek yogurt
- 1 1/2 cups shredded zucchini, squeezed dry
- 1 cup cooked quinoa
- 2 eggs, beaten
- 1 teaspoon vanilla extract

Direction

- Preheat oven to 375 degrees F (190 degrees C). Line 2 muffin tins with paper liners.
- Combine whole wheat pastry flour, brown sugar, cinnamon, baking powder, baking soda, salt, cloves, allspice, ginger, and nutmeg in a bowl.
- Mix Greek yogurt, zucchini, quinoa, eggs, and vanilla extract together in a bowl. Add flour mixture; mix until batter is well blended.
- Spoon batter into the prepared muffin tins.
- Bake in the preheated oven until tops are lightly browned and a toothpick inserted into the center comes out clean, about 30 minutes.

Nutrition Information

- Calories: 78 calories
- Total Fat: 0.8 g
- Cholesterol: 17 mg
- Sodium: 158 mg

- Total Carbohydrate: 14.1 g
- Protein: 3.8 g

256. Quinoa Cranberry Salad with Pecans

"A very easy salad and a nice twist on the usual cranberries-pecans salad with contrasting flavors and textures. Nice in the fall/winter with a bowl of pumpkin soup!"

Serving: 6 | Prep: 5 m | Cook: 15 m | Ready in: 1 h 20 m

Ingredients

- 1 cup quinoa, rinsed and drained
- 2 cups water
- 1/2 cup chopped toasted pecans
- 1/2 cup dried cranberries
- 1 tablespoon olive oil
- 2 tablespoons lemon juice
- salt and pepper to taste

Direction

- Bring the quinoa and water to a boil in a saucepan over high heat. Reduce heat to medium-low, cover, and simmer until the quinoa is tender, and the water has been absorbed, about 15 to 20 minutes. Scrape into a mixing bowl, and cool to warm, about 20 minutes.
- Once the quinoa has cooled, stir in the pecans, cranberries, olive oil, and lemon juice; season to taste with salt and pepper to taste. Let stand at room temperature for 1 hour before serving.

Nutrition Information

- Calories: 222 calories
- Total Fat: 11 g
- Cholesterol: 0 mg
- Sodium: 8 mg
- Total Carbohydrate: 27.9 g
- Protein: 4.7 g

257. Quinoa Fennel Pilaf

Serving: Makes 8 servings | Prep: 20 m | Cook: 35 m

Ingredients

- 1 cup quinoa
- 1/2 small white onion, finely chopped
- 1 celery rib, cut into 1/4-inch dice
- 1 carrot, cut into 1/4-inch dice
- 1 small fennel bulb (sometimes called anise), trimmed, cored, and cut into 1/4-inch dice
- 1 tablespoon unsalted butter
- 1 1/2 cups water

Direction

- Rinse quinoa in a bowl in at least 5 changes of water, rubbing grains and letting them settle before pouring off water, until water runs clear. Drain in a fine sieve.
- Cook onion, celery, carrot, and fennel in butter in a 3-quart heavy saucepan over moderate heat, stirring occasionally, until onion is softened, 5 to 6 minutes. Add quinoa and sauté over moderately high heat, stirring, until lightly toasted, 2 to 3 minutes. Add water and salt and pepper to taste and cook over moderately low heat, covered, until quinoa is tender and liquid is absorbed, 12 to 15 minutes.

258. QuinoaMushroom Frittata With Fresh Herbs

Used as healing compounds since the early days of medicine, herbs have strong scents and flavors that indicate the presence of unique phytonutrients. Study after study shows that traditional healers were right: these plants are medicine. This simple dish brings some serious plant power with the fresh herbs, mushrooms, olives, and quinoa. Mushrooms also contain unique phytonutrients, helping you round out this meal. For your next brunch, serve up some healing!

Serving: Serves 6

Ingredients

- 3/4 cup uncooked quinoa (or 1 1/2 cups cooked)
- 6 large pasture-raised eggs
- 1/2 cup grated Parmesan cheese
- 1/4 cup chopped fresh basil
- 2 tablespoons chopped fresh chives or tarragon
- 1 teaspoon minced fresh thyme leaves
- 1/4 teaspoon freshly ground black pepper
- 4 green onions or garlic scapes, thinly sliced
- 1 cup sliced mushrooms such as maitake, shiitake, or chanterelle, brushed clean and sliced
- Olive oil
- 1/4 cup assorted pitted olives, whole or chopped

Direction

- Cook the quinoa according to the package instructions. Set aside.
- In a large bowl, whisk the eggs, then stir in the quinoa, Parmesan, herbs, pepper, green onions or garlic scapes, and mushrooms.
- Coat a medium, ovenproof skillet with a thick layer of olive oil. Place over medium high heat, add the egg mixture, and sprinkle with the olives. Cook for 2 to 3 minutes without stirring.
- Preheat the broiler with the rack in the second position from the top. Broil the frittata until the top is lightly browned and the eggs have firmed up in the center, 3 to 4 minutes.
- Remove the frittata from the oven and let it rest for 3 minutes. Loosen the edges with a spatula and cut into 6 wedges. Serve immediately.

Nutrition Information

- 232 Calories
- 13g Protein
- 14g Carbohydrates
- 14g Fat (6g Saturated)
- 295mg Cholesterol
- 2g Sugars
- 2g Fiber
- 409mg Sodium
- Selenium = 65%
- Vitamin K = 51%
- B12 = 39%
- Choline = 35%
- Zinc = 33%

259. Red Quinoa and Avocado Salad

"A tasty combination of quinoa, avocado, cumin, and lime juice with fresh veggies for a delicious meal!"

Serving: 2 | Prep: 5 m | Cook: 15 m | Ready in: 50 m

Ingredients

- 1/3 cup red quinoa
- 2/3 cup water
- 1 cup cherry tomatoes, halved
- 1/2 cup diced cucumber
- 1/4 cup diced red onion
- 2 tablespoons lime juice
- 1/2 teaspoon ground cumin seed
- salt and pepper to taste
- 2 cups baby spinach leaves
- 1 avocado - peeled, pitted and sliced

Direction

- Bring the quinoa and water to a boil in a saucepan over high heat. Reduce heat to

- medium-low, cover, and simmer until the quinoa is tender, and the water has been absorbed, about 15 to 20 minutes. Spread into a mixing bowl, and refrigerate until cold.
- Once the quinoa has chilled, gently stir in the tomatoes, cucumber, and onion. Season with lime juice, cumin, salt, and pepper; stir to combine. Divide the spinach leaves onto salad plates, and top with the quinoa salad. Garnish with the avocado slices to serve.

Nutrition Information

- Calories: 311 calories
- Total Fat: 17.3 g
- Cholesterol: 0 mg
- Sodium: 46 mg
- Total Carbohydrate: 37.1 g
- Protein: 8.1 g

260. Red Quinoa and Tuscan Kale

"We love quinoa, especially red quinoa. I like kale (the kids weren't so sure about kale). The kids loved this dish! Everyone had seconds, even my picky eater. The combination of salty, sweet, and savory was awesome. Keeping in mind that I do the pinch-here-pinch-there style of cooking, this is easily adjusted to your personal taste. Next time I make this, I will be adding in some capers . . . because we like capers!"

Serving: 6 | Prep: 15 m | Cook: 20 m | Ready in: 35 m

Ingredients

- 2 1/2 cups water
- 1 cup red quinoa
- 3 red bell pepper, diced
- 1 bunch kale, cut into 1-inch pieces
- 3 tablespoons coconut oil
- 1/2 sweet onion, diced
- 2 tablespoons minced garlic
- 1/2 cup crumbled feta cheese
- 1/4 cup toasted slivered almonds
- 1 lemon, juiced and zested
- 1 tablespoon olive oil
- sea salt to taste
- fresh cracked black pepper to taste

Direction

- Bring water to a boil in a saucepan; add quinoa and red bell pepper. Return water to a boil, place cover on the saucepan, reduce heat to low, and cook for about 10 minutes; add kale and continue cooking until quinoa is tender, about 5 minutes more.
- Heat coconut oil in a skillet over medium-high heat. Sauté onion and garlic in hot oil until the onion is translucent, about 5 minutes; transfer to a large bowl. Stir feta cheese, almonds, lemon juice, lemon zest, and olive oil with the onion mixture; add quinoa mixture and stir. Season mixture with sea salt and cracked black pepper.

Nutrition Information

- Calories: 316 calories
- Total Fat: 16.9 g
- Cholesterol: 11 mg
- Sodium: 235 mg
- Total Carbohydrate: 34.6 g
- Protein: 10.1 g

261. Red Quinoa Pilaf with Caribbean Flavors

"A tasty quinoa dish with the zing of lime and a depth of tropical and not-so-tropical flavors. Goes great with jerk-style grilled meats!"

Serving: 8 | Prep: 30 m | Cook: 20 m | Ready in: 50 m

Ingredients

- 1 cup red quinoa, rinsed and drained
- 2 cups water
- 1 pinch salt
- 1 cup frozen shelled edamame, thawed
- 1 unripe mango, shredded
- 1 red bell pepper, diced

- 1 serrano chile pepper, minced
- 6 green onions, chopped
- 1/4 cup sliced almonds
- 1/4 cup dried cranberries
- 1/4 cup fresh shaved coconut
- 3 tablespoons chopped fresh cilantro
- 1/2 cup lime juice
- 2 tablespoons balsamic vinegar
- 1 pinch salt and ground black pepper to taste

Direction

- Place the quinoa into a saucepan over medium-high heat, and toast the quinoa in the dry pan, shaking the pan frequently, until the quinoa is dry and giving off a roasted fragrance, 2 to 5 minutes. Stir in water and a pinch of salt, bring to a boil, cover, reduce heat, and simmer the quinoa for about 10 minutes.
- Stir in the edamame, mango, bell pepper, and serrano chile, cover, and simmer the mixture until the water has been absorbed and the quinoa is fluffy, about 5 more minutes. Stir in the green onions, almonds, cranberries, coconut, cilantro, lime juice, balsamic vinegar, and salt and pepper. Bring the mixture back to a simmer, and serve hot.

Nutrition Information

- Calories: 178 calories
- Total Fat: 5.4 g
- Cholesterol: 0 mg
- Sodium: 66 mg
- Total Carbohydrate: 27.9 g
- Protein: 7 g

262. Rice and Quinoa Breakfast Pudding

"A warm breakfast pudding with more texture than regular oatmeal. It tastes great the same day you make it, and heats up well for those rushed work mornings. Top with blackberries, blueberries, dried cranberries, raisins, toasted coconut, or nuts."

Serving: 2 | Prep: 10 m | Cook: 20 m | Ready in: 30 m

Ingredients

- 1 1/2 cups cooked quinoa, divided
- 1 1/2 cups cooked brown rice, divided
- 1 1/2 cups almond milk
- 1 tablespoon honey
- 1 tablespoon brown sugar
- 1 teaspoon salt
- 1 egg
- 1 tablespoon vanilla extract, or more to taste
- 2 teaspoons pumpkin pie spice

Direction

- Combine 1 cup quinoa, 1 cup brown rice, almond milk, honey, brown sugar, and salt in a pot over medium heat; stir until almond milk is heated through, about 5 minutes.
- Whisk egg in a small bowl. Mix in some of the hot milk mixture to gradually warm up the egg to room temperature.
- Pour egg mixture into the saucepan. Add remaining 1/2 cup quinoa, 1/2 cup brown rice, vanilla extract, and pumpkin pie spice. Bring to a boil; reduce heat and simmer until mixture begins to thicken, 10 to 15 minutes. Scoop mixture into 2 serving bowls.

Nutrition Information

- Calories: 495 calories
- Total Fat: 8.7 g
- Cholesterol: 93 mg
- Sodium: 1338 mg
- Total Carbohydrate: 86.6 g
- Protein: 14 g

263. Rice Cooker Chicken Quinoa with Sundried Tomatoes

"Sun-dried tomatoes and curry mix well in this lightly flavored dish."

Serving: 1 | Prep: 15 m | Cook: 45 m | Ready in: 1 h

Ingredients

- 1 (6 ounce) chicken breast, cut into 1/2-inch cubes
- 3/4 cup water
- 3/8 cup white quinoa
- 1/4 cup chopped onion
- 1/4 cup sun-dried tomatoes, cut into strips
- 2 cloves garlic, minced
- 1/2 teaspoon curry powder
- ground black pepper to taste

Direction

- Stir chicken breast cubes, water, quinoa, onion, sun-dried tomatoes, garlic, curry powder, and ground black pepper together in the bowl of a rice cooker.
- Cook on white rice setting according to manufacturer's directions.

Nutrition Information

- Calories: 472 calories
- Total Fat: 8 g
- Cholesterol: 88 mg
- Sodium: 367 mg
- Total Carbohydrate: 55.4 g
- Protein: 45 g

264. Ricks Sauteed Salmon over Quinoa

"Sauteed salmon over quinoa, spinach, shallots, garlic, and olive oil."

Serving: 1 | Prep: 10 m | Cook: 10 m | Ready in: 20 m

Ingredients

- 3 tablespoons olive oil, divided
- 1 (3 ounce) fillet salmon fillet
- 1 shallot, finely diced
- 1 clove garlic, thinly sliced
- 4 ounces fresh spinach, roughly chopped
- 1/2 cup cooked quinoa
- salt and ground black pepper to taste
- 1 lemon wedge

Direction

- Heat a skillet over high heat and add 1 tablespoon olive oil. Add salmon, cover, and cook 4 minutes.
- Heat another skillet over medium heat. Add remaining olive oil, shallot, and garlic. Cook until slightly browned, about 2 minutes. Add spinach.
- Turn salmon over. Cook, uncovered, until fish flakes easily with fork, an additional 4 minutes. Toss spinach until wilted; add quinoa. Season with salt and pepper and mix well.
- Plate spinach-quinoa mixture and lay salmon on top. Add lemon wedge.

Nutrition Information

- Calories: 649 calories
- Total Fat: 46 g
- Cholesterol: 36 mg
- Sodium: 299 mg
- Total Carbohydrate: 44.9 g
- Protein: 25.5 g

265. Roasted Butternut Squash Quinoa with Pumpkin Seeds

"Tired of the same old side dish for the holidays? Wow your family and friends with this simple yet unique side that is sure to please. The crunch from the pumpkin seeds, texture from the quinoa, and the earthiness from the roasted squash really sets this one apart."

Serving: 6 | Prep: 5 m | Cook: 29 m | Ready in: 34 m

Ingredients

- 3 tablespoons unsalted butter, melted
- 1 teaspoon dried thyme
- 1 teaspoon rubbed sage
- 1 teaspoon light brown sugar
- 1 1/2 cups 1-inch cubes peeled, seeded butternut squash
- 1 tablespoon olive oil
- 1 1/2 cups quinoa, rinsed and drained
- 3 cups Swanson® Chicken Broth
- 1/2 cup raw pumpkin seeds

Direction

- Preheat oven to 350 degrees F (175 degrees C). Lightly oil a 9x13-inch baking dish.
- Mix the warm melted butter, thyme, sage, and sugar together in a small bowl.
- Place cubed butternut squash in prepared baking dish. Drizzle with seasoned butter. Roast uncovered in preheated oven until tender, about 20 minutes.
- Heat oil in a skillet over medium heat. Toast quinoa in oil until light brown, about 5 minutes. Add Swanson(R) Chicken Broth to quinoa and bring to a boil. Cover and turn heat to low. Cook for 10 minutes without disturbing. Remove from heat and let sit covered until broth is absorbed, about 3 minutes.
- Stir the quinoa and pumpkin seeds into the roasted squash.

Nutrition Information

- Calories: 314 calories
- Total Fat: 16.2 g
- Cholesterol: 18 mg
- Sodium: 487 mg
- Total Carbohydrate: 34.9 g
- Protein: 9.8 g

266. Roasted Sweet Potato Quinoa Salad

"Purple sweet potatoes add beautiful color to the mix in this healthy, fresh tasting, zesty salad!"

Serving: 4 | Prep: 25 m | Cook: 35 m | Ready in: 1 h 20 m

Ingredients

- Salad:
- 2 cups water
- 1 cup quinoa, rinsed
- 2 sweet potatoes, peeled and cubed
- 2 tablespoons olive oil
- 1 cup chopped broccoli
- 1 yellow bell pepper, diced
- 1 red bell pepper, diced
- 1/2 cucumber - peeled, seeded, and chopped
- Dressing:
- 1/4 cup extra-virgin olive oil
- 2 tablespoons maple syrup
- 1/2 lemon, juiced
- 1/2 lime, juiced
- salt and ground black pepper to taste
- 1/2 cup chopped cilantro

Direction

- Preheat oven to 400 degrees F (200 degrees C).
- Bring water and quinoa to a boil in a saucepan. Reduce heat to medium-low, cover, and simmer until quinoa is tender, 15 to 20 minutes. Set aside to cool.
- Toss sweet potatoes in olive oil on a baking sheet.
- Roast in the preheated oven until tender, 20 to 25 minutes. Set aside to cool.

- Mix broccoli, yellow pepper, red pepper, and cucumber in a large bowl; stir in quinoa and sweet potatoes.
- Whisk extra-virgin olive oil, maple syrup, lemon juice, lime juice, salt, and pepper in a small bowl. Mix dressing into salad; garnish with cilantro.

Nutrition Information

- Calories: 445 calories
- Total Fat: 23.6 g
- Cholesterol: 0 mg
- Sodium: 93 mg
- Total Carbohydrate: 52.1 g
- Protein: 8.3 g

267. Robins Quinoa with Mushrooms and Spinach

"I do pilates over my lunch break a couple of times a week, and this is the perfect thing to eat after it. It's way better than the usual lean-cuisine, and way better for you. Plus, it's super-cheap to make and you get three lunches out of it, easily."

Serving: 3 | Prep: 25 m | Cook: 25 m | Ready in: 50 m

Ingredients

- 1 tablespoon olive oil
- 1/2 onion, chopped fine
- 1 teaspoon minced garlic
- 1 cup quinoa
- 1/2 cup white wine
- 1 3/4 cups chicken broth
- 2 teaspoons balsamic vinegar
- 1 teaspoon chopped fresh thyme
- 1 tablespoon olive oil
- 1 (8 ounce) package sliced mushrooms
- 4 teaspoons balsamic vinegar
- 1/4 cup white wine
- 1/4 cup chicken broth
- 1 teaspoon chopped fresh thyme
- salt and pepper to taste
- 1 (10 ounce) bag washed spinach leaves
- 1/4 cup crumbled goat cheese

Direction

- Heat olive oil in a saucepan over medium heat. Add onion and garlic, cook and stir until the onion has softened and turned translucent, about 5 minutes. Stir in quinoa until well blended.
- Pour in 1/2 cup white wine and cook, stirring, until absorbed by the quinoa, about 30 seconds. Stir in 1 3/4 cups chicken broth, 2 teaspoons balsamic vinegar, and 1 teaspoon chopped thyme. Bring to a boil over medium-high heat, then reduce heat to medium-low, cover, and simmer until the quinoa is tender, about 15 minutes.
- Meanwhile, heat 1 tablespoon olive oil in a skillet over medium-high heat. Add the mushrooms and cook until lightly browned, about 5 minutes. Pour in 4 teaspoons balsamic vinegar, 1/4 cup white wine, 1/4 cup chicken stock, and 1 teaspoon chopped thyme. Reduce heat to medium-low, cover, and simmer until the mushrooms soften, about 5 minutes.
- Once the quinoa has cooked, stir in the mushroom mixture, and season to taste with salt and pepper. Remove quinoa from the heat and stir in spinach leaves, which will wilt. Transfer to a serving dish and sprinkle with crumbled goat cheese.

Nutrition Information

- Calories: 433 calories
- Total Fat: 16.5 g
- Cholesterol: 10 mg
- Sodium: 167 mg
- Total Carbohydrate: 47.3 g
- Protein: 15.7 g

268. Saffron Quinoa with Dried Cherries and Almonds

Saffron rice is an indispensable accompaniment in Persian cuisine, and it tastes just as good made with fluffy quinoa. Crushing and steeping the saffron in hot water brings out its full flavor and color. If you have coconut oil on hand, the naturally sweet flavor pairs nicely with the cherries and almonds.

Ingredients

- 1/4 teaspoon saffron threads (optional)
- 3 tablespoons coconut oil or olive oil, divided
- 1 1/2 cups sliced almonds
- 1 teaspoon ground cinnamon
- Pinch of cayenne pepper
- 1 3/4 teaspoons kosher salt, divided
- 1 medium onion, chopped
- 2 cups quinoa
- 1 1/2 cups dried cherries

Direction

- Crush saffron, if using, with the handle of a wooden spoon (or crush between your fingers) in a small bowl until a powder forms. Add 1 Tbsp. hot water. Swirl gently; set aside to steep.
- Heat 1 Tbsp. oil in a large pot over medium-high. Add almonds, cinnamon, cayenne, and 1/4 tsp. salt and cook, stirring occasionally, until toasted and fragrant, about 2 minutes. Using a slotted spoon, transfer almonds to a small bowl; reserve oil in pot.
- Heat oil in pot over medium-high. Add onion and remaining 2 Tbsp. oil and 1 1/2 tsp. salt, reduce heat to medium, and cook until onion is light brown and translucent, about 5 minutes. Add quinoa and cook, tossing to coat, until fragrant and beginning to brown, 1–2 minutes.
- Stir in 4 cups water, cover pot, and bring to a boil. Reduce heat to low and simmer until quinoa is cooked and water is absorbed, 20–30 minutes. Remove from heat, sprinkle cherries over, cover, and let sit 10 minutes.
- Transfer 2 cups quinoa mixture to a medium bowl. Reserve 1/2 cup toasted almonds, then toss remaining almonds with remaining quinoa mixture and transfer to a platter. Toss quinoa in bowl with saffron water until coated, then garnish platter with saffron quinoa. Top with remaining toasted almonds.
- Do Ahead   Quinoa, with cherries, can be cooked 3 days ahead. Transfer to a resealable container and chill. Reheat over low on stovetop or in a 300°F oven until warmed.
- Cooks' Note: If you can't find dried cherries, substitute dried cranberries.

Nutrition Information

- Calories: 271
- Total Fat: 11 g (17%)
- Saturated Fat: 4 g (18%)
- Sodium: 169 mg (7%)
- Total Carbohydrate: 38 g (13%)
- Protein: 7 g (14%)
- Fiber: 4 g (17%)

269. Savory Rice and Quinoa Pilaf

"Pretty, delicious, and can easily be personalized. Freeze leftovers for a quick side dish ready in minutes."

Serving: 6 | Prep: 10 m | Cook: 25 m | Ready in: 35 m

Ingredients

- 6 cups vegetable broth
- 2 cups basmati rice
- 1 cup quinoa
- 2 tomatoes, chopped (optional)
- 1/4 cup raisins (optional)
- 1 tablespoon chopped fresh parsley
- 1 teaspoon salt
- 1 teaspoon ground black pepper
- 1/2 teaspoon ground allspice
- 1/2 teaspoon dried sage

Direction

- Bring vegetable broth to a boil in a large saucepan. Stir in basmati rice, quinoa, tomatoes, raisins, parsley, salt, pepper, allspice, and sage. Reduce heat and simmer until broth is absorbed and quinoa is tender, about 20 minutes.

Nutrition Information

- Calories: 386 calories
- Total Fat: 3.1 g
- Cholesterol: 0 mg
- Sodium: 853 mg
- Total Carbohydrate: 80 g
- Protein: 10.4 g

270. Scots Thai Soup

"This soup began as something else that evolved as it was being cooked. After tasting it a few times, it needed something else. So the Thai red curry paste, lime juice, and coconut milk were added after cooking for 4 hours. That was the magic! Everyone who tried it was very satisfied, except one who didn't care for anything spicy. This isn't overpoweringly spicy, just enough heat tamed by the lime juice and coconut milk. Have fun!"

Serving: 10 | Prep: 25 m | Cook: 4 h 15 m | Ready in: 12 h 40 m

Ingredients

- 2 quarts vegetable broth
- 1 cup dried red beans
- 1 cup quinoa, or more to taste
- 1 cup pearl barley, or more to taste
- 1 stalk celery, chopped
- 1 tomato, diced
- 6 cloves garlic (or more to taste), peeled and chopped
- 1 red chile pepper, sliced
- 1/2 green bell pepper (or more to taste), cut into 1-inch pieces
- 1/2 cup chopped green onion, or more to taste
- 2 ounces Thai red curry paste
- 1 (1 inch) piece fresh ginger root, peeled and thinly sliced (or more to taste)
- 3 tablespoons chicken bouillon powder, or more to taste
- 2 tablespoons dried Italian seasoning, or more to taste
- 2 tablespoons ground black pepper
- 2 teaspoons dried chives
- 2 teaspoons onion powder
- 2 teaspoons garlic powder
- 1 (5.6 ounce) can coconut milk
- 2 tablespoons fresh lime juice

Direction

- Place the red beans into a large container and cover with several inches of cool water; let soak 8 hours to overnight.
- Drain and rinse beans. Put beans in a slow cooker; add quinoa, barley, celery, tomato, garlic, red chile pepper, green bell pepper, green onion, curry paste, ginger, chicken bouillon, Italian seasoning, black pepper, chives, onion powder, and garlic powder to the beans.
- Cook on High, stirring occasionally, until the beans and barley are tender, about 4 hours. Stir coconut milk and lime juice into the soup; cook 15 minutes more.

Nutrition Information

- Calories: 248 calories
- Total Fat: 3.1 g
- Cholesterol: < 1 mg
- Sodium: 821 mg
- Total Carbohydrate: 45.5 g
- Protein: 11.1 g

271. Seeded Flatbread

"We love the wonderful nutty flavor of this bread and wanted to replace the sandwich rounds I was still buying. When sliced, they're the perfect size for a tuna sandwich or for toasting with butter and jam. Store in a plastic bag."

Serving: 16 | Prep: 30 m | Cook: 15 m | Ready in: 1 h 45 m

Ingredients

- 1 cup bread flour
- 1 cup spelt flour
- 1/4 cup brown sugar
- 2 tablespoons sesame seeds
- 1 tablespoon quinoa
- 1 tablespoon sunflower seeds
- 1 tablespoon millet
- 1 tablespoon oats
- 1 tablespoon flax seeds
- 3/4 cup warm milk
- 1 tablespoon olive oil
- 2 teaspoons bread machine yeast

Direction

- Mix bread flour, spelt flour, brown sugar, sesame seeds, quinoa, sunflower seeds, millet, oats, and flax seeds together in a bowl.
- Combine milk and oil in the bread pan of a bread machine, add flour mixture. Make a well in the center of the flour mixture; pour in yeast. Knead dough according to manufacturer's instructions.
- Turn out dough on a floured work surface. Punch down and separate into 16 pieces. Flatten into 5-inch diameter flatbreads.
- Place flatbreads on 2 baking sheets; cover with plastic wrap. Let sit in a warm place until risen, about 1 hour. Remove plastic wrap.
- Preheat oven to 350 degrees F (175 degrees C).
- Bake in the preheated oven until golden brown, about 15 minutes. Cool slightly; slice in half.

Nutrition Information

- Calories: 104 calories
- Total Fat: 2.6 g
- Cholesterol: <1 mg
- Sodium: 7 mg
- Total Carbohydrate: 17.4 g
- Protein: 3.3 g

272. Seedy Cherry Quinoa Bars

Serving: Makes 12

Ingredients

- 1 cup chopped almonds, toasted
- 1/2 cup rinsed raw quinoa
- 1/4 cup raw pumpkin seeds
- 1/4 cup raw sunflower seeds
- 1 cup dried tart cherries
- 2 tablespoons brown rice syrup
- 3/4 teaspoon kosher salt
- 2 tablespoons water
- One 8x8" baking pan, Parchment paper

Direction

- Coat 8x8" baking pan with nonstick vegetable oil spray; line with parchment, leaving overhang on all sides. Toast 1 cup chopped almonds, 1/2 cup rinsed raw quinoa, 1/4 cup raw pumpkin seeds, and 1/4 cup raw sunflower seeds on a rimmed baking sheet in a 350° oven, stirring occasionally, until golden brown, 10–12 minutes. Let cool. Reduce oven temperature to 200°. Process 1 cup dried tart cherries, 2 tablespoons brown rice syrup, 3/4 teaspoon kosher salt, and 2 tablespoons water in a food processor until smooth. Transfer to a medium bowl and stir in toasted almond mixture. Press firmly into prepared pan and bake until no longer sticky, 20–25 minutes. Let cool, then cut into bars.

273. Sesame Kale Glow Bowl

"This simple, nourishing and healthy 'glow bowl' is one that we all need to have in our recipe box. Its' been my weekday go-to because it's quick, tasty and perfect for Meatless Mondays or anytime you need extra greens."

Serving: 3 | Prep: 15 m | Cook: 25 m | Ready in: 40 m

Ingredients

- 2 cups water
- 1 cup quinoa
- 1 tablespoon coconut oil
- 1/2 red onion, chopped
- 3 cups torn kale leaves
- 2 cups broccoli florets
- 4 ounces tempeh, crumbled
- 1 clove garlic, minced
- 2 tablespoons sesame seeds
- 2 tablespoons water
- 2 tablespoons tamari
- 1 lime, juiced
- 1 1/2 teaspoons Dijon mustard
- 1 teaspoon minced fresh ginger
- 1/2 teaspoon ground black pepper
- 1 pinch red pepper flakes (optional)

Direction

- Bring 2 cups water and quinoa to a boil in a saucepan. Reduce heat to medium-low, cover, and simmer until quinoa is tender and water has been absorbed, 15 to 20 minutes.
- Heat coconut oil in a small saucepan over medium-high heat; sauté red onion until lightly browned, 2 to 3 minutes. Add kale, broccoli, tempeh, and garlic; sauté until kale is wilted, about 3 minutes.
- Whisk sesame seeds, 2 tablespoons water, tamari, lime juice, Dijon mustard, ginger, black pepper, and red pepper flakes together in a bowl; pour over kale mixture and cook for 2 minutes.
- Spoon quinoa into serving bowls and top with kale mixture.

Nutrition Information

- Calories: 434 calories
- Total Fat: 16 g
- Cholesterol: 0 mg
- Sodium: 794 mg
- Total Carbohydrate: 56.7 g
- Protein: 21.6 g

274. Shrimp and Quinoa

"This delicious shrimp, quinoa, and vegetable recipe can be eaten hot as a main dish or cold as a salad."

Serving: 4 | Prep: 15 m | Cook: 40 m | Ready in: 55 m

Ingredients

- 1 1/2 cups water
- 1 cup uncooked quinoa
- 2 tablespoons olive oil
- 1 red onion, chopped
- 1/2 green bell pepper, chopped
- 1/2 cup sliced fresh mushrooms
- 6 fresh asparagus spears, trimmed and chopped
- 1/4 cup golden raisins
- 1 tablespoon minced fresh ginger root
- salt and pepper to taste
- 1 pound medium shrimp - peeled and deveined
- 1 lime, juiced
- 2 tablespoons olive oil
- 1/2 cup chopped Italian flat leaf parsley

Direction

- In a large pot, bring the water to a boil, and stir in the quinoa. Cover, reduce heat to low, and simmer 15 minutes. Remove from heat, and set aside 10 minutes, or until all liquid has been absorbed.
- Heat 2 tablespoons olive oil in a skillet over medium heat, and sauté the onion and green bell pepper until tender. Mix in the mushrooms, asparagus, raisins, and ginger, and continue cooking until asparagus is tender. Season with salt and pepper. Mix in

the shrimp, and cook 5 minutes, or until opaque.
- In a large bowl, mix the quinoa with the lime juice and remaining 2 tablespoons olive oil. Toss with the skillet mixture and parsley to serve.

Nutrition Information

- Calories: 457 calories
- Total Fat: 18.3 g
- Cholesterol: 173 mg
- Sodium: 179 mg
- Total Carbohydrate: 43.6 g
- Protein: 31.1 g

275. Shrimp Quinoa

"A delicious stir fry-like dish that includes vegetables and shrimp."

Serving: 4 | Prep: 25 m | Cook: 20 m | Ready in: 45 m

Ingredients

- 1 cup uncooked quinoa, rinsed
- 1 1/2 cups chicken broth
- 2 tablespoons olive oil
- 3 cloves garlic, minced
- 1 onion, diced
- 1 red bell pepper, diced
- 8 spears fresh asparagus, trimmed and cut into 1 inch pieces
- 1 cup sliced fresh mushrooms
- 1/4 cup raisins
- 1 tablespoon minced fresh ginger root
- 1 pound uncooked medium shrimp, peeled and deveined
- 1 tablespoon lemon juice
- salt and pepper to taste

Direction

- Bring the quinoa and chicken broth to a boil in a saucepan over high heat. Reduce heat to medium-low, cover, and simmer until the quinoa is tender about 15 minutes. Turn off the heat, and let the remaining liquid absorb into the quinoa.
- Meanwhile, heat the olive oil in a large skillet over medium heat. Stir in the garlic, onion, and red bell pepper; cook and stir until the onion has softened and turned translucent, about 5 minutes. Add the asparagus, mushrooms, raisins, and ginger; continue cooking until the asparagus is tender. Stir in the shrimp, and cook until the shrimp have turned pink and are no longer translucent in the center.
- Stir the lemon juice into the quinoa, then toss the quinoa with the shrimp and vegetable mixture. Season to taste with salt and pepper before serving.

Nutrition Information

- Calories: 378 calories
- Total Fat: 10.6 g
- Cholesterol: 173 mg
- Sodium: 207 mg
- Total Carbohydrate: 44.7 g
- Protein: 27.1 g

276. Simple Mexican Quinoa

"This is my new favorite quinoa dish. It is super simple."

Serving: 5 | Prep: 10 m | Cook: 20 m | Ready in: 30 m

Ingredients

- 2 cups water
- 1 cup quinoa
- 1 (12 ounce) package frozen corn and black bean vegetable blend (such as Archer Farms®)

Direction

- Bring water and quinoa to a boil in a saucepan. Reduce heat to medium-low, cover, and simmer until quinoa is tender and water is absorbed, 15 to 20 minutes.

Place vegetable blend in a microwave-safe bowl; microwave until heated through, about 5 minutes. Stir vegetable blend into quinoa.

Nutrition Information

- Calories: 184 calories
- Total Fat: 2.4 g
- Cholesterol: 0 mg
- Sodium: 5 mg
- Total Carbohydrate: 32.8 g
- Protein: 7.7 g

277. Simple Savory Quinoa

"A savory side dish, tasty yet simple, with carrots, celery, onions and quinoa. I always cut my veggies really small, more like mincing because I don't like chunky veggies. It is always optional to cut this small. This would probably taste great with rice as well."

Serving: 3 | Prep: 15 m | Cook: 30 m | Ready in: 45 m

Ingredients

- 2 tablespoons olive oil
- 1 stalk celery, finely chopped
- 2 carrots, sliced
- 1 small onion, minced
- 1 clove garlic, minced
- 1 cup vegetable stock
- 1/2 cup uncooked quinoa, rinsed
- 1/4 teaspoon dried basil
- 1 teaspoon ground turmeric
- 1 teaspoon lime juice
- salt to taste

Direction

- Heat the olive oil in a saucepan over medium heat. Stir in the celery, carrots, onion, and garlic. Cook and stir until the onion has softened and turned translucent, about 5 minutes. Stir in the vegetable stock, quinoa, basil, and turmeric. Bring to a simmer, then reduce heat to low, cover, and simmer 25 to 30 minutes until the quinoa is tender and has absorbed the liquid. Once done, stir in the lime juice, and season to taste with salt to serve.

Nutrition Information

- Calories: 227 calories
- Total Fat: 11.1 g
- Cholesterol: 0 mg
- Sodium: 195 mg
- Total Carbohydrate: 27.3 g
- Protein: 5.2 g

278. Skillet Chicken and Quinoa with Fresh Salsa

"A filling and fresh dish. Topping with the homemade salsa is a must!"

Serving: 4 | Prep: 20 m | Cook: 41 m | Ready in: 1 h 1 m

Ingredients

- Homemade Salsa:
- 4 Roma tomatoes, seeded and diced
- 1/2 red onion, finely chopped
- 1/2 cup chopped fresh cilantro
- 1 fresh jalapeno pepper, chopped
- 1/2 lime, juiced
- Skillet Chicken and Quinoa:
- 2 cups chicken broth, divided
- 1/2 cup quinoa, rinsed
- 2 tablespoons olive oil
- 1 sweet onion, chopped
- 1 pound ground chicken
- 1 (15 ounce) can black beans, drained and rinsed
- 1 cup prepared salsa
- 2 tablespoons chili powder
- 2 cloves garlic, minced
- 1 lime, juiced
- 2 avocados, halved and pitted
- salt and ground black pepper to taste

Direction

- Mix tomatoes, red onion, cilantro, jalapeno pepper, and juice of 1/2 lime together in a bowl. Cover and place in the refrigerator.
- Combine 1 cup chicken broth and quinoa in a small pan. Bring to a boil. Reduce heat, cover, and simmer until chicken broth is absorbed, about 15 minutes. Remove from heat.
- Heat olive oil in a large skillet over medium heat. Cook and stir sweet onion until softened, about 5 minutes. Add chicken; cook and stir until no longer pink, 6 to 8 minutes. Stir in cooked quinoa, remaining 1 cup chicken broth, black beans, prepared salsa, chili powder, and garlic. Simmer over low heat for 10 minutes.
- Remove skillet from heat. Squeeze lime juice all over. Divide among serving bowls. Top each serving with homemade salsa and 1 avocado half. Season with salt and pepper.

Nutrition Information

- Calories: 597 calories
- Total Fat: 25.8 g
- Cholesterol: 69 mg
- Sodium: 1547 mg
- Total Carbohydrate: 55.2 g
- Protein: 41.1 g

279. Slow Cooked Chicken Stew

"Slow cookers are so great for those times when you want a fuss-free dinner. You can literally throw everything in it and leave it all day so you have a lovely wholesome meal waiting for you at dinner time."

We left this stew in the slow cooker for 8 hours on a low heat but if you want it ready bit sooner than that, you can turn the heat up to medium and it should be ready in about 4 hours."

Serving: 8 | Prep: 20 m | Cook: 7 h 5 m | Ready in: 7 h 25 m

Ingredients

- 1 teaspoon olive oil
- 1 onion, chopped
- 3 cloves garlic, minced
- 4 skinless, boneless chicken breasts
- 1 (32 fluid ounce) container vegetable broth
- 1 (14.5 ounce) can diced tomatoes
- 2 sweet potatoes, diced
- 1 cup uncooked quinoa
- 1 teaspoon ground black pepper
- 5 mushrooms, chopped
- 2 teaspoons dried oregano
- 2 teaspoons curry powder
- 5 green onions, chopped
- 1 bay leaf

Direction

- Heat oil in a skillet over medium heat; stir in onion and garlic. Cook and stir until onion and garlic have softened and turned translucent, about 5 minutes.
- Place chicken breasts in the bottom of a slow cooker; add onion, garlic, vegetable broth, diced tomatoes, sweet potatoes, quinoa, green onions, mushrooms, curry powder, oregano, pepper, and bay leaf and mix well. Cook on Low until chicken is tender, 7 to 8 hours.
- Discard bay leaf. Remove chicken; shred using 2 forks and place back into the stew, mixing well before serving.

Nutrition Information

- Calories: 210 calories

- Total Fat: 3.5 g
- Cholesterol: 29 mg
- Sodium: 356 mg
- Total Carbohydrate: 27.8 g
- Protein: 16.3 g

280. Slow Cooker Chicken Curry with Quinoa

"Chicken, quinoa, and apples, combine in this tasty, easy curry!"

Serving: 6 | Prep: 30 m | Cook: 4 h | Ready in: 4 h 30 m

Ingredients

- 1 1/2 pounds diced chicken breast meat
- 3/4 cup chopped onion
- 1 1/4 cups chopped celery
- 1 3/4 cups chopped Granny Smith apples
- 1 cup chicken broth
- 1/4 cup nonfat milk
- 1 tablespoon curry powder
- 1/4 teaspoon paprika
- 1/3 cup quinoa

Direction

- Place the chicken, onion, celery, apple, chicken broth, milk, curry powder, and paprika into a slow cooker; stir until mixed. Cover, and cook on Low for 4 to 5 hours. Stir in the quinoa during the final 35 minutes of cooking. Serve when quinoa is tender.

Nutrition Information

- Calories: 185 calories
- Total Fat: 3.1 g
- Cholesterol: 59 mg
- Sodium: 75 mg
- Total Carbohydrate: 14.4 g
- Protein: 24.4 g

281. Slow Cooker Quinoa Sweet Potato Chicken

"Easy hearty and healthy stew. Serve with a hunk of crusty bread."

Serving: 6 | Prep: 15 m | Cook: 8 h | Ready in: 8 h 15 m

Ingredients

- 2 (14.5 ounce) cans chicken broth
- 2 1/2 cups chopped cooked chicken, or more to taste
- 1 (28 ounce) can petite-cut diced tomatoes with garlic and olive oil
- 2 (16 ounce) cans red kidney beans, drained and rinsed
- 1 (15 ounce) can black beans, drained and rinsed
- 2 large sweet potatoes, peeled and cut into cubes
- 1/2 cup quinoa
- 1 tablespoon dried minced onion
- 1 tablespoon chili powder
- 1 teaspoon minced garlic
- 1/4 teaspoon red pepper flakes
- salt and ground black pepper to taste

Direction

- Stir chicken broth, chopped chicken, tomatoes, kidney beans, black beans, sweet potatoes, quinoa, minced onion, chili powder, minced garlic, red pepper flakes, salt, and black pepper together in a slow cooker.
- Cook in the slow cooker set to Low for 8 hours.

Nutrition Information

- Calories: 533 calories
- Total Fat: 4.9 g
- Cholesterol: 53 mg
- Sodium: 1965 mg
- Total Carbohydrate: 86.8 g
- Protein: 36.7 g

282. Soft Polenta with Spicy Tomato Sauce

"Polenta should be served soft from the pot, or chilled and then pan-fried. Wild mushrooms, cheese, fresh herbs, and olives are good additions to this grain. If you can get a hold of it, try ricotta salata in place of the Parmesan cheese. If you don't want to use quinoa, you can simply use an equivalent amount of cornmeal in its place."

Serving: 4 | Prep: 20 m | Cook: 40 m | Ready in: 1 h

Ingredients

- 1 quart water
- 1/2 cup stone ground cornmeal
- 1/2 cup quinoa
- 1/2 teaspoon salt
- 2 tablespoons olive oil
- 2 cups minced onion
- 1 large portobello mushroom, chopped
- 3 cloves garlic, minced
- 2 (14.5 ounce) cans stewed tomatoes
- 1/4 cup sherry
- 1/2 teaspoon crushed red pepper flakes (optional)
- 1 teaspoon dried oregano
- salt and pepper to taste
- 3 cups chopped green onions
- 1/2 cup grated Parmesan cheese
- 1/4 cup shaved Parmesan cheese

Direction

- In a small bowl whisk together 2 cups water with the cornmeal, quinoa and salt. Bring the remaining 2 cups water to a boil in a heavy saucepan. Stir the cornmeal mixture into the boiling water, and continue stirring. Be careful! The polenta may spit and sputter and the hot bits of polenta can burn. Turn the heat to very low and cook the polenta for 40 minutes; stirring with a wooden spoon every 10 minutes.
- Make the tomato sauce while the polenta cooks: Heat olive oil in a large saucepan over medium heat, add the onions. Cook the onions for about 5 minutes, stirring often, until they have softened. Stir in the chopped mushrooms and the garlic, sauté for 5 minutes. Then add the tomatoes, sherry, chili flakes and oregano. When the sauce comes to a boil turn the heat to low. Simmer the sauce for 30 minutes; season with salt and pepper.
- When the polenta has cooked for 40 minutes, sprinkle the green onions and grated cheese into the polenta. Stir well. Mound the polenta on plates, make a well in the center of each mound and ladle in the tomato sauce. Garnish with the shaved cheese.

Nutrition Information

- Calories: 395 calories
- Total Fat: 13.7 g
- Cholesterol: 13 mg
- Sodium: 1090 mg
- Total Carbohydrate: 56.8 g
- Protein: 15.1 g

283. Solterito De Quinua Quinoa Solterito

In Peru, Quinoa is one of the most nutritious grains cultivated by our ancestors, which we are once again sharing with the world.

Serving: Serves 4 | Prep: 10 m | Cook: 10 m

Ingredients

- 1 1/3 cups quinoa grains, cooked
- 4 ounce queso fresco, cubed
- 1/2 cup corn kernels, cooked (or frozen corn, defrosted)
- 3/4 cup fava beans, shelled and boiled (or frozen favas, defrosted)
- 1 small onion, diced
- 1 tomato, diced
- 1 rocoto chile, seeded, membrane removed, and chopped
- 1 yellow chile, seeded, membrane removed, and chopped
- 1 tablespoon chopped parsley
- 1 tablespoon chopped huacatay leaves

- 3/4 cup black olives, cut in strips
- 4 tablespoons white wine vinegar
- 5 tablespoons vegetable oil
- 1/2 teaspoon dried oregano
- Salt and pepper

Direction

- Place all the ingredients together in a bowl.
- Mix together well and season with salt and pepper to taste.
- Serve.
- Cooks' Note: If you can't find the specific Peruvian chiles called for here, substitute your favorites. Jalapeño is a decent choice. Substitute half cilantro and half mint if you can't find huacatay leaves.

Nutrition Information

- Calories: 545
- Total Fat: 31 g (47%)
- Saturated Fat: 6 g (28%)
- Cholesterol: 20 mg (7%)
- Sodium: 590 mg (25%)
- Total Carbohydrate: 53 g (18%)
- Protein: 17 g (34%)
- Fiber: 8 g (33%)

284. Southwestern Quinoa Salad

"A healthy grain salad with lots of fresh flavor."

Serving: 8 | Prep: 30 m | Cook: 15 m | Ready in: 1 h 25 m

Ingredients

- 1 cup quinoa
- 1 tablespoon butter
- 2 cups chicken broth
- 1/2 cup diced green bell pepper
- 1/2 cup diced red onion
- 1 cup corn
- 1 (15 ounce) can black beans, drained
- 1/4 cup chopped cilantro
- 1 large tomato, diced
- 1/2 cup fresh lime juice, or to taste
- 2 tablespoons red wine vinegar
- 2 tablespoons olive oil
- 1 tablespoon adobo seasoning
- 1/2 cup feta cheese
- salt and black pepper to taste

Direction

- Rinse the quinoa thoroughly under cold water, and drain. Melt butter in a large saucepan over medium heat, and cook and stir the quinoa until the water has evaporated and the quinoa is lightly toasted, about 3 minutes. Pour in the chicken broth, bring to a boil, reduce heat to low, and simmer until the quinoa has absorbed all the broth, about 10 minutes. Cool quinoa in refrigerator at least 10 minutes.
- Mix together green pepper, red onion, corn, black beans, cilantro, tomato, lime juice, red wine vinegar, olive oil, adobo seasoning, and feta cheese in a large salad bowl. Lightly stir in the quinoa, and season with salt, pepper, and additional lime juice to taste, if desired. Chill the salad at least 30 minutes before serving; serve cold.

Nutrition Information

- Calories: 195 calories
- Total Fat: 9.8 g
- Cholesterol: 18 mg
- Sodium: 197 mg
- Total Carbohydrate: 22.1 g
- Protein: 6.3 g

285. SpanishStyle Quinoa

"This quinoa dish is a delicious and higher protein alternative to Spanish rice. This is a nice side dish to a Mexican meal, or it can be used as a filling in burritos. I like my food on the less-salty side, so you may have to adjust the seasonings to your taste."

Serving: 8 | Prep: 20 m | Cook: 40 m | Ready in: 1 h

Ingredients

- 2 tablespoons vegetable oil
- 1 cup uncooked quinoa
- 1 medium onion, finely chopped
- 3 cloves garlic, minced
- 1 small green bell pepper, chopped
- 1 (8 ounce) can tomato sauce
- 2 1/2 cups water
- 1 teaspoon chili powder
- 1/4 teaspoon garlic powder
- 1/4 teaspoon ground cumin

Direction

- Heat the vegetable oil in a large saucepan over medium-high heat. Stir in the quinoa, onion, garlic, and green pepper. Cook and stir 5 to 10 minutes until the onion is tender, and the quinoa has lightly toasted. Stir in the tomato sauce and water, then season with the chili powder, garlic powder, and cumin. Bring to a boil, then reduce heat to medium-low, cover, and simmer until the quinoa is tender, and the liquid is absorbed, about 30 minutes. Stir the quinoa occasionally as it cooks.

Nutrition Information

- Calories: 126 calories
- Total Fat: 4.9 g
- Cholesterol: 0 mg
- Sodium: 154 mg
- Total Carbohydrate: 17.5 g
- Protein: 3.7 g

286. Speedy Mexican Black Beans and Quinoa

"A super-speedy simple supper the whole family will love. Full of Mexican flavor, but not too spicy. The ingredients are great to keep on hand in the pantry so you can whip this up on those busy nights."

Serving: 6 | Prep: 10 m | Cook: 25 m | Ready in: 40 m

Ingredients

- 5 1/2 cups water, divided
- 2 cups quinoa
- 3 teaspoons chicken bouillon granules, divided
- 2 (15 ounce) cans black beans, rinsed and drained
- 1 (10 ounce) can diced tomatoes and green chiles (such as RO*TEL® Chunky)
- 1/2 teaspoon ground cumin
- 1/2 teaspoon ground coriander
- 1/8 teaspoon garlic powder
- 1/8 teaspoon cracked black pepper
- 1/2 (8 ounce) package shredded Monterey Jack cheese

Direction

- Bring 4 cups water to a boil in a medium saucepan. Stir in quinoa and 2 teaspoons chicken bouillon. Reduce heat to medium-low, cover, and simmer until water is absorbed and quinoa is tender, 20 to 25 minutes.
- Meanwhile, combine remaining 1 1/2 cups water and 1 teaspoon bouillon with black beans, diced tomatoes, cumin, coriander, garlic powder, and pepper in another medium saucepan. Bring to a boil. Reduce heat to medium and cover. Simmer until quinoa is ready.
- Remove quinoa from heat and let sit for 5 minutes. Spoon the quinoa into bowls. Top with the seasoned beans and Monterey Jack cheese.

Nutrition Information

- Calories: 418 calories
- Total Fat: 9.8 g
- Cholesterol: 17 mg

- Sodium: 1027 mg
- Total Carbohydrate: 62.1 g
- Protein: 21.7 g

287. Spiced Quinoa

"This recipe combines pungent Mediterranean and Indian flavors for a quick and delicious side dish."

Serving: 4 | Prep: 20 m | Cook: 25 m | Ready in: 45 m

Ingredients

- 1 tablespoon olive oil
- 1 small onion, chopped
- 1 clove garlic, minced
- 3/4 cup quinoa
- 1 1/2 teaspoons curry powder
- 1/2 teaspoon salt
- 1/2 teaspoon black pepper
- 1/2 teaspoon cumin
- 1/4 teaspoon cinnamon
- 1 1/2 cups chicken stock
- 1 (14 ounce) can garbanzo beans, drained and rinsed
- 1/2 cup toasted pine nuts
- 1/2 cup raisins, soaked in hot water and drained (optional)

Direction

- Stir together the olive oil, onion, and garlic in a saucepan over medium heat until the onion has softened and turned translucent, about 5 minutes. Stir in the quinoa, curry powder, salt, pepper, cumin, cinnamon, and chicken stock. Bring to a boil, then reduce heat to medium-low, cover, and simmer 20 minutes until the quinoa is tender.
- Once the quinoa has finished cooking, stir in the drained garbanzo beans, toasted pine nuts, and raisins. Serve warm or cold.

Nutrition Information

- Calories: 440 calories
- Total Fat: 15.6 g
- Cholesterol: < 1 mg

- Sodium: 851 mg
- Total Carbohydrate: 64.8 g
- Protein: 14.8 g

288. Spiced Quinoa Porridge

"A simple, delicious, and nutritious way to serve quinoa, hot or cold. Serve with milk, soy milk, or cream."

Serving: 6 | Prep: 5 m | Cook: 15 m | Ready in: 25 m

Ingredients

- 4 cups water
- 2 cups quinoa
- 1/2 cup raisins
- 1/2 cup golden raisins
- 1 (1.5 fluid ounce) jigger spiced dark rum
- 1 teaspoon freshly ground Vietnamese cinnamon
- 6 tablespoons maple syrup

Direction

- Bring water to a boil in a saucepan. Add quinoa, raisins, golden raisins, and rum; reduce heat and simmer, covered, until water is absorbed, about 10 minutes. Remove from heat and keep covered, about 5 minutes.
- Fluff quinoa mixture with a fork and stir in cinnamon. Ladle into 6 serving bowls; top each with 1 tablespoon maple syrup.

Nutrition Information

- Calories: 360 calories
- Total Fat: 3.6 g
- Cholesterol: 0 mg
- Sodium: 13 mg
- Total Carbohydrate: 71.9 g
- Protein: 8.9 g

289. Spicy Chicken Quinoa

"We are trying to eat healthier, but we still want flavorful, so I came up with this recipe. My family loves it! Great served with chips, stuffed in half a zucchini (and baked), in a tortilla, or just by itself!"

Serving: 4 | Prep: 10 m | Cook: 35 m | Ready in: 45 m

Ingredients

- 1 cup chicken broth
- 1/2 cup quinoa
- 1 pound ground chicken
- 1/2 teaspoon garlic powder
- 1/4 teaspoon cayenne pepper
- 2 teaspoons olive oil, divided
- 1 zucchini, diced
- 1 (15 ounce) can corn, drained
- 1 (15 ounce) can black beans, rinsed, drained
- 1 (14.5 ounce) can diced tomatoes with green chile peppers, drained
- 1 cup salsa
- 3/4 cup shredded Mexican cheese blend

Direction

- Bring chicken broth and quinoa to a boil in a saucepan. Reduce heat to medium-low, cover, and simmer until quinoa is tender and water is absorbed, 15 to 20 minutes.
- Mix chicken, garlic powder, and cayenne pepper together in a bowl.
- Heat 1 teaspoon olive oil in a large skillet over medium heat. Cook and stir chicken mixture in hot oil until chicken is cooked through, 5 to 10 minutes. Drain and discard grease. Transfer chicken mixture to a bowl.
- Heat remaining 1 teaspoon olive oil in the same skillet over medium-high heat. Cook and stir zucchini in hot oil until softened, about 4 minutes. Add cooked quinoa, chicken mixture, corn, black beans, tomatoes, and salsa to skillet; cook, stirring, until heated through and flavors have combined, 5 to 10 minutes. Sprinkle cheese over the top. Cover skillet and cook until cheese melts, 1 to 2 minutes.

Nutrition Information

- Calories: 566 calories
- Total Fat: 17 g
- Cholesterol: 95 mg
- Sodium: 2017 mg
- Total Carbohydrate: 62.1 g
- Protein: 45.9 g

290. Spicy Quinoa and Spinach Pulao Pilaf

"This spicy quinoa pulao with Indian flavors is made with quinoa rather than rice for added protein!"

Serving: 4 | Prep: 15 m | Cook: 20 m | Ready in: 35 m

Ingredients

- 2 tablespoons olive oil
- 1 teaspoon cumin seeds (jeera)
- 2 teaspoons minced garlic
- 1 1/2 teaspoons ground cumin (jeera)
- 1 1/2 teaspoons ground coriander (dhana)
- 1 1/2 teaspoons chile powder
- 1 teaspoon minced ginger
- 3/4 teaspoon minced Thai chile pepper
- 1/4 teaspoon pav bhaji masala
- 1/4 teaspoon ground turmeric (haldi)
- 1 yellow onion, diced
- 1 1/2 vine-ripened tomatoes, diced
- 4 cups finely chopped fresh spinach
- 3 cups water
- 1 1/2 cups uncooked quinoa
- 1 cup chopped fresh cilantro, or to taste
- 1 lemon, cut into wedges

Direction

- Heat olive oil in a large wok over medium heat. Add cumin seeds and let sizzle for 30 seconds. Add garlic, ground cumin, coriander, chile powder, ginger, chile pepper, pav bhaji masala, and turmeric; sauté until fragrant, about 30 seconds. Stir in onion; sauté until translucent, about 5 minutes. Stir in tomatoes

and cook until the tomato smell goes away. Mix in spinach; cook until wilted, 2 to 3 minutes.
- Pour water and quinoa into the wok. Bring to a simmer; cook, stirring occasionally, until water is absorbed, 8 to 12 minutes. Garnish with freshly chopped cilantro and lemon wedges.

Nutrition Information
- Calories: 359 calories
- Total Fat: 11.7 g
- Cholesterol: 0 mg
- Sodium: 47 mg
- Total Carbohydrate: 55.3 g
- Protein: 12.2 g

291. Spicy Quinoa Bean and Pepper Salad

"Incredibly tasty dish that even non-quinoa lovers will love! Add other veggies and peppers to taste. This can be served either hot or cold."

Serving: 4 | Prep: 20 m | Cook: 35 m | Ready in: 55 m

Ingredients
- 1 teaspoon chile oil
- 1 onion, chopped
- 3 cloves garlic, chopped
- 1 large red bell pepper, chopped
- 3/4 cup red quinoa
- 1 1/2 cups vegetable broth
- 1/2 teaspoon chipotle pepper powder, or more to taste
- 1/4 teaspoon cayenne pepper
- 1 (15 ounce) can black beans, rinsed and drained
- 1 cup frozen corn kernels (optional)

Direction
- Heat oil in a saucepan over medium heat. Cook and stir onion and garlic in hot oil until lightly browned, 5 to 7 minutes; add chopped red pepper and continue to cook and stir until slightly tender, 1 to 2 minutes.
- Stir quinoa with the onion mixture. Pour vegetable broth into the saucepan; season with chipotle pepper powder and cayenne pepper. Bring the broth to a boil. Cover the saucepan, reduce heat to low, and simmer until the quinoa is tender, about 20 minutes.
- Stir black beans and corn into the quinoa mixture; simmer until the beans and corn are heated through, about 5 minutes more.

Nutrition Information
- Calories: 309 calories
- Total Fat: 3.9 g
- Cholesterol: 0 mg
- Sodium: 588 mg
- Total Carbohydrate: 57 g
- Protein: 13.7 g

292. Spicy Vegan Lentil Quinoa Soup

"A vegan mix of lentil and quinoa with carrot, mushroom, and celery in a spicy soup."

Serving: 4 | Prep: 10 m | Cook: 45 m | Ready in: 55 m

Ingredients
- 4 cups water
- 1 cup chopped celery
- 1 cup dry lentils
- 1/2 cup quinoa
- 1/2 cup chopped carrots
- 1/2 cup mushrooms
- 1 tablespoon chili powder
- 1 tablespoon cumin
- 1 tablespoon ground ginger

Direction
- Combine water, celery, lentils, quinoa, carrots, mushrooms, chili powder, cumin, and ginger

in a saucepan. Cover saucepan and cook soup over medium-low heat until vegetables and lentils are tender, 45 to 60 minutes.

Nutrition Information

- Calories: 277 calories
- Total Fat: 2.7 g
- Cholesterol: 0 mg
- Sodium: 70 mg
- Total Carbohydrate: 47.9 g
- Protein: 16.6 g

293. Spinach Quinoa Burgers

"After having one of these burgers at a local catering place, I had to adapt my own version! These are extremely filling and taste great with chipotle mayonnaise and sliced cheese! These may be refrigerated or frozen for later use."

Serving: 4 | Prep: 25 m | Cook: 28 m | Ready in: 58 m

Ingredients

- 2/3 cup beef broth
- 1/3 cup dry quinoa
- 1 (10 ounce) package frozen chopped spinach, thawed and drained
- 1/2 cup chopped onion
- 1/2 cup shredded Parmesan cheese
- 2 cloves garlic, or more to taste
- 1/2 cup fresh bread crumbs
- 1 teaspoon salt
- 1 teaspoon red pepper flakes
- 1/2 teaspoon garlic powder
- 1/4 teaspoon fresh ground black pepper
- 2 egg whites
- 1 egg
- cooking spray
- 4 hamburger buns

Direction

- Bring beef broth to a strong boil in a saucepan over high heat. Stir in quinoa; reduce heat to low and cover. Cook until broth is absorbed, about 15 minutes. Remove from heat; let stand for 5 minutes. Fluff with a fork; let cool.
- Chop spinach in a food processor; transfer to a bowl. Chop onion, Parmesan cheese, and garlic in the food processor; add to the spinach. Mix in cooled quinoa, bread crumbs, salt, red pepper flakes, garlic powder, and black pepper. Add egg whites and egg; stir burger mixture to combine.
- Shape burger mixture into 4 equal patties. Heat a skillet over medium-high heat and coat with cooking spray. Cook patties until cooked throughout, 4 to 6 minutes per side. Serve on hamburger buns.

Nutrition Information

- Calories: 336 calories
- Total Fat: 8.6 g
- Cholesterol: 55 mg
- Sodium: 1305 mg
- Total Carbohydrate: 47.2 g
- Protein: 18.2 g

294. Spinach Tomato and Feta Quinoa Salad

"A quick and healthy side dish alternative to rice and pasta. It will make a quinoa-lover out of anyone. Thanks to the salty feta and sweet Campari tomatoes, my kids even like it!"

Serving: 4 | Prep: 10 m | Cook: 15 m | Ready in: 1 h

Ingredients

- Salad:
- 2 cups water
- 1 teaspoon chicken bouillon granules
- 1 cup multi-colored quinoa
- 2 cups roughly chopped spinach
- Dressing:
- 3 tablespoons almond oil
- 2 tablespoons extra-virgin olive oil
- 2 tablespoons champagne vinegar
- 1 teaspoon dried thyme
- 1 teaspoon dried basil
- 1 teaspoon minced garlic

- 1/4 teaspoon kosher salt
- Salad Ingredients:
- 3 on-the-vine tomatoes (such as Campari®), diced
- 1/2 cup crumbled feta cheese, divided
- freshly ground black pepper to taste

Direction

- Bring water and bouillon to a boil in a saucepan. Add quinoa, reduce heat to low, cover, and cook until water is absorbed, about 15 minutes. Transfer quinoa to a bowl and cool slightly, 5 to 10 minutes. Stir spinach into quinoa and refrigerate until completely cooled, at least 30 minutes.
- Whisk almond oil, olive oil, vinegar, thyme, basil, garlic, and salt together in a bowl until dressing is smooth.
- Stir tomatoes, 1/2 of the feta cheese, and dressing into cooled quinoa until evenly coated; top with remaining feta cheese and ground black pepper.

Nutrition Information

- Calories: 388 calories
- Total Fat: 23.9 g
- Cholesterol: 17 mg
- Sodium: 446 mg
- Total Carbohydrate: 34.6 g
- Protein: 10.3 g

295. Sriracha Quinoa Burger Melt

"Looking to take a break from meat? This is a delicious alternative. You will not be disappointed by the flavors!"

Serving: 4 | Prep: 25 m | Cook: 1 h 15 m | Ready in: 3 h 40 m

Ingredients

- 2/3 cup water
- 1/2 cup cooked black beans
- 1/3 cup uncooked quinoa
- 4 teaspoons extra-virgin olive oil, divided
- 1/2 red onion, diced
- 3/4 cup fine dry bread crumbs
- 1/4 cup chile-garlic sauce (such as Sriracha)
- 3 tablespoons all-purpose flour
- 1 teaspoon ground black pepper
- 1/2 teaspoon salt
- 1/2 cup shredded pepper jack cheese
- 2 tablespoons margarine, or as needed
- 3/4 cup crushed buttery round crackers
- 1 tomato, sliced
- 1/2 red bell pepper, chopped
- 1 pinch dried thyme
- 1 small red potato, thinly sliced
- 1/4 teaspoon garlic powder
- 1/4 teaspoon chili powder
- 4 slices Emmentaler cheese, torn into 4 pieces
- 4 ciabatta rolls, split and toasted

Direction

- Place water, black beans, and quinoa in a small pot; bring to a simmer and cook until quinoa is tender, about 20 minutes. Place mixture into a bowl; mash with a fork.
- Heat 2 teaspoons olive oil in a small skillet over medium heat; stir in onion and sauté until onion has softened and turned translucent, about 5 minutes. Reduce heat to medium-low, and continue cooking and stirring until the onion is very tender and dark brown, about 15 minutes.
- Stir onion, bread crumbs, chile-garlic sauce, flour, black pepper, and salt into quinoa mixture; stir in pepper jack cheese. Shape quinoa mixture into patties, place in freezer until firm, about 1 hour.
- Melt margarine in a microwave-safe shallow bowl in the microwave, about 15 seconds on High. Place crushed buttery crackers in a separate shallow bowl. Remove patties from freezer, dip into margarine to coat, and dredge in crushed crackers to coat evenly. Place quinoa patties on a small baking sheet; refrigerate for 1 hour.
- Preheat oven to 400 degrees F (200 degrees C).
- Toss tomato slices and red pepper in a bowl with 1 teaspoon olive oil and thyme; place in a

single layer on a baking sheet. Toss potato slices with remaining olive oil, garlic powder, and chili powder in a bowl; place potatoes on the baking sheet.
- Roast vegetables in the preheated oven until peppers and tomatoes are tender and potatoes are golden brown, about 10 minutes.
- Bake patties until heated through, turning once, about 20 minutes. Layer each patty with Emmentaler cheese, potato chips, Emmentaler cheese, roasted tomato, Emmentaler cheese, roasted red pepper, and Emmentaler cheese. Return patties to the oven; bake until cheese is melted, about 5 minutes. Serve on ciabatta rolls.

Nutrition Information

- Calories: 719 calories
- Total Fat: 31.2 g
- Cholesterol: 44 mg
- Sodium: 1941 mg
- Total Carbohydrate: 82.6 g
- Protein: 26.2 g

296. SteelCut Oats and Quinoa Breakfast

"The best make-ahead breakfast! Full of fiber and protein will keep you full all morning. Keeps in the fridge for up to a week."

Serving: 4 | Prep: 5 m | Cook: 20 m | Ready in: 40 m

Ingredients

- 3 cups water
- 1/2 cup quinoa
- 1/2 cup steel-cut oats
- 2 tablespoons almond meal
- 2 tablespoons flaxseed meal
- 1 tablespoon ground cinnamon

Direction

- Bring water to a boil in a saucepan; add quinoa and oats. Simmer, stirring frequently, until water is absorbed and quinoa is tender, 15 to 20 minutes.
- Stir almond meal and flaxseed meal into quinoa mixture; pour into a glass container and top with cinnamon. Let cool, about 15 minutes. Transfer to the refrigerator.

Nutrition Information

- Calories: 191 calories
- Total Fat: 4.7 g
- Cholesterol: 0 mg
- Sodium: 8 mg
- Total Carbohydrate: 30.6 g
- Protein: 7.6 g

297. Stovetop Butternut Squash and Chicken Stew with Quinoa

"This all-in-one-pan fall stew is made with chicken, sausage, butternut squash and apples. Serve with warm biscuits or bread."

Serving: 6 | Prep: 30 m | Cook: 35 m | Ready in: 1 h 5 m

Ingredients

- 1/2 teaspoon salt
- 1 teaspoon freshly ground black pepper
- 1 pound chicken tenderloins
- 2 tablespoons all-purpose flour
- 1 tablespoon olive oil
- 1 clove garlic, minced
- 1 onion, diced
- 1/2 cup diced red bell pepper
- 2 links precooked apple chicken sausage, sliced into rounds
- 3 cups chicken stock, divided
- 1 tablespoon minced fresh tarragon
- 1/2 teaspoon rubbed sage
- 1/2 teaspoon garam masala
- 2 cups butternut squash - peeled, seeded, and cubed
- 1 cup diced carrots
- 2 celery ribs, chopped
- 1 apple - peeled, cored and diced

- 1 cup quinoa, rinsed and drained
- 1 tablespoon butter

Direction

- Season chicken tenderloins with salt and black pepper; pat into flour in a shallow bowl until lightly coated. Heat olive oil in a skillet over medium-high heat. Cook tenderloins, until browned, turning once, about 5 minutes per side. Remove from pan and set aside.
- Reduce heat to medium-low; add garlic, onion, red bell pepper, and apple chicken sausage. Cook and stir until garlic and onion are fragrant and sausage is slightly browned, about 2 minutes. Pour in 1/2 cup chicken stock to deglaze the pan, scraping up browned bits. Add tarragon, sage, and garam masala; simmer for 2 more minutes.
- Slice the chicken tenderloins into 1-inch pieces. Add chicken, remaining chicken stock, butternut squash, carrots, celery, and apple to pan; cover and bring to a boil. When stock is boiling, push ingredients to the edge of the skillet and add quinoa to the center of the pan. Cover and simmer over low heat until vegetables are soft and quinoa is cooked, about 20 minutes.
- Mix in butter; stir the stew until slightly thickened, 3 to 5 minutes. Adjust seasoning to taste.

Nutrition Information

- Calories: 353 calories
- Total Fat: 11.9 g
- Cholesterol: 83 mg
- Sodium: 747 mg
- Total Carbohydrate: 36.5 g
- Protein: 25.6 g

298. Stuffed Peppers with Quinoa

"We tweaked this from several stuffed pepper recipes to come up with a yummy version that tastes even better reheated for lunch the next day. This is a great side dish with fish. You could use vegetable broth to make it vegetarian."

Serving: 6 | Prep: 20 m | Cook: 1 h 5 m | Ready in: 1 h 25 m

Ingredients

- 3 red bell peppers, sliced lengthwise
- 1 tablespoon olive oil
- 1 onion, finely chopped
- 1 tablespoon minced garlic
- 1 teaspoon ground cumin
- 1 teaspoon salt
- 1/2 teaspoon ground black pepper
- 1 (16 ounce) can diced tomatoes, drained and juice reserved
- 1 cup chicken broth
- 3/4 cup quinoa
- 1/2 carrot, grated
- 1 (14 ounce) can black beans, rinsed and drained
- 1 (6 ounce) package fresh spinach, or more to taste
- 1/2 cup shredded Mexican cheese blend

Direction

- Preheat oven to 375 degrees F (190 degrees C). Grease a 9x13-inch baking dish and arrange red bell peppers in dish.
- Roast peppers in the preheated oven until tender, about 30 minutes.
- Heat olive oil in a skillet over medium heat; cook and stir onion until softened, 5 to 10 minutes. Add garlic, cumin, salt, and black pepper to onion; cook and stir until fragrant, about 1 minute more.
- Mix tomatoes, chicken broth, quinoa, and carrot into onion mixture; cook until quinoa is tender, about 12 minutes. Stir black beans and spinach into quinoa mixture, adding reserved tomato juice if mixture is dry. Spoon quinoa mixture into roasted red peppers and top with Mexican cheese blend.

- Bake in the oven until cheese is melted, about 15 minutes.

Nutrition Information

- Calories: 258 calories
- Total Fat: 7.8 g
- Cholesterol: 12 mg
- Sodium: 1038 mg
- Total Carbohydrate: 35.2 g
- Protein: 12.1 g

299. Stuffed Red Pepper with Quinoa and Chickpeas

"This is a very healthy, vegetarian main course with lots of protein from the chickpeas and quinoa. The flavors in this recipe are a blend of Persian and Mediterranean. Very easy to make and super satisfying! This freezes really well for a dinner or lunch later on (goat cheese and all!)"

Serving: 4 | Prep: 15 m | Cook: 45 m | Ready in: 1 h

Ingredients

- 1 teaspoon olive oil, or as needed
- 1 1/3 cups water
- 2/3 cup quinoa
- 1 (16 ounce) can garbanzo beans (chickpeas), drained and rinsed
- 1 (16 ounce) can stewed tomatoes (such as Del Monte® Stewed Tomatoes with Onions, Celery, and Green Peppers)
- 1/4 cup walnut pieces
- 1/2 cup golden raisins
- 1 bunch green onions, sliced, white parts and tops separated
- 1/2 lemon, juiced
- 1/2 teaspoon chili powder
- 1/4 teaspoon garlic powder
- 1/4 teaspoon dried mint leaves
- 1 pinch ground cinnamon
- 2 large red bell peppers, halved lengthwise, seeds and membrane removed
- 1/4 cup crumbled goat cheese

Direction

- Preheat oven to 350 degrees F (175 degrees C). Grease a 9x13-inch baking dish with olive oil.
- Bring water and quinoa to a boil in a saucepan. Reduce heat to medium-low, cover, and simmer until quinoa is tender and water has been absorbed, 15 to 20 minutes.
- Mix garbanzo beans, stewed tomatoes, walnuts, raisins, white parts of green onions, lemon juice, chili powder, garlic powder, mint, and cinnamon together in a bowl; stir in cooked quinoa.
- Arrange red bell pepper halves, hollow-side facing upwards, in the prepared baking sheet. Spoon quinoa mixture into each red bell pepper half.
- Bake in the preheated oven until bell peppers are tender, about 30 minutes. Spoon a few teaspoons of drippings from the bottom of the baking dish over each stuffed pepper; top each with 1 tablespoon goat cheese and green parts of green onions.

Nutrition Information

- Calories: 469 calories
- Total Fat: 12.4 g
- Cholesterol: 7 mg
- Sodium: 654 mg
- Total Carbohydrate: 73.5 g
- Protein: 16.3 g

300. Stuffed Red Peppers with Quinoa Mushrooms and Turkey

"Kid-friendly red bell peppers stuffed with ground turkey and quinoa."

Serving: 8 | Prep: 30 m | Cook: 1 h 30 m | Ready in: 2 h

Ingredients

- 2 cups water
- 1 cup uncooked quinoa
- 1 tablespoon olive oil

- 1 onion, diced
- 1 pound ground turkey
- salt and ground black pepper to taste
- 12 mushrooms, chopped, or more to taste
- 1 (24 ounce) jar tomato sauce, or more to taste
- 1 (6 ounce) can tomato paste
- 8 large red bell peppers - tops, seeds, and membranes removed
- 1 (8 ounce) package shredded Cheddar cheese, or to taste

Direction

- Bring water and quinoa to a boil in a saucepan. Reduce heat to medium-low, cover, and simmer until quinoa is tender, 15 to 20 minutes.
- Heat olive oil in a large skillet over medium heat. Add onion and cook until softened, about 5 minutes. Add turkey and season with salt and pepper; cook and stir until turkey is no longer pink, 5 to 7 minutes. Add mushrooms and cook until softened, about 5 minutes.
- Preheat the oven to 350 degrees F (175 degrees C).
- Transfer cooked turkey mixture to a large bowl. Add cooked quinoa, tomato sauce, and tomato paste. Stir well; add additional tomato sauce as needed, until filling has the consistency of a casserole.
- Arrange red bell peppers in a baking dish and spoon an equal amount of filling into each.
- Bake in the preheated oven for 45 minutes. Remove from oven and top each stuffed pepper with Cheddar cheese. Continue baking until cheese is melted, about 10 minutes more.

Nutrition Information

- Calories: 389 calories
- Total Fat: 17.4 g
- Cholesterol: 71 mg
- Sodium: 850 mg
- Total Carbohydrate: 34.6 g
- Protein: 25.8 g

301. Summer Squash and Red Quinoa Salad with Walnuts

For this pretty side or meatless main salad, use medium and small squash for the best flavor. Quinoa and walnuts (or a grain and nut of your choosing) add heft.

Serving: Makes 4 to 6 servings | Prep: 20 m | Cook: 35 m

Ingredients

- 1/2 cup red or other quinoa, rinsed in a fine-mesh sieve, drained
- 2 teaspoons kosher salt plus more for seasoning
- 1 pound assorted summer squash
- 2 tablespoons finely grated Parmesan plus 1/4 cup shaved with a peeler
- 1 teaspoon finely grated lemon zest
- 2 tablespoons fresh lemon juice
- 1 tablespoon Sherry vinegar
- 6 tablespoons extra-virgin olive oil
- Freshly ground black pepper
- 1/2 cup flat-leaf parsley leaves
- 1/2 cup walnuts, toasted
- 1/4 cup fresh basil leaves, torn

Direction

- Bring quinoa and 4 cups water to a boil in a medium saucepan. Season with salt, cover, reduce heat to medium-low, and simmer until quinoa is tender but not mushy, 12-15 minutes. Drain; return quinoa to hot saucepan. Cover and let sit for 15 minutes. Uncover; fluff with a fork and let cool.
- Cut squash into 1/8"-thick slices, some lengthwise and some crosswise. Transfer to a large bowl, season with 2 teaspoons salt, and toss to coat. Let sit until slightly wilted, about 15 minutes. Rinse under cold water and drain well. Pat dry with paper towels.
- Whisk grated Parmesan, zest, juice, and vinegar in a medium bowl. Gradually whisk in oil. Season dressing with salt and pepper.

- Combine squash, quinoa, parsley, walnuts, and basil in a large bowl. Pour dressing over; toss to coat. Garnish with shaved Parmesan.
- Per serving: 350 calories, 29 g fat, 3 g fiber
- Nutritional analysis provided by Bon Appétit

302. Super Breakfast Apple and Quinoa Oatmeal

"Delicious warm breakfast, or anytime treat, that tastes kinda like oatmeal but with a nuttier flavor that blends well with the apples. Packs a bigger punch of protein to keep you fuller longer than oatmeal. May drizzle a little extra half half on cereal if desired."

Serving: 1 | Prep: 10 m | Cook: 8 m | Ready in: 18 m

Ingredients

- 1 apple, peeled and diced
- 3 tablespoons granular sucralose sweetener (such as Splenda®)
- 1/2 teaspoon apple pie spice
- 1 tablespoon water (optional)
- 1 cup cooked quinoa
- 1/4 cup fat-free half-and-half

Direction

- Place apple, sweetener, and apple pie spice in a saucepan over medium heat; cook and stir until apple is cooked through, 5 to 8 minutes. Add water if needed to keep apples from sticking. Mix quinoa and half-and-half into apple mixture; cook until warmed through, 3 to 5 minutes.

Nutrition Information

- Calories: 334 calories
- Total Fat: 4.7 g
- Cholesterol: 3 mg
- Sodium: 103 mg
- Total Carbohydrate: 65.4 g
- Protein: 10.1 g

303. Super Pasta e Ceci

"Traditional Italian ditalini pasta and chickpeas made even better and faster by adding Barilla® Tomato and Basil sauce, cooked quinoa, and shrimp for a savory meal."

Serving: 3 | Prep: 15 m | Cook: 30 m | Ready in: 45 m

Ingredients

- 1 cup Barilla® Ditalini
- 1 cup Barilla® Tomato Basil Sauce
- 2/3 cup water
- 1/3 cup quinoa
- 2 tablespoons olive oil
- 1 carrot, minced
- 1 celery stalk, minced
- 1 small onion, minced
- 2 cups cooked chickpeas, liquid reserved
- 1 jalapeno pepper, seeded and minced (optional)
- 1 teaspoon salt
- 1/4 cup nutritional yeast
- 2 cups boiling water, or more if needed
- 18 cooked shrimp, shelled
- 3 tablespoons chopped fresh flat-leaf parsley
- 1 tablespoon extra-virgin olive oil

Direction

- Bring water and quinoa to a boil in a saucepan. Reduce heat to medium-low, cover, and simmer until quinoa is tender, 15 to 20 minutes. If all water has not been absorbed, drain.
- Heat oil in a large pot. Add carrots, celery, and onion; cook and stir until vegetables soften and onions begin to turn translucent, 3 to 5 minutes. Add chickpeas with liquid and cooked quinoa. Stir in jalapeno pepper. Add tomato sauce, salt, and nutritional yeast; stir to combine.
- Slowly pour in 2 cups boiling water; add ditalini. Continue to stir; add more water only if needed. Cook until ditalini are al dente, 9 to 10 minutes. Mixture should have a stew-like consistency. Add shrimp; cook and stir until shrimp are heated through, 1 more minute.

- Divide among serving bowls; top with fresh, chopped parsley and a drizzle of extra-virgin olive oil.

Nutrition Information

- Calories: 2776 calories
- Total Fat: 38.5 g
- Cholesterol: 4033 mg
- Sodium: 6210 mg
- Total Carbohydrate: 123.1 g
- Protein: 460 g

304. Suzys Special Red Quinoa

"Red Quinoa flavored with Chinese five-spice powder."

Serving: 4 | Prep: 10 m | Cook: 20 m | Ready in: 30 m

Ingredients

- 2 cups water
- 1 1/2 teaspoons butter
- 1 tablespoon Chinese five-spice powder
- 1/4 teaspoon ground ginger
- 1/4 teaspoon black pepper
- 1 cube beef bouillon
- 1 cup red quinoa, rinsed and drained

Direction

- Place the water, butter, five-spice powder, ginger, black pepper, and beef bouillon cube into a saucepan over medium heat, and bring to a boil. Stir the mixture to dissolve the bouillon cube, then add the quinoa. Reduce heat to a simmer, cover, and cook until all the water is absorbed, about 20 minutes.

Nutrition Information

- Calories: 173 calories
- Total Fat: 4.2 g
- Cholesterol: 4 mg
- Sodium: 239 mg
- Total Carbohydrate: 28.3 g
- Protein: 5.8 g

305. Sweet Potato Quinoa Patties

"These are kind of like a twist on falafel. Goes well in pita bread. Enjoy with a generous sprinkling of fresh thyme leaves and some finishing salt! You can use vegan butter instead of coconut oil, if desired."

Serving: 4 | Prep: 15 m | Cook: 15 m | Ready in: 30 m

Ingredients

- 1 tablespoon extra-virgin olive oil
- 1 yellow onion, diced
- 3 cloves garlic, crushed
- 1 tablespoon chopped fresh thyme
- 2 cups mashed sweet potatoes
- 2 cups cooked quinoa
- sea salt to taste
- freshly cracked black pepper to taste
- 1 tablespoon coconut oil, or as needed

Direction

- Heat olive oil in a large skillet over medium-low heat; cook and stir onion with a pinch of salt in hot oil until onion is translucent, 5 to 10 minutes. Add garlic; cook and stir until fragrant; about 1 minute. Stir in thyme and cook for about 30 seconds; transfer mixture to a large bowl.
- Stir sweet potatoes, quinoa, sea salt, and black pepper together with onion mixture until well-combined. Divide mixture into golf-ball size balls and press into patties.
- Heat coconut oil in a nonstick skillet over medium-high heat. Cook patties in hot oil until browned, about 2 minutes per side.

Nutrition Information

- Calories: 316 calories
- Total Fat: 9 g
- Cholesterol: 0 mg
- Sodium: 184 mg
- Total Carbohydrate: 52.6 g
- Protein: 7.1 g

306. Tabbouleh Salad with Quinoa and Shredded Carrots

"Great summer recipe. When unexpected company comes, everything I need can be picked from the garden."

Serving: 4 | Prep: 15 m | Cook: 15 m | Ready in: 1 h

Ingredients

- 2 cups water
- 1 pinch salt
- 1 cup quinoa
- 1 tomato, chopped
- 1/2 cup shredded carrot
- 1/2 cup minced green onion
- 1/4 cup minced fresh mint
- 1/4 cup minced fresh parsley
- 5 tablespoons lemon juice
- 1/4 cup olive oil
- 1/2 teaspoon salt
- 1/8 teaspoon ground black and red pepper blend (such as Penzey's®)

Direction

- Bring water and a pinch of salt to a boil in a saucepan. Add quinoa to water, reduce heat to medium-low, cover, and simmer until quinoa is tender and water has been absorbed, about 15 minutes. Cool.
- Stir cooled quinoa, tomato, carrot, green onion, mint, and parsley together in a bowl.
- Whisk lemon juice, olive oil, 1/2 teaspoon salt, and ground pepper together in a small bowl until dressing is smooth. Pour dressing over quinoa mixture and toss to coat. Cover the bowl with plastic wrap and refrigerate until flavors combine, about 30 minutes.

Nutrition Information

- Calories: 300 calories
- Total Fat: 16.3 g
- Cholesterol: 0 mg
- Sodium: 314 mg
- Total Carbohydrate: 33.2 g
- Protein: 7 g

307. TexMex Quinoa Salad

"This versatile salad can be served warm in a tortilla, or as a filling for tacos and burritos."

Serving: 10 | Prep: 20 m | Cook: 20 m | Ready in: 2 h 40 m

Ingredients

- 1 cup quinoa
- 2 cups water
- 1 teaspoon kosher salt
- 1/4 cup fresh lime juice
- 2 tablespoons olive oil
- 1/8 teaspoon ground black pepper
- 1 (14 ounce) can diced tomatoes with green chile peppers, drained
- 1 (14 ounce) can garbanzo beans, drained and rinsed
- 1 bunch cilantro, chopped
- 2 avocados, cubed
- 1/4 cup crumbled cotija cheese

Direction

- Bring quinoa, water, and salt to a boil in a saucepan. Reduce heat to medium-low, cover, and simmer until the quinoa is tender, 20 to 25 minutes. Meanwhile, stir together the lime juice, olive oil, pepper, diced tomatoes, and garbanzo beans. When the quinoa is done, stir it into the tomato mixture, then cool in refrigerator until cold, about 2 hours
- When the quinoa is cold, fluff with a spoon, and gently fold in the cilantro, avocados, and cheese.

Nutrition Information

- Calories: 219 calories
- Total Fat: 11.1 g
- Cholesterol: 3 mg
- Sodium: 515 mg

- Total Carbohydrate: 25.7 g
- Protein: 6.3 g

308. Toasted Quinoa Granola

"Quick and easy. Sprinkle a few tablespoons of this nutty-tasting granola on yogurt. Quinoa is high in protein."

Serving: 10 | Prep: 15 m | Cook: 15 m | Ready in: 45 m

Ingredients

- 1 cup quinoa
- 1 tablespoon pure maple syrup
- 1 tablespoon olive oil
- 1 teaspoon ground cinnamon
- 1/4 cup flax seed

Direction

- Preheat oven to 350 degrees F (175 degrees C). Spray a baking sheet with cooking spray.
- Rinse and thoroughly drain the quinoa. In a large bowl, stir together the maple syrup, olive oil, and cinnamon; mix in the quinoa and flax seed until the grains are thoroughly coated. Spread the mixture out as thinly as possible on the prepared baking sheet.
- Toast the granola in the preheated oven until lightly golden brown, about 15 minutes, stirring every 5 minutes. Let cool completely before storing in an air-tight container.

Nutrition Information

- Calories: 94 calories
- Total Fat: 3.6 g
- Cholesterol: 0 mg
- Sodium: 1 mg
- Total Carbohydrate: 14 g
- Protein: 3.4 g

309. Tomato and Spinach Quinoa Skillet

"Great as a flavorful side dish or as a base of a meal if you add chicken, shrimp, or tofu."

Serving: 4 | Prep: 10 m | Cook: 20 m | Ready in: 30 m

Ingredients

- 4 cups chicken broth
- 1 (12 ounce) box quinoa
- 3 Roma tomatoes, chopped
- 3 cups fresh spinach
- 1/4 cup pesto
- 1/4 cup grated Parmesan cheese

Direction

- Bring chicken broth and quinoa to a boil in a saucepan. Reduce heat to medium-low, cover, and simmer until most of the broth is absorbed, 10 to 15 minutes.
- Stir tomatoes, spinach, and pesto into the quinoa. Simmer until remaining chicken broth is absorbed and quinoa is tender, about 5 minutes. Sprinkle Parmesan cheese over quinoa mixture.

Nutrition Information

- Calories: 437 calories
- Total Fat: 14.3 g
- Cholesterol: 14 mg
- Sodium: 1180 mg
- Total Carbohydrate: 58.8 g
- Protein: 18.6 g

310. TomatoMint Quinoa Salad

"Even for non-vegetarians, quinoa is a great change to rice or pasta. I've been trying to think of more dishes using quinoa and came up with this salad."

Serving: 4 | Prep: 40 m | Cook: 15 m | Ready in: 1 h 55 m

Ingredients

- 2 1/2 cups water
- 1 1/4 cups quinoa
- 1/3 cup raisins
- 1 pinch salt
- 2 medium tomatoes, diced
- 1 medium onion, minced
- 10 radishes, quartered
- 1/2 cucumber, diced
- 2 tablespoons sliced almonds, toasted
- 1/4 cup chopped fresh mint
- 2 tablespoons chopped fresh parsley
- 1 teaspoon ground cumin
- 1/4 cup lime juice
- 2 tablespoons sesame oil
- salt to taste

Direction

- Bring water to boil in a small saucepan. Pour in quinoa, raisins, and a pinch of salt. Cover, and let simmer for 12 to 15 minutes, then remove from heat, and allow to cool to room temperature.
- Toss together the tomatoes, onion, radish, cucumber, and almonds in a large bowl. Stir in the cooled quinoa, then season with mint, parsley, cumin, lime juice, sesame oil, and salt. Chill 1 to 2 hours before serving.

Nutrition Information

- Calories: 346 calories
- Total Fat: 11.8 g
- Cholesterol: 0 mg
- Sodium: 178 mg
- Total Carbohydrate: 53.3 g
- Protein: 9.5 g

311. Tropical Coconut Quinoa Pudding

"This dairy-free dessert is creamy and indulgent but balanced by using whole grain quinoa instead of traditional white rice. The bright coconut and mango accents will have you thinking of a sunny island beach even on the coldest day of winter!"

Serving: 6 | Prep: 10 m | Cook: 20 m | Ready in: 1 h 30 m

Ingredients

- 2 cups water
- 1/4 teaspoon salt
- 1 cup uncooked whole grain quinoa, well rinsed
- 1 (14 ounce) can coconut milk
- 1/2 cup granulated sugar
- 3 eggs
- 1/4 cup lime juice
- 2 teaspoons finely grated lime zest
- 2 teaspoons vanilla extract
- Gay Lea Real Coconut Whipped Cream
- Chopped fresh mango
- Toasted coconut

Direction

- Bring water and salt to a boil in a medium saucepan with a tight fitting lid set over medium heat. Add quinoa; cover and cook over low heat for 15 minutes or until fluid is absorbed.
- Meanwhile, whisk coconut milk with sugar, eggs, and lime juice. Stir into quinoa. Return pan to medium heat and cook, stirring constantly for 5 to 7 minutes or until thickened. Remove from heat; stir in lime zest and vanilla.
- Cool to room temperature; transfer to the refrigerator and chill completely. (Pudding can be reserved in a covered container for up to 3 days.)
- Spoon into bowls and garnish with a generous amount of coconut whipped cream, mango, and toasted coconut.

Nutrition Information

- Calories: 397 calories
- Total Fat: 19.8 g
- Cholesterol: 93 mg
- Sodium: 156 mg
- Total Carbohydrate: 49.1 g
- Protein: 8.9 g

312. Tropical Quinoa

"A super-easy, sweet side dish that goes great with fish, shrimp, or light chicken dishes."

Serving: 4 | Prep: 20 m | Cook: 10 m | Ready in: 30 m

Ingredients

- 1/2 cup uncooked quinoa, rinsed
- 1 cup water
- 1/4 cup chopped dried pineapple
- 1/4 cup chopped dried mango
- 1/4 cup sweetened coconut flakes
- 1/4 cup dry-roasted macadamia nuts, chopped
- 1 tablespoon hot mango chutney
- 2 tablespoons regular mango chutney

Direction

- Mix the quinoa and water in a saucepan over medium heat, and bring to a boil. Cover, reduce heat, and simmer until all the water is absorbed, 10 to 12 minutes. Remove from heat, and stir in the dried pineapple, dried mango, coconut flakes, macadamia nuts, hot and regular mango chutney until thoroughly combined. Serve hot.

Nutrition Information

- Calories: 238 calories
- Total Fat: 10.5 g
- Cholesterol: 0 mg
- Sodium: 145 mg
- Total Carbohydrate: 33.9 g
- Protein: 4.1 g

313. Tropical Quinoa Salsa Salad

"I just added this recipe to my lunch menu. They loved it. I hope you do too!"

Serving: 12 | Prep: 30 m | Cook: 15 m | Ready in: 1 h 45 m

Ingredients

- 1 1/2 cups water
- 3/4 cup quinoa
- 1 1/3 cups cubed seeded watermelon
- 1 cup sliced red bell pepper
- 1 cup sliced cucumber
- 3/4 cup sliced red onion
- 1 small mango - peeled, seeded, and chopped
- 1/4 cup drained pineapple tidbits, juice reserved
- 1 bunch cilantro leaves, chopped, a few leaves reserved for garnish
- Dressing:
- 3 tablespoons white wine vinegar
- 3 tablespoons honey
- 2 tablespoons reserved pineapple juice from the can
- 2 tablespoons lime juice
- 3 cloves garlic, minced
- 1/4 cup canola oil
- salt and ground black pepper to taste
- 4 slices lime
- 1 jalapeno pepper, thinly sliced

Direction

- Bring water and quinoa to a boil in a saucepan; reduce heat to medium-low, cover, and simmer until quinoa is tender and water has been absorbed, about 15 minutes. Refrigerate until cold, about 1 hour.
- Stir cooled quinoa, watermelon, bell pepper, cucumber, red onion, mango, pineapple, and chopped cilantro leaves together in a large bowl.
- Whisk wine vinegar, honey, pineapple juice, lime juice, and garlic together in a small bowl;

drizzle in canola oil, whisking constantly. Pour dressing over quinoa mixture; toss gently to combine. Place salad in a serving bowl; garnish with lime slices, jalapeno slices, and reserved cilantro leaves.

Nutrition Information

- Calories: 125 calories
- Total Fat: 5.5 g
- Cholesterol: 0 mg
- Sodium: 19 mg
- Total Carbohydrate: 18.3 g
- Protein: 2.2 g

314. Turkey and Quinoa Meatballs

"I developed this recipe with turkey and quinoa, but have since used it successfully with just about every type of ground meat and variety of grain. The addition of grains not only adds nutritional value and keeps the texture light, but also helps those on a budget stretch a small amount of quality meat into a bigger meal. It's simple, clean, nutritious eating but will please even the pickiest of meatloaf lovers. Make extra grains and serve those alongside a green salad, steamed asparagus, or roasted vegetables. Enjoy!"

Serving: 5 | Prep: 35 m | Cook: 20 m | Ready in: 55 m

Ingredients

- 1 tablespoon olive oil
- 1 1/2 cups chopped celery
- 1/2 large onion, chopped
- 2 tablespoons minced garlic
- 1 1/3 cups tomato ketchup
- 1/3 cup balsamic vinegar
- 1/3 cup low-sodium soy sauce
- 1 1/2 pounds ground turkey
- 1 1/2 cups cooked quinoa
- 2 eggs
- 1 tablespoon dried parsley
- 1 teaspoon dried sage
- 1/2 teaspoon ground black pepper
- 1/2 teaspoon salt

Direction

- Preheat oven to 375 degrees F (190 degrees C).
- Heat oil in a large skillet over medium heat. Add celery, onion, and garlic; cook, stirring occasionally, until softened but not browned, 5 to 7 minutes. Remove from heat.
- Mix ketchup, balsamic vinegar, and soy sauce together in a small bowl.
- Combine turkey, quinoa, eggs, parsley, sage, black pepper, and salt in a large bowl. Add celery mixture and 1/3 cup of the ketchup mixture; mix until well-combined.
- Spread 1/3 cup of the ketchup mixture on the bottom of two 9-inch square baking dishes. Form turkey mixture into meatballs with damp hands. Pour remaining 1/3 cup of the ketchup mixture over the meatballs.
- Bake in the preheated oven until meatballs are no longer pink in the center and ketchup mixture is thickened, 15 to 20 minutes.

Nutrition Information

- Calories: 419 calories
- Total Fat: 16.4 g
- Cholesterol: 175 mg
- Sodium: 1657 mg
- Total Carbohydrate: 35.8 g
- Protein: 34.7 g

315. Turkey and Quinoa Meatloaf

"I always found turkey meatloaf to be quite disappointing. The flavor is usually lacking as well as the texture. Well, I have developed this version that has a great texture and a surprisingly good flavor (my brother couldn't even tell that it wasn't beef)! The secret is the quinoa, which adds wonderful texture and is much nuttier than breadcrumbs. I hope you enjoy this recipe!"

Serving: 5 | Prep: 30 m | Cook: 50 m | Ready in: 1 h 20 m

Ingredients

- 1/4 cup quinoa

- 1/2 cup water
- 1 teaspoon olive oil
- 1 small onion, chopped
- 1 large clove garlic, chopped
- 1 (20 ounce) package ground turkey
- 1 tablespoon tomato paste
- 1 tablespoon hot pepper sauce
- 2 tablespoons Worcestershire sauce
- 1 egg
- 1 1/2 teaspoons salt
- 1 teaspoon ground black pepper
- 2 tablespoons brown sugar
- 2 teaspoons Worcestershire sauce
- 1 teaspoon water

Direction

- Bring the quinoa and water to a boil in a saucepan over high heat. Reduce heat to medium-low, cover, and simmer until the quinoa is tender, and the water has been absorbed, about 15 to 20 minutes. Set aside to cool.
- Preheat an oven to 350 degrees F (175 degrees C).
- Heat the olive oil in a skillet over medium heat. Stir in the onion; cook and stir until the onion has softened and turned translucent, about 5 minutes. Add the garlic and cook for another minute; remove from heat to cool.
- Stir the turkey, cooked quinoa, onions, tomato paste, hot sauce, 2 tablespoons Worcestershire, egg, salt, and pepper in a large bowl until well combined. The mixture will be very moist. Shape into a loaf on a foil lined baking sheet. Combine the brown sugar, 2 teaspoons Worcestershire, and 1 teaspoon water in a small bowl. Rub the paste over the top of the meatloaf.
- Bake in the preheated oven until no longer pink in the center, about 50 minutes. An instant-read thermometer inserted into the center should read at least 160 degrees F (70 degrees C). Let the meatloaf cool for 10 minutes before slicing and serving.

Nutrition Information

- Calories: 259 calories
- Total Fat: 11 g
- Cholesterol: 121 mg
- Sodium: 968 mg
- Total Carbohydrate: 15.2 g
- Protein: 25.3 g

316. Turkey Quinoa and Zucchini Mini Meatloaves

"Great recipe for healthier meal prepping. Can be cooked, wrapped, and frozen individually.
This recipe can also be baked in a toaster oven at the same temperature."

Serving: 6 | Prep: 20 m | Cook: 50 m | Ready in: 1 h 15 m

Ingredients

- 1 cup water
- 1/2 cup quinoa, rinsed well
- 1 medium zucchini
- 1 teaspoon olive oil
- 3/4 cup sambal oelek (Indonesian chile sauce), divided
- 1 small red onion, finely chopped
- 2 large egg whites
- 3 cloves garlic, minced
- 1 tablespoon chopped fresh parsley
- 1 teaspoon dried Italian seasoning
- 1/2 teaspoon salt
- 1/2 teaspoon ground black pepper
- 1 pound ground skinless turkey breast
- 3 tablespoons stone-ground mustard

Direction

- Bring water and quinoa to a boil in a saucepan. Reduce heat to medium-low, cover, and simmer until quinoa is tender, 15 to 20 minutes.
- Shred the zucchini using a cheese grater over a lint-free kitchen towel. Wrap the zucchini in

- the towel and wring out as much water as possible.
- Preheat the oven to 350 degrees F (175 degrees C). Line a baking sheet with aluminum foil and swab with olive oil.
- Place the zucchini in a large bowl. Add 1/4 cup chile sauce, red onion, egg whites, garlic, parsley, Italian seasoning, salt, and pepper. Add quinoa and turkey; mix well to combine. Divide mixture into 6 parts and shape into small loaves. Space them evenly on the baking sheet.
- Combine the remaining 1/2 cup chile sauce with mustard. Spread a heaping spoonful over each loaf.
- Bake in the preheated oven until meatloaves are hot on the inside and sauce has darkened in color, 30 to 35 minutes. Remove from oven and let rest, at least 5 minutes.

Nutrition Information

- Calories: 239 calories
- Total Fat: 6.3 g
- Cholesterol: 47 mg
- Sodium: 605 mg
- Total Carbohydrate: 30.6 g
- Protein: 22.5 g

317. Turkey Quinoa Baked Burgers

"The most moist, spicy, and flavorful turkey burger you will ever have. The quinoa gives the ground turkey the texture of a beef burger. Serve on a bun and use whatever favorite burger topping you like!"

Serving: 8 | Prep: 20 m | Cook: 50 m | Ready in: 1 h 10 m

Ingredients

- 1 cup water
- 1/2 cup quinoa
- 1 tablespoon olive oil
- 1 onion, finely chopped
- 5 cloves garlic, finely chopped
- 1/2 cup Worcestershire sauce, divided
- 2 eggs
- 2 tablespoons barbeque sauce (such as Sweet Baby Ray's®)
- 2 tablespoons hot pepper sauce
- 1 tablespoon seasoned salt (such as LAWRY'S®)
- 2 teaspoons ground black pepper
- 2 pounds lean ground turkey
- 3 tablespoons brown sugar

Direction

- Preheat the oven to 350 degrees F (175 degrees C). Line a glass baking dish with aluminum foil.
- Bring water and quinoa to a boil in a saucepan. Reduce heat to medium-low, cover, and simmer until quinoa is tender, 15 to 20 minutes. Let cool.
- Heat oil in a skillet over medium heat. Cook and stir onion until translucent, about 5 minutes. Add garlic; cook until fragrant, about 1 minute.
- Combine cooked quinoa, onion mixture, 1/4 cup Worcestershire sauce, eggs, barbeque sauce, hot sauce, seasoned salt, and black pepper in a large bowl. Whisk together. Add ground turkey and mix well with hands. Form patties and place in the prepared baking dish.
- Mix remaining 1/4 cup Worcestershire sauce and brown sugar together in a bowl to make a paste. Spoon on top of the patties.
- Bake patties in the preheated oven until no longer pink in the center, 35 to 45 minutes.

Nutrition Information

- Calories: 289 calories
- Total Fat: 12.2 g
- Cholesterol: 130 mg
- Sodium: 732 mg
- Total Carbohydrate: 19.3 g
- Protein: 25.9 g

318. Uncle Bobs Soybean Bread

"I use an old large slow cooker for my mixing bowl, this way I don't need to dirty up a bunch of different bowls or counters. The soybeans and quinoa give this bread great texture. I use an electric coffee grinder to grind up the soybeans."

Serving: 12 | Prep: 30 m | Cook: 45 m | Ready in: 5 h 50 m

Ingredients

- 1 cup bread flour
- 2 cups warm water (110 degrees F)
- 1 (.25 ounce) package active dry yeast
- 1/2 cup dried soybeans
- 1 1/2 teaspoons salt
- 3 cups bread flour
- 2 tablespoons quinoa
- 1 tablespoon olive oil

Direction

- In a large bowl or crock pot, dissolve yeast and 1 cup flour in water. Cover with plastic wrap or a pot lid and let stand for 2 hours.
- Coarsely grind the soybeans in a food processor or blender. Stir soy beans and 1 cup flour into the yeast mixture. Let stand for 2 hours.
- Stir in the salt and remaining flour, 1/2 cup at a time, beating well after each addition. When the dough has pulled together, turn it out of the slow cooker and knead 1 1/2 tablespoons quinoa into the dough. Form into a loaf and place in a lightly greased 9x5 inch loaf pan. Sprinkle the remaining quinoa on top of the loaf. Brush or drizzle on the olive oil. Cover and let rise until loaf is just above the top of the loaf pan. Meanwhile, preheat oven to 400 degrees F (200 degrees C).
- Bake in preheated oven for 45 minutes, or until loaf sounds hollow when tapped on the bottom. Let cool before slicing.

Nutrition Information

- Calories: 53 calories
- Total Fat: 2.8 g
- Cholesterol: 0 mg
- Sodium: 291 mg
- Total Carbohydrate: 3.7 g
- Protein: 3.3 g

319. Vegan Curry Quinoa Salad

"The original recipe was a non-vegan version I found at another food website. I've made some major overhauls to the original recipe, I feel that I can call it my own. I took the dish to a recent vegan potluck dinner and it was a huge hit! Lots of flavor. Serve warm or at room temperature."

Serving: 8 | Prep: 30 m | Cook: 20 m | Ready in: 50 m

Ingredients

- 2 1/3 cups water
- 1 1/3 cups quinoa
- 6 ounces vegan sour cream (such as Tofutti®)
- 1/4 cup curry powder
- 2 tablespoons freshly squeezed lime juice
- 2 teaspoons finely grated peeled fresh ginger
- 1 1/2 teaspoons salt
- 1/2 teaspoon ground black pepper
- 6 tablespoons vegetable oil
- 1 (1 pound) firm-ripe mango, cut into 1/2-inch chunks
- 1 cup salted roasted peanuts, chopped
- 1 red bell pepper, chopped
- 2/3 cup chopped fresh mint
- 1 jalapeno chile, seeded and minced

Direction

- Combine water and quinoa in a saucepan over high heat. Cover and bring to a boil. Reduce heat to low. Cook until water has been absorbed, about 15 minutes.
- Whisk sour cream, curry powder, lime juice, ginger, salt, and black pepper together in a large bowl. Add oil; whisk thoroughly. Toss with the quinoa, mango, peanuts, red bell pepper, mint, and jalapeno.

Nutrition Information

- Calories: 419 calories
- Total Fat: 25.4 g

- Cholesterol: 0 mg
- Sodium: 711 mg
- Total Carbohydrate: 41.8 g
- Protein: 10 g

320. Vegan Mexican Quinoa Bowl with Green Chile Cilantro Sauce

"Quinoa gets tossed with red bell peppers, black beans, romaine, and red onions, then smothered in a dairy-free sauce with a jalapeño kick. An easy meal!"

Serving: 4 | Prep: 30 m | Cook: 20 m | Ready in: 50 m

Ingredients

- Vegan Green Chile Cilantro Sauce:
- 1 cup unsalted raw cashews
- 1 (4 ounce) can chopped green chile peppers
- 1/4 cup hemp milk
- 1/2 jalapeno pepper with seeds, or more to taste
- 1/2 teaspoon salt
- 1 1/4 cups chopped fresh cilantro
- 3 cups water
- 1 1/2 cups quinoa
- 2 romaine hearts, chopped
- 2 (15 ounce) cans black beans, rinsed and drained
- 3 cups chopped red bell pepper
- 1/2 cup chopped red onion
- 2 avocados, chopped

Direction

- Combine cashews, green chile peppers, hemp milk, jalapeno pepper, and salt in a blender; process until smooth.
- Pour cashew mixture into a small bowl; stir in 1 cup cilantro.
- Bring water and quinoa to a boil in a saucepan. Reduce heat to medium-low, cover, and simmer until quinoa is tender, 15 to 20 minutes.
- Divide romaine lettuce among 4 bowls. Top with quinoa, black beans, red bell pepper, and onion. Drizzle cilantro sauce on top. Garnish with remaining 1/4 cup cilantro and chopped avocados.

Nutrition Information

- Calories: 694 calories
- Total Fat: 20.5 g
- Cholesterol: 0 mg
- Sodium: 1476 mg
- Total Carbohydrate: 101.5 g
- Protein: 31.3 g

321. Vegan Quinoa and Guac Bowl

"Mmmm...this vegan recipe is so delicious and guilt-free! Even if you're not vegan, I whole-heartedly believe in giving your body a break from eating meat once in a while with a perfectly light dish like this one."

Serving: 4 | Prep: 15 m | Cook: 30 m | Ready in: 55 m

Ingredients

- 1 (15 ounce) can pinto beans, rinsed and drained
- Quinoa:
- 2 1/2 cups water
- 2 cups quinoa
- 1/2 teaspoon kosher salt
- Veggie Bowl:
- 1 tablespoon olive oil
- 1 red bell pepper, sliced
- 1 yellow bell pepper, sliced
- 1/2 teaspoon ground black pepper
- 4 cups lettuce leaves
- 1 cup vegan shredded cheese blend
- 1 avocado - peeled, pitted, and sliced
- 1/4 cup vegan sour cream

Direction

- Heat pinto beans in a saucepan over low heat until hot, 5 to 7 minutes.
- Bring water, quinoa, and salt to a boil in a saucepan and simmer until quinoa is tender and water is absorbed, 15 to 20 minutes.

- Remove from heat and set aside to cool, about 10 minutes.
- Heat olive oil in a skillet over medium heat. Add red bell pepper, yellow bell pepper, and black pepper; cook and stir until bell peppers are softened but still crisp, about 10 minutes.
- Toss quinoa, pinto beans, and lettuce together in a bowl. Top with pepper mixture, vegan cheese, avocado, and vegan sour cream.

Nutrition Information

- Calories: 623 calories
- Total Fat: 23.5 g
- Cholesterol: 0 mg
- Sodium: 846 mg
- Total Carbohydrate: 78.2 g
- Protein: 24.6 g

322. Vegan Quinoa Chili

"Amazing chili is a great vegan main dish that cooks all in one pot!"

Serving: 8 | Prep: 20 m | Cook: 40 m | Ready in: 1 h

Ingredients

- 1 tablespoon olive oil
- 1 onion, chopped
- 3 carrots, chopped
- 1 red bell pepper, chopped
- 1 jalapeno pepper, seeded and chopped
- 4 cloves garlic, chopped
- 2 (28 ounce) cans tomatoes
- 2 (15 ounce) cans black beans
- 2 (15 ounce) cans chickpeas
- 1 cup quinoa
- 2 teaspoons garlic salt
- 2 teaspoons chili powder
- 1 teaspoon ground cumin

Direction

- Heat olive oil in a large saucepan over medium heat. Add onion, carrots, red bell pepper, and jalapeno pepper. Cook and stir until tender, about 5 minutes. Add garlic and cook until fragrant, about 2 minutes. Add tomatoes, black beans, chickpeas, quinoa, garlic salt, chili powder, and cumin. Reduce heat to low and cook until quinoa is tender and chili is heated through, 30 minutes to 1 hour.

Nutrition Information

- Calories: 340 calories
- Total Fat: 4.7 g
- Cholesterol: 0 mg
- Sodium: 1379 mg
- Total Carbohydrate: 62.3 g
- Protein: 15.4 g

323. Vegan Quinoa Oatmeal

"I use cacao nibs (low-carb roasted and coarsely ground cocoa beans) for my morning oatmeal. You can get them online or in select health food stores."

Serving: 1 | Prep: 5 m | Cook: 15 m | Ready in: 20 m

Ingredients

- 1/4 cup quinoa
- 1/4 cup rolled oats
- 2 tablespoons flaked coconut
- 2 tablespoons cacao nibs
- 1 tablespoon molasses
- water to cover

Direction

- Combine quinoa, oats, flaked coconut, cacao nibs, and molasses in a pot; cover with water. Bring to a boil and cover. Reduce heat and simmer until quinoa and oats are soft, 10 to 15 minutes. Add more water, 1 tablespoon at a time, if oatmeal becomes too dry.

Nutrition Information

- Calories: 459 calories

- Total Fat: 15.2 g
- Cholesterol: 0 mg
- Sodium: 68 mg
- Total Carbohydrate: 71.8 g
- Protein: 9.7 g

324. Vegan Quinoa Stuffed Peppers

"A vegan and gluten-free spin on stuffed peppers. I don't enjoy the Mexican flavors usually associated with quinoa, so this recipe closely resembles the flavor of a standard beef-and-rice stuffed pepper, minus the fat but with complete protein and lots of veggies! Sometimes there may be enough stuffing left over for a fifth pepper, but honestly, I like the stuffing plain, too!"

Serving: 4 | Prep: 30 m | Cook: 42 m | Ready in: 1 h 12 m

Ingredients

- 1 (14.5 ounce) can vegetable broth
- 1/4 cup water (optional)
- 1 bay leaf
- 1 cup quinoa, rinsed
- 1 (6 ounce) can tomato paste (optional)
- 1 teaspoon dried parsley
- 1/2 teaspoon salt (optional)
- 1/2 teaspoon paprika
- 1/2 teaspoon dried oregano
- 1/2 teaspoon dried basil
- 1/4 teaspoon dried thyme
- cooking spray
- 4 large green bell peppers - tops, seeds, and membranes removed
- water to cover
- 1 tablespoon olive oil
- 4 carrots, finely chopped
- 1 onion, finely chopped
- 2 stalks celery, finely chopped
- 2 cloves garlic, chopped
- 2 large white mushrooms, sliced

Direction

- Combine broth, water, and bay leaf in a small saucepan; bring to a boil. Add quinoa. Reduce heat to low; cover and simmer until liquid is absorbed, 12 to 15 minutes. Discard bay leaf. Stir in tomato paste, parsley, salt, paprika, oregano, basil, and thyme.
- Preheat the oven to 350 degrees F (175 degrees C). Coat a 10x15-inch baking pan with cooking spray.
- Cut a thin slice from the bottom of each green bell pepper so it stands upright, if necessary. Fill a 4-quart Dutch oven with enough water to cover the peppers and bring to a boil. Add peppers and cook until tender but firm, about 2 minutes. Drain and rinse with cold water.
- Heat olive oil in a large nonstick skillet over medium-high heat. Add carrots, onion, celery, and garlic; sauté until tender, about 6 minutes. Add the cooked quinoa; cook and stir until heated through, about 2 minutes. Remove from heat and add mushrooms. Spoon mixture into peppers and place into the prepared pan.
- Bake, uncovered, in the preheated oven until peppers are tender, 20 to 25 minutes.

Nutrition Information

- Calories: 315 calories
- Total Fat: 7.1 g
- Cholesterol: 0 mg
- Sodium: 910 mg
- Total Carbohydrate: 55.6 g
- Protein: 11.3 g

325. Vegetarian Quinoa Frittatas

"This a healthy option for a side to another dish or all on its own. You can eat it hot or cold. And it is great for making ahead to have something quick to eat later."

Serving: 6 | Prep: 15 m | Cook: 45 m | Ready in: 1 h 5 m

Ingredients

- 1 1/2 cups water

- 1 cup quinoa
- 1 teaspoon olive oil
- 2 tablespoons chopped fresh rosemary
- 1 1/4 cups shredded zucchini
- 1 cup shredded mozzarella cheese
- 3/4 cup drained and rinsed black beans
- 6 tablespoons shredded Parmesan cheese, divided
- 2 eggs
- 2 egg whites
- 1/4 teaspoon ground white pepper

Direction

- Combine water, quinoa, and olive oil in a saucepan; bring to a boil. Stir rosemary into the quinoa mixture. Reduce heat to medium-low, cover, and simmer until quinoa is tender and water is absorbed, 15 to 20 minutes.
- Preheat oven to 400 degrees F (200 degrees C). Grease 6 muffin cups.
- Mix quinoa mixture, zucchini, mozzarella cheese, black beans, 1/4 cup Parmesan cheese, eggs, egg whites, and white pepper together in a large bowl. Spoon mixture into each muffin cup and top with remaining Parmesan cheese.
- Bake in the preheated oven until set in the middle and edges are golden brown, 25 to 30 minutes. Cool for 5 minutes in the muffin cups.

Nutrition Information

- Calories: 238 calories
- Total Fat: 8.7 g
- Cholesterol: 78 mg
- Sodium: 353 mg
- Total Carbohydrate: 24.3 g
- Protein: 15.6 g

326. Veggie Almond and Raisin Quinoa Salad

"The original recipe is from a friend, and I modified it by adding some ingredients to the recipe. Since it has an abundance of goodness in it, I'll often eat it alone as a meal. I've also served this as a side dish with bbq chicken or lamb shish-kabobs."

Serving: 12 | Prep: 15 m | Cook: 20 m | Ready in: 1 h 5 m

Ingredients

- 1/2 cup sliced almonds
- 4 cups vegetable stock
- 2 cups quinoa
- 1 English cucumber, diced
- 15 grape tomatoes, quartered
- 1 bunch fresh flat-leaf parsley, stemmed and leaves finely chopped
- 1 orange bell pepper, diced
- 3/4 cup crumbled feta cheese
- 1/2 cup raisins
- 1/4 cup chopped black olives
- 4 scallions, white and light green parts, chopped
- 1/2 cup fresh lemon juice
- 1/2 cup olive oil

Direction

- Preheat oven to 350 degrees F (175 degrees C). Spread almonds onto a baking sheet.
- Bake almonds in the preheated oven until lightly toasted and fragrant, 5 to 10 minutes.
- Bring vegetable stock and quinoa to a boil in a saucepan. Reduce heat to medium-low, cover, and simmer until quinoa is tender and stock has been absorbed, 15 to 20 minutes. Transfer quinoa to a bowl and refrigerate until chilled, about 30 minutes.
- Mix almonds, cucumber, tomatoes, parsley, orange bell pepper, feta cheese, raisins, olives, and scallions into quinoa.
- Whisk lemon juice and olive oil together in a bowl; pour over quinoa mixture and stir until quinoa mixture is coated.

Nutrition Information

- Calories: 282 calories
- Total Fat: 15.4 g
- Cholesterol: 8 mg
- Sodium: 292 mg
- Total Carbohydrate: 30.2 g
- Protein: 7.5 g

327. Veggie Quinoa

"I blundered into this delicious mix of ingredients while trying to use up leftover vegetables in the fridge. Even friends who 'don't like vegetarian cooking' have enjoyed it. I like the slightly bitter taste of unwashed quinoa (just check for unwanted debris before you use it), but most recipes call for rinsed quinoa."

Serving: 2 | Prep: 10 m | Cook: 25 m | Ready in: 35 m

Ingredients

- 1 cup vegetable broth
- 1/2 cup uncooked quinoa
- 2 teaspoons olive oil
- 2 teaspoons minced garlic
- 1/2 cup broccoli florets
- 1/2 cup diced firm tofu
- 1/4 cup vegetable broth
- 1/4 cup sliced mushrooms
- 1 cup chopped fresh spinach

Direction

- In a medium saucepan, bring 1 cup vegetable stock to a boil. Stir in the quinoa and reduce heat to low. Cover and simmer for 20 minutes.
- While quinoa is cooking, heat olive oil in a skillet over medium heat. Add the garlic, broccoli florets, and tofu. Stir for a minute, then cover and steam over low heat for 2 minutes. Stir in 1/4 cup vegetable broth, mushrooms, and spinach. Cover and cook over medium heat until the mushrooms are soft and spinach is wilted, about 3 minutes.
- Stir the vegetable-tofu mixture into the cooked quinoa. Cover, and allow to sit for 10 minutes before serving.

Nutrition Information

- Calories: 282 calories
- Total Fat: 10.8 g
- Cholesterol: 0 mg
- Sodium: 315 mg
- Total Carbohydrate: 34.9 g
- Protein: 13.3 g

328. Veggie Quinoa Bake

"I came across some quinoa bake recipes online and decided to put my spin on them, using ingredients I had on hand. This recipe is very flexible so you can add or subtract veggies and other ingredients as you wish. Serve with sour cream, avocado, and hot sauce."

Serving: 8 | Prep: 15 m | Cook: 1 h 15 m | Ready in: 1 h 45 m

Ingredients

- 3/4 cup dry black beans
- 4 cups water
- 2 cups tri-colored quinoa
- 1 tablespoon vegetable oil
- 1 red onion, diced
- 1 red bell pepper, diced
- 2 cloves garlic, minced
- 1 pinch cumin
- 1 1/2 cups frozen grilled corn (such as Trader Joe's®)
- 1/2 cup chopped fresh cilantro, divided
- salt and ground black pepper to taste
- 2 cups shredded Colby Jack cheese, divided
- 3/4 cup spicy green salsa, or more to taste
- 1 tablespoon tomato paste
- 3/4 cup hot water
- 2 scallions, thinly sliced

Direction

- Place black beans in a multi-functional pressure cooker. Add enough water to cover by a few inches. Close and lock the lid. Select high pressure according to manufacturer's instructions; set timer for 20 minutes. Allow 10 to 15 minutes for pressure to build.
- Release pressure using the natural-release method according to manufacturer's instructions, about 10 minutes. Unlock and remove lid. Drain black beans and rinse out the pot.
- Combine 4 cups water and quinoa in the pressure cooker pot. Close and lock the lid. Select Brown Rice function and set timer for 8 minutes. Allow 5 to 10 minutes for pressure to build.
- Release pressure carefully using the quick-release method according to manufacturer's instructions, about 5 minutes. Unlock and remove lid. Remove pot carefully using oven mitts, fluff quinoa with a fork, and let cool.
- Preheat the oven to 375 degrees F (190 degrees C).
- Heat oil in a large skillet over medium heat. Add onion, red bell pepper, garlic, and cumin; cook and stir until softened and fragrant, about 5 minutes. Stir in corn until heated through, 3 to 5 minutes. Remove from heat and stir in 1/4 cup cilantro. Season with salt and pepper.
- Stir black beans, onion mixture, 1 cup Colby Jack cheese, and green salsa into the pot of quinoa. Spread mixture in a large baking dish.
- Dissolve tomato paste in 3/4 cup hot water. Drizzle over the quinoa mixture. Sprinkle remaining Colby Jack cheese evenly over the top.
- Bake in the preheated oven until cheese is melted, about 25 minutes. Garnish with remaining cilantro and scallions.

Nutrition Information

- Calories: 414 calories
- Total Fat: 15.8 g
- Cholesterol: 33 mg
- Sodium: 384 mg
- Total Carbohydrate: 50.9 g
- Protein: 19.1 g

329. Veggie Quinoa Burgers

"This veggie burger is packed with veggie and quinoa goodness including lots of meatless protein. A great alternative to a beef burger and just as hearty and filling. It can be cooked on the grill or baked in the oven. The egg and cheese may be left out to make this recipe vegan."

Serving: 8 | Prep: 30 m | Cook: 15 m | Ready in: 45 m

Ingredients

- 1/2 cup quinoa
- 1 cup water
- 2 teaspoons olive oil
- 4 carrots, peeled and minced
- 2 stalks celery, minced
- 1/2 red bell pepper, minced
- 1 onion, minced
- 4 cloves garlic, minced
- 2 tablespoons minced fresh ginger root
- 2 cups minced fresh mushrooms
- 1 (19 ounce) can kidney beans, rinsed and drained
- 1/2 bunch fresh dill, chopped
- 2 cups chopped fresh spinach
- 1 egg (optional)
- 1/2 cup dry bread crumbs
- 2 tablespoons sesame oil
- 4 slices shredded mozzarella cheese
- salt and ground black pepper to taste
- 1 tablespoon olive oil

Direction

- Preheat an outdoor grill for high heat and lightly oil the grate.
- Combine quinoa and water in a saucepan and bring to a boil. Reduce heat to low, place lid on saucepan, and cook until water is completely absorbed, about 15 minutes; Remove from heat and set aside to cool.

- Heat 2 teaspoons olive oil in a skillet over medium-high heat. Cook and stir carrots, celery, red bell pepper, onion, garlic, ginger, and mushrooms in the hot oil until softened, about 10 minutes; set aside to cool.
- Mash kidney beans with a fork in a large bowl; add quinoa and the carrot mixture to the means and mix.
- Mix dill, spinach, egg, bread crumbs, sesame oil, mozzarella cheese, salt, and pepper into kidney bean mixture; shape into 8 patties.
- Brush the 1 tablespoon olive oil evenly both sides of each patty.
- Arrange the patties into a large baking dish.
- Grill on preheated grill until hot in the center, 7 to 8 minutes per side.

Nutrition Information

- Calories: 263 calories
- Total Fat: 10.7 g
- Cholesterol: 32 mg
- Sodium: 336 mg
- Total Carbohydrate: 31.1 g
- Protein: 12 g

330. Warm Cinnamon Raisin Quinoa

"When ready to eat, place a portion of the quinoa into a bowl, drizzle with maple syrup and top with chia seeds, raisins, and nut butter."

Serving: 4 | Prep: 10 m | Cook: 20 m | Ready in: 30 m

Ingredients

- 2 cups almond milk
- 1 cup quinoa
- 1 teaspoon ground cinnamon
- 5 vanilla beans
- 1 cup raisins
- 2 tablespoons chia seeds, or to taste
- 2 tablespoons ground flax seeds, or to taste

Direction

- Bring almond milk and quinoa to a boil in a saucepan. Add cinnamon and vanilla beans; reduce heat and simmer, stirring occasionally, until all liquid is absorbed, about 15 minutes. Remove vanilla beans from quinoa.
- Spoon quinoa into bowls; top each with raisins, chia seeds, and ground flax seeds.

Nutrition Information

- Calories: 419 calories
- Total Fat: 6.7 g
- Cholesterol: 0 mg
- Sodium: 88 mg
- Total Carbohydrate: 84.6 g
- Protein: 9 g

331. What I Did With Quinoa

"This is a protein-packed main dish. Especially good for Lap-Band® recipients. I can no longer eat rice and am always looking to increase my protein intake. This recipe is tweaked from another. I liked it so much, I decided to share it. Check it out. This is my first time writing a recipe. Hope I did it well. Happy eating!"

Serving: 4 | Prep: 15 m | Cook: 40 m | Ready in: 1 h 15 m

Ingredients

- 1 cup quinoa
- 1 tablespoon canola oil
- 1 small onion, chopped
- 1 red bell pepper, chopped
- 1 head garlic, chopped
- 2 cups chicken broth
- 1/4 cup sofrito (such as Goya®)
- 1 teaspoon ground cumin
- 1 teaspoon dried cilantro
- salt and ground black pepper to taste
- 1 cup frozen corn kernels
- 1 tablespoon canola oil
- 1 pound ground chicken
- 1 teaspoon adobo seasoning

- 1/2 teaspoon garlic powder
- 1/2 teaspoon ground cumin
- 1 (15 ounce) can black beans, drained
- 1/2 cup sofrito (such as Goya®), or to taste

Direction

- Soak quinoa in a bowl of water for 20 minutes; drain.
- Heat 1 tablespoon canola oil in a frying pan over medium heat; sauté onion, red bell pepper, and garlic until soft, 5 to 10 minutes.
- Combine chicken broth, quinoa, 1/4 cup onion mixture, 1/4 cup sofrito, 1 teaspoon cumin, cilantro, salt, and pepper in a saucepan; bring to a boil. Cover saucepan with a lid, reduce heat, and simmer until quinoa is tender and liquid is absorbed, about 20 minutes. Stir corn into quinoa mixture and cook until corn is warmed, about 5 minutes.
- Heat 1 tablespoon canola oil in a skillet over medium heat; cook and stir chicken, adobo seasoning, garlic powder, 1/2 teaspoon cumin, salt, and pepper together until chicken is no longer pink, 5 to 10 minutes.
- Mix quinoa mixture, remaining onion mixture, black beans, and 1/2 cup sofrito into chicken mixture; cook until heated through, 2 to 3 more minutes.

Nutrition Information

- Calories: 589 calories
- Total Fat: 18.3 g
- Cholesterol: 69 mg
- Sodium: 734 mg
- Total Carbohydrate: 64 g
- Protein: 43.6 g

332. Zesty Quinoa Salad

"This bright and colorful salad is a great summertime recipe (or anytime you want to feel like it's summertime). Light and citrusy, it's a whole new way to enjoy quinoa. Lime juice and cilantro give a refreshing kick, while quinoa and black beans provide tasty vegan protein. If you're not vegan, add even more protein by adding chunks of chicken or turkey. Yum!"

Serving: 6 | Prep: 20 m | Cook: 10 m | Ready in: 30 m

Ingredients

- 1 cup quinoa
- 2 cups water
- 1/4 cup extra-virgin olive oil
- 2 limes, juiced
- 2 teaspoons ground cumin
- 1 teaspoon salt
- 1/2 teaspoon red pepper flakes, or more to taste
- 1 1/2 cups halved cherry tomatoes
- 1 (15 ounce) can black beans, drained and rinsed
- 5 green onions, finely chopped
- 1/4 cup chopped fresh cilantro
- salt and ground black pepper to taste

Direction

- Bring quinoa and water to a boil in a saucepan. Reduce heat to medium-low, cover, and simmer until quinoa is tender and water has been absorbed, 10 to 15 minutes. Set aside to cool.
- Whisk olive oil, lime juice, cumin, 1 teaspoon salt, and red pepper flakes together in a bowl.
- Combine quinoa, tomatoes, black beans, and green onions together in a bowl. Pour dressing over quinoa mixture; toss to coat. Stir in cilantro; season with salt and black pepper. Serve immediately or chill in refrigerator.

Nutrition Information

- Calories: 270 calories
- Total Fat: 11.5 g
- Cholesterol: 0 mg
- Sodium: 675 mg

- Total Carbohydrate: 33.8 g
- Protein: 8.9 g

- Total Fat: 18.7 g
- Cholesterol: 18 mg
- Sodium: 1265 mg
- Total Carbohydrate: 81.3 g
- Protein: 26.9 g

333. Zucchini Noodle and Cannellini Bean Quinoa Bowl

"Instead of requiring the oven during the hot zucchini and tomato season, here is a way to serve up some of your favorite summer produce, packed with protein and flavor, quickly and right in the frying pan. This recipe serves 2 but can easily be doubled or tripled depending on your garden bounty and dinner guests!"

Serving: 2 | Prep: 20 m | Cook: 19 m | Ready in: 39 m

Ingredients

- 2 zucchini, spiralized
- 2 cups water
- 1/2 teaspoon salt
- 1 cup quinoa, rinsed
- 1 tablespoon vegetable oil
- 1 clove garlic, minced
- 1 cup drained and rinsed canned cannellini beans
- 1 cup cherry tomatoes, halved
- 1/2 cup freshly grated Parmesan cheese
- salt and ground black pepper to taste

Direction

- Cut zucchini into noodles using a spiralizer.
- Combine water and salt in a saucepan; bring to a boil. Add quinoa and simmer, covered, until water is absorbed, 10 to 15 minutes.
- Heat oil in a skillet over medium heat. Add garlic; cook for 30 seconds. Add cannellini beans; cook until heated through, about 1 minute. Stir in zucchini noodles and cook until noodles are crisp-tender, 3 to 5 minutes. Add cherry tomatoes and Parmesan cheese. Serve over the prepared quinoa. Season with salt and pepper.

Nutrition Information

- Calories: 596 calories

Index

A

Acorn squash, *62-63, 66*

Allspice, *145-146, 163, 171-172*

Almond, *12-13, 16, 22-23, 47, 51-52, 54, 60-61, 64-65, 67, 69, 91-94, 97, 101-102, 108, 116, 118, 122, 132, 138-139, 143, 162, 166-167, 171, 173, 185-187, 195, 204, 207*

Almond extract, *92*

Almond milk, *22-23, 64, 139, 167, 207*

Amaranth, *15, 29, 91-92*

Anise, *164*

Apple, *12-13, 23, 39, 43, 48, 54, 62-64, 77-78, 96-97, 110, 132-133, 139, 141, 147, 152, 178, 187-188, 191*

Apple juice, *23, 139, 141*

Apricot, *122, 147-148*

Asparagus, *38-39, 51, 83, 118, 121-122, 138, 156, 174-175, 197*

Avocado, *17, 19, 21, 24-25, 43, 46, 58-59, 69, 73, 78-79, 83, 98-99, 115, 121, 123, 142-143, 165-166, 176-177, 193, 201-202, 205*

B

Bacon, *15, 81, 132*

Baking, 12, 15-16, 18, 23-25, 27-28, 32-36, 43, 45, 56, 58, 61-66, 69, 75, 84, 90-92, 94-97, 102, 106, 112, 115-117, 123, 125, 128, 134, 144-146, 152, 163, 169, 173, 186-190, 194, 197-199, 203-204, 206-207

Baking powder, *12, 64-65, 91-92, 106, 145-146, 163*

Balsamic vinegar, *16, 84, 87, 103, 130, 138, 153, 167, 170, 197*

Banana, *16-17, 71, 97, 139*

Barley, *65-66, 112, 172*

Basil, 16, 26, 38-41, 51-52, 74-78, 80-81, 87, 93-94, 103, 108, 165, 176, 185-186, 190-191, 203

Basmati rice, *171-172*

Bay leaf, *40, 49, 137, 177, 203*

Beans, 16, 18-20, 27-31, 34, 36, 41-42, 54, 58-61, 73, 82, 88-89, 93, 98-99, 101, 105, 108-111, 119-121, 127-128, 136, 151-152, 157, 172, 176-184, 186, 188-189, 193, 200-202, 204-209

Beef, 20, 28, 30, 65, 71, 80, 89, 93, 103-104, 112, 127-128, 133-134, 185, 192, 197, 199, 203, 206

Berry, *21, 139*

Biscuits, *187*

Black beans, 18-20, 30-31, 34, 58-59, 73, 88-89, 98-99, 109-111, 119-121, 127-128, 176-178, 180-181, 183-184, 186, 188, 201-202, 204-206, 208

Black pepper, 11, 16-21, 23, 25-41, 43, 46-50, 53-54, 56-61, 66-68, 72-78, 82, 84-87, 89, 92, 95-96, 98-99, 104-105, 107-113, 115-116, 118-119, 122-123, 127-128, 130-131, 134, 136-138, 141-144, 146-149, 151-155, 158-161,

165-169, 171-172, 174, 176-178, 180-182,

185-188, 190, 192-193, 196-202, 205-209

Blackberry, *20, 167*

Blueberry, *22-23, 71, 82, 167*

Bread, 19-20, 27, 29, 33, 33, 57-58, 61, 64-65, 70, 75-77, 83, 90, 115, 120-121, 124, 127,

136, 147, 151, 173, 178, 185-187, 192, 200, 206-207

Breadcrumbs, *134, 197*

Broccoli, 13, 23-24, 32, 49-50, 56-57, 70, 83, 100-102, 107, 111, 120, 122-123, 143, 162,

169-170, 174, 205

Broth, 14-15, 17, 19-21, 25, 27-28, 31-32, 34, 37-41, 43, 45, 48, 50-53, 58, 62, 65, 73,

80-81, 86, 88-89, 93, 95, 98-104, 106-107, 111, 114, 118-119, 126, 128-129, 132-133,

136-137, 143-145, 149-150, 152-157, 160-161, 169-172, 175-178, 180, 183-185, 188, 194,

203, 205, 207-208

Brown rice, *15, 24, 44, 60, 64, 66, 75, 123, 167, 173, 206*

Brown sugar, 44, 63, 70, 102, 128, 145-146, 163, 167, 169, 173, 198-199

Brussels sprouts, *58*

Bulgur wheat, *67*

Buns, *115, 185*

Burger, 19-20, 92, 96-97, 105, 114-115, 120, 124, 130, 185-186, 199, 206

Butter, 11-12, 16-18, 25, 31-32, 36-38, 43, 50, 53-56, 58, 62-65, 69-70, 80, 83, 94, 96-97,

100, 111, 113, 115, 120, 124, 128, 136, 145, 150-151, 155, 159-160, 164, 169, 173, 180,

188, 192, 207

Butternut squash, *27, 144, 147-148, 155, 159, 169, 187-188*

C

Cabbage, *14, 28, 72, 91, 100, 153-154*

Cake, 12, 29, 44, 64, 97, 112, 125

Cannellini beans, *73, 127, 209*

Capers, *166*

Cardamom, *53, 120*

Carrot, 13-14, 24, 28-31, 34, 37-40, 42-43, 47, 54, 70, 73, 77-78, 82, 91, 93, 95, 98, 100,

105, 108, 113-114, 120, 123-124, 131-133, 136-137, 143-144, 149-150, 153, 156, 159,

164, 176, 184, 187-188, 191, 193, 202-203, 206-207

Carrot cake, *29*

Cashew, *50, 120-122, 141, 201*

Cauliflower, *31-32, 34, 83, 120*

Cayenne pepper, 11, 19, 21, 67, 70-71, 82, 92, 94, 111, 127, 133, 142, 145-146, 159, 161,

171, 183-184

Celery, 11, 29, 37, 39-40, 54-55, 62-63, 73, 82, 92, 107-108, 110, 118-119, 131, 133, 137,

142-143, 152-153, 164, 172, 176, 178, 184, 187-189, 191, 197, 203, 206-207

Champagne, *11, 185*

Chard, *124, 126, 161*

Cheddar, 18, 23-26, 32, 34, 61, 84, 89, 96-97, 100, 111, 122-123, 190

Cheese, 16-18, 23-26, 32-35, 38-39, 41, 45, 47-51, 56-59, 61-64, 68, 71, 74-79, 83-85, 87,

89-90, 92, 96-97, 100-104, 109, 111, 116-119, 121-125, 127, 129-130, 132-135, 140-141,

146, 148-149, 155, 157-158, 160, 165-166, 170,

179–181, 183, 185–190, 193–194, 198, 201–202, 204–207, 209

Cherry, 59, 65, 68, 85, 125, 140, 165, 171, 173, 208–209

Cherry tomatoes, *59, 65, 68, 125, 165, 208–209*

Chicken, 13, 15–17, 19, 21, 23–28, 30, 34–43, 45–48, 50–53, 57, 62, 65, 69, 71–72, 74, 79–81, 84–85, 88–90, 93–94, 98–100, 102–103, 107, 113, 126–127, 132–133, 135, 137–138, 143–144, 150, 153–157, 160, 168–170, 172, 175–178, 180–183, 185, 187–188, 194, 196, 204, 207–208

Chicken breast, 13, 21, 25, 27, 35, 39–41, 72, 84, 89, 100, 113, 155–156, 168, 177–178

Chicken soup, *37, 39, 89*

Chicken stock, 35–37, 40, 47, 53, 69, 72, 89–90, 94, 127, 138, 150, 160, 182, 187–188

Chicken thigh, *89–90*

Chickpea, 29, 41, 51–52, 55, 82, 130, 138, 157, 189, 191, 202

Chickpea flour, *130*

Chipotle, *109–110, 128–129, 184–185*

Chips, 12, 17, 59, 69, 72, 128, 183, 187

Chives, 31–32, 42, 83–85, 94, 113, 165, 172

Chocolate, *12, 34, 64, 69, 128*

Chocolate cake, *64*

Chopped tomatoes, *55, 134*

Chorizo, *36, 128*

Chutney, *86, 196*

Ciabatta, *186–187*

Cider, 24, 43, 54, 62, 64, 77–78, 95–96, 110, 128, 149

Cinnamon, 12, 16–17, 22, 34, 44–46, 48, 53, 62–63, 66, 71, 93, 95, 97, 106, 116, 120, 122, 128, 135, 138–139, 145–147, 163, 171, 182, 187, 189, 194, 207

Cloves, 11–12, 14, 17–18, 25, 27–28, 33, 36–38, 42–43, 45, 50–53, 57–58, 61–62, 65, 67, 69, 72–73, 83–84, 86, 88, 91, 93, 95, 98–100, 103–105, 107, 109, 111, 114, 117–118, 120, 124, 126–128, 131, 133, 136, 138, 142, 145–147, 149, 152–153, 158–159, 161, 163, 168, 172, 175–177, 179, 181, 184–185, 192, 196, 198–199, 202–203, 205–206

Cocoa powder, *12, 64, 116*

Coconut, 12–14, 16–17, 44–46, 51, 60, 64, 69, 76, 89–90, 96–97, 100, 102, 106, 108, 116, 132, 135, 137, 166–167, 171–172, 174, 192, 195–196, 202

Coconut cream, *64*

Coconut milk, *16–17, 44–46, 89–90, 108, 132, 172, 195*

Coconut oil, 12–14, 45–46, 51, 69, 96–97, 100, 102, 106, 116, 132, 135, 137, 166, 171, 174, 192

Coffee, *65, 200*

Coriander, *45–46, 53, 60–61, 110, 159, 181, 183*

Corn oil, *86*

Cottage cheese, *71*

Couscous, *40, 51, 54–55, 82, 119, 129, 159–160*

Crab, *130*

Crackers, *39, 186*

Cranberry, 11, 47–49, 55, 60–61, 81, 95, 104, 116, 141–143, 147–148, 155, 157, 164, 167, 171

Cream, 17, 21, 23–26, 35, 42, 50–51, 58, 64, 73, 89, 94, 111, 121–123, 182, 195, 200–202, 205

Cream cheese, *25–26*

Crumble, *42, 63*

Cucumber, 24, 57, 67, 74, 78–79, 85–87, 101–102, 113–114, 123, 129–130, 144, 148–150, 153–154, 165–166, 169–170, 195–196, 204

Cumin, 11, 18–19, 21, 29, 34, 37, 42, 53, 55, 58–61, 68, 72–73, 82, 89, 93, 98–99, 101, 109–115, 118–121, 127–129, 134, 144, 150, 157, 159, 163, 165–166, 181–184, 188, 195, 202, 205–208

Curd, *123*

Curly kale, *65*

Currants, *77, 150*

Curry, 45–47, 52–55, 60, 66, 85–86, 89–90, 101, 108, 114–115, 158, 168, 172, 177–178, 182, 200

Curry paste, *55, 89–90, 108, 172*

Curry powder, 45, 47, 52–54, 60, 66, 85–86, 101, 114–115, 158, 168, 177–178, 182, 200

D

Dark chocolate, *34, 69*

Date, *95–96, 132–133*

Dijon mustard, *48, 56, 58, 71, 77–78, 105, 118, 130, 140–141, 154, 174*

Dill, 15, 28, 43, 50, 65, 68, 76–77, 112–113, 149, 206–207

Dried apricots, *122, 147*

Dried cherries, *85, 171*

Dried fruit, *77, 142*

E

Egg, 12–14, 19–20, 25–26, 28, 33–34, 44, 61, 64–65, 69, 71, 75–77, 83, 90, 92, 96–98, 100, 103, 105–106, 111–112, 116–117, 120–121, 124–125, 130–132, 134, 139, 145–146, 151, 163, 165, 167, 185, 195, 197–199, 204, 206–207

Egg wash, *75*

Egg white, *25–26, 64–65, 139, 185, 198–199, 204*

English muffin, *115*

Evaporated milk, *57*

F

Falafel, *192*

Fat, 11–58, 60–90, 92–209

Fennel, *68, 164*

Feta, 17, 41–42, 45, 47–49, 56, 59, 74, 76–79, 87, 118, 129–130, 132, 148–149, 157, 166, 180, 185–186, 204

Fish, 80, 90, 134, 154, 161, 168, 188, 196

Fish sauce, *90*

Five-spice powder, *192*

Flank, *68*

Flatbread, *112, 173*

Flour, 12, 24, 34, 44, 57, 63–65, 70, 75, 91–92, 96–97, 106, 112, 130, 132, 139, 145–146, 151, 163, 173, 186–188, 200

Fruit, 20–21, 63, 77, 102, 122, 141–142

G

Garam masala, *50, 147, 187–188*

Garlic, 11, 13–21, 25–29, 31, 33–43, 45–46, 49–53, 55–59, 61–63, 65, 67, 69, 72–73, 75–77,

  80, 83–84, 86, 88–89, 91–95, 98–101, 103–111, 114–115, 117–122, 124–131, 133–134, 136,

  140–143, 145–147, 149–150, 152–155, 157–163, 165–166, 168, 170, 172, 174–179, 181–189,

  192, 196–199, 202–203, 205–209

Ghee, *118–119*

Ginger, 12–14, 25, 45, 62–63, 71, 86, 93, 100–101, 105–106, 120, 123–124, 131, 138, 145–146,

  154–155, 158–159, 163, 172, 174–175, 183–184, 192, 200, 206–207

Gouda, *33*

Grain, 15, 18, 20, 24, 29, 33, 37, 39, 41, 44, 47, 51, 61, 65–66, 68, 70, 80–83, 86–87, 91, 96,

  103, 111–112, 114–115, 123–125, 129, 135, 137, 139, 142–144, 147, 149, 152, 158–161,

  164, 179–180, 190, 194–195, 197

Grapefruit, *142–143*

Grapes, *66–67, 131*

Grapeseed oil, *67*

Green beans, *27, 36, 108, 120*

Ground almonds, *12*

Ground ginger, *12, 71, 86, 93, 101, 106, 145–146, 159, 163, 184, 192*

Gruyère, *83*

Guacamole, *69, 73, 121*

H

Halloumi, *68*

Ham, *104–105*

Harissa, *45*

Heart, *123–124, 201*

Herbes de provence, *58*

Herbs, 51, 67, 80, 83, 93, 103, 112, 159, 165, 179

Hoisin sauce, *20*

Honey, 12–13, 16–17, 25, 43, 48–49, 54, 58, 65, 68–69, 88, 96–97, 102, 106, 113, 116, 118,

  122, 131–133, 135, 142–143, 167, 196

J

Jam, *173*

K

Kale, 13, 26, 32–34, 45, 53–54, 61–62, 65–66, 73, 76–79, 101, 105, 115, 143, 166, 174

Ketchup, *26, 115, 197*

Kidney, *42, 73, 119, 178, 206–207*

Kidney beans, *42, 73, 119, 178, 206–207*

L

Lamb, *204*

Leek, *80, 101–102*

Lemon, 17, 21–23, 29, 33, 35, 41–43, 45, 47–49, 51–52, 54–57, 65–68, 70, 72, 74–82, 84–85,

  87, 93, 105, 110, 113–115, 118, 120, 122–123, 129–

130, 138–139, 142–145, 148–150, 154, 159, 161, 164, 166, 168–170, 175, 183–184, 189–190, 193, 204

Lemon juice, 17, 21, 23, 29, 33, 41–43, 45, 47–49, 51–52, 55–57, 65–68, 70, 72, 76–82, 84–85, 87, 93, 105, 113–114, 118, 129–130, 138–139, 142–145, 148–150, 154, 159, 161, 164, 166, 170, 175, 189–190, 193, 204

Lemongrass, *89–90*

Lentils, 45–46, 48–49, 53, 60, 68, 76–77, 93–94, 113–115, 126, 184–185

Lettuce, *29, 43, 46, 59, 107, 115, 201–202*

Lime, 18–19, 25, 41, 43, 46–47, 49, 58–59, 66–67, 69, 73, 76, 88, 99, 107–108, 112–113, 134, 136, 142–143, 148, 150, 157–158, 165–167, 169–170, 172, 174–177, 180, 193, 195–197, 200, 208

Lime juice, 18–19, 25, 41, 43, 46–47, 49, 59, 67, 69, 73, 76, 88, 99, 107–108, 112–113, 136, 142, 148, 150, 157–158, 165–167, 170, 172, 174, 176–177, 180, 193, 195–196, 200, 208

M

Macadamia, *196*

Mango, 11, 43, 53, 85–86, 158, 166–167, 195–196, 200

Mango chutney, *86, 196*

Maple syrup, 22–23, 48, 95, 97, 105, 122, 139, 169–170, 182, 194, 207

Margarine, *186*

Marjoram, *40, 50–51*

Marmalade, *14*

Marshmallow, *128*

Mayonnaise, *23–24, 29, 76–77, 120, 134, 185*

Meat, 16, 26, 35–38, 41, 67, 71, 96, 115, 132, 137, 147, 161, 166, 178, 186, 197, 201

Milk, 12, 15–17, 22–24, 44–46, 57, 61, 64–65, 70, 89–90, 97, 102, 106, 108, 122, 132, 135, 139, 167, 172–173, 178, 182, 195, 201, 207

Millet, *15, 70, 173*

Mince, *28*

Mint, 57, 60–61, 67, 93–94, 138, 142–143, 149–150, 153, 158–159, 180, 189, 193, 195, 200

Mirin, 24

Miso, 91

Molasses, *45–46, 64–65, 91–92, 94, 202*

Mozzarella, 16, 33, 39, 62–63, 75, 84, 92, 125, 133–134, 146, 204, 206–207

Muffins, 106, 111, 115–116, 132, 139, 145, 163

Mushroom, 35, 65–66, 89–91, 93–94, 122–124, 126–127, 135, 137, 140, 147, 150–152, 160–162, 165, 170, 174–175, 177, 179, 184, 189–190, 203, 205–207

Mustard, 14, 48, 56, 58, 71, 77–78, 86, 88, 104–105, 113, 115, 118, 130, 140–141, 154, 174, 198–199

Mustard oil, *88*

N

Nachos, *118*

Noodles, *100, 209*

Nori, *24, 123–124*

Nut, 31, 33, 55–56, 77, 82, 141–142, 147, 152, 163, 167, 182, 190, 196, 207

Nutmeg, 12, 22–24, 50, 62–63, 97, 122, 145–146, 163

O

Oatmeal, *22, 122, 167, 191, 202*

Oats, 12–13, 69, 95–98, 102, 114–116, 173, 187, 202

Oil, 12–20, 25–34, 36–43, 45–52, 54–73, 75–81, 83–93, 95–123, 125–138, 140–144, 146–166,

168–171, 173–209

Olive, 15–18, 25–34, 36–43, 47–49, 51–52, 54–70, 73, 76–81, 83–85, 87–93, 95–99, 101–102,

104–108, 110, 112–123, 125–129, 131, 133–135, 137–138, 140–144, 146–166, 168–171,

173–180, 182–183, 185–194, 197–208

Olive oil, 15–18, 25–34, 36–41, 43, 47–49, 51–52, 54–70, 73, 76–81, 83–85, 87–93, 95–99,

101–102, 104–108, 110, 112–123, 125–129, 131, 133–135, 137–138, 140–144, 146–166,

168–171, 173–180, 182–183, 185–194, 197–208

Onion, 11, 13–15, 17–19, 21, 25–37, 39–43, 45–54, 56–57, 59–63, 66, 69, 71–74, 76, 78,

80–101, 103–111, 113–129, 131, 133–138, 140–142, 144–156, 158–168, 170–172, 174–193,

195–199, 201–203, 205–208

Orange, 14, 18, 49, 52, 85, 110, 112, 129, 141, 156, 204

Orange juice, *49, 85, 110, 156*

Oregano, 11, 26–27, 40, 47, 68, 73, 77–78, 87, 89, 94, 108–110, 118–119, 125, 127–129,

133–134, 163, 177, 179–180, 203

P

Paella, *35*

Paprika, 21, 28, 36–37, 40, 45, 72–73, 88, 115, 127–129, 159, 178, 203

Parfait, *20–21*

Parmesan, 23–24, 33, 35, 38–39, 48, 50–51, 74–75, 83–84, 96–97, 116–117, 124, 127,

134–135, 140, 160, 165, 179, 185, 190–191, 194, 204, 209

Parsley, 17, 37, 39, 41–42, 50–52, 54–56, 65, 67, 74–77, 79–80, 82, 84–85, 93, 101–102, 105,

114–115, 118, 125, 127–128, 134, 136, 144–145, 148–150, 153–155, 157, 160, 171–172,

174–175, 179, 190–193, 195, 197–199, 203–204

Parsnip, *107*

Pasta, 16, 28, 38, 42, 74, 185, 191, 195

Pastry, *163*

Peanut butter, *11, 25, 69, 100, 136*

Peanut oil, *71–72, 103, 158*

Peanuts, *13, 31–32, 69, 100, 108, 158, 200*

Pearl barley, *172*

Peas, 40, 53–54, 70, 95, 108, 120, 131, 160

Pecan, 12, 48, 55, 60, 77, 97, 142, 155, 161–162, 164

Pecorino, *160*

Peel, *21–22, 28, 97*

Pepper, 11, 16–21, 23–43, 45–63, 65–78, 80–82, 84–90, 92, 94–101, 103–123, 125–131,

133–138, 140–149, 151–172, 174–193, 196–209

Pesto, *47, 101–103, 112, 132, 194*

Pie, *87, 156, 167, 191*

Pine nut, *33, 55–56, 82, 147, 152, 182*

Pineapple, *60, 76, 103, 196*

Pineapple juice, *60, 196*

Pinto beans, *201–202*

Pistachio, *58*

Pizza, *112*

Plum, *148*

Polenta, *179*

Pomegranate, *20, 57–58, 103–104*

Pomegranate juice, *103*

Poppy seeds, *141*

Pork, *28, 104, 147*

Potato, *11, 25–27, 50, 64–65, 71, 97, 116–117, 120, 134, 161–162, 169, 178, 186–187, 192*

Potato wedges, *134*

Poultry, *152*

Prune, *31–32, 131*

Pulse, *94, 106–107, 112, 133, 135*

Pumpkin, *96–97, 106, 116, 156, 164, 167, 169, 173*

Pumpkin seed, *96–97, 116, 169, 173*

Q

Quinoa, *11–209*

R

Radish, *58–59, 195*

Rainbow chard, *126*

Raisins, 29, 51–52, 54, 60–61, 76, 93, 97, 101, 108, 139, 142, 145–147, 152, 156, 163, 167,

171–172, 174–175, 182, 189, 195, 204, 207

Raspberry, *20, 39*

Red lentil, *45, 53, 114*

Red onion, 17, 19, 25, 31, 43, 47, 59–60, 66, 74, 78, 81–82, 84–85, 87, 99, 101, 107, 110, 115,

129, 138, 148, 153–154, 165, 174, 176–177, 180, 186, 196, 198–199, 201, 205

Red wine, 17, 19, 34, 68, 74, 113, 119, 131, 135, 141, 144, 154, 180

Red wine vinegar, *17, 19, 68, 74, 113, 119, 131, 141, 144, 154, 180*

Rice, 14–16, 22, 24, 29, 35, 40, 44, 60, 62–66, 75, 88–89, 91, 100, 103–104, 111–114, 119,

123–124, 131, 138, 145, 154, 159–160, 167–168, 171–173, 176, 181, 183, 185, 195, 203,

206–207

Rice flour, *63–65*

Rice pudding, *16*

Rice vinegar, *24, 100, 104, 113–114*

Rice wine, *14*

Ricotta, *116–117, 133–134, 179*

Risotto, *50, 83, 135, 140, 150*

Roast chicken, *42*

Roasted vegetables, *56*

Rosemary, *36, 73, 94, 104, 112, 158, 204*

Rum, *182*

S

Safflower oil, *141*

Saffron, *36, 159, 171*

Sage, *94, 137, 158, 169, 171-172, 187-188, 197*

Salad, *11, 14, 16-17, 19, 29, 38-39, 41-42, 46-49, 51, 53, 55-60, 66-68, 70-71, 74, 76-79,*
   81-82, 84-88, 93-94, 101, 105, 110, 112-113, 118-119, 122, 129-132, 136, 140-144,
   148-151, 153-154, 164-166, 169-170, 174, 180, 184-186, 190, 193, 195-197, 200, 204, 208

Salmon, *33, 48, 71, 161, 168*

Salsa, *11, 36, 73, 89, 176-177, 183, 196, 205-206*

Salt, *11-12, 14-29, 31-70, 72-73, 75-87, 89, 91-92, 94-125, 127-129, 131-135, 137-155,*
   157-159, 161-180, 182, 185-188, 190-193, 195-203, 205-209

Sausage, *36-37, 127, 133, 144, 187-188*

Savory, *53, 93, 127, 166, 171, 176, 191*

Sea salt, *15, 21-22, 24, 36-37, 41-42, 51, 56, 59, 77-78, 82-83, 87, 101-102, 108-109,*
   113-114, 116, 124, 134, 138-139, 148-149, 152, 166, 192

Seafood, *154*

Seasoning, *11, 16, 51, 55, 67, 80, 86, 88, 96-97, 114-115, 121, 137, 141, 152, 172, 180-181,*
   188, 190, 198-199, 207-208

Seaweed, *24, 123*

Seeds, *13, 20-21, 25, 33-34, 36, 56-58, 64-65, 69-71, 78, 91-94, 96-97, 102-106, 116, 122,*
   132-133, 140-141, 169, 173-174, 183, 189-190, 201, 203, 207

Sesame oil, *13, 20, 25, 55, 61, 71, 100, 131, 142, 195, 206-207*

Sesame seeds, *13, 25, 64-65, 70, 96-97, 104-105, 173-174*

Shallot, *31, 41-42, 45, 55-56, 65, 79, 93, 107, 114, 137, 142-143, 168*

Sherry, *31, 179, 190*

Sherry vinegar, *31, 190*

Shiitake mushroom, *91, 94, 140*

Snapper, *134*

Soda, *12, 64, 145-146, 163*

Sole, *74-75*

Soup, *11, 23-24, 27, 35, 37, 39-40, 50, 54, 56, 65-66, 72-73, 89-90, 94-95, 107, 122-123,*
   127, 136, 153, 164, 172, 184-185

Soy sauce, *13-14, 25, 55, 71, 96-97, 100, 103-106, 112-113, 131, 135-136, 154-155, 162, 197*

Spaghetti, *84*

Spelt, *65, 91-92, 96-97, 173*

Spelt flour, *91-92, 96-97, 173*

Spices, *88, 110, 120, 122, 128, 142, 146*

Spinach, *15, 25, 30-35, 38-40, 67, 84-86, 90, 92, 104, 107, 110, 115, 120, 127, 151-152,*
   165-166, 168, 170, 183-186, 188, 194, 205-207

Squash, *27-28, 55-56, 62-63, 66, 129, 144-148, 155, 159, 163, 169, 187-188, 190-191*

Steak, *68, 103-104*

Stew, *45-46, 91, 127, 129, 159, 177-178, 187-188, 191*

Stilton, *141*

Stock, *11, 35-37, 40, 47, 50-51, 53-54, 65, 69, 72, 86, 89-90, 94, 127, 137-138, 147-148,*

150-152, 160, 170, 176, 182, 187-188, 204-205

Stuffing, *147-148, 152, 203*

Sucralose, *191*

Sugar, 12, 14, 18, 24, 42, 44, 55, 62-64, 69-70, 92, 102, 119, 124, 128, 139-140, 145-146,

163, 165, 167, 169, 173, 195, 198-199

Sunflower seed, *33, 56, 64-65, 70, 78, 82, 96-97, 116, 140, 173*

Sweet potato, *11, 25-26, 50, 71, 97, 116-117, 134, 161-162, 169, 192*

Swiss chard, *126, 161*

Syrup, 22-23, 48, 95, 97, 105, 122, 139, 169-170, 173, 182, 194, 207

T

Tabasco, *136*

Taco, 17, 58-59, 88, 121, 128, 193

Tahini, *41-42, 68, 96-97*

Tamari, *91, 174*

Tapioca, *64-65*

Tarragon, *67, 165, 187-188*

Teriyaki, *131*

Teriyaki sauce, *131*

Thyme, 26, 30-32, 39, 50-51, 94, 104, 108, 116-118, 127, 133, 137, 140, 145, 160, 165,

169-170, 185-186, 192, 203

Tofu, 71-72, 91, 112, 123, 128, 194, 205

Tomato, 16-18, 27, 30-31, 35-36, 38-39, 41-42, 45-47, 55-59, 65, 68-69, 72-74, 79-80,

86-90, 92, 98-103, 108-110, 115, 117-121, 125-130, 132-134, 136, 143, 146, 148-152,

153-154, 157, 159, 165-166, 168, 171-172, 176-181, 183-191, 193-195, 197-198, 202-206,

208-209

Tomato juice, *36, 188*

Turkey, 30-31, 35, 84, 105, 117-119, 147, 152, 157-158, 189-190, 197-199, 208

Turkey breast, *35, 198*

Turmeric, *51, 54, 113, 120, 159, 176, 183*

Turnip, *27-28*

V

Vanilla extract, *12, 23, 64, 92, 96, 102, 116, 132-133, 139, 145, 163, 167, 195*

Vegetable oil, 14, 18-19, 33-34, 50, 75, 86, 89, 104, 109, 111, 120, 126, 128-130, 133, 136,

142, 153, 156, 180-181, 200, 205, 209

Vegetable stock, *11, 37, 50-51, 54, 137, 147-148, 176, 204*

Vegetables, 11, 28, 30, 37-38, 41, 54, 63, 66, 68, 87, 91-92, 95, 98-100, 107, 112, 120, 124,

129, 135, 144, 146, 148, 152, 154, 156, 159, 162-163, 175, 185, 187-188, 191, 197, 205

Vinegar, 11, 14, 16-17, 19, 24, 31, 43, 48-49, 51-52, 54, 58, 62-65, 68, 74-75, 77-78, 84-87,

95-97, 100, 103-105, 110, 113-114, 119, 128-131, 138, 140-142, 144, 149, 153-154, 167,

170, 180, 185-186, 190, 196-197

W

Walnut, 48-49, 85, 101-102, 104, 106, 131-133, 136, 141, 145-146, 156-157, 189-191

Walnut oil, *106*

Wasabi, *29*

Watercress, *66, 141*

Watermelon, *196*

Whipping cream, *50*

White pepper, *204*

White sugar, *12, 14, 24, 42, 55, 62-64, 119*

White wine, *48, 50, 58, 85-86, 140, 147, 161, 170, 180, 196*

White wine vinegar, *48, 58, 85-86, 140, 180, 196*

Wild mushrooms, *65, 179*

Wild rice, *29*

Wine, *14, 17, 19, 24, 34, 48, 50-51, 58, 61, 68, 74, 85-86, 113, 119, 131, 135, 140-141, 144, 147, 154, 161, 170, 180, 196*

Worcestershire sauce, *26, 90, 93-94, 118-119, 198-199*

Y

Yam, *143-144, 147*

Yeast, *51, 64-65, 70, 77-78, 93-94, 113, 173, 191, 200*

Z

Zest, *18-19, 22, 43, 47, 52, 74-76, 80-82, 85, 110, 115, 118, 134, 141-143, 166, 190, 195*

Conclusion

Thank you again for downloading this book!

I hope you enjoyed reading about my book!

If you enjoyed this book, please take the time to share your thoughts and post a review on Amazon. It'd be greatly appreciated!

Write me an honest review about the book – I truly value your opinion and thoughts and I will incorporate them into my next book, which is already underway.

Thank you!

If you have any questions, **feel free to contact at:** *cheflilyli@gmail.com*

Lily Li
http://www.thecookingmap.com/lily-li

Printed in Great Britain
by Amazon